Wandering Soul

WANDERING SOUL

The Dybbuk's Creator, S. An-sky

GABRIELLA SAFRAN

Harvard University Press
Cambridge, Massachusetts, and London, England   2010

Library of Congress Cataloging-in-Publication Data

Safran, Gabriella, 1967–
Wandering soul : the Dybbuk's creator, S. An-Sky / Gabriella Safran.
    p. cm.
  Includes bibliographical references and index.
  ISBN 978-0-674-05570-4 (alk. paper)
  1. An-Sky, S., 1863–1920. 2. Authors, Russian—Biography. I. Title.
  PJ5129.R3Z84 2010
  839'.18309—dc22
  [B]   2010017208

To William and Marian Safran,
and to Michael, Eva, and Frieda Kahan

Contents

Note on Names, Dates, and Transliteration

I refer to my subject as "Shloyme-Zanvl" or "Rappoport" when describing his childhood and youth. When I reach his mature period, I refer to him for the most part as "An-sky" (or "Semyon"). I hope that this evolution, which seems to me true to the man himself, will not confuse the reader. I give dates according to the Russian Julian calendar for events in Russia and according to the Gregorian calendar for events in Europe, except as noted otherwise, until January 31, 1918. I often follow my subjects in giving both dates. For dates after the Bolshevik government brought Russia into chronological alignment with the West, I use the Gregorian calendar consistently. For places within the Russian Empire, I give the Russian names that An-sky himself used, even when they differ from contemporary usage; however, for places in Congress Poland and Galicia, I give Polish names. Russian personal names and words are transliterated according to Library of Congress style, but I prefer final *-sky* to *-skii*, use the first names Semyon, Fyodor, and Pyotr, and eliminate the soft sign in names. Yiddish is transliterated per YIVO (Institute for Jewish Research) style. In the body of the text, I spell familiar personal and place names as they usually appear in English. Unless indicated otherwise all translations are mine.

Map of An-sky's Travels

Legend:

— Western border of the Russian Empire until 1914
▨ Russian occupation of Austria-Hungary in 1915
▨ Pale of Jewish Settlement
--- Province borders

BALTIC SEA

BLACK SEA

Tamerfors
Terioki
St. Petersburg
Pskov
Riga
Dvina River
Kuzhi
Dvinsk · Osveia
VITEBSK
Moscow
Kovno
Ushachi
Vitebsk · Liozno
Königsberg
Verzhbolovo
Vilna
Lepel · Chashniki
Smolensk
Minsk
Mogilev
Tula
Białystok
MOGILEV
Efremov
Warsaw
Grodzisk
Elets
Otwock
Kobrin
Skierniewicz
Brest-Litovsk
Gomel
Pinsk
CHERNIGOV
Liuboml
Chernigov
Zamość
Lutsk
Rovno
Korets
VOLYNIA
Kiev
Tarnów
Sokal
Dubno
Zdolbunov
Zhitomir
Fastov
Dębica
Krystynopol
Radivilov
Sudilkov
Tuchów
Lvov
Brody
Miropol
Skvira
Gorlice
Kremenets
Berdichev
Ruzhin
GALICIA
Tarnopol
Starokonstantinov
KIEV
Skałat
Proskurov
Dnepr River
Kałusz
Kopyczyńce
Podwołoczyska
Czortków
Husiatyn
Ekaterinoslav
Slavianoserbsk
Śniatyn
PODOLIA
EKATERINOSLAV
Sadagora
Krasnopol
Czernowitz
BUKOVINA
Kishinev
Odessa

And there are homeless souls that find no rest, and so they enter living bodies to purify themselves. Such a soul is called a dybbuk. . . .

S. An-sky, The Dybbuk, Act 2

Prologue

I have neither a wife, nor children, nor a house, nor even an
apartment, nor belongings, nor even any settled habits . . . the only
thing that connects me firmly to these dimensions is my nation.

    —S. An-sky, undated autobiographical fragment

T WAS EARLY FEBRUARY OF 1915, and a fifty-one-year-old writer
who called himself Semyon Akimovich An-sky was traveling
through the war zone in disguise.[1] A few months earlier the Russian army had occupied Galicia, a poor province on the far eastern edge
of the Austro-Hungarian Empire, home to Jews, Poles, Germans, and Ruthenians. Rumors were reaching Petrograd, the Russian imperial capital,
that along with defending the motherland, the army was burning Jewish
homes, taking Jews hostage, and beating, raping, and killing them. The
leaders of the Jewish Committee to Help War Victims (known by its Russian initials, EKOPO) had asked An-sky, a well-known journalist and
ethnographer, to travel to the embattled area and investigate these charges.
Although Jews were usually excluded from working for the officially recognized aid organizations in the occupied territory, An-sky, an old revolutionary with friends in many political parties, used his connections to get
a posting. In his aid worker's uniform, wearing a sabre and a fur hat with
Red Cross insignia, he resembled an army officer. No one guessed that his
legal name was not his Russian-sounding pseudonym but the obviously
Jewish Shloyme-Zanvl Rappoport.

On the evening of February 7, An-sky arrived in the town of Tuchów
in Galicia and headed for the synagogue. In the dim evening light, he saw
that the benches and the pulpit had been destroyed, the walls were bare,
the floor covered with scraps of prayer books, broken glass, hay, and
what he realized was human excrement. The next morning, An-sky saw
the town in daylight and found the destruction "indescribable." Most of
the Jewish houses had been burnt and the streets were filled with trash.

The hundred Galician Jewish families who inhabited the town had taken flight and only twenty Jews remained. An old woman who had fled from nearby Dębica said that the Russian soldiers had opened the cabinets in the synagogue walls. "They took the Torah scrolls," she sobbed. "They threw them under the horses' hooves."[2]

The very next evening, February 8, An-sky was invited with other aid workers to a "spectacle" performed by the Russian soldiers stationed nearby under the command of a Colonel Nechvolodov. The soldiers' performance combined songs, dances, jokes, and dramatic readings of poems and stories. Despite the jarring contrast with the previous day's spectacle of destruction, An-sky confessed to his diary that the soldiers' performance touched him. He listened to their Ukrainian songs and felt a connection between the plight of these twenty young men and the music. "There was so much deep, strong sadness in their situation." As he listened, An-sky imagined all the horror that these soldiers had already seen and that lay ahead for them. The soldiers then began to sing merrier songs in Russian, and An-sky began to see them as bold, brave, and strong. He mused on the effect that the songs had on him. "You can hear the phrase 'death to our enemies' so many times and it doesn't make an impression. But here you feel the whole terrible real meaning of these words, on the lips of people who just yesterday went into hand-to-hand combat with the enemy and will do it again tomorrow." After the performance, the officers offered their guests dinner with wine, cognac, toasts and speeches, even ice cream. The aid workers left late.[3]

An-sky told his diary that he felt sympathy for all the people he met in Galicia, the ruined Jews as well as the Russian soldiers who were systematically burning down Jewish homes. True, the worst violence against Jews was the fault of Cossack regiments, mounted soldiers from communities that historically defended Russia's borderlands, but it could have been Colonel Nechvolodov's soldiers who had burned the Jewish homes of Tuchów and shat in the synagogue. Still, An-sky could shift quickly from sympathy for the Jews of Tuchów to admiration for the soldiers. He drank cognac and ate ice cream with Colonel Nechvolodov, and he felt the emotional power of the soldiers' music. Whatever these soldiers had done, he admired their boldness, bravery, and strength, and he appreciated the songs that communicated their heroism so strongly. He recognized the soldiers as possible destroyers *and* as human beings. For him, both the Russian soldiers and the Galician Jews had stories to tell and songs to sing that helped them survive and make sense of their difficult experiences. An-sky was absorbed by their words and wanted to preserve their art.

In An-sky's world, it was not clear whether a person could be both a Russian and a Jew, but judging from An-sky's diary, the contradictions between his Russian and his Jewish sympathies troubled him only occasionally. Throughout his life, he was attentive to the experiences of the moment and fully absorbed in hearing the people with whom he was speaking. Perpetually underfed, he craved only tea with sugar, cigarettes, and an empathetic response from the people he met, which he could almost always elicit; strangers tended to trust him immediately and tell him their stories. These habits, which he had since youth, made him a successful journalist and ethnographer but a maddeningly inconsistent human being. Because he could see the merits in both sides of an argument, he succeeded in maintaining friendships with people in opposing political parties, and sometimes he could reconcile them. Even in his politically riven era, An-sky was usually forgiven his mixed loyalties in person, though not in print. Whether he was writing letters to old friends or new loves, political propaganda, articles for Russian or Yiddish newspapers and journals, stories, poems, or plays, he anticipated his audience's reaction and spoke in words that could reach them. He left a large and sometimes brilliant corpus of work, fiction and nonfiction, in Russian and Yiddish. From the storehouse of his experiences, he chose details that would resonate with his readers. He was adept at assuming the voices that the occasion demanded.

An-sky grew up as a Yiddish speaker in a largely Jewish shtetl (market town), but he moved to a big city as a teenager, mastered Russian, and soon began a career as a Russian journalist and then as a Socialist Revolutionary activist. Starting seven or eight years before the outbreak of World War I, his mixed Russian and Jewish loyalties became less tenable and he began to need to take sides. He made many such choices as he reworked his Russian wartime diaries, letters, and newspaper articles into a Yiddish memoir of his time as an aid worker, under the title *The Destruction of Galicia*. With his Yiddish readers in mind, he muted his own Russian sympathies; he presented himself as a witness to the violence against the Jews and as an investigator determined to debunk the rumors of Jewish treachery that were spread by the authorities and used to justify the army's brutality. He described the devastated Tuchów synagogue in print much as he had in his diary, but omitted his own sense of intimacy with the Russian soldiers and officers soon after, depicting some of them as anti-Semitic; he avoided mention of the soldiers' songs that he had found so moving.[4] His mixed sympathies in Galicia looked simpler in his memoir.

As An-sky traveled through Galicia, he was carrying a draft of what would become his best-known work, the play *The Dybbuk,* which he had begun in 1913. Khonen, the play's hero, dies after summoning the Devil to help him win the hand of his beloved Leah. Because his soul can find no peace in the afterworld, he returns as a dybbuk, a character from Jewish folklore, who possesses Leah's body. An-sky put much of his own restlessness into Khonen, whose geographical and spiritual wanderings and ability to take on a new form parallel those of his creator. Khonen could embody the paradoxes at the heart of An-sky's activities. A dedicated revolutionary, An-sky worked for the destruction or radical reform of old ways of life, but he also yearned to find a place for himself inside the traditional structures. Khonen similarly longs for acceptance in Leah's wealthy family, but his actions destroy her and her family's hope of continuity.

Like Khonen and the dybbuk he became, An-sky did not fit neatly into his society's categories, and he wrote about the discomfort of being in between. Love and marriage, the themes of the play, posed a painful conundrum for their author. An-sky wrote passionate letters to men as well as women. His frustrated relationships with both, his occasional outbursts of anger about sex, and some of the silences in his friends' memoirs suggest that as he felt pulled among ethnic and political loyalties, he also wrestled with his sexuality. His place in the class system troubled him too. Like Khonen, he was the poor son of a single mother, hoping that his wits would make rich Jews accept him and upset when they did not. His solitariness, his poverty, and his sympathies made him an outsider, and he spoke over and over of yearning for "soil" where he could be sure that his steps would make an impression; the metaphor he used to express his longing for a home revealed his debt to the Russian Populists who idealized the peasants' tie to the land, and it prefigured his own late flirtations with Zionism.

Class, education, and the empire's byzantine laws limited An-sky's options, but he resisted, refusing with all his might to accept a small life. Like the hero of his play, he was drawn to forbidden knowledge. Khonen left the shtetl to study the kabbalah, Jewish mysticism, with a distant master, and An-sky left his home to study Slavic peasants and revolutionary theory. And as Khonen insisted that kabbalah would give him what he wanted even while fellow students in yeshiva (a school of higher rabbinic learning) questioned his daring, so An-sky believed in the goodwill of poor Russians toward Jews even when many of his friends began to doubt it and retained his loyalty to his Socialist Revolutionary Party even after it was clear that their cause was lost.

Being like a dybbuk, an archaic character restless and fluid in its identity and loyalties, contributed to An-sky's success in the quintessentially modern occupations he chose. As an ethnographer, he worked to blend in among Russians and Jews. As a journalist, he got interviews from people who disagreed with him. As a revolutionary propagandist, he could display the political engagement inherent in his ethnographic and journalistic work; he could celebrate heroism in others and aspire to it himself. And as a relief worker, that cousin of the ethnographer, the journalist, and the revolutionary, he shifted—as relief workers a century later continue to do—from self-aggrandizing to self-effacing views of his own effectiveness.[5] It may be that audiences' thrilled rediscovery of An-sky in the late twentieth and early twenty-first centuries, the proliferation of publications and performances of his work, reflect the value his readers find in his outsiderly eye; those who are uncertain of their own place in the present or in history respond to his sense of not belonging, to his sense of his own falseness and his yearning for the authenticity he glimpsed in others. But to celebrate him as an outsider is to ignore the pain of the dybbuk, who longs for purification and for rest. An-sky used his nearly supernatural abilities to charm people as he tried to attain proof of his acceptance.

In his own evaluation of his life he stressed what was *not* there, emphasizing his lack of the things that bind other people to their conventional private existences. "I have neither a wife, nor children, nor a house, nor even an apartment, nor belongings, nor even any settled habits." By insisting on his rootlessness, he was claiming a place in the Russian intellectual tradition. The early-nineteenth-century nobleman Pyotr Chaadaev had been locked up as a madman for publishing his famous "Philosophical Letter," in which he described Russians in almost the same terms that An-sky used to describe himself: "It seems we are all in transit. No one has a fixed sphere of existence; there are no proper habits, no rules. We do not even have homes. We have nothing that binds, nothing that awakens our sympathies and affections; nothing that endures; nothing that remains."[6] Russian writers whom An-sky read, such as Fyodor Dostoevsky, responded to Chaadaev by asserting that while the nation as a whole was not homeless, its *intelligentsia,* intellectuals whose Westernized education divorced them from the experience of the peasant majority, were indeed rootless and needed to return "home" to traditional culture.

For An-sky, Chaadaev's metaphor was real. Like the dybbuk, he was ageless as well as restless, existing outside the chronology that governed the lives of others, remaining forever a kind of adolescent, full of potential, nothing binding him to any older version of himself. He was free to reinvent himself as persistently as he revised his old stories, poems, and articles, which he would pick up every few years, rework, translate from Russian to Yiddish or Yiddish to Russian, and republish. He responded to his own sense of rootlessness and absence—he spoke of a terrifying "emptiness" at the center of his own identity—by imagining himself as a hero whose ability to negate his own identity made him better able to help those in need, to hear their words and write powerfully about them. Paradoxically, he wanted both to vanish and to be famous, to be celebrated for his modesty and his mastery of words. These contradictory goals led him to revise not only his writings, but also his literary persona, his most elaborate multimedia creation. Born Shloyme-Zanvl Rapoport, he always preferred the spelling "Rappoport." After he adopted the pseudonym Semyon Akimovich An-sky at the age of 28 years and a few months, he lived largely under that name until he died, 28 years and a few months later. He signed many of his private as well as his professional letters "An-sky" or "Semyon," and he signed his will both "An-sky" and "Rappoport," thus claiming his multiple identities.[7]

He was a gifted ethnographer, some of whose ideas about folklore bear the traces of his own fluid identity. The anthropologists of his era wanted to locate cultures along an evolutionary progression; folklorists argued about whether tales and songs were remnants of a shared corpus of ancient myths or traces of specific historical events; and Russian Populist ethnographers studied the peasants' lore to help them resist capitalism and imagine revolution. Earlier than others, An-sky described folklore as the dynamic product of interactions among people and nations. He grasped that the stories people tell depend on who is listening, and he strove to vanish into the background as he heard them, to be indistinguishable from the people he was studying. At the same time, folklore collecting offered the possibility of heroic action, and he wanted to save the cultures and the people he studied.

As he shifted between Russian and Jewish selves, he told different stories about his past. He and others used the years he spent among Russian peasants and miners, his arrests, and his revolutionary work to symbolize his connection to the *narod*, the Russian folk. They used his encounters with Jewish causes célèbres—his newspaper articles about the Dreyfus Affair in France in the 1890s, the 1906 Bialystok pogrom, the Beilis blood libel trial in Kiev in 1913, and ultimately the wartime violence against the Galician Jews—to symbolize his demonstrative return to Jewishness. His collection of folklore, first the songs of the Russian miners in the Donets Basin, then Jewish lore, made him appear a conduit for what his era saw as the authentic feelings of the folk, be they Russian or Jewish. His own evident emotion, as when he heard the lament of the Jewish woman in Tuchów and the songs of the Russian soldiers, made people feel that more than other intellectuals, An-sky truly understood the Russian Empire's poor. As the possessed Leah speaks in Khonen's voice, so An-sky was believed to speak in the voices of the poor whose lore he collected. He was described as a *meshulekh,* a messenger from another world who appears in *The Dybbuk* to explain the plot in mystical terms.[8]

The idea that An-sky was a living conduit to the world of the folk, be they Jewish or Russian, is supported by much of his best-known published work and by almost all the memoir literature. He is depicted, as well, as a returnee, someone who first cast aside his Jewish roots for Russian causes, then, repentant, reclaimed his Jewish identity and loyalties. However, his newspaper articles, drafts, letters, and diaries reveal a rebellious and protean figure, more like Khonen than Leah or the Messenger, never able to limit himself to a single set of loyalties; the sources expose him as a self-reviser who drew on his own genuine but conflicting emotions to produce first one, then another story about who he was, what he had seen, and how he felt about it. As in February 1915, he had multiple sympathies, and only through careful editing and a canny appreciation for the demands of different readers could he tailor his experiences into narratives that spoke to distinctive audiences.

An-sky's unwillingness to be tied down made him unusual, but also prototypical of his generation of Jews. The Jews of Eastern Europe would leave a corner of their houses unpainted to remember the destruction of the temple in Jerusalem and to remind themselves that they were in diaspora, not at home. In An-sky's time, the metaphor of the wandering Jew became ever more real. Jews traveled urgently throughout the Pale of Settlement (the Western provinces of the Russian Empire, where they had historically lived and to which they were, for the most part, legally confined), doing business, looking for work, following family, moving from the shtetl to the city or (more rarely) back again. Quotas on university enrollment in the Russian Empire pushed Jewish youth to study in Germany, Switzerland, and France, and the adventurous or desperate left Europe altogether for the New World or sometimes Palestine. In an empire where the majority were peasants, the Jews stood out for their physical and cultural mobility, in spite of the restrictions of the Pale. As religion grew less compelling, ambitious turn-of-the-century Jews like An-sky shed spiritual for secular loyalties: to Russian high culture and literature; to Western European learning and the professional qualifications it could bring; to a panoply of radical parties that promised to destroy the barriers separating Jew from Christian, poor from rich; and eventually, to the new ideologies of Jewish socialism, Zionism, and the belief that the old culture could be transformed into something that would unite and strengthen a downtrodden community. Hesitating among all their options, a cohort of the Russian Jews of the last generations before the 1917 revolution were culturally homeless, and An-sky could stand in for all of them, as reaf-firmed by his success as a journalist, an editor, a public speaker, and a radical activist, occupations where such Jews were overrepresented.

An-sky responded to the options that modernity offers by trying on first one self, then another. In spite of his many shifts, though, he retained a consistent core: the urge to use the power of language to save something or someone, and the desire simultaneously to disappear and to be recognized for his heroic action. An-sky's ability to transform himself and his stories, to move freely among professions, identities, and loyalties, made him both an eccentric and an emblem of the intelligentsia of his age. With his restless mind and soul, he could embody all the richness of Russian and Jewish art and intellectual life in the final years of the empire.

CHAPTER ONE

A Bad Influence

It's hard for a human being to live among cattle!
> —Karl-Ludwig Börne, quoted in the diary of Shloyme-Zanvl
> Rappoport, 1881

O NE DAY IN 1878, two adolescent boys, one rich and one poor, were sweating in the Jewish bathhouse in the Russian provincial capital of Vitebsk. Fourteen-year-old Shloyme-Zanvl Rappoport, a rangy boy with thick dark hair, and thirteen-year-old Chaim Zhitlowsky, a shorter, fairer, curly haired child, had met a few months earlier. Chaim's grandfather owned a candy shop, and his father Joseph was a wealthy lumber merchant who traded within and beyond the Russian Empire. Shloyme-Zanvl's father Aron traveled on business, buying and selling forest land, and was rarely and after a certain point never home; his wife Chana ran a tavern to support her son and his two older sisters, Basya and Sora-Rysia (Sarah). Lying on the warm, slippery wooden benches in the steam room, the two boys imagined their futures. Chaim predicted smugly that—like his own father—he would marry a wealthy bride, a girl with a dowry of ten thousand rubles. Thirteen years later, Shloyme-Zanvl still remembered his intense feelings that day: "I got angry from the depths of my soul." Greeting the birth of Chaim's child, he wrote that he had moved on: "Now, in truth, I'm not angry. I'm even happy for you." Shloyme-Zanvl would travel a long way after 1878, not only out of Vitebsk but symbolically away from what he saw as the confined spaces of Jewish traditional life to a broader perspective, from which he could look back with a mix of irony and nostalgia. Yet his memory of his childhood in Vitebsk Province, and his passionate lifelong friendship with Chaim, would shape the way he saw himself and what he could become.[1]

Shloyme-Zanvl remembered the bathhouse because it was one of the centers of Jewish life in Vitebsk, one node in a geography that included

Jews and Christians, peasants and merchants, cities, shtetls, and villages, Russia, Europe, and Asia, all the people and places that would matter to him over his lifetime. Jews in the Russian Empire, like their Christian neighbors, built heated bathhouses and developed customs around them. The Jewish bathhouse where Shloyme-Zanvl and Chaim sat included a bathing room where attendants would help you wash, a steam room where you could be beaten with birch branches, and a *mikveh,* a ritual bathing pool. Jewish men usually washed on Fridays, before the start of the Sabbath, and women on Wednesdays or Thursdays. Married Jewish women were obligated to immerse themselves in the mikveh each month after they menstruated, before they could have sex with their husbands; without a bathhouse, Jews would be unable to fulfill the commandment to "be fruitful and multiply" and traditional Jewish life would be impossible. *The Dybbuk*'s Khonen would visit the mikveh for repeated, ascetic immersions. The Russian bathhouse also existed between the material and spiritual worlds: girls gathered there at midnight and carried out rituals to learn whom they would marry, just as Shloyme-Zanvl and Chaim sought to peer into their own marital futures. The Russian bathhouse even had a mischievous guardian spirit, the *bannik,* who had to be propitiated with gifts and polite words.[2]

Vitebsk had enough Jews to maintain at least one large bathhouse. The city was positioned ideally for the commerce that supported Chaim's family so well and Shloyme-Zanvl's so badly. It had existed since 1021 as a trading center, near the thick forests of today's Belarus, where the Vitba River (after which the town was named) flows into the broad Dvina River and on to the Baltic Sea. Ancient highways linked it to Smolensk, Novgorod, Kiev, and even Byzantium; Moscow was less than 300 miles away. From the 1860s, Vitebsk was at the crossroads of the train line tying St. Petersburg in the north to Kiev, Odessa, the Black Sea, and Asia in the south, and the line connecting Moscow in the east to Riga, the Baltic Sea, and Europe in the west. Jews lived in the city from the late sixteenth century, working as craftsmen, merchants, and middlemen for Polish aristocrats and enjoying the protection of the Polish kings. Vitebsk and its Jews were incorporated into the Russian Empire with the first partition of Poland in 1772, and although the Russian rulers were ambivalent about their new non-Christian subjects, both Vitebsk itself and its Jewish population grew quickly. By 1897, the city had 65,000 residents; the nearby forests supplied materials for the bustling lumber business, shipyards, and paper factories where they worked. Over half the population— some 34,420 people—were Jews. The city belonged to the empire, and Russian culture occupied an honored place in it: the ringing of church bells measured the days, cathedral towers marked the skyline, and Eastern Orthodox believers and loyal soldiers proceeded through the streets on church festivals and national holidays. But the city at the end of the nineteenth century was full of not just churches and government offices but also Jewish shops; by 1909 it had two synagogues and over sixty prayer houses. As the artist Marc (Movshe) Chagall, another Vitebsk Jew, recalled, Jews were everywhere, "running back and forth in circles, or just walking aimlessly."[3]

Chaim lived in the center of town, on Castle Street, which had once led to an ancient fortress. People arranged to meet on his street, strolled down it, and admired the two- and three-story stone houses with their elegant painted facades and the goods in the ground-floor shop windows. The Zhitlowsky family's three-story house, with nineteen windows in front, was right by the Dvina. It belonged to his father and uncle; the family occupied the second floor, and they rented the third to a Russian police colonel. At home, they enjoyed all the warmth of traditional Jewish holidays and food and many of the riches of secular culture, for increasingly as Chaim and his eight younger siblings grew up and his father grew wealthier, his family embraced non-Jewish civilization. They rarely interacted with Christians as equals: they encountered Russians, Poles, and Germans as city officials to be feared and bribed, teachers to be placated, servants to be commanded, customers and suppliers to be bargained with, but almost never friends. Nonetheless, the Zhitlowsky family, like other Jewish families in their position in the last decades of the nineteenth century, found Russian culture alluring and took pride in their own mastery of it. They had a library full of Russian books, and they hosted evening gatherings where music was performed and Russian poetry read. Moscow was so near—Vitebsk was closer to it than any other major city in the Jewish Pale of Settlement—and St. Petersburg a direct train ride away; artists on tour took the train from the empire's capitals to perform in Vitebsk's City Theater, which held 600 people.[4]

Moscow was close, but the rural parts of Vitebsk Province were close too. Behind the grand facades on Castle Street were courtyards with horses, cows, and chickens brought from the countryside for sale. Many of the Jews of Vitebsk were themselves from shtetls, and they returned frequently. Shloyme-Zanvl had been born on October 15, 1863, in Chashniki, a shtetl in the Lepel district at the province's southern border. In 1897 it had 4,590 inhabitants, of whom 3,480 (about 75 percent) were Jews, craftsmen and merchants who served the needs of the Slavic peasants in the nearby countryside. The family's move to Vitebsk may have followed the father's departure, since single mothers often went to bigger cities where they could find better work. Chaim's father Joseph was born in Vitebsk, but he married a woman from Ushachi and the young couple lived for a few years there with her family; Chaim was born there in the spring of 1865, before they returned to Vitebsk. Chagall, born in 1887, a generation after Chaim and Shloyme-Zanvl, had roots in yet another shtetl, Liozno.[5]

Like Chagall, Shloyme-Zanvl lived on one of the poorer streets of the city. His mother's tavern was on a side street near the Vitba River, and her clients were poor Jews and Christians. It was an easy walk from Castle Street, but growing up in the tavern, Shloyme-Zanvl saw "wild scenes from Russian private and family life," things that Chaim knew of only from books. He learned to value the exposure that poverty gave him to the lives of other poor people, and he eventually wrote about what he had seen. He used his own childhood to claim legitimacy as a witness, telling another writer, "I was born and lived till age 18 in a tavern, so I know all these poor people and not-so-poor ones very well in this setting and very badly outside of it."[6]

In a sketch he wrote in his twenties, Shloyme-Zanvl described a tavern much like his mother's, from the perspective of a young Jewish tavern-keeper named Chanka, the diminutive form of his own mother's name. Together with her grandmother Malka, she serves poor peasants and craftsmen, pathetic men and women who fight and waste their money on drink. "The beggar runs in for a drink the earliest, then the worker and craftsman, then the clerk, and after that the rest of the drinkers. But the first sale of the day will always be to a beggar." The narrator sympathizes with the clients, disapproves of the tavernkeepers' greed, and registers the Jews' horror when a peasant beats his wife and a mother strikes her child. The tavernkeepers are disgusted by their clients' alcoholism. When a customer tells Malka that she would like to buy something to eat along with her vodka, the old lady is surprised and delighted.[7]

Shloyme-Zanvl undoubtedly did see scenes like these in his mother's tavern. The ethnographic perspective of his writing is that of the barkeeper who can listen in on customers' conversations, and it may have grown out of a childhood spent observing people different from his own family. He depicted Chanka the young tavernkeeper as an amateur ethnographer. After a fistfight during which the peasant Aksinia is beaten, she weeps and Chanka comforts her by giving her the first words of folk songs:

> Directing a concentrated, steady gaze at her, she said quietly, "Aksinia, listen! 'Oh . . . they caught. . . .' Well?" And bending over her, she continued to look at her expectantly.

Aksinia immediately stopped complaining and called out loudly, sobbing, striking her hand against the floor at each word:

Oh! They caught! A bird! Wait!
And! Will you escape! The net!
And! I've been trapped! By you!

"Aksinia, listen! 'The Devil take!. . . .' Well?" Chanka interrupted her in the same manner and tone.

Aksinia immediately cut short her "song" and began to call out:

The Devil take my cart!
All four wheels!

"Aksinia! 'Oh my cigarette, my friend! . . .' Well?"

Oh my cigarette, my secret friend!
I love you with all my soul!
I am the karing of harararts!

Aksinia still sang plaintively, but was much calmer. She sang two or three more songs under the compelling look and gestures of Chanka until she calmed down completely. Then Chanka helped her get up and took her to the kitchen.

The Jewish tavernkeeper knows the Slavic folk songs better than the peasant herself, and she uses her knowledge to heal her. Each line that Chanka sings is the beginning of a well-known song, while Aksinia's lines are drunken distortions of the lyrics. When Chanka gets Aksinia to sing, she connects her with a tradition that provides an antidote to the violence in her life. The tavern enabled Shloyme-Zanvl to think of folklore as a force for communal healing, a vision that would inspire him throughout his life, and it allowed him to imagine folk songs as the dynamic product of interactions among Jews and Slavs.[8]

Jewish tavernkeepers were often criticized for providing the conditions under which peasants could drink. Shloyme-Zanvl's sketch confirmed that Jews earned money from alcoholic peasants, but suggested that they had no desire to harm their customers. He sidestepped the Russian stereotype that depicted Jewish tavernkeepers as greedy exploiters and the Jewish stereotype that the peasants were simply drunken boors. Instead, he saw the tavern as offering the possibility of peaceful relations and comfort taken in traditional culture.

Shloyme-Zanvl and Chaim came from different homes, but one day not long before Chaim turned thirteen, they met on the street and started talking. Impulsively, Chaim invited Shloyme-Zanvl to hear him give his bar mitzvah *drash* (a speech about a biblical text) and come to the celebratory meal afterward. Over the next four years, the two boys spent as much time together as they could. They played games, building and defending a "temple" and pretending to be firemen, but they devoted most of their energy to reading and talking. On Castle Street, Chaim's friends joined their discussions. Shmuel (Samuil) Gurevich, a boy a bit younger than Chaim whose father was also a wealthy lumber merchant and who lived across the street from the Zhitlowskys, had a practical disposition and a warm heart; he was generous with his family's money (and later his own) to help his impecunious friends. Masha Reinus was Chaim's slightly younger cousin. Because her father was having financial problems, she had come from Elets, in central Russia south of Moscow, to live with the Zhitlowskys and help care for Chaim's sisters and brothers; she later worked for the Gurevich family. Masha was sensible, "a girl with a man's brain," as the family thought. On the Sabbath, when she had free time, Chaim and his friends sought her opinion, and when the boys got carried away over some idea she chided them for their "calflike rapture." Another friend, Berl (Boris) Reinus, Masha's cousin on her father's side, was full of intelligence and willpower. Like many Jewish boys and girls, kept out of high school by the quota system or unable to afford the fees, he decided to study for the high school exams on his own. He mastered everything quickly, even new languages: after a short time with his Latin and French textbooks, he could read Tacitus and Victor Hugo in the original. He threw himself just as passionately into arguments, where he could be poisonously sarcastic.[9]

Education first divided, then united Chaim and Shloyme-Zanvl. Chaim was enrolled in a gymnasium, a Russian-language high school where he remembered tension between the liberal German principal and the more conservative, even anti-Semitic students (the Jewish students, in contrast, were all "political"). Shloyme-Zanvl's mother could not afford to send him to school beyond *heder,* the one-room elementary school for reading the Talmud that most shtetl boys went through. Listening to the patrons in his mother's tavern, Shloyme-Zanvl understood the languages of the street: Vitebsk Yiddish, with its "Litvish" (Lithuanian) accent and strong Russian influences, the Belorussian speech of peasants recently arrived from the countryside, the Russian of the city administrators, and perhaps the Polish that, a century after the partitions, could still be heard here and there. He had no formal non-Jewish education, but police records noted that he learned to read Russian at home. Chaim helped him with this, and Shloyme-Zanvl reminisced about "taking dictation" from his younger friend, mastering the standard literary language that a gymnasium education offered the city's well-heeled children, whose families knew that speaking and writing the Russian of the empire's center would distinguish them from their provincial peers. Writing mattered: what would make Shloyme-Zanvl stand out later was not that he could read Russian (his sister Sora-Rysia could too) but that he could write correctly.[10]

The boys also studied Jewish texts together. Chaim was tutored in Talmud study at home, but he would meet Shloyme-Zanvl at a local study house to read Talmud. The boys used the Hebrew and Aramaic skills they gained there for other purposes: to read the works of the Haskalah (the Jewish enlightenment movement), Hebrew poems, novels, and articles by Jewish men (and a very few women) who longed to refashion Jewish literature and Jewish life on a "modern" Western European model. They read the *maskilim* (adherents of the Haskalah), Hebrew writers born twenty to thirty years before them and raised deep inside a tradition that they urged their readers to step away from in order to enter the broader world of secular learning. In his 1876 autobiography, *The Sins of Youth,* Moses Leyb Lilienblum depicted the life of a thinking man within the traditional Jewish community as an unending cycle of torments. Everyone around him believed whole-heartedly, but he doubted the existence of God—and his loss of faith was also a loss of community. When he aired his doubts, the elders branded him an atheist and tried to have him exiled to Siberia. Some of the Jews of Shloyme-Zanvl's generation responded to Lilienblum with passionate sympathy. David Frishman, a writer born three years earlier than Shloyme-Zanvl who would eventually publish the Hebrew translation of *The Dybbuk,* could not sleep after reading *Sins of Youth:* "It was perhaps the most extraordinary confession of a human being I had read in all my life." For Chaim and Shloyme-Zanvl, though, reading Lilienblum was probably less of a shock than it had been to Frishman. Chaim's father Joseph was a worldly merchant who read Haskalah literature himself, so when his son dipped into modern Hebrew literature, he knew he was not rebelling against his family; Shloyme-Zanvl's father was not around to defy.[11]

The boys' Russian reading had more subversive potential. At first, Chaim and Shloyme-Zanvl read romantic novels, written in Russian or translated from French. Shloyme-Zanvl's favorite was Victor Hugo. Reading *Les misérables,* he learned that anyone could aspire to heroic self-sacrifice. "To be superb it is not necessary to carry, like Yvon, the ducal morion, or to have in one's hand, like Esplandian, a living flame, or, like Phyles, the father of Polydamas, to have brought back from Ephyra a suit of armor given by the king of Corinth; it is enough to give one's life for a conviction or a loyalty." Chaim and Shloyme-Zanvl loved the radical edge in Heinrich Heine and Ludwig Börne, two early-nineteenth-century German satirists of Jewish origin who were popular among the maskilim. They dipped into Haskalah works in Russian: Sora-Rysia, who shared the boys' political inclinations, had a bound copy of old issues of the Odessa newspaper *Rassvet* (Dawn) from the 1860s, and Chaim and Shloyme-Zanvl pored over its stories of Jews making their way into Russian culture.[12]

From there, the boys moved on to modern Russian literature and the radical critics who interpreted it. Even in the relatively liberal 1870s, the censor did not permit open discussion of political questions, so the public learned from politically engaged critics how to read between the lines and find the veiled politics in fictional works. In 1862, Ivan Turgenev published *Fathers and Children,* an account of the life and death of the brash young medical student Evgeny Vasilievich Bazarov. The brilliant radical literary critic, Dmitry Pisarev, then twenty-two years old, wrote a review explaining to young people such as Shloyme-Zanvl how to use Turgenev's book as a model for what contemporaries called a "nihilist" lifestyle. He pointed out Bazarov's lack of sentiment or superstition: "As an empiricist, Bazarov acknowledges only what can be felt with the hands, seen with the eyes, tasted by the tongue, in a word, only what can be examined with one of the five senses." Pisarev praised Bazarov's uncompromising "realism," even though it made him discount what others see as beauty. Although Bazarov dies what Pisarev saw as a noble death—poisoned by infection from a corpse he had been dissecting—the critic did not insist that his readers follow his example to the letter. "We must live while we are alive, eat dry bread if there is no roast beef, know many women if it is not possible to love a woman, and, in general, we must not dream about orange trees and palms, when under foot are snowdrifts and the cold tundra."[13]

In trying to model their own lives on Pisarev, Shloyme-Zanvl and Chaim were typical of their generation. By the time Shloyme-Zanvl used the experiences of his teens in his fiction, he would give ironic descriptions of yeshiva students who became so obsessed with Pisarev that they memorized his literary-critical articles as one would memorize Talmudic passages. When he was a teenager himself, though, he took his Pisarev seriously. Shloyme-Zanvl and Chaim, like Jewish and non-Jewish readers throughout the empire, drew a powerful political energy from their readings of Pisarev and his comrades. And along with Shmuel, Boris, Masha, and Sora-Rysia, they combined their reading of literature with social theory, absorbing the radical critique of capitalism and concluding that the commerce that supported so many of the Jews of Vitebsk—including their own parents—was immoral.[14]

Their parents' very lifestyle was unethical, as Shloyme-Zanvl, Chaim, and many of their contemporaries (including Vladimir Lenin) learned from *What Is to Be Done?* This 1863 novel by Pisarev's friend Nikolai Chernyshevsky describes a group of "new people" who reject all the old rules, especially those governing sex and marriage. The heroine, Vera Pavlovna, who is married to one man but loves another, sets up a sewing collective to employ liberated ex-prostitutes. The most radically new hero, Rakhmetov, rejects sex altogether as a distraction from the revolutionary cause. He also eats raw meat and sleeps on a bed of nails to toughen himself up. Shloyme-Zanvl and Chaim saw *What Is To Be Done?* as "the holiest of all the holy writings" and dreamed of setting up a commune of their own. Chernyshevsky's vision of communal free love made no allowances for children and could not be easily reconciled with the Jewish emphasis on marriage and procreation; the obvious conclusion was that Jewish tradition was wrong. Shloyme-Zanvl, who had reacted so angrily in the bathhouse when his friend mentioned marriage, and sometimes wrote mournfully of his loneliness, at other points referred to his bachelor state as though he were one of Chernyshevsky's heroes. He told Chaim he had once thought it was a sin "to forget about all people for the sake of your own family," and he admitted his suspicion that he might belong to the small number of people in the world "who are able to live not just for the sake of their stomachs . . . who are able to give themselves to some good cause," but who are "scattered, dispersed, broken, poor, exhausted." Even Shloyme-Zanvl's chain-smoking fit Chernyshevsky's model: Rakhmetov's one vice is good cigars.[15]

Once he and his friends had rejected his parents' values, Chaim did not see why he should continue attending the snobby gymnasium they had chosen for him. He began to skip school and spend days in the town library or the drafty attic of Shloyme-Zanvl's house, where they could sit in a hideout the older boy had rigged up and smoke strong cigarettes, cheap at seven kopecks per hundred. Shloyme-Zanvl had dreams of studying on his own and passing the gymnasium exams, and he and Chaim did a few math problems together each day, but soon they returned to talking about their favorite writers. They skipped their prayers and took long walks along the Vitba, through Christian neighborhoods where they could smoke on Sabbath without attracting attention; later, they started to smoke on Sabbath openly, where their parents could see. Finally, they began to preach their radicalism to others. Shloyme-Zanvl wrote a play about the evils of the heder, and the two boys began to publish a Yiddish newspaper, which they called *Vitebsker gleklekh* (The Bells of Vitebsk), a nod to the émigré Alexander Herzen's famous radical journal, *Kolokol* (The Bell). Shloyme-Zanvl wrote nonfiction, Chaim fiction. Demonstrating his liberal values and his interest in the non-Jewish world, Shloyme-Zanvl wrote an obituary for Dr. Kenig, a local German who had treated the Jews of the town.[16]

For Chaim, his parents stood for everything bad and bourgeois. They sat at the dinner table and talked about how to pickle cucumbers and marinate mushrooms, and the teenage Chaim squirmed at their petty materialism. His mother called in the tailor to let out the family's clothes when they gained weight, which she saw as a sign of their good fortune; gratefully and superstitiously, she murmured a formula to avert the evil eye, and Chaim was appalled. When his father told a risqué joke at the table, Chaim was disgusted at his crudeness. Chaim shared these feelings with Shloyme-Zanvl, whom he viewed as fortunate to have avoided this sort of morally tainted upbringing. Instead, the distraction of his harried mother and the absence of his father made the poorer boy, alone in his attic den, into "a free Cossack."[17]

Shloyme-Zanvl himself was not so sure he was lucky to have a life unlike Chaim's. He rarely wrote or spoke about his childhood or his parents, whereas Chaim remembered them vividly: Chana Rappoport as hard-working, poor, and honest, and Aron Rappoport as a self-important petty tyrant, snobby about his lineage and his status as a *cohen* (a descendent of the biblical priestly class), who came back to his family so rarely that his son barely knew him. Some of Shloyme-Zanvl's early story drafts feature a family like his own, with an industrious mother, two older daughters, and a younger son. The children sympathize with their mother and are intrigued by but fearful of an older male figure (an uncle, a grandfather) who appears rarely. There and in his 1884 novel *History of a Family*, Shloyme-Zanvl wrote critically of a way of life common among Jews, in which mothers needed to earn money and run the home. These texts suggest suppressed anger at his own father and pity for his mother.[18]

He used more elements of his own childhood in a later story, "In a Jewish Family" (1896): money problems, estranged parents, a mostly absent father, a lonely son who is drawn to non-Jewish culture. The son, Leybka, rebels against his heder and his teacher, who beats him for dancing with Christian peasant children. Leybka's parents have little sympathy for him, but the family's servant, Chana, defends him. She is an alternative mother for Leybka, because when he had been ill at the age of five, he was given a new name signifying life (Chaim) and officially sold to Chana, so as to fool the Angel of Death: "He would show up with instructions to take the soul of Leyb, son of Malka, and find in his place Chaim, son of

Chana. . . . The trick worked, the angel returned empty-handed, and Leybka got better." The story was published in Yiddish as "Chana the Cook," drawing attention to Shloyme-Zanvl's use, once again, of his mother's name. The Chana in that story is an *agunah,* an abandoned (literally chained or anchored) wife, prevented by Jewish law from remarrying; when he gave his mother's name to this character, Shloyme-Zanvl suggested that his mother may actually have been an agunah, the classical object of the pity of the maskilim, who saw the plight of abandoned wives as a perfect example of the flaws in the rabbinic legal system. There is no evidence on what terms Shloyme-Zanvl's father left his mother, whether he was expected back, whether she even wanted him to return; but we know that cases of abandoned wives increased during Shloyme-Zanvl's childhood, as husbands sought to avoid the expenses associated with divorce and took advantage of greater mobility to leave their wives. Want ads in Jewish newspapers in the Russian Empire testified to the frequency of husbands leaving their wives and traveling through the Pale of Settlement. Shloyme-Zanvl's father may or may not have been among them, but the story indicates that his son understood all the reasons why it might be better to be Chaim, like his rich friend, than Leybka, and why he and his family should be pitied, not envied.[19]

In spite of all his radical convictions, Shloyme-Zanvl recognized that Chaim offered a path to a better existence. He understood the arguments condemning rich lumber merchants such as Joseph Zhitlowsky and their bourgeois family life, and it took him a decade to forgive Chaim for boasting in the bathhouse about his wealth. This did not prevent him from constantly asking his younger friend for loans and treasuring the gifts—such as his excellent written Russian—that Chaim could give him only because of his family's money. In spite of his fantasy that he was a Rakhmetov type, a self-denying "new man" who could bear any hardship, he saw his friendship with Chaim as liberating and he thanked the younger boy for "setting me on the path out of the tavern's dirt." When the boys were teenagers, Chaim's and Shmuel's parents, blaming Shloyme-Zanvl for their sons' defiance, finally forbade the older boy to enter their homes. Chaim saw the episode as funny, but Shloyme-Zanvl, who would go on to write stories and plays ("On a New Course," *Father and Son*) where parents come to understand the wisdom of their children's radical choices, may not have agreed. He had charmed Chaim and his friends, and although he knew why Chaim criticized his own parents, it probably mattered to him to charm them as well.[20]

Chaim continued to be susceptible to his friend's charisma. At one point the two boys developed an elaborate parlor trick. When a group of friends

were gathered, chatting in a darkened room, Shloyme-Zanvl would sit in a
corner by a lamp and announce that he could read minds. He invited
everyone present to write a question on a piece of paper, fold it, and put
it in front of him. He picked up someone's paper, held it, still folded, to
his forehead, and gave an answer, then unfolded the paper and read the
question, which always matched his answer perfectly. The key to the
hoax was Chaim, who told Shloyme-Zanvl his question in advance.
Shloyme-Zanvl always began by answering Chaim's question, then pretended to read that one out loud, while really reading the question that
he would answer next; he opened Chaim's paper last. "Even though I
was his partner in the game," Chaim remembered, "I was still strongly
affected by the mystical atmosphere that he created." Chaim knew just
how much Shloyme-Zanvl loved mystification and play-acting; at the
same time, he believed that in a sense, his friend really could see into the
souls of others, and that his unerring intuitions about people's feelings
explained his ability to maintain friendships with men and women who
were very different from him.[21]

The boys' parlor game showcased Shloyme-Zanvl's acting ability and
Chaim's loyalty to him. Shloyme-Zanvl was well aware of the social gap
between him and his friends—an awareness heightened, undoubtedly,
when the Zhitlowskys and the Gureviches chased him from their homes—
but he stayed close to both Chaim and Shmuel. The adolescent need for
acceptance among his wealthier friends may have honed his ability to
make himself over to suit his circumstances, a chameleon quality that he
never lost. Had Chaim been less faithful, though, the parlor trick, and
much else in Shloyme-Zanvl's life, would have failed. Shloyme-Zanvl's
long-repressed anger at his friend's mention of a rich bride suggests he
knew how much rested for him on Chaim's friendship, and he always
feared losing it; he would return to the subjects of class difference and
arranged marriage in *The Dybbuk*. No matter how charming he was, no
matter how cleverly he could read people's minds, no matter how well he
knew the radical theory that told him his experience was more valuable
than theirs, he never forgot that he was essentially a fatherless child,
raised in a dirty tavern, whose rich friends might abandon him at any
moment.

As with other Jews in Vitebsk Province, Shloyme-Zanvl's daily activities
were governed by Jewish law and custom: he ate kosher food, visited the
bathhouse regularly, learned to read the Talmud, and observed the holidays and the Sabbath (until he deliberately flouted it by smoking). Such
regular Jewish practice was easy in Vitebsk, where Judaism came in two

varieties: Hasidism, a mystical movement developed in the eighteenth century by a series of charismatic leaders who emphasized ecstatic prayer, rather than study, as a means to reach the divine, and Mitnaged (literally, opposition), a movement that rejected Hasidism as irrational and insisted on the importance of text study. Along with its sixty Hasidic prayer houses, Vitebsk boasted a renowned Mitnaged yeshiva. Although the leaders of the two movements worked against each other in the late eighteenth century, by Shloyme-Zanvl's time they got along with little strife. Mixed marriages were not uncommon, including that of Zhitlowsky's parents, whose father had been brought up in Mitnaged, while his mother was from a Hasidic family. In the shtetls around Vitebsk, the Mitnaged movement could not compete with Hasidism, particularly the Chabad, or Lubovitch, movement founded by a local mystic, Shneur Zalman of Liady (born in 1745 in Liozno). The name of this movement is an acronym of the Hebrew words *hokhma* (wisdom), *bina* (understanding), and *daat* (knowledge), which symbolize the intellectualism that distinguishes Chabad from other Hasidic strains.[22]

During his early years in Chashniki, Shloyme-Zanvl was probably exposed to Chabad Hasidism. He may have been drawing on his own life when the narrator in his 1892 story, "Mendel the Turk," used poetic terms to describe the evening shadows and muted chanting in a Hasidic prayer house that "brought back memories from my own distant childhood." On Sabbath, during the break between the afternoon and evening prayers, the men would tell legends of the *tsaddiks*, the founders of Hasidism, and their wondrous feats. They would sing wordless songs and prayers, prolonging the Sabbath as the prayer house darkened and the stars came out. Boys would listen to the stories and songs, and some would twist towels into "bombs" that they would throw at the congregants. Shloyme-Zanvl remembered that the victims easily forgave their tricks.

> The kind-hearted congregant would further express his warm feelings toward the youngsters by taking a mischievous little boy on his knees, stroking his head as tenderly as if he were his own son and singing all the while. He didn't even look to see who his captive was. The startled child would be silenced by this unexpected benevolence from a stranger. His heart would beat with joy, and he would smile contentedly, grateful for the gentle hand on his head.

Grateful for a man's attention, this child evokes Shloyme-Zanvl's own childhood longing. Boys are usually brought into the world of male Hasidic spirituality by their fathers. Without a father, Shloyme-Zanvl would have found it hard to enter, but he could have listened from the outside to the songs and stories in the Chabad prayer house. Like Chaim's house on Castle Street, this was an intact community where he could not be sure he was welcome.[23] His increasing interest in Hasidism as an adult—when he moved from collecting Hasidic songs and stories from friends to collecting on his own in Vitebsk Province to mounting a full-scale ethnographic expedition to the sources of Ukrainian Hasidism—may have grown out of the longing for that community (a whole room of substitute fathers) that he expressed in this story.

Whether or not he felt at home in the Chabad prayer house in Chashniki, Shloyme-Zanvl lived with Hasidism and it left a trace on his behavior. He chain-smoked as he read, wrote, and talked with friends; the habit, and the rapturous terms in which he sometimes described it, recall not just Chernyshevsky's Rakhmetov but also the Hasidic belief that tobacco use can bring one closer to holiness. More broadly, as Hasidism uses ascetic means to attain ecstatic states that promise access to the divine, so Shloyme-Zanvl lived an ascetic life and experienced moments of ecstatic communication, not with God, but with other human beings. As a political propagandist, he may also have been influenced by Hasidism, whose initial radicalism consisted in its leaders' insistence on reaching out to ignorant and illiterate Jews.[24]

Hasidic roots and the ability to reach a wide audience were only two of the things that Shloyme-Zanvl shared with Marc Chagall. Both men grew up in poor Vitebsk families, but both became friends with wealthier boys who shared their ambitions and interests and gave them opportunities their own parents could not. Chagall's wealthy friend and fellow art student, Viktor Mekler, introduced him into his own circle of Russian-speaking young people from the center of town; he eventually married a friend of one of them, Berta (Bella) Rosenfeld, whose father, a jeweler, was the Zhitlowskys' Castle Street neighbor. Like Shloyme-Zanvl, Chagall as a youth embraced Russian culture and turned indifferently away from Jewishness in general and Hasidism in particular, but both men would become famous as cultural revivalists who drew on Jewish sources to produce art with a broad modern appeal. The coincidence emerges from the advantages of a youth spent in Vitebsk, where the shtetls and the Russian capitals both felt close and a child could grow up to become a mediator between them. Marc Chagall and Shloyme-Zanvl Rappoport both knew firsthand the "authentic" Jewish life of the hinterlands, Shloyme-Zanvl from his early years in Chashniki and Chagall from his summer visits back to Liozno; both also knew Russian well, and the experiences of their youth helped them intuit the desires of big-city audiences.[25]

Shloyme-Zanvl's Vitebsk years ended early in 1881. At seventeen, he traveled about thirty miles east to another place where Jews were in the majority, Liozno, the shtetl where the founder of Chabad had been born and Chagall's mother still lived. It was only half the size of Chashniki: in 1897, it had a population of 2,474, including 1,665 Jews. Shloyme-Zanvl worked there as a private tutor of secular subjects, hiding his radicalism from the Jewish leaders of the town while doing his best to lead their children astray. He kept a diary in the form of a letter to Chaim, where he recorded how it felt to live on his own for the first time; he was already thinking like a writer, trying to preserve his impressions for future use. "My head is full! Scene after scene, one better than the next." He worried that he was too busy to get it all down: "Certainly a lot is missing and I will certainly forget a lot." He wrote about things he had never seen before—such as a woman's death—as well as recounting his dreams, his anxieties, and his vows to be more frugal.[26]

He felt far superior to the traditional Jews of Liozno. Börne, he remembered, had written, "It's hard for a human being to live among cattle!" He felt like the lone human among Jews who were far more conservative than those he had shocked in Vitebsk by smoking on the Sabbath. In Liozno, Shloyme-Zanvl noted glumly, even smiling at a Jew who was not wearing a skullcap would make people think you were a dangerous liberal, reading secular books instead of studying rabbinic texts made you a heretic, and thinking that learning Russian was as important as studying the Talmud made people see you as an apostate. Isolated among "cattle," the teenager turned inward. He wrote about staying up all night in his room. "The devils only know (or even they don't know) how many cigarettes I smoked. I saw one vision after another, each more beautiful than the next." When morning came, he finally fell asleep and had strange dreams of his friends back in Vitebsk until a happy interruption: three letters from home arrived at once.[27]

If he wanted to convince the traditional townspeople to hire him as a tutor, Shloyme-Zanvl found that he would have to play the role of an observant, synagogue-going young man. "You have to go to *shul* [synagogue]," his landlord told him. "To shul?" he asked, horrified. "Yes . . . to shul. You have to . . . you must go to shul!" Shloyme-Zanvl went to the shul and reacted with scorn. "The shul was like a stable where there are horses." As for the ark holding the scrolls of the Torah, even to describe it would be to "desecrate the holy places." He started to pray, then noticed two boys giving him funny looks, pulling each other by their coattails, and giggling, until a synagogue official came up to them and yelled, "Pray!"[28]

The boys were not the only ones to guess that Shloyme-Zanvl was out of place in the shul. Another man of about 30, sensing his true inclinations, revealed himself as a secret ally. He offered his hand and asked Shloyme-Zanvl, "Do you already have some lessons set up?"

"Very few," Shloyme-Zanvl answered. "Almost none."

"It would have to be hard here," his new friend agreed. "People are cursed here. Come, I'll try to do something about it."

He took Shloyme-Zanvl away and explained that he was a *melamed*, a heder teacher who for now had to "dance to the tune" of the conservative shtetl parents. He made Shloyme-Zanvl a list of families that he could approach, and offered to go with him. Shloyme-Zanvl refused, saying that he didn't want to trouble the older man.[29] The encounter with the melamed showed him that this seemingly sleepy shtetl was a land ripe for rebellion, where insurgents lurked everywhere, recognizable to each other through subtle signs. Even while Shloyme-Zanvl stood in the shul and mouthed the prayers, something in his tone, stance, or style made it obvious to the melamed that he was a fellow rebel, as opposed to the "cattle." The boys pulling each others' coattails may also have guessed that although he billed himself as a Russian tutor, Shloyme-Zanvl really wanted to teach the children of the town to read the heretical books of the maskilim and the Russian radicals, to abandon the religious regulations governing their parents' lives, and to dedicate themselves to ideals their parents would find abhorrent.

What is remarkable is that Shloyme-Zanvl did find work. In the early 1880s, even in as traditional a bastion of Hasidism as Liozno, Jewish parents wanted their children to read and write Russian. Even though they knew that Russian could be the gateway for dangerous ideas, and even though they must have been suspicious of the tutor from Vitebsk, they saw what he had to offer as so crucial that they were willing to invite him into their homes and leave him alone with their children. The seeds of change had been sown even before Shloyme-Zanvl arrived in town. For over a decade, Jewish parents had already been hiring *shraybers* (literally, writers), poorly paid tutors to teach their children the basics of Russian and sometimes German. These tutors themselves often barely knew the languages they taught, though they did not necessarily claim to train their students to do more than write neatly. Nonetheless, Shloyme-Zanvl's first encounters with his future employers were difficult. When he went door to door to find tutoring work, Shloyme-Zanvl found the householders unappealing. He went into one house and saw a man in an undershirt with a stubbly beard eating at a table. Faced with the man's "cunning smile," he could not decide how to begin. "I heard that you need . . . a . . . tutor for your children," he forced himself to say, turning red and feeling his head begin to spin. "I am a tutor from Vitebsk."[30]

Shloyme-Zanvl would look back with a mix of admiration and irony at his adolescent self: "I abounded in dashing self-reliance and was greatly inspired by the high ideals which lit up my vision." He knew that he would have to conceal his radical ideals if he wanted to succeed in spreading enlightenment among the young people. "To avoid provoking malicious acts against me from the start, I put on a mask of piety and showed that my only purpose was to earn my keep. I played my role well, I obtained lessons, and soon I was in contact with several boys." But the secret agent was unable to maintain his cover for long. One source of his undoing was his diary. He usually hid it away, but one day he forgot to lock the box where he kept it, and his landlady's daughter came in and found it. Highly amused by Shloyme-Zanvl's sarcastic comments about her neighbors, she invited a group of friends over and read portions of the diary out loud. The next day, Shloyme-Zanvl, who knew nothing of his unexpected publicity, went to the home of two of his students and was greeted by their furious mother. "Listen here, you teacher!" she yelled. "I hired you to teach my girls to read and write, but not for you to write down that my Yakhninka's nose is dirty, and that my Fridinka has big teeth, and that I go about in a bedraggled dress. I can assure you that even if I wear a bedraggled dress, whatever I put in the garbage is worth more than you and your fine learning. And you can go back where you came from! Teachers like you I don't need!" Fortunately for him, his landlady's daughter had only read a few of his diary entries. At the next homes he visited, his students' parents greeted him, as he recalled, "not only without anger and abuse, but with even more friendliness than usual. These women, rolling with laughter, begged me to let them read how I described their neighbors."[31]

The exposure of his diary was only the beginning of Shloyme-Zanvl's troubles. On March 1, 1881, Tsar Alexander II was assassinated by a group of revolutionaries that included one Jewish woman. Six weeks later, pogroms (violent riots) began in the south of the empire. In big cities and small towns along the railway lines, mobs of men attacked Jewish property and sometimes Jews themselves; during the two-year wave of pogroms, between 50 and a few hundred Jews were killed. There were no pogroms in Vitebsk Province or anywhere in the northern part of the Pale of Settlement. Jewish radicals such as Shloyme-Zanvl and his friends reacted to the pogroms in various ways. A few welcomed the news of peasant unrest, believing that the violence against Jews would soon become

violence against landowners and would lead to full-scale revolution. Increasingly over time, others—and the revolutionary parties as a whole—
condemned the pogroms. News of the pogroms shocked Chaim and inspired him to reimagine Jewish life in Eastern Europe. He would eventually
become a maverick Jewish cultural leader, an advocate of a secular Jewish identity based on Yiddish. Shloyme-Zanvl himself was apparently
unaffected by the news; he did not mention the 1881–1882 pogroms in
his letters or memoirs. When the Liozno elders learned of the violence
against Jews in the south, they became convinced that the real cause was
the growing disregard among the young for religious traditions: in His
anger, God had sent the pogroms to punish the Jews.[32]

Meanwhile, some of the teenage boys in town had begun to meet in
Shloyme-Zanvl's room late on Friday nights to discuss their ideas. He
lent them books, which they read secretly. Among them was *Sins of
Youth*. One of Shloyme-Zanvl's young friends stayed up all night reading
Lilienblum's account of alienation from his father's religious worldview
and his eventual rejection by the community. Like many of the heroes of
maskilic fiction and autobiography, the boy brought *Sins of Youth* to the
study house in the morning to read it under cover of the Talmud—then,
unfortunately, fell asleep. The forbidden book was discovered by a pious
student who happened upon the line, "Who can prove there is a God?"
Although the boy awoke and snatched the volume away, the damage
had been done. In the ensuing furor, a dozen secular books were found
in people's homes and publicly burned. Shloyme-Zanvl comforted the
culprit, telling him that the punishment for reading forbidden books was
itself a heroic act with religious significance: "Calming him, I proved to
him that his and his brother's sufferings were a sort of self-sacrifice for
Kiddush ha-Shem [sanctification of the name, or martyrdom as an expression of devotion to Judaism]—on behalf of the Haskalah. This reasoning encouraged him." The boy may have felt better, but one of the
shtetl fathers threatened Shloyme-Zanvl that if he did not leave immediately, the police would be bribed to remove him.[33]

Shloyme-Zanvl took his advice and left quickly, but the few months he
spent in Liozno became a touchstone for him: in novels, short stories,
and a memoir, he would return half a dozen times to the theme of radical
Russian tutors going underground in conservative shtetls, always reevaluating the meaning of the events he saw and his own role in them, and
distancing himself increasingly from his teenage sense of the tremendous
importance of his task. In 1881, though, Shloyme-Zanvl truly believed in
the sacredness of his mission to radicalize the youth of Liozno. The shtetl
elders saw reading forbidden texts as a dangerous transgression, and

Shloyme-Zanvl agreed with them that the written or spoken word was a powerful weapon. A picture of him and Chaim from the winter of 1882 conveys this youthful feeling of self-importance. Shloyme-Zanvl's dark hair is carefully parted and combed to the side, and he wears a bowtie knotted at his neck, a clean shirt, and a solemn expression. Both boys—who look younger than their seventeen and nineteen years, respectively—have uncovered heads, a public marker of their rejection of Jewish tradition. Even as a teenager, Shloyme-Zanvl impressed his friends with his idealism: Samuil remembered him from this period as less worldly than other boys, shocked, for example, by seeing a woman sit on a man's lap in public.[34]

Earnest though he was, Shloyme-Zanvl, as he came increasingly to recognize, was a poor conspirator, his mission to Liozno a failure. He loved observing the shtetl folk, and he succeeded, at least at first, at pretending to be one of them. But the thrill of playing a role, and the delight of knowing he was able to charm and persuade people—the parents who hired him to teach their children, the angry melamed, the landlady's daughter, and later the children who met in his room to discuss Lilienblum—made him lose focus on his real task of fomenting rebellion. He made mistakes, leaving his diary for the taking, and lending *Sins of Youth* to a child too young to take care of it. In Liozno as in Vitebsk, he was more attentive to the effort to please the people in his immediate vicinity than to his own long-range plans, and he may have already suspected that if he really wanted to influence people, he would be able to do it better in print than in person.

When the community leaders chased him out of Liozno, Shloyme-Zanvl went to Dvinsk, on the western edge of Vitebsk Province. There he decided to turn to practical work, work with his hands. He tried blacksmithing and bookbinding, and stuck longer with the latter. A later co-worker reported that Shloyme-Zanvl never acquired more than the most basic skills of the bookbinder's craft, but the point for him may not have been to become a master bookbinder, but rather to demonstrate to himself and others that he was not the kind of Jew that the maskilim criticized, versed in rabbinic literature but unable to perform any productive work. At the same time, Shloyme-Zanvl tried to break into a different profession by drafting his first novel in Yiddish, *History of a Family,* where he acted on the beliefs that he had once discussed with Chaim and Samuil: fiction was serious stuff, whose purpose was not psychological analysis or romantic entertainment (certainly it should not discuss sex) but a means of transmitting truths that readers needed to know.[35]

He was inspired by a newspaper article about a Jewish ditchdigger who died in an accident at work; his widow demanded that his employer compensate her for his death and ended up receiving 40 rubles. In successive versions of the novel, Shloyme-Zanvl explored themes that fascinated him: self-reform, physical labor, relations between workers and their superiors, the problems of single mothers, and the power of a written or spoken word of protest. His hero, Moisei, leaves the study of rabbinic texts for physical labor as a ditchdigger. The transition from Talmudist to laborer turns him from a "machine," a person who looked "more like a calf than like a man," into a strong father and husband. Yiddish and Russian-Jewish fiction in the late 1870s featured many male characters, by contrast, who could not support their families. Shloyme-Zanvl's story differed both in the depiction of Sora, Moisei's wife, as an effective agent in her own right, and in the depiction of a husband who succeeds in breaking from tradition and finding a job.[36]

In creating a literary hero who abandons Talmud study and begins a "new life" of physical labor, Shloyme-Zanvl acted on the values he shared with other Russian Jewish reformers. One year before he started writing the novel, in 1880, several wealthy Russian Jews created ORT (Society for the Spread of Labor among Jews) to assist Jewish craftsmen, train Jewish children in crafts, and raise money to establish Jewish agricultural schools and farming communities. The ORT founders wanted to combat the poverty of the Russian Jews, and they agreed with the Imperial government that Jews needed to be weaned away from study and commerce and made into "productive" workers. The "productive" work that Moisei chooses reflects the options available in 1881. The founders of ORT either envisioned the Jews of the Pale as building on the artisan work that they already did, or, like the Russian author Lev Tolstoy, they imagined that agricultural labor would allow Jews—along with other disaffected intellectuals—to achieve redemption. It would be unrealistic to imagine Moisei turning straight from Talmudist to farmer, but when he made him a ditchdigger, Shloyme-Zanvl had him do the next best thing: choose an urban job that provided intimate contact with the earth.

In the novel, this choice does not ensure Moisei's happiness. A ditch collapses on him as he works, and soon after he is dug out of the ground, he dies. He is buried on a dark night, and the narrator intones, "A dark night, a dark life, a dark death!"[37] The tragedy leads to changes of all sorts. One of Sora's sisters, Khiena, becomes a prostitute to support her family and gives birth to a child out of wedlock; she later finds happiness with an enlightened man who forgives her for her past. Another sister, Lia, shocks her father by choosing a husband for herself, a modern Jew who dresses in European clothing. After a lawsuit, Berkin, the business-man responsible for Moisei's death, is forced to give Sora 200 rubles, which she uses to open a store. Women, thus, prove capable of making choices that ensure the survival of their families.

The Yiddish publisher Shloyme-Zanvl approached rejected his book manuscript because it looked unlikely to sell. Yiddish fiction publishing had been developing gradually in the Russian Empire since the mid-nineteenth century, as maskilic writers produced satirical stories meant to entertain the Yiddish-speaking masses and simultaneously to point out their faults and inspire them to reform. Some of these satires sold well, such as Y. Y. Linetski's *The Polish Youth,* a runaway best-seller in the late 1860s and early 1870s that lampooned the heder system. Others, includ-ing the brilliantly inventive works of Yankev Sholem Abramovitsh (aka Mendele Moykher Sforim), such as *The Nag* and *The Jew,* were admired by a small maskilic audience but did not reach the broad public at which they were aimed. Yankev Dinezon, a Warsaw writer who would later be-come Shloyme-Zanvl's close friend, had a huge success in the 1877 *Dark Young Man,* a sentimental potboiler that sold 10,000 copies. Nakhum Shaykevitsh (aka Shomer) followed up on Dinezon's success with a series of suspenseful romantic novels full of "extraordinary events," unlikely adventures, and improbable plot twists, and a wide Yiddish reading public devoured them: in 1889 alone, 96,000 copies of Shomer's novels were printed by various publishers, while Sholem Rabinovitsh (Sholem Aleichem) printed only 3,200 copies of his more earnest, maskilic jour-nal, *Di yudishe folksbibliotek* (The Jewish People's Library). There was no room for Shloyme-Zanvl's *History of a Family* in the Yiddish publish-ing world of the early 1880s: it was neither the sort of thriller that Shomer's audience enjoyed nor the kind of comic satire that Linetski had produced and Mendele had perfected.[38]

As he tried to find an audience, Shloyme-Zanvl switched languages, having grasped that his dark depiction of the lives of the poor in *History of a Family* was more marketable to the Russian reader of the early 1880s. Even before the abolition of serfdom in 1863, Russian writers had been producing fiction and reportage about the poor folk in the country-side, and by the early 1880s, writers such as Gleb Uspensky were special-izing in the sort of bleak realism that Shloyme-Zanvl had created in his novel. One of the sons in the Ostrom family, Jewish friends in Dvinsk, translated it into Russian and sent it to a Russian-Jewish journal in St. Petersburg, *Voskhod* (The Dawn).[39]

Shloyme-Zanvl left Dvinsk for another shtetl about the size of Liozno, Osveia, where, again, he gave Russian lessons. In late 1883, he boasted to Samuil about the money he was making, but complained about boredom in his new home: he missed both the "society of freethinkers" and the "antagonism" of the pious.[40] A few months later, he left Osveia and Vitebsk Province altogether, and began moving farther and farther away from the battlefield where pious Jews and freethinkers fought over the souls of their children.

CHAPTER TWO

To the Salt Mines

I beg you, tell me, *what should I do with my life?* Point me toward a field where I can use it to bring some benefit to the people.

> —Shloyme-Zanvl Rappoport, letter to Nikolai Mikhailovsky,
> October 19, 1887

I N THE FALL OF 1884, at almost twenty-one Shloyme-Zanvl Rappoport became a published Russian writer when *History of a Family* came out in the last four monthly issues of *Voskhod*, under "Pseudonymous." A *Voskhod* reviewer the next year praised the novel and its writer, "the broad range of his pen and the complete objectivity of his story . . . his sense for truth and his talent."[1] Literature had taught the teenage Rappoport to rebel. With the publication of his novel, he had become a writer, albeit a nameless one, and entered the class of people who, he believed, were changing the world. At the same time, he was ready to leave the province of his birth to spend seven years wandering the Russian Empire, trying to confirm his heroism to himself and everyone else.

He returned briefly to Vitebsk in 1884, perhaps to observe *shiva,* the seven-day period of mourning, for his mother. He went on to Moscow to see his father Aron, who had been working there; Chaim Zhitlowsky thought his friend wanted to put a symbolic end to his childhood by bidding farewell to a father who had played the role of a "Menachem Mendl" from the stories of Sholem Aleichem, a character with an infinite supply of get-rich-quick schemes, each leaving him—and his long-suffering wife—poorer than before.[2] Aron had once worked for the wealthy Poliakov family, Jewish philanthropists who made their money as financiers and investors building the Russian railway system. Their success did not benefit Aron Rappoport, who had fallen on hard times. He joked with his son about his plans to marry a rich widow, and tried to convince him to stay in Moscow and use his Russian skills to help with some new scheme. Father and son discovered that they had things in common; they stayed up late drinking and talking, cheerfully unconcerned that they had no idea where they would spend the night.

Sitting for a picture at that time, Shloyme-Zanvl's hair was longer than before and combed back from the brow. He already had a full beard and mustache. Aron's coat was longer than his son's, more traditional, but neither one wore a skullcap, suggesting that Aron was not observant and that life was easier for a man who was not obviously Jewish. He may have had permission to reside in Moscow when he had worked for the Poliakovs, but once that stopped, his residency status, as a Jew outside the Pale, would have become less clear, and it would have been in his interest to avoid the attention of the police. The photograph hints that as he moved farther away from Jewish traditions, Shloyme-Zanvl Rappoport encountered little resistance from his father, but their shared distance from the past did not make the two men close. For about five years after their 1884 reunion, Shloyme-Zanvl and Aron Rappoport corresponded. Writing in a literate Yiddish peppered, like his son's, with Russian words, Aron chided Shloyme-Zanvl for his unsettled way of life. The father worked to convince the son to settle down, forget his radical ideas, and earn a living: "It's already time for you to come to your senses and not be smarter than the whole world." Aron wanted Shloyme-Zanvl to get an office job with a good salary; presumably, he could then send his father more money or follow through on the plans they periodically discussed for Aron to move in with him—plans that were never carried out.[3]

After his visit with Aron, Shloyme-Zanvl remained outside the Pale of Settlement. Like *The Dybbuk*'s Khonen, he wandered. Instead of returning to Vitebsk Province he went to Tula, south of Moscow, where he had an uncle whose status as an army veteran gave him permission to live outside the Pale. Had he chosen to, Rappoport could have joined the many pilgrims who visited Yasnaya Polyana, the nearby estate of the world-renowed novelist Count Lev Tolstoy. In 1897, a few years after Rappoport's time there, Tula had a population of more than 100,000 but only some 2,000 Jews, who had established a single prayer house.[4] After a short time in Tula, Rappoport again moved on, this time to a place with an even smaller Jewish population, a village near the city of Efremov, where he taught the children of a Jewish friend, who may have secured him residence permission as an employee.

Zhitlowsky was certain that Rappoport was drawn to village life for ideological reasons. The implications of a radical young man moving to a village were clear to anyone who, like Rappoport and Zhitlowsky, had come of age in the Russian Empire of the 1870s. When the serfs were freed in 1861, literate people had turned their collective attention to the enormous population of the countryside, trying to understand who these newly liberated people—the narod—were. The picture they saw was in flux. Because of the poor productivity of the soil and the short growing season in much of the Russian lands, peasants under serfdom had often earned money on the side, traveling to urban areas to work in factories. After the emancipation, when heavy redemption payments for the land were imposed on peasant communities—sometimes exceeding the amount of money that could be eked out of the land—migrant labor became essential.[5] Thus peasants were increasingly exposed to urban culture and the cash economy, and their lives began to change.

Many Russian intellectuals reacted to the enormous cultural and economic changes in the countryside with nostalgia for the peasants' traditional ways. Whether he read religious nationalist writers such as Dostoevsky, radical realists and critics such as Gleb Uspensky and Nikolai Mikhailovsky, or Tolstoy, Rappoport would have learned that the Russian village was a fascinating place, home to archaic communal structures that might have revolutionary potential, inhabited by men and women who might be able to provide their educated and urban "betters" unsullied examples of honesty, innocence, and virtue, though it was equally possible that they were losing these qualities and needed to preserve them.

All these ideas were associated with Russian Populism. Some who called themselves or were called by others Populists thought that intellectuals needed to teach, observe, or emulate peasants, and all Populists agreed that urban intellectuals needed to repay a moral debt to the rural folk. Populists were convinced of the virtue of the traditional way of life of the Russian narod, even while they decried the feudalism under which it had arisen. The left wing of Populism was fascinated by the socialism of the philosopher Pyotr Lavrov, who believed that any revolution in Russia would have to rely on the peasants; Russian Populists were unwilling to accept the mechanistic view of Karl Marx that history follows a predetermined path, moving inevitably from feudalism to capitalism to socialism. Deeply suspicious of modernization, they accepted Herzen's assertion that Russia could evolve toward socialism without passing through capitalism. One of the most dramatic manifestations of Russian Populist belief was the "Going to the People" movement in the summer of 1874, when more than a thousand young, educated Russians went to the countryside to teach the peasants, to study their way of life, and in some cases, to try to convince them to rebel.[6]

When Rappoport moved to the village near Efremov in the mid-1880s, Zhitlowsky saw him as reenacting the summer of 1874, playing the role of a Russian *intelligent* who owed a debt to the peasants and wanted to repay it by living among them and working in their behalf. Both

Zhitlowsky and Rappoport had already rejected the materialism and historical determinism of the Marxist Social Democrats. In 1888, Rappoport wrote mockingly of what must have been a brief phase when he accepted the Marxist view that history obeyed "scientific" laws and the world "seemed to be some kind of heaven, full of the pure water of the social democrats." By 1884, having stopped reading Hebrew, he was reading in Russian about the peasants. Among the available Populist groupings, he was attracted to the moderates known as the Black Repartition; the name refers to the Russian village custom of periodically dividing up or repartitioning land among families according to their increase or decrease in size.[7]

The summer of 1874 had produced few results, and while some Black Repartition members reacted to it by trying harder to educate the peasants, other Populists turned to more violent methods of bringing down the Tsarist regime. In the late 1870s, the members of the radical Populist movement of the People's Will came to believe that the assassinations of officials they blamed for repressive policies—which they called "terrorism"—would be an effective and justified way to change the government. On January 24, 1878, a few months before Rappoport and Zhitlowsky first met, a young woman, Vera Zasulich, shot and wounded the St. Petersburg municipal governor, Fyodor Trepov, to punish him for ordering the brutal flogging of a young prisoner who had neglected to remove his hat in the governor's presence. Astonishingly, a jury acquitted Zasulich that April and Russian society celebrated her as a heroine. She became a model for the adherents of the People's Will, who assassinated other officials in the next few years and succeeded in 1881 in killing Alexander II, the tsar who had freed the serfs.

Alexander III, his son and successor, suppressed the revolutionary movement harshly; the thirteen years of his reign (1881–1894) were marked by counterreform and censorship. His officials, paranoid about where the next terrorist's bomb would land, arrested and punished on the slightest suspicion: they were particularly frightened of the Poles and the Jews in the empire's western borderlands. But Tsarist decrees could not distract society from the peasants' troubles. Members of the intelligentsia who subscribed to the program of "small deeds" tried, like Rappoport, to improve the peasants' lives, going from the towns to the countryside to work as teachers, doctors, or veterinarians. At the same time, the revolutionary movement, driven further underground, continued to develop. Indeed, the government's policies had the opposite of the desired effect: by imposing restrictions on students, Poles and Jews, journalists and their newspapers, the government created an atmosphere where anger grew and no number of arrests could stop it.[8] Not just in St. Petersburg and Moscow but in the provinces as well, many people—workers and students, Jews, Poles, and Russians—grew increasingly restive.

Although the Populists and the Tsarist government disagreed on most issues, they shared a sense that the largely illiterate narod could be easily exploited by literate people. Since the sixteenth century, the Jews in Polish lands, a relatively literate minority, had acted as middlemen between landowners and peasants, overseeing agricultural work, purchasing crops for resale, running taverns as Chana Rappoport had, and working as tailors, shoemakers, and carpenters. With the Polish partitions of the late eighteenth century, the Russian Empire abruptly acquired some 500,000 new Jewish subjects, who continued to work with the peasants as they had before. Russian officials often blamed the peasants' poverty, drunkenness, and unrest on what they saw as these shrewd and greedy non-Christians. The Pale of Settlement was meant to protect the Christians of the heartlands from the Jews, and within the Pale, a shifting array of laws limited Jewish contact with peasants. With emancipation, the peasants no longer had the "protection" of their owners, and they appeared yet more vulnerable to Jewish exploitation.[9]

Given these assumptions, the wave of pogroms that had broken out when Rappoport was in Liozno in 1881 made sense to many government officials, who saw the frustrated peasants as punishing the Jews for exploiting them. After briefly considering that the pogroms might have been caused by radical propaganda, the authorities concluded that the Jews themselves were to blame. In August 1881, Interior Minister Count Nikolai Ignatev explained to the new tsar, Alexander III, that the pogroms were the result of the Jews' trade monopoly. "Because of their clannishness and solidarity, all but a few of them have bent every effort not to increase the productive forces of the country but to exploit the native inhabitants, and primarily the poorer classes. This provoked the protest of the latter, finding such deplorable expression in acts of violence." He advised the tsar to "remove the abnormal conditions which now exist between Jews and natives and protect the latter from that pernicious activity which . . . was responsible for the disturbances." The People's Will agreed with the government about the logic of the peasants' punishment of the Jews who oppressed them and issued a proclamation in September 1881 welcoming the pogroms, but the Black Repartition opposed them, insisting that the peasants' problems were the fault of the government and pogroms only served the regime by fostering ethnic strife.[10]

Rappoport was influenced by two Populist writers known for the brutal honesty of their depictions of peasants. Nikolai Mikhailovsky admitted the tremendous gap between his own values and those of the peasants: "Upon my desk stands a bust of [the literary critic Vissarion] Belinsky which is very dear to me, and also a chest with books with which I have spent many nights. If Russian life with all its ordinary practices breaks into my room, destroys my bust of Belinsky, and burns my books, I will not submit to the people from the village; I will fight." After the 1881–1882 pogroms, Mikhailovsky wrote a long article, "The Heroes and the Mob," on peasant mob violence. He concluded that the peasant tendency to follow a pogrom "hero" or rabble-rouser could be blamed on capitalism itself: "A hero, emerging all of a sudden amidst people who . . . live a meaningless routine life, easily becomes for them an experience of irresistible force, stifling their critical faculties and arousing them, instead, to irrational imitation."[11]

Even more than Mikhailovsky, Gleb Uspensky was known for the bleakness of his depictions of lower-class life, but he too believed in the virtue of traditional peasant ways. Rappoport knew the 1882 essay, "The Power of the Soil," where Uspensky used the language of folklore to protest against capitalism and the changes it brought to rural ways. He insisted that the peasants will remain powerful only so long as they are "from head to foot and from the surface to the depths suffused and illuminated by the heat and the light that waft to them from Moist Mother Earth." Moist Mother Earth is an ancient Slavic folkloric concept, a creature imagined to nourish humanity, her children: throughout Rappoport's lifetime, peasants ratified oaths by swallowing a mouthful of earth, measured boundary lines by walking along them with soil on their heads, and protected villages from cattle disease by plowing a furrow around them to release the vital energy of the earth. Uspensky retells a *bylina* (a folk lay) that draws on these folk beliefs about the power of the soil. The hero Sviatogor meets a peasant with a bag over his shoulder, and no matter how fast Sviatogor rides, he cannot catch him. The peasant puts down the bag and Sviatogor tries to lift it, but he can barely move it off the ground, while he sinks in the earth to his knees. The weight of the bag is "from Moist Mother Earth" and the peasant is Mikula, who draws strength from the earth, his mother: "The power of the land is so enormous that scarlet blood comes to the hero's face when he tries to move it by a hair's-breadth, but the *narod* carry that force as easily as an empty bag."[12]

Although it was ideologically satisfying to live in a village near peasants, Rappoport did not keep his tutoring position for long. His employers' daughter had converted from Judaism to Christianity in order to marry a local man. (The Russian Empire did not permit civil marriage,

nor could a Christian convert to Judaism.) The woman's family continued to see her regularly. She herself felt ambivalent about her choice,
frequently coming to her parents' house and crying in front of the ark in
which they kept a Torah. Her unhappiness created tension in the house.
Finally, in a burst of anger, her father grabbed the younger children's
Russian textbooks out of their hands, tore them up, and sent their tutor—
Rappoport—away. The episode, with its dramatic denouement, may have
improved in Zhitlowsky's telling, but it shows that in the village, Rappoport had found a place where Jews interacted with Christians in ways
influenced and manifested by the written word, whether the Torah or the
textbooks.[13] As in Liozno, where maskilic novels threatened an old way
of life, this story demonstrates that in Rappoport's world, books possessed tremendous destabilizing power.

Rappoport followed the railroad line south in March 1885 to another
place where Jews and Slavs interacted. The expanding industry in the
Donets Basin–Dnepr Bend mining region led to its ethnic diversity. Migrants from central Russia toiled alongside Ukrainian peasants in mines
and mills; Jews from the north moved south to work as artisans, clerks,
and shop- or tavernkeepers. By 1897, Jews constituted 35 percent of the
population in Ekaterinoslav, the region's largest city. Relations between
Jews and Christians in the mining region were often troubled, with devastating pogroms in 1883 and 1892, in spite of consistent police efforts
to prevent violence.[14] Rappoport spent six years, until late 1891, in Ekaterinoslav and elsewhere in the region, sometimes teaching children in
Jewish families, sometimes working with his hands. At the same time, he
performed his own "small deeds," reading to peasants and miners, observing them, and writing about them.

Rappoport moved periodically from tutoring work to manual labor
not as an ideological statement but out of real economic need. He was at
times on the edge of starvation. In fall 1886, after the police asked him to
leave the town of Krasnopol, he lived "very badly, without a roof, food,
or clothing, speaking literally," until he found another teaching job. He
told Zhitlowsky that he wished he could save money but doubted that,
"with my character," he would succeed, although he had lined up enough
lessons to earn 35 rubles a month. In June 1888, he begged Zhitlowsky
to send him 130–140 rubles and offered in exchange to translate anything at all: "I need money terribly, otherwise I'll never get myself out of
this whirlpool."[15]

Because "no easier work could be found," he decided to try the mines.
After two weeks of trudging from one mine to another, seeking work and

being rejected, he felt that he was beginning to change, taking on a new identity, as he always had in response to new surroundings. He was becoming physically tougher, getting used to sleeping on bare boards and hearing the bosses treat him rudely, reacting as calmly "as any Russian worker." The Russian Empire was full of such men and women, moving from the village to the town and back, looking for work, living on the edge. They included peasants and workers, Jews, Christians, and Muslims. Rappoport was not the only Russian writer to draw literary inspiration from a period of wandering: his eventual acquaintance Maxim Gorky (Alexsei Peshkov) also spent the 1880s on the road, drifting from job to job, educating himself by voracious reading and often reading to the illiterate folk he met, and just like Rappoport, Gorky would begin a writing career in earnest, under a pseudonym, in 1892. Anton Chekhov gave a glimpse of these drifters in an 1887 story, "The Tumbleweed": "If one could imagine the whole Russian land, what a multitude of the same kind of tumbleweeds, seeking a better place, were walking the highways and byways or, waiting for sunrise, drowsing in coaching inns, taverns, hotels, on the grass under the sky. . . ."[16]

The well-paid work in the mines drew many applicants, particularly in fall and winter when the peasants were not needed in the fields, and Rappoport began to lose hope. Everywhere he went, he was told that he was unneeded, and he began to wonder whether, as the child of poor parents, he had any reason to expect a welcome anywhere. He wondered if the ideas of Thomas Robert Malthus applied to him: "'A person who arrives in a world that is already occupied, if his parents are not in a position to feed him or if society is not in a position to use his labor, has not the smallest right to demand any kind of sustenance, and in truth, he is superfluous on the earth. There is no seat for him at the great feast of the world.'" Just as he reached despair, he was saved by chance. Two workers in a salt-processing factory, caught in a brawl, were summoned home to their village to stand trial. The boss who had just told Rappoport there was no work turned back to him. Hearing that he could read, drank little, and (most important) had no village to call him back in the summer, he offered him a salary of 18 rubles a month to work in the salt mill and asked if he could start immediately. Offer in hand, Rappoport felt that he was "at the feast . . . I felt good and peaceful, and I felt firm soil under my feet." He looked at the crowd of workers happily, knowing soon he would be among them. The next morning he was up at 5 A.M. to start work, but it turned out that he was not needed till the following day. Rather than spending the day at the tavern, he decided to talk his way into the mines themselves. The foreman, skeptical at first, eventually let him go down the shaft. Rappoport was amazed by the eerie subterranean world. "For a minute I felt that I was in some legendary underground palace. In the light of some ten lamps, everything—the walls, the ceiling, the hill [of wet salt]—sparkled like millions of diamonds, stunning in its amazing beauty."[17]

The work he had gotten was simple, but exhausting. Rappoport made sure that the milled salt was poured into bags, he moved the bags away, and he weighed them. He calculated that each day he moved some 2,000 bags of salt, each weighing about 200 pounds. "There was not even half a minute to rest. As soon as you dragged one sack off and weighed it, the next one was already full." He blistered his hands on the sacks and felt excruciating pain when salt got in the wounds, but because the salt prevented infection, they soon healed. When he started the work, he felt terribly thirsty, no matter how much water he drank. After he got used to the air in the mill, he discovered that no food—not even salted herring—tasted salty.[18]

He was intrigued by the other workers, especially the miners. They sang songs in the tavern and on the street, and Rappoport wrote down the lyrics:

> We work day and night;
> It's like doing hard time.
> Day and night with candles
> We pull death behind us!

The work was hard, but the pay was good:

> Only God in heaven is with us,
> We know no need!

For Rappoport and other Populists, such songs confirmed the horror of the miners' life. Uspensky read these songs, ignored the workers' high pay, and insisted they showed that alienation from the soil drives men to despair and alcoholism. "His life from his youth to his grave will be wasted, without the tiniest use to him, with the most mathematical precision. They pilfer it from him bit by bit. They pluck it away in the factories, the plants, the mines." Like Uspensky, Rappoport saw the capitalism driving the mining industry as a "dark force" built on "a frightening pile of dried-out human bones."[19]

In 1887, Rappoport started an article about the mining industry. Although miners earn more money than peasants, he argued, they should be pitied because their work prevents them from settling down; peasants who work in the mines are morally ruined by the unnatural conditions. Using tables and figures, he demonstrated that miners become uprooted from agriculture, but find no roots in the mines themselves: unless it is very large, a mine is eventually worked out and the miners forced to move on. Alexander Fenin, a local mining engineer, found such attitudes common: "Russian public opinion . . . considered the miner's life tantamount to imprisonment with hard labor and dwelled on the unsatisfactory living conditions." Fenin felt that when contrasted with the brutality of village life, the miners' lifestyle had some advantages, but rates of murder, serious assault, and rape were in fact far higher in Ekaterinoslav Province than in similarly urbanized places elsewhere in Russia; workers fought each other on holidays and paydays, for entertainment or revenge, across or within ethnic lines, frequently in conjunction with binge drinking. Miners from central Russia tended not to bring their families south because the environment was more dangerous than in the village: theirs was a brutal world of alcohol, gambling, prostitution, and violence.[20]

In the mines as in the factories, peasants picked up new ways: they spent their cash on clothing and food unknown in the village, and they began to imagine their own future differently, questioning family structures such as early marriage and obedience to one's father. Each small rebellion paved the way for the abandonment of what the Populists saw as the Russian peasants' unique ancient culture in favor of a morally suspect, consumer-driven modernity. Thus Rappoport wrote that even though full-time work in the mines offered workers high pay, they were right in refusing to abandon farming for good. Peasants continued to cherish their landholdings, no matter how small, and they were willing to migrate to distant Siberia in hopes of getting more land. "And meanwhile here in Russia, two steps away from the migrants, the coal industry bosses for decades have been offering the people wages and a refuge— but no one accepts their offer!" Rappoport was sure that the peasants who did become full-time miners had fallen under the sway of a pernicious system calculated to turn them into alcoholic drones unable to question the bosses' will. "All this, like slime, sucks in the weaker worker who comes from his home with the best intentions; it depraves him, forces him to forget his home, his family, his village, his agricultural interests, and it turns him into 'a pure miner,' in the full ugly meaning of the word." Miners who never go back to the village, Rappoport wrote, turn into "some kind of nomadic tribe, torn away from one shore but not having reached the other."[21]

Rappoport's writings on the life of the miners expose the contradictions in his vision of Russians and Jews. Whereas he himself, when he came to the salt mines looking for work, had no agricultural commitments and no attachment to a village to tie him down and provide him with an unchanging moral code, Rappoport was horrified to see that peasants were in the same situation as he was. In Liozno, he had tried to lure boys away from their own traditions and beliefs. As Lilienblum had testified, such self-reform was painful, and Rappoport later used the same words to describe the *maskilim* that he had once used for the miners: yeshiva students who learned to read Russian became "an entire generation of broken and bruised survivors who had left one shore behind and never reached the other."[22] Rappoport described their boldness as heroic, indeed essential for Jewish survival, but when he encountered this same kind of rebelliousness among the miners, this same willingness to challenge the patriarchal structure and the traditional mores, he was appalled.

Even while he criticized the miners' ways, Rappoport was the first person in Russia to collect and transcribe their folk songs. The folklorists of his era shared the Populist scorn for industrialization and saw only rural songs and legends as authentic folklore. The dominant "mythological" school held that the folklorist's task was to gather the remains of old myths in order to reconstruct the "authentic" lore of the past. While Rappoport, especially in his twenties, shared the Populist anxiety about capitalism, he was already willing to accept the validity of new songs, produced in an industrial setting; he already saw the creation of folklore as dynamic and ongoing, not fixed. His pioneering expansion of the definition of folklore to include workers' songs points to his own ideological flexibility. Ultimately, among miners as among Jews, his impulse to listen sympathetically to other people's stories and songs, to try to fit in among them seamlessly, was stronger than any of his ideological convictions.

Although Rappoport described the miners' move away from the old ways in dark terms, he contributed to one aspect of the change in rural life: the peasants' increasing access to the printed word. In the winter and spring of 1887, he read and wrote letters for peasants in a village in the Slavianoserbsk region of Ekaterinoslav Province. Some peasants who could not support their families were considering migrating to the Ural Mountains or beyond. They were desperate for reliable information about their destination, and Rappoport was stunned by the effect rumors had on them. One told him about some families bound for the Amur River. Having traveled 8000 miles and with 500 left to go, they met a group of returning migrants who told them that the Amur land would give a good harvest for one year only. "Even if it lies fallow for 12 years, nothing will grow on it—once it's been turned over once, it becomes like ash, even weeds won't grow. Under the influence of these stories the emigrants turned back."[23]

Longing to improve their lives but terrified that things would only get worse, would-be migrants sought out written information about conditions in the eastern territories. Every letter from a settler and every scrap of official information was read and reread, discussed, interpreted, memorized. "It was remarkable to see the attention with which the peasants listened to such a 'paper': most of them remembered all the details on the first reading, but still no one would grow tired of hearing it ten times." Even more than letters, the peasants yearned to find signed or sealed "official orders" from the government.[24] Trust was needed for poor peasants to take the enormous risk of selling their homes and investing everything in a long journey into unknown territory. Skeptics in the village taunted them, saying "Ural—*Vral*": in Russian, "the Urals" and "he lied" are only one letter apart, and the coincidence suggested that the promises about a better life in the east might turn out to be a big lie.

The peasants asked the literate Rappoport to help them learn the truth. Klim Sh-ko, a middle-aged landless peasant with an "extremely benevolent but somehow tormented and suffering expression," came to him with a crumpled, dirty piece of paper, a "King Solomon," used to tell fortunes: one dripped wax on the sheet, then read the words associated with the number where it fell. Klim's wax fell on a numeral and Rappoport read the associated prophecy knowing it was nonsense, but Klim listened tensely, his eyes sparkling. "It means it's good?" he asked in a lightly trembling voice. "It means, praise God?" "What are you trying to predict, Klim?" Rappoport asked. He learned that Klim and a few other village men had sent to the village of Petropavlovka for a copy of the "travel certificate" that, according to a letter from a settler, would guarantee its holder an array of free goods and privileges on arrival in the Urals: fifty-four acres per person, thirty trees for building, thirty rubles, and freedom from taxes for ten years. Klim told Rappoport of his hopes and fears. When the peasants talked about migration, they sometimes pictured an apocalyptic scene where there would be no end to their wanderings. "I don't know if you all [the literate] say this, if they write about this in the newspapers, but we've been saying that a time will come when people will wander all over the world like ants, one here, another there, and it won't be possible to help it. It will be hard to live, people will go east, it will get bad there, people will go west, and you won't be able to live there either." Peasant rumors about migration involved apocalyptic images of bitter water, ashen soil, and famine. Peasants also believed messianic rumors, telling stories of a future when the land would be wrested away from the big landowners and all inequities would be set right; perhaps all money would disappear.[25]

Even while he dismissed these fantastic rumors, Rappoport was intrigued by the power they wielded. A returning migrant told him that rumors could predict the future or even make things happen. "It's all nonsense!" Rappoport said. "Empty chatter!"

"Chatter!" the peasant said. "No, it's not! When people start to talk about something, at first it seems that it's nonsense, rubbish—and then sooner or later it comes out just as it was said . . . Chatter! After all, no one believed that they would free the serfs, right? But they freed us. . . . No! The rumor has started—that means it's going to happen!"[26]

Perhaps when Rappoport heard this returning migrant insist on the power of the spoken word, he was reminded of Sora in his *History of a Family,* who managed to wrest justice from the rich Berkin simply by voicing her complaint. Although in this interchange it was Rappoport who questioned the power of spoken words to change reality, his peasant interlocutor voiced an opinion that Rappoport sometimes defended. During his time in the South, Rappoport worked to give both peasants and miners access to the written word, which seemed even more powerful than the spoken one. He left the salt-processing plant and went back to tutoring, but maintained contact with miners, writing about them and their folklore. He carefully choreographed the public readings that he gave for peasants on Sundays or holidays and for miners in the evenings after work. He was sure that because he shared his listeners' lifestyle, his presence did not inhibit them "from saying frankly and freely, with the expressions that were characteristic of them, what they thought both about the books and their heroes, people of different estates." He limited his own participation in the reading, giving no explanations, asking no questions, and making no effort to stop unrelated conversations. He left it to the listeners to choose the reading material and when possible deputized one of them to read. With his awareness that the audience influences the tale, he articulated ideas about folklore collection that ethnographers would adopt only in the twentieth century.[27]

When Rappoport wrote that he posed no questions, gave no explanations, and wanted his listeners to choose the reading material, he was claiming that he had once more donned a disguise that allowed him to fit in among people unlike himself. At the same time, he was pointing out the differences between his methods and those of other intellectuals. Public readings by peasants or reform-minded intellectuals were common in the countryside. In the decades after the emancipation, it became increasingly clear that peasants would benefit from literacy, and schools spread. At the same time, intellectuals became concerned about the kind of books the peasants read or heard. They complained that rather than immersing themselves in the classics, the peasants preferred *lubki,* cheap illustrated romances and adventure stories. Activists spent years regularly reading to peasants, talking to them about the stories they had heard, and observing their reactions. A Kharkov schoolmistress, Khristina Alchevskaia, published a three-volume collection titled *What to Read to the Peasants,* containing some stories peasants had been observed to enjoy and others Alchevskaia herself thought morally uplifting.[28]

Like Alchevskaia (whom he read and admired), Rappoport thought carefully about what he was doing. By the spring of 1889, he had drafted an entire book on peasant literacy and peasant literature. There he explained that intellectuals usually adopted one of three attitudes toward peasant literacy: the urge to imbue the peasants with the intellectuals' own high culture; the Tolstoyan impulse to insist that the peasants' way of life is better than the intellectuals' and the intellectuals should imitate them, not teach them; and Rappoport's clear favorite, the Populist desire to avoid these two extremes and to dedicate oneself to "unselfish service to the folk." Rappoport had always been fascinated by Tolstoy, but more convinced by Uspensky and Mikhailovsky. By the time he wrote his book on folk literacy, he had found in the writings of Uspensky, Mikhailovsky, and the early Tolstoy the lesson that the folk needed not a teacher "who would like to rebuild the entire structure of folk life" but "an enlightener to help it fight the unfavorable phenomena and conditions that threaten it, to cast the light of knowledge on the folk's own rooted foundations and all the conditions of contemporary life."[29] That is, intellectuals should serve the narod by helping it learn about its own traditions, so it could survive without adopting urban culture wholesale. Rather than trying to convince peasants to read highbrow literature, intellectuals should create a new literature especially for the peasants, drawing on literary forms they recognized, such as Russian Orthodox saints' lives. Whereas Rappoport had written about the miners as though they really could simply reject modernity and all it implied, his approach to cultural change in the literacy book was more nuanced: he saw change as inevitable but wanted to soften the impact and help the peasants cope with it by drawing on the healing power of their own folklore.

Rappoport wrote as though he were a conduit between the peasants and the capitalist world, a filter to eliminate harmful elements before they could reach the narod, and an empty vessel to be filled with peasant content that he could then convey to the outside world. When he stressed the difference between himself and Alchevskaia or the other intellectuals who interrupted their public readings with explanations and concluded them with questions, Rappoport defined himself as a person who fit in seamlessly in the countryside, a fly on the wall, an ethnographer privy to the conversations of the peasants, rather than a teacher wanting to mold them. He depicted himself as a person who could gain the trust of peasants such as Klim Sh-ko, who would sit in his room till midnight, talking about his difficult life and listening to sad stories that brought tears to his eyes.[30]

Given the violent history of Christian-Jewish relations in the mining region, one might wonder whether a Jew could really gain complete trust among the peasants, but Rappoport wrote about his talks with Klim without mentioning his Jewishness. He hinted at it in a passage where one peasant complained that the village authorities were "christened— but worse than the Christless! You could convince a Jew, but not them. . . ."[31] In relaying this comment, Rappoport suggested that he had moved seamlessly into the world of the peasants, although he still noticed the peasants' attitudes toward Jews. Whereas his attempt in Liozno to disguise himself as what he was not—a pious youth—proved as unsuccessful as it was insincere, Rappoport described himself as more successful in the village, perhaps because his attempts to behave like the peasants reflected his own convictions.

In trying to become like the peasants, Rappoport was following Tolstoy's insistence on the peasants' moral superiority; in the 1880s, Tolstoy spoke for the radical view that aristocrats should live like their former serfs, imitating the peasants' diet, fashion, family structure, and beliefs. In his 1882 *Confession,* which Rappoport was reading in 1886, Tolstoy concluded that only thus could an educated person attain inner peace. "In opposition to what I saw in our circle, where a whole life is spent in idleness, amusement, and dissatisfaction, I saw among the people whole lives passed in heavy labor, and they were happier with life than the wealthy."[32] Thus when Rappoport wrote to Zhitlowsky in stark terms of his own poverty in spite of his hard work, he was not just asking his rich friend for money; he was also presenting himself in the terms that the most famous writer of his era had identified with the peasantry and everything good.

As if to symbolize the addition of a Russian peasant identity to his old Jewish one, Rappoport gave one 1888 letter to Zhitlowsky two signatures: he signed the body of the letter "Solomon," the Russian form of Shloyme, and the postscript "Semyon Akimovich," which sounded much more Russian than "Solomon Aronovich." Eventually, for Rappoport and for his friends, that new first name and patronymic came to symbolize his closeness to the Russian people. His revolutionary friend Victor Chernov wrote that the miners themselves named Rappoport, as though they had become his surrogate parents. In a world where Ostaps and Osmans became Osip; Ibrahims, Abram; Friedrichs, Fedor; and Hirshes, Grigory, Solomons were called Semyon. "My Solomon [Aronovich] Rappoport became Semyon Akimovich. He kept his new, russified name as a touching reminder of his mining period. For he had managed to grow fond of the miners . . . what simplicity, freshness of soul and naiveté!" For the rest of his life, Rappoport would repeat this explanation of the origin of "Semyon Akimovich," and his listeners would accept the story as Chernov had.[33] His new first name and patronymic symbolized his magic ability to cross over the barrier separating the intelligentsia from the masses and the Jew from the Russian narod.

The magic may not have worked with everyone as well as it did with Klim Sh-ko. Zhitlowsky was skeptical about it: he was certain that no matter how hard he tried, his friend could not fit in perfectly among the narod, and the barrier between them was symbolized by the peasants' inability or refusal to call him by name. "In the eyes of the folk he still remained if not an absurd foreigner then a strange and surprising person. The peasants and the workers did not know 'what to eat him with' [how to understand him, what category to put him in]. . . . The peasants used to call him to his face 'vona' ('that one')." Shloyme/Semyon told Zhitlowsky, "I like the peasants for their simple life of work, their naiveté, their poverty, their sense of justice, lack of greed and so on and so on." He admitted, though, that new name or not, he had not succeeded in merging completely with the narod. "I need soil where each of my footsteps will make an impression. . . . I have settled in a Russian village; I have given myself to it already halfway and hope to give myself soon entirely."[34] For Semyon to truly become part of the village, he would have to take one more step, giving himself to the village entirely by converting to Christianity; this would change his legal status and make it easier for him, from an administrative as well as a cultural perspective, to live among peasants.

But already in 1888, Rappoport was ambivalent about rejecting Jewishness and skeptical that he could be clearly defined as either a Jewish nationalist or a socialist internationalist. He spoke ruefully of a period when he "thought that a Jewish intellectual had no right to give himself to a handful of the people who are close to him by birth and forget about the rest." He told Zhitlowsky, who had already begun to devote his attention to specifically Jewish problems, that he was torn between the nonethnic, "cosmopolitan" stance of a revolutionary and a national loyalty to the Jews over other groups. "You think that I am much more of a cosmopolitan than I really am. There is a lot of feline, that is, patriotic feeling in me. More than once I've been bitten by the national bug—bitten in such a way that I was unhappy. But each of these episodes ended in nothing. The fact is that I can't find good ground for action in Jewish life."[35] He explained his decision to work among peasants as a result of circumstance, not conviction. If he could have found "good ground for action"—meaning the possibility of carrying out effective propaganda or education work—among Jews, then he would have done so, but given that was impossible, he was committed to working with the peasants even while he retained his Jewish legal status.

The new name, "Semyon" or "Semyon Akimovich," which he went on to use in published writing and intimate correspondence for the rest of his life, may have functioned better in the literary world than in the village or the salt-processing factory where he acquired it. Indeed, in many ways, literature made it possible for Shloyme to become Semyon. The fantasy of unification with the village that his friends celebrated in their anecdotes could be realized best in Semyon's own writings. Both Rappoport and Zhitlowsky wrote about his urge to fit into the village, using imagery of land and water. Zhitlowsky wrote that his friend wanted to flow "into the stream" of the peasantry, and in an 1887 sketch "Rain," Rappoport suggested that alienation such as his could be overcome precisely through contact with the Russian land. The sketch begins in the second person; "you" are in the steppe during a heat wave, watching the crops die, feeling helpless. The narrative switches to the first person, and the narrator reveals his own uncertain status in this place. "I am foreign here. . . . They want no help or welcome from you."[36] But when it finally rains, both the land and the narrator are transformed: as rain and teardrops flow down his face, he feels happy and knows that he finally belongs. The centrality of rain and soil in Rappoport's language suggests that he understood the Russian peasantry in the terms Uspensky had used in "The Power of the Soil." Rappoport wrote about his desire to penetrate into the soil of the village as though he shared the pagan Slavic belief in Moist Mother Earth. Through the healing power of rain and soil, he could become one with the land and those who worked it.

Although Rappoport wrote stories in which a literate Jew could flow unimpeded into the stream of Russian village life, reality and the police did not accommodate his fantasy. Whatever his name, in the late 1880s Rappoport had become one of the people he had once described to Zhitlowsky as living not "for the sake of their stomachs" but "for some great cause." By conducting public readings, listening to Klim's sad stories, and helping migrants understand government documents, he was doing his best to improve the lives of the peasants. From the point of view of the authorities, these activities, especially the public readings, were suspicious. The revolutionaries of the 1880s, who were doing their best to radicalize workers and peasants, often began by reading them nonpolitical fiction, then moved on to illicit works of political philosophy. Public readings in the countryside, though common, were technically illegal: they only became legal in the 1890s, and even then only from a restricted list of books. Thus the police would have had reasons to suspect Rappoport of conducting his readings with an ulterior motive, and Zhitlowsky agreed that his friend had worked among the peasants, "of course, in the interest of socialist propaganda."[37]

The police acted several times on their suspicions. Most often they simply told Rappoport to leave town, chasing him out of Krasnopol in 1886 and, to judge by his many changes of address in the next five years, other villages as well. He was officially accused of a crime for the first time on November 15, 1888, and soon thereafter arrested, jailed, interrogated, and again sent out of town. The episode, a few weeks after his twenty-fifth birthday, was traumatic. In January 1889, Rappoport was still in shock.

> What a lot I have gone through in the last few days: the search of my lodgings, the arrest, prison, four days of interrogation; looking through the papers that were returned to me. . . . Finally, the necessary, inescapable life in a new city that I do not know (Starodub), with no friends, nowhere to stay, no means; the search for low-paid tutoring jobs, the suspicious glances of the liberals. . . .

The police found nothing to prove Rappoport was a revolutionary, but their investigation of his books and papers confirmed their suspicions of his "political unreliability," and they suggested that he be placed under regular surveillance, which was officially instituted on September 3, 1890. From late 1888, the police opened many of his letters and recorded the names he mentioned, his correspondents' addresses, his literary influences and projects, and even his mood (one police clerk diligently noted that in December 1889, Rappoport wrote to a friend, "I'm feeling blue").[38]

Arrest, interrogation, and resettlement were meant to intimidate Rappoport and deter him from public readings, but they had the opposite effect. In January 1891, the Ekaterinoslav Province police chief filed a report that Rappoport had been gathering peasants and workers and reading them "some kind of books, purportedly with the goal of educating the dark masses." Rappoport may already have had contact with revolutionaries between 1885 and 1891: groups of the People's Will and Social Democratic sympathizers were active in Ekaterinoslav, and many Jews like him—russified, semi-educated, born in the northwest—belonged to both movements; they tended to shift around both geographically and in their allegiances. Like him, they were aware of the specific disabilities that the Jews of the empire faced, but they assumed that these could be resolved only after a revolution that would bring down the entire Tsarist system and grant civil rights to all the peoples of the empire.[39] However, considering the readiness of the police to punish radicals, especially Jewish ones, on very little evidence, particularly after the attempt to assassinate Alexander III on March 1, 1887, the fact that Rappoport was neither jailed for long nor exiled to Siberia when he was arrested in late 1888 indicates that at that time, he was in fact doing nothing more provocative than conducting public readings. But the early experience of arrest, when the state began to consider him a criminal, may have pushed him further toward revolution.

Over time, Rappoport and his friends transformed the story of his arrest into a rite of passage and a confirmation of his membership in the radical literary intelligentsia. In Zhitlowsky's retelling, Rappoport seized the opportunity during his interrogation to lecture the policeman about the latest publications on peasant literacy. Later, he retold a bit of folklore collected from the policeman himself. A poor musician meets a wild animal in the woods and realizes he can keep it from attacking only by playing his fiddle. First one string breaks, then another, and the musician, playing on his last string, is terrified. The policeman told Rappoport that his endless speech about peasant literacy reminded him of the musician's fiddling—while the interrogator himself was clearly the animal.[40] This version of the story of his arrest indicated that if Rappoport was indeed a threat to the Tsarist system, that danger was bound up with his abilities as an observer and a raconteur. Over his time in the South, Rappoport came to believe that by developing these abilities and confirming his identity as a writer, he could confront the contradictions in his life: whether he truly belonged in the village, whether one should preserve traditional ways of life or reform them. For the tutor and sometime laborer Shloyme-Zanvl Aronovich Rappoport, these issues posed questions that could be answered in the Russian writings of Semyon Akimovich.

Throughout his time in the South, Rappoport invested time and energy in his writing, almost all in Russian. He was not ideologically opposed to publishing in Yiddish, and he reached out to the nascent world of Yiddish publishing. In August 1889, he visited the man who would become Russia's best-known Yiddish writer. The comic genius Solomon Rabinovich (better known as Sholem Aleichem) was then living in Kiev and editing his new literary almanac, *Di yudishe folksbibliotek*, modeled on the Russian "thick journals" that combined fiction and nonfiction. Rabinovich was not interested when Rappoport told him of a project of Zhitlowsky's to publish world classics in Yiddish, nor was he particularly enthusiastic about the manuscript Rappoport offered him—and Rappoport, in turn, was not impressed by Rabinovich, describing him as "dry; a man of business, with no time to spare."[41] Regardless of his attitude toward Yiddish publishing per se, Rappoport must have found Rabinovich, in 1889 a rich man who invested in the stock market as well as writing prolifically, too bourgeois for his ascetic tastes and Rabinovich's attitude toward literature too commercial. Rappoport's serious literary efforts, like his emotional investments, continued to be in Russian.

Rappoport lived a passionate life through his correspondence. In 1888, seven years after he had left Vitebsk, his relationship with Chaim Zhitlowsky was still the focus of his desires and fears. He and his friend sent each other angry letters, which they later destroyed, and after they reconciled, Rappoport wrote of his strong feelings and his despair when they were not reciprocated. "Chaim, Chaim, how could I not love you, how could I not want to meld with you into a single soul? For a long time you were everything for me. You replaced my family, God, life, a woman, and now you are and will remain for [me] the closest person on earth. How could I not love you? That is why I am so sensitive to your every insult." His enduring love for Chaim made the sense of exclusion and anger stronger. "I will still reprove you. Not because you didn't write for a long time—that's your nature—but because you have so little sensitivity and delicacy toward me. Did you understand, did you know how I was waiting for your answers to my last letters? No? That is a lack of sensitivity." He concluded this letter with a plea for money, possibly in exchange for translation work.[42]

Just as he yearned for proof of Chaim's love, so Rappoport longed to be accepted as a writer. He wanted desperately to publish his stories and articles, and he feared that if he could not elicit a response to his words— whether from the friend who had replaced all other people for him, or from a publisher—he and his life would have no meaning. In the fall of 1886 he sent two short stories to a newspaper that rejected them. In the fall of 1887, he was upset that the Petersburg journal *Severnyi Vestnik* (Northern Herald) had returned an article about local miners that he had spent half a year writing. Each rejection was devastating: "Every such blunt blow on my nerves and soul after months of feverish work and passionate expectation defeated me for weeks and months, so that I wouldn't be able to start anything new, to do anything. . . . Every time, I would think, Should I leave all this and set my life on a new path?"[43]

Finally he found a new tactic: instead of sending unsolicited manuscripts to journals, he, like many other Russian young people with literary ambitions, decided to send them in advance to a well-known writer who might help him improve his work and then find a place to publish it. On October 19, 1887, four days after his twenty-fourth birthday, he wrote to Mikhailovsky about his efforts to dedicate his life to Populist ideals and service to the narod. He told the famous writer about the success of *History of a Family* in 1884 and the rejections ever since. Now he was living in the South, where, he wrote, "I didn't just learn about the miners' work and life, but I deeply felt the whole punishing weight of that life and that work, all the scandalous, burning injustices that suffuse the bosses' attitudes to the miners." The experience inspired an article, again rejected. He appealed to Mikhailovsky desperately, confessing that writing was the only way he could fill a personal void that he feared more than anything else. "For many reasons, my life has developed in such a way that if writing were removed from it, such emptiness would appear that it would simply horrify me. But the editor's last response has powerfully shaken my faith that I am able to serve the people with my pen. I beg you, tell me, *what should I do with my life?* Point me toward a field where I can use it to bring some benefit to the people." Because he had learned from Mikhailovsky's writings, he turned to him now in his despair. "Do not refuse to advise me. When I was confident in myself I did not ask for advice, but now my life has been shrouded in an oppressive, heavy darkness from which I cannot escape. I feel that I will fall without moral support, without advice from one of those on whose works I myself developed."[44] Rappoport tried in this letter to describe himself as an authoritative source on the miners, exaggerating the time he had spent in the Donets Basin (to four years, not two and a half years) and writing that he had worked in the mines himself, a claim he never repeated in print.

Mikhailovsky did not answer the letter. After waiting almost six months, Rappoport decided to approach another of his idols and wrote in April 1888 to Uspensky. This time he took a different tack, telling Uspensky that he had given up on publishing on the miners himself but was worried that the horrors he had seen would never be made public: "I saw that terrible life of several thousand people from so close that I am tortured by the thought that no one knows about it. . . . If that manuscript stays with me, it will tear me up and torment me."[45] He offered to give the manuscript to Uspensky and asked him to publicize the material described there however he could.

Uspensky, unlike Mikhailovsky, responded sympathetically to the unknown young writer and agreed to look at his manuscripts. Rappoport sent two substantial articles and one shorter one, on the life of miners, the peasant migrants, and the Jewish tavern. Uspensky read two of the pieces immediately and wrote back encouragingly: "I found them positively magnificent, intelligent, sensible and fair. Just in a few places the language is not right." He agreed that Rappoport's sketches could indeed educate readers about conditions in the countryside, but urged him to work to convey his characters' dialect in literary Russian. The tavern sketch needed more background: "You must expand it, say a few words about the place and the working population of the city and how and why such inveterate drunkards appear." Uspensky promised to ask the editors of *Russkaia Mysl'* (Russian Thought) if they would be interested in the piece on migrants.[46]

Rappoport was thrilled. The specter of a life of terrible emptiness was replaced with the dream of life as a writer, a heroic public figure. In one long letter after another, he told Uspensky how much his encouragement meant. He read Uspensky's letter over and over all night, and then, feeling terribly agitated, went outside, where it was growing light. Suddenly, he told Uspensky, he understood everything. "Your letter had said to me, 'it's starting.' That bright, heavenly, good thing that I had desired and worked for so strongly, and whose achievement I was already starting to doubt, was seriously beginning. . . . I deeply felt how little I have earned your help, how far I had sunk 'in unclean slime,' and how I do not love the narod as deeply and passionately as I wished and should have." He was seized by a burning feeling, a desire to give himself entirely to the people, "with my whole life, my whole soul, all my thoughts, and thus make my life pure and clear." The sense of blissful union with the people was unsustainable, and Rappoport recounted the rest of his morning in a less ecstatic vein. He heard a noise and went to the tavern, where he saw two drunk tramps beating up a smaller tramp. In a Tolstoyan mood, Rappoport intervened on behalf of the smaller man. The fighters turned to him. One said, "A-ah! And who called you here?" and hit him hard; the other did the same. "I don't know what I would have done at another time," Rappoport told Uspensky, "but my soul felt so bright then that these blows did not anger me. For some reason, they seemed funny."[47]

Still in an ecstatic mood, Rappoport told Zhitlowsky about Uspensky's letter. "What can you say about this, my dear brother—this is a turning point in my life!" Actually, it was a slow turning point. In the late 1880s, Uspensky was experiencing symptoms of severe mental illness. He would suddenly feel compelled to leave Petersburg and travel to other cities, then return home immediately, and he fell into periods of depression when he could accomplish little. He sent Rappoport's article on the life of the miners to a friend and never managed to retrieve it. When he included the miners' songs that Rappoport had sent him in an article of his own in April 1889, Rappoport was displeased; Uspensky apologized that he had done it only because "the editors had their knives at my throat." He explained that he had been in a psychiatrist's care, and his condition kept him from devoting much attention to getting Rappoport's manuscripts published. With his help, though, the piece on migrants finally came out in early 1890 as "To New Lands," under the pseudonym "S. Vidbin," in what Uspensky called a "modest little journal," *Trud* (Labor). Rappoport probably meant the pseudonym to refer to the Vitba (or Vidba) River in Vitebsk; he had already experimented with other pseudonyms based on his hometown. Uspensky himself, though, interpreted the pseudonym as coming from the verb *videt'*, "to see," advertising Rappoport's legitimacy as an eyewitness.[48]

Rappoport knew that if he wanted a real writing career, he would need to travel north to St. Petersburg, the center of the intellectual and publishing worlds. In the fall of 1886, he had already been asking Zhitlowsky to find out "what documents and papers I would need to have the right to live in Petersburg." During almost all of his lifetime, only certain categories of Jews were granted special permission to live in cities such as Petersburg, outside the Pale of Settlement: soldiers and retired soldiers, domestic servants, prostitutes, graduates of institutions of higher education, merchants of the first guild, and certain craftsmen. Rappoport belonged to none of these groups, but he continued dreaming of going to Petersburg.[49] He never got the right papers, and finally he stopped waiting for them. In the fall of 1891, he set out for Petersburg and a new career as a writer.

In Rappoport's world, that move meant he could claim a new heroic role, based on his readings of Jewish and Russian writers. Like Pisarev and Lilienblum, he could stake out a position as an ascetic writer, outside the traditional patriarchal society, who could threaten it and might succeed in destroying it. At the same time, paradoxically, like Mikhailovsky and Uspensky, he could become a defender of everything good about tradition and an enemy of capitalist modernity. Both these literary models, in spite of the differing ideologies that they entailed, confirmed the advantages of Rappoport's congenital restlessness. If he was so sensitive to the ways both miners and maskilim were adrift, sailors who had left one shore but could not reach the other, that may have been because he too could fit in perfectly nowhere, neither among Russians nor among Jews. As a writer, though, he could profit from his own intermediary status.

He had once contrasted his perspective from inside a Jewish bathhouse in his Vitebsk adolescence to his more mature view from the broader perspective of Ekaterinoslav Province. With the move out of the Pale to Petersburg, Shloyme-Zanvl Rappoport could leave traditional Jewish space even farther behind. He was ready to begin a different and much more public stage of his life, under the pseudonym "Semyon Akimovich An-sky." That persona, of course, was a literary creation, constructed by the words that Rappoport wrote and spoke. But the An-sky persona relied on the ways that Rappoport had constructed and lived the first part of his life, before adopting his pseudonym. Rappoport's identification with the poor, his hope that his solitary life might help him aspire to great things, and his ability to imagine himself as now an insider, now an outsider, in both Russian and Jewish spheres, were all part of the literary self that he began to create in earnest in late 1891.

A Revolutionary Has No Name

The revolutionary . . . does not have his own interests, affairs, feelings, habits, property, not even a name. Everything in him is absorbed by a single, exclusive interest, a single thought, a single passion—the revolution.

—Mikhail Bakunin and Sergei Nechaev, "Catechism of the Revolutionary"

WHEN HE ARRIVED in St. Petersburg early in the winter of 1892, Rappoport began to live out his dreams. For almost a decade, he had tried to publish his stories and articles in the mainstream Russian press and faced rejection after rejection. Once he reached the capital, his backlog of manuscripts began to come out in *Russkoe Bogatstvo* (Russian Wealth), his byline appearing in seven of the twelve issues of the year. Mikhailovsky had just taken over the leadership of this "thick journal," which became the standard-bearer of the Populist movement and the intelligentsia tradition. As Rappoport remembered, "For all of living, honorable, and conscious Russia, *Russkoe Bogatstvo* was not just a periodical speaking for social-revolutionary Populism, but the symbol of an unshakeable adherence to principle, the incarnation of the highest civic courage and nobility." Before he came to Petersburg, Rappoport had longed for approval, especially from the Russian radical writers who were his heroes. Now he was on close terms with Uspensky, Mikhailovsky, the editor Sergei Krivenko, and their circle of Populist intelligentsia. Zhitlowsky thought that the winter and spring that Rappoport spent in Petersburg in 1892 were "the happiest days in his entire long-suffering life."[1] After all the years when he did not feel fully accepted, he had come to rest among people he admired.

But it may not have been so easy for him to find a stopping place in Petersburg, even though for Rappoport as for other subjects of the Russian tsar, the city would have seemed a logical place for the realization of fantasies. It was built on the marshy ground at the cold, damp edge of the Finnish Gulf, in the first decades of the eighteenth century, at the order of

Tsar Peter the Great and at a tremendous cost in human lives. The squares, monuments, and public buildings were designed on a vast scale meant to display the Russian Empire's power and wealth, while the pastel, Venetian-style palaces, the delicate bridges over canals modeled after Amsterdam, and the light reflecting on the water during the long, glimmering northern summer evenings gave the city an improbable beauty. Dostoevsky, who called Petersburg "the most abstract and pre-meditated city in the entire world," was one of the many Russians who wrote about how the empire's capital confronted the viewer with the power of the human imagination.[2] The promise of the modern city that you can transform yourself, as Rappoport had already done several times, seemed more tempting here than anywhere else. But Petersburg constantly frustrated such ambitions. The lives of the legitimate residents of the city were controlled by strict rules and hierarchies, and the police strove even harder here than elsewhere to exclude anyone without the right papers. Indeed, while the facts of Rappoport's publications in 1892 show an unknown writer succeeding in breaking into the circle of the radical intelligentsia, after he left the city, he and his friends told stories about his time there that suggest that Petersburg may never have offered the refuge he craved.

In January and February 1892, Rappoport published "A Sketch of the Coal Industry in the South of Russia" in *Russkoe Bogatstvo*. First, though, he needed to resolve a technicality: his pen name. Neither "Pseudonymous," under which he had published *History of a Family* in 1884, nor "S. Vidbin," which he had used in *Trud* in 1890, satisfied him. He told his radical friend Victor Chernov that using his own name, Solomon Rappoport, had made him feel somehow "ashamed," and when he published *History of a Family,* he was relieved to hear that he could use a pseudonym, a notion he took literally when he chose to sign his novel "Pseudonymous." Later he decided that that choice had been a mistake, but the question of what to use instead remained. He liked the simplicity and modesty of the pseudonyms of the radical writers he admired. "Just think about it: Uspensky himself signed his work 'G. U.' for a long time, or 'G. Ivanov.' Or Vasily Pavlovich Vorontsov: for his whole literary life he was the simplest possible thing, 'V. V.' And Nikolai Frantsevich Danielson, Karl Marx's friend and correspondent? Just 'Nikolai -on.' And if you want, Dobroliubov did better than anyone else: what could be simpler and more modest than his signature, '-bov'?" Finally, Uspensky himself resolved the question for his protégé. He chose the initials of the first name and patronymic that Rappoport had used among the miners, "Semyon Akimovich." Then, "at random," he wrote "An," paused for a moment, added a hyphen, and put the ending "-sky." "How is this?" he asked Rappoport, who recalled, "I was delighted—I took a tremendous liking to it, undoubtedly just because it had been written by his hand and in his handwriting. So ever since then I have been S. A. An-sky."[3]

In accepting his new name, the young writer was affirming that he belonged to a new community. When the miners named him "Semyon Akimovich," that meant that they had accepted him, and now Uspensky's circle accepted him too. Anger at his biological father may have made him reluctant to use "Rappoport," and Uspensky, as a better father, had provided a new name that even rhymed with his own. This pseudonym was a password that gave Rappoport entry into two entire new families: Uspensky's own and that of the writers at *Russkoe Bogatstvo.* An-sky was a literary novice, but as in Liozno and among the miners, he was adept at picking up the language and mannerisms of others. He showed Chernov that he knew about the Russian literary canon when he recited the names whose greatness made him feel small by comparison: "Turgenev, or Pisemsky, or Ostrovsky." He demonstrated his mastery of the radical canon and its codes when he noted that the radical critic Nikolai Dobroliubov published under "-bov" and Vasily Vorontsov, a writer on economic issues, used "V. V." When he took Uspensky's suggestion, he made it clear to his new patron that he shared the ideology behind the radicals' choice of names, the urge for the individual to avoid attention. The 1868 "Catechism of the Revolutionary," a statement by Mikhail Bakunin and Sergei Nechaev, articulated this urge in extreme form: "The revolutionary . . . does not have his own interests, affairs, feelings, habits, property, not even a name. Everything in him is absorbed by a single, exclusive interest, a single thought, a single passion—the revolution."[4] Because An-sky too wanted to be anonymous, his new friends could see that he was a good radical.

Although writers have used pseudonyms since ancient times, they have rarely done so in such numbers as in Tsarist Russia, where the opposition between them and the state was taken for granted by both parties. To avoid the attention of the authorities, writers either published their works unsigned or used pseudonyms that would let clever readers guess their identity: names based on their initials, hometown, or ancestry, comic foreign-sounding names, adjectives meant to describe them (i.e., Gorky, "bitter," and Bedny, "poor"), or mystifying expressions (the Decembrist Gavriil Batenkov used the mathematical symbol for the square root of minus one). In the second half of the nineteenth century, most of the contributors to radical journals such as *Sovremennik* (The Contemporary) and *Otechestvennye Zapiski* (Fatherland Notes) used false names, often selected or invented by a friend or publisher.[5] When he told the story of his pseudonym, An-sky was showing that he had entered the subculture of radical Russian writers.

An-sky's favorite pseudonyms were those that revealed as little as possible, such as Dobroliubov's choice "-bov," and the pseudonym that Uspensky devised displayed its refusal to divulge the author's identity. Although An-sky told Chernov that Uspensky chose *A* and *N* "at random," they are the first letters in *Anon.* or *Anonymous* (*Anonim*), an implication only slightly disguised by the addition of *sky*: "An-sky" sounded like "Mr. Anonymous." The new name effaced Rappoport's Jewishness, along with everything else about him. Since he had already used the byline "Pseudonymous," it made sense for Rappoport to continue to hide his name by becoming "Anonymous-sky." The hyphen, which he used throughout his career in Russian and Yiddish, highlighted the name's artificiality. An-sky's contemporaries noticed his pseudonym's emptiness; in 1910, when a writer for the anti-Jewish *Novoe Vremia* (New Times) reported on the twenty-fifth anniversary of An-sky's literary activity, he mocked him for being unable, over all that time, "to find a last name" more conventional than "An-sky": "If this is a pseudonym, it has something missing."[6]

Incomplete or not, this pseudonym gave An-sky entry into the Petersburg Populist intelligentsia. He appealed to his new friends as a member of a group that fascinated them: the intelligentsia "from the folk," literate, semi-educated rural people who shared the principles of the urban Populists but could speak to peasants in their own language and be accepted by them. An-sky was only one of Uspensky's folklore-collecting correspondents, a group that included several actual peasants. Uspensky cared about helping beginning writers of this kind get published, because he believed it would be wrong to ignore these "*formerly unknown voices* from the folk masses." An-sky, who had introduced himself to Uspensky as a laborer who had only recently begun to study Russian, qualified as just such a "previously unknown voice." To judge by Uspensky's enthusiastic interpretation of "Vidbin" as something like an eyewitness, An-sky had calculated right in his self-presentation.[7]

After the sketch on the coal industry in the January and February issues of *Russkoe Bogatstvo,* An-sky's sketch set in a Jewish tavern, "Hangover" (a version of "In 'The Depths' "), appeared in the March issue, and four long articles on peasant literacy followed in the July through October issues (republished two years later as a book, *Sketches on Folk Literature*). An additional sketch about the sale of sheep, slated for publication, was forbidden by the censor. These pieces were all in the Populist spirit. The coal industry article emphasized that the mines were corrupting innocent peasants and destroying their culture. "Hangover" showed that the alcohol the Jewish tavernkeeper sells the peasants leads to their moral and physical degradation, a problem she recognizes but cannot solve. The peasant literacy book addressed the search for reading material for peasants: An-sky argued there that peasants need stories that reflect their own values, not inaccessible highbrow literature or books that could lead them to become too modern too fast. The censored story about sheep told of speculators who take advantage of peasants.[8] All the articles An-sky published in 1892 suggested that readers must try to rescue the peasants and their culture by slowing down the spread of capitalism in the countryside.

An-sky's *Russkoe Bogatstvo* articles, like his pseudonym, advertised his successful assimilation; there was no way to tell from them that their author was a Jew who could not even write Russian until his teens. In his private correspondence too, An-sky did his best to transform himself into a person whose dedication to the Russian peasants could never be questioned. In a letter he wrote to Uspensky in February 1892, An-sky distanced himself from the sort of Jews whom the Populists suspected of taking advantage of peasants. "I see only one possible solution to the Jewish question. To remove from the Jews, in the most radical way, all possibility of exploiting the population, and especially to protect the defenseless peasant village from them, but at the same time to open the door for them to agricultural work. It seems to me there's no other solution."[9] This vision of Jewish reform would have seemed attractive to Uspensky, who was not personally hostile to Jews. Uspensky had written warmly about a Jewish coachman who yearned to buy land and work it, and An-sky's letter echoed that image of a would-be Jewish farmer, but went even farther by urging that all Jews be offered that option. In this letter, An-sky did his best to show Uspensky that his loyalties to the narod and to the ideology of *Russkoe Bogatstvo* were firmly in place.

Also in 1892, An-sky began working on some of his mature stories, including "Twenty Years Old," a story of a hungry would-be student. While the *Russkoe Bogatstvo* articles testified that An-sky had found an ideological home among the Petersburg Populists, this story suggested that he was also trying to locate himself within the city's literary tradition. It imitates the opening chapters of one of the best-known works of fiction set in St. Petersburg, Dostoevsky's 1866 *Crime and Punishment*. Like Dostoevsky's hero Raskolnikov, the narrator of "Twenty Years Old" is a starving student who relies on tutoring to support himself but has run into hard times and lost his regular pupils. Like Raskolnikov, he is in debt to his landlady and obsessed by money—and like Raskolnikov, when he gets money, he immediately gives it away to a family with a sick mother and small children. Like Raskolnikov, he considers going to a fellow student to get help, but changes his mind. And like Raskolnikov, he is obsessed by thoughts of what others might say about him. Raskolnikov is furious with injured pride when he learns that his sister is willing to sacrifice herself to help him, and An-sky's narrator suffers from the same kind of pride and inability to accept help from a young woman:

> Several times the sentence was on the tip of my tongue: "Annushka, by the way, give me something to eat," but it did not come out of my mouth. It was exactly that "By the way." I had come to ask for bread for hungry people, and *by the way* I would satisfy my own hunger. No, I can't even ask Annushka in this way! And she, as though on purpose, did not guess herself that she should offer me something to eat.[10]

When he created a hero who anticipates his interlocutors' criticism and responds to what he imagines they might say rather than to what they actually say, An-sky was experimenting with Dostoevsky's signature style of dialogue and interior monologue, the self-accusatory tones of the young man from the provinces who is nearly driven mad by his exposure to the possibilities and the dangers of the big city. As An-sky worked to convince the *Russkoe Bogatstvo* writers to accept him, he must have felt, as Raskolnikov did, the weight of other people's eyes upon him and the difficulty of guessing what they were thinking. The story that he started in 1892 reflected both the temptation and the risk of St. Petersburg for Shloyme-Zanvl Rappoport as he tried to transform himself into the Russian writer S. A. An-sky.

The biggest problem with the transformation of Shloyme-Zanvl Rappoport into a Petersburg writer was that as a Jew, he was not allowed to live in the city at all. He often told the story of his first night there. He went straight from the train station to Uspensky's house, where the two men sat up late talking. Only after he left did Rappoport realize that without residence permission, he could not go to a hotel. He decided to walk around the streets until the morning. Swaying from exhaustion at 3 A.M., he heard a voice he knew. Uspensky himself, unable to sleep and still thinking over his meeting with the young writer, had gone for a walk.

"Why are you walking around here?" Uspensky asked.

"I'm wandering," Rappoport explained.

"Why? Why aren't you at home?"

"I have no home."

"A hotel?"

"I have no residence permission. . . ."

Uspensky was shocked. As An-sky would retell the episode, Uspensky had known in theory about Jews' restriction to the Pale, but this was his first personal encounter with it. He brought Rappoport back to his own house and put him to sleep in his own bed. Exhausted from his hours of walking, Rappoport fell asleep, but later woke up and saw Uspensky sitting by the bed, crying. From then on, Uspensky took personal responsibility for Rappoport's well-being and literary fate.[11]

The sight of Uspensky's tears in his presence—and his own welcome into the writer's bed—must have profoundly affected Rappoport. He reacted to the people he met with open emotion, and he craved emotional responses from others to match his own. Uspensky's reaction mattered especially, because his letters had made Rappoport see himself differently, freeing him, if only briefly, from the oppressive voices in his mind telling him that he was "a failure, a superfluous man." Before he met Uspensky, he had written to tell him that he believed that once he spoke to the older writer, his life would "lose its 'temporary' character."[12] Now he had proof that he and his stories had moved Uspensky, as borne out by the offer of a bed where he could finally sleep. Zhitlowsky's and Gurevich's parents may have chased him out of their homes, but now Rappoport had been let into a more important house than theirs.

When Rappoport met him, Uspensky was celebrated as the author of powerful depictions of the brutality of peasant life, the degeneracy of urban existence, and the falsity of the promise of progress. He was renowned for his sympathy for the oppressed, and he exemplified the intelligentsia virtues of moral clarity and the refusal to compromise. That this man was so visibly moved by his own plight must have awoken a powerful emotion in Rappoport himself, reinforcing the bond he already felt with this surrogate father. He eventually transferred his emotions about Gleb Uspensky to his wife and children. After he left Petersburg, Uspensky's wife Alexsandra sent him a new edition of Uspensky's novel *The Customs of Rasteriaeva Street,* and he stayed up until 2:30 A.M. reading it, feeling as though he had "returned after a long absence to my native town and seen my relatives, friends, places that were full of dear memories for me." He kept a special album for pictures of the Uspensky family, and he told Alexsandra, "At a sad moment, when my spirit is low, I look at that album and my soul becomes higher, better, clearer."[13]

For many years after 1892, An-sky and his friends retold the story of Uspensky's tears, for this anecdote made the young Jew's acceptance by the Petersburg intelligentsia a matter of public record. The tears showed that An-sky had encountered one of Uspensky's best-known qualities, his sadness. In clinical terms, Uspensky's sadness was part of his mental illness.

His strong feelings frequently manifested themselves in public: at the celebration of the twenty-fifth anniversary of his writing career in 1887, his
intense emotion had made him unable to read his most recent work out
loud, though the crowd still applauded enthusiastically. Whether or not
they knew he was being treated for what may have been clinical depression, Uspensky's friends often pointed out his sadness. In their writings
and their experience interacting with him, especially during the early
stages of his disease, that sadness did not seem pathological. Vladimir
Korolenko at *Russkoe Bogatstvo* wrote, "Perhaps that remarkable sensitivity revealed the illness that was already near . . . But at that time such
an idea never entered my head, even more so since the sadness and sensitivity produced a single whole that was too attractive to seem ill."[14] By
retelling the story of his terrible agitation in his own presence, An-sky let
his listeners know that he had met the real Uspensky.

The anecdote also cast a new light on the "Jewish question." The sympathy so powerfully expressed in Uspensky's writing was directed at the
suffering people of Russia, first among them the peasantry. When he cried
for An-sky, he symbolically extended his famous sympathy for the oppressed to include a new group, the Jews, their limited rights symbolized
by the residence restrictions confining them to the Pale. Uspensky's tears,
by creating an equation between Jews and peasants, legitimized the suffering of the Jews and opposed the stereotype that the Jews were themselves oppressors, guilty of contributing to the peasants' misery. When
An-sky cast himself as the Jewish object of the sad gaze of the famous
writer, he suggested that he stood for all the Jews of the empire. Chernov,
in his own retelling of the anecdote, brought this political subtext to the
surface with a metaphor from the New Testament. He compared Uspensky to Doubting Thomas and the Jews to the crucified and resurrected
Jesus, citing John 20:25 to describe Uspensky's reactions when he ran
into An-sky on that dark Petersburg street: for the first time, Uspensky
was "placing his fingers on the nail wounds" of Jewish life. Chernov
ended with An-sky awakening to see Uspensky's tears and wondering,
"Was it long ago that this quiet, wordless weeping for the fate of another,
an orphaned nation, had begun?"[15] The story as Chernov told it symbolized not just that the Petersburg radicals accepted Rappoport, but that
they accepted him *as a Jew,* that there was no contradiction between his
identities as a Jew and as a Russian radical. The anecdote echoes Rappoport's 1887 sketch "Rain," where the narrator first feels that he will
never fit in among the peasants, then, as his tears mix with the falling
rain, realizes that he does belong; Uspensky's tears too dissolve the barriers of ethnicity.

The story also carried a broader cultural weight. By relating an incident in which he wanders the streets of the empire's capital all night, An-sky created a connection between himself and some of the city's most famous Russian writers, who had depicted that very scene in their works. Alexander Pushkin's poem "The Bronze Horseman," Nikolai Gogol's story "The Overcoat," Dostoevsky's story "White Nights," and his novel *Crime and Punishment* all combine depictions of the city's magnificence with heroes who wander the streets at night, their perceptions clouded by madness of one sort or another, hopelessly challenging the omnipotent state. Wandering, sleepless nights and exhaustion were real elements of An-sky's life, which he would lend to his hero Khonen. But his well-read interlocutors, seeing these familiar images set in the capital, would have understood that the story legitimized An-sky as a typical Petersburg writer, that is, a member of the Russian intelligentsia who opposed the regime and felt ambivalent about the Westernization of Russian ways represented by the city itself.[16]

Ironically, it was precisely as a Jew that An-sky experienced the alienation typical of the Petersburg intellectual, for the story of his nighttime stroll belonged, in fact, to two literary categories, one Russian and one Jewish: the classic Petersburg tale, and the accounts of Jews living illegally in the capital. For economic and other reasons, Jews were drawn to those parts of Russia where they were forbidden to live, especially Petersburg, and they found myriad ways to stay: they acquired false papers; they bribed doormen and policemen; they registered as the servants of Jewish families who did have residence permission; they joined professions (photographers, prostitutes) that had special dispensation to live outside the Pale; most effectively, they changed their legal status by converting to Christianity (sometimes paying a professional to take the required catechism exam).[17] An-sky's story of wandering the streets until he found a sympathetic non-Jew to take him in identified him as a victim of the Tsarist regime, a poor Jew himself and a comrade to the other poor Jews of the empire. The Jewish residence restrictions undermined the Petersburg tale of Pushkin and Gogol, transforming it from a modern fable of alienation into news from the police blotter. The expulsion of the Jews of Moscow the year before, in 1891, would have made An-sky's fears sound justified. The Jews who heard An-sky tell his story would undoubtedly have appreciated the irony, as would non-Jews who—like Uspensky—grasped what Jews went through to stay in the capital.

There is no way to know whether An-sky himself grasped all the possible meanings for his nighttime stroll in early 1892. His mention of the "Jewish question" in his February 1892 letter to Uspensky suggests that when the two men had met a few weeks earlier, the topic of Rappoport's Jewishness had come up, but his assertions in the letter about the danger that Jews pose to peasants complicate the picture that emerges from the anecdote, of Jews as primarily victims of the regime. As An-sky told and retold the anecdote over a lifetime, he must have begun to see it—and his entire time in Petersburg—differently.

He would also retell the story of how he chose his *Russkoe Bogatstvo* byline; whereas he told Chernov that "An-sky" symbolized his connection to Uspensky, he later insisted that it tied him instead to his mother, Chana (Anna) Rappoport. He had given his mother's name to his fictional heroines, from the sympathetic tavernkeeper in "Hangover"/"In 'The Depths' " to the agunah in "In a Jewish Family"; the sound of Khonen, in *The Dybbuk*, echoes Chana; and he eventually began to claim his mother's name for himself as well. He did so in print first of all in early 1902, when he began to publish Yiddish verse and revolutionary propaganda under a new pseudonym, "Z. Sinanni," or *syn Anny*, "Anna's son."[18] (The name pointed to an alternative father as well as a reclaimed mother: he sometimes spelled it with only one *N* as "Sinani," linking himself to his friend Boris Sinani, Uspensky's psychiatrist, a Petersburg intellectual of Karaite origin.) This pseudonym suggests that An-sky was taking a few careful steps away from the persona he had created in 1892.

He took more steps away when he started to tell his friends that his pseudonym resulted from a mistake. One memoirist wrote that "the hyphen in An-sky [instead of Ansky] was the error of a typesetter who took the crossbar in the Russian *N* [which looks like *H*] for a little line." This story of the misspelled name that stuck forever sounds like a Gogolian absurdity—and if the typesetter had actually mistaken an *N* for a hyphen, then the pseudonym would have ended up as "A-sky," not "An-sky." This unlikely story may be a corruption of a somewhat more probable version, whereby the *Russkoe Bogatstvo* editors rejected "Rappoport" as too frequent, so the young writer suggested "Annensky," after his mother. "I wanted," he told a friend, "to convince my mother, who grieved over my departure for the society of others, that my connection to this woman who personified my own Jewish heritage was not only not broken but rather would be made closer and stronger in my future work. But because the well known Populist N. F. Annensky was already publishing in *Russkoe Bogatstvo*, it had to be changed to 'An-sky.' " This An-sky has little in common with the radical writers who sought anonymity in order to serve the narod and evade the attention of the regime; he is bound by personal ties, demonstratively embracing his family and through them the Jewish people. The depiction of an attachment to Jewish culture arising after a period of alienation evokes an ancient archetype: the *baal tshu-vah,* literally "master of return," meaning a prodigal son, a person who has left Judaism or committed a sin but has since returned to tradition and repented.[19] An-sky depicted himself in this story as a baal tshuvah, and when he linked that image to the pen name of his entire career, he suggested that his literary work should be read as an expression of a "return" to Jewishness that began in 1892 with his choice of pseudonym. His pseudonym functioned at first as a password giving him access to the Petersburg intelligentsia; later, he would transform it into a shibboleth that allowed him into Jewish communities as well.

Such contradictions filled An-sky's tales of his months in Petersburg. Although in his letter to Uspensky he presented the Jews as exploiters, his anecdote about meeting his patron demonstrated that Jews were instead victims of the regime. And although comparison of the anecdotes he told about his pseudonym indicates that the connection to his mother's name became important to him only later, he would insist that he already had it in mind in 1892. As we will see, at some points, particularly around 1910, An-sky would tell the story of his own life as a perfect ricochet of departure from the Jewish fold followed—after around 1900—by return. When he retold his anecdotes of 1892, he moved the moment of "return" back in time, in spite of all evidence to the contrary, to the year when he adopted his pseudonym and his literary career began in earnest.

An-sky's false dating and inconsistent stories reflected his constant need to make himself over to find acceptance among new groups of people. Perhaps, in his Vitebsk youth, he could not master the role of a wealthy teenager who belonged on Castle Street, but his next attempts at disguise, as a pious young man in Liozno, then a simple Russian worker in the Donets Basin, worked better. In Petersburg, he managed to transform himself into a member of the Russian Populist intelligentsia; as he retold his anecdotes about his months there, he began to carve out a new identity as a Jewish cultural and political activist. His shifting Petersburg stories are well suited to his location. Russian literary tradition depicts that city as a construction of masks and facades, where nothing is what it seems. Dostoevsky's Raskolnikov takes on the identity of a radical intellectual, only to go almost mad when he realizes the moral emptiness of his new self. In shifting from depicting himself in Petersburg as a successful assimilator to claiming he was already a baal tshuvah when he arrived, An-sky followed the tradition that makes that city the site of repeated self-transformations. Indeed, the revelation that An-sky did not feel at home in this city identified him as a legitimate denizen of Petersburg. In "The Noise of Time," the poet Osip Mandelstam's memoir of an 1890s

Petersburg Jewish childhood, he wrote of his feeling that the city's magnificence was a sham, "a brilliant covering thrown over an abyss."[20] He
echoed Pushkin, Gogol, Dostoevsky, and the other writers who described
their city as a stage set that may come down at any moment.

An-sky belonged to a generation of Russian and Jewish writers for
whom the distinction between life and art, or private life and politics,
was hazy if it existed at all. People in his milieu took it for granted that
one's literary texts illustrated one's life and one's life illustrated one's literary texts.[21] For An-sky himself, this assumption was more true than for
most. As we remember, he had written to Mikhailovsky that "my life has
developed in such a way that if writing were removed from it, such an
emptiness would appear that it would simply horrify me." Whereas other
writers might in fact have elements in their lives that could not be brought
into conformity with their literary and political ideals, An-sky had nothing but his work—no family, no home, not even any regular habits. All he
had was his ideals and the stories that he told about them.

In telling and retelling his 1892 anecdotes, An-sky constructed a literary
identity, using the techniques he knew. Like the two most brilliant Yiddish
writers who were his contemporaries, Sholem Rabinovich (or Sholem
Aleichem) and Sholem Yankev Abramovich (or Mendele Moikher Sforim),
An-sky created a pseudonym that was part of a carefully designed literary
persona; his Russian audience differed from their Yiddish one, but his
sense of the malleability of identity was similar.[22] He created his persona as
he created his literary texts, making ruthless revisions. Just as his writing
always remained within the parameters of mainstream Russian literature,
so his persona was determined by the available Russian genres. The persona that he created with his 1892 stories fits into the Petersburg tradition,
identifying its creator as a typical Russian *intelligent,* terribly conscious of
his own rootlessness. At the same time, An-sky's 1892 anecdotes under-
mine the Petersburg tradition by reminding their audience that the Jewish
reality of legal repression was no literary conceit.

Whether or not he had become a typical Petersburg writer, An-sky's stay
in the city was short. At some point in the summer of 1892, he left the
city that he had dreamed of for so long, not to return until 1906. The
timing of the departure points to its likely cause: the materialization of
the metaphor of Petersburg as a literally maddening abyss, before his
very eyes. Uspensky's mental condition worsened precipitously in the
spring of 1892. At the end of June, Sinani told Krivenko that the writer
was suffering from delusions of persecution and was convinced that
many of his friends had been killed or committed suicide. "To my horror,

my study and careful observation of him have made it impossible for me to deceive myself that his disease might not be as serious as it had seemed on my last visit to Petersburg. . . . God, how hard it is to accept this fact!" In July, Uspensky was admitted to a private mental hospital in St. Petersburg, where he stayed until September, when he fell into another depression and attempted suicide. On September 21, he entered the Kolmovskaia mental hospital near Novgorod; apart from a respite the following year, he remained hospitalized until his death on March 24, 1902.[23] This tragic withdrawal of his patron must have contributed to An-sky's decision to leave the city in the summer of 1892.

There were other reasons to leave. He could have been nervous about the law, although in fact an arrest warrant would not be issued for him until 1894, as a result of information the police received about his activities abroad. He told some people that he left because he wanted to become acquainted with the life of European workers. He also wanted to see Zhitlowsky again, and he was pursuing Masha Reinus, the cousin who had lived with Zhitlowsky's family in the center of Vitebsk. She was studying in Switzerland, and An-sky had been corresponding with her. After a few weeks in Berlin (which he disliked), An-sky went to Bern, where he had a happy reunion with Zhitlowsky. His first meetings with Masha went well, but things did not develop as he had wished, and she finally told him she had realized that her letters had given him a false impression of her feelings for him.[24] Once again, he had tried to get conclusive proof of his acceptance from a member of the family on Castle Street, and once again, he had been shown the door.

An-sky was devastated by Reinus's rejection. He cabled Zhitlowsky on October 2 to meet him at the Bern train station, writing cagily, "I just received a telegram saying that I must immediately leave for Russia. This is my own personal business." At the station, he told his friend that he had decided to go back to Russia, "to drown psychologically in the sea . . . in the great sea of the Russian people." Again, he was imagining erasing his old self—and this time, nothing would stand in his way. The implications were clear: if Masha (and, symbolically, Zhitlowsky's family) would not have him, then he would find solace among other people. He was hinting at his willingness to convert to Christianity and thus remove the legal barrier separating him from the narod.[25]

Zhitlowsky persuaded An-sky to change his mind: instead of going back to Russia, he went to Paris. The idea that An-sky could be so easily convinced to go west rather than east, farther from Russia instead of closer, might seem improbable, but the point was not the destination, but the flight. At other moments, An-sky wrote that when he felt rejected, his urge was to flee. Some sixteen years later, he would draft a letter to his second wife, Edia Glezerman, then traveling in Europe, articulating similar emotions. When she did not write to him for two weeks, he wrote that "I decided that if I didn't get a letter from you I'd write that I understood your silence as a break with me, and I'd go . . . I don't know where myself, abroad, to the south, anywhere, so that somewhere, in complete solitude, I'd be able to get through that truly terrible condition that I was in."[26]

If An-sky had those same emotions after his rejection by Reinus as he left the Bern train station in October 1892, and if he was still reeling from similar emotions after Uspensky's hospitalization a couple of months earlier, then he may have gone to Paris seeking something quite different from what other people sought there. The Paris of the 1890s, at the beginning of the Belle Epoque, home of the cabaret and the can-can, was the capital of Europe's intellectual and popular culture. Paris offered Russian émigrés economic opportunity, political freedom, and the pleasures of a burgeoning consumer culture. An-sky was looking not for that, but for an emotional refuge. He would find what he looked for, and more as well.

CHAPTER FOUR

A Propagandist's Education

If writing press reports is something like a whale, then like the
prophet Jonah, I'm lying in the belly of that whale.
        —Letter from S. An-sky to Chaim Zhitlowsky, November 9, 1898

I N THE FALL OF 1892, An-sky arrived in Paris. He had enjoyed a
winter and spring of success as a writer in Petersburg under Uspensky's patronage, but now Uspensky was hospitalized and An-
sky needed to figure out how to continue without him, in a foreign city
where he knew almost no one. He found work in a factory and as a typesetter, but he still had to ask Zhitlowsky for loans. He was homesick and
unhappy, and blamed himself for his ill temper. One day when his mood
was especially bad, he remembered a time when he was in the woods
with a little girl. "She picked a berry and said happily, 'A berry, a berry!'
I said, 'Throw it away, it's nasty!' She looked at me and at the berry and
said calmly, 'It's you, brother. You have nasty eyes.' That's it, my eyes
have become nasty." Depression made him passive, and it was hard to
write; instead, he read, worked a little, and observed.[1] As he gradually
began to write again and to be published, he confronted the gap between
his ideal of heroic writers who serve the people with their pen and the
"nasty" reality of the competitive consumer culture of Paris.

Paris was more complicated than he had expected. "Every Russian,"
An-sky wrote, "has his own dream of Paris."[2] For radicals such as himself, Paris was still the capital of the 1789 revolution, where the Bastille
had fallen and new ideas about freedom and equality were taken seriously. Here Russian writers who would have been imprisoned under the
tsar published books and journals that were then smuggled back into
Russia. The most prominent Russian radical in Paris at the time was
Pyotr Lavrov, whose ideas about the obligation of educated people to
improve the lives of the peasants so inspired the Populists. Arrested after

an 1866 attack on the tsar (to which he had no connection) and exiled to a small town north of Moscow, Lavrov had written his famous *Historical Letters* there and then escaped to Western Europe. Since 1870 he had been editing Russian journals and writing copiously in philosophy, sociology, history, mathematics, and other fields. In his early seventies by the time An-sky arrived in France, Lavrov was the only person An-sky really admired in the Russian emigration. He was a figure worthy to replace Uspensky as An-sky's patron and mentor, and before long he did so.

But Paris was not all about freedom and high ideals. By the time An-sky arrived, the latest manifestation of the French revolution—the socialist government that directed the Paris Commune for two months in the spring of 1871—had been crushed in a bloody street war, and the Vendôme column, erected by Napoleon to celebrate the victory at Austerlitz and then dismantled in May 1871 by the Communards, had been rebuilt, cementing the revolution's defeat. The strength of French conservatism became increasingly evident in the 1890s, as the Dreyfus Affair exploded and divided Parisian society. And even as the French authorities tolerated foreign radicals, the government of the Third Republic entered into an alliance with the Russian Empire in 1894, celebrated with Tsar Nicholas's visit to Paris in 1896.

Paris was an exciting place to be at the end of the century. The Eiffel Tower completed for the 1889 World's Fair represented the promise of technological innovation, as did the Pasteur Institute, a government-funded medical research organization established in 1887, one of whose directors was Ilia Mechnikov, a Russian émigré and Lavrov's friend. New technologies of communication and transportation were on display: from 1891, bicycles got cheaper and became accessible to the middle class; automobiles eventually followed, and people could move faster and farther than ever before. Gramophones and records (on wax cylinders) were on sale, and in a Paris cellar in 1895, a paying audience watched a motion picture for the first time. What you could see and hear no longer depended on who you were or where and when you lived. Henri de Toulouse-Lautrec and other artists used lithography to make bright posters luring audiences to Paris's *cafés chantants* (nightclubs) and cabarets where workers, shop owners, and foreigners could drink together. By 1896, Singer-made sewing machines produced ready-to-wear clothing for men and then for women. If modernity meant the breakdown of limits keeping different kinds of people distinct and apart, or limits to human movement, sight, and hearing, then Paris was its capital.[3]

Paris was also home to diverse people—French and immigrant, wealthy, working-class, and poor—who fascinated An-sky. Between 1880 and

1925, approximately 100,000 Jewish immigrants came to France from Eastern Europe, and the majority settled in Paris, working in the burgeoning garment industry and crowding into the traditionally Jewish quarter, the Marais, in the Third Arrondissement. Like garment workers elsewhere, they took home piecework: parents and children worked together, using leased sewing machines. An-sky's life had much in common with that of other Russian Jewish immigrants. He too did manual labor in his rented home. In June 1894, when the Russian police learned that the revolutionary newspaper *Russkii Rabochii* (The Russian Worker) was typeset in his Paris room, they issued a warrant to arrest him, should he ever return to the empire.[4]

During An-sky's eight years in the city, he moved at least ten times around the Fifth Arrondissement on the Left Bank, where Russian students and other émigrés gathered on Thursdays in Lavrov's apartment at 328 rue St. Jacques for tea, cookies, and nightlong discussions. Like other immigrants, An-sky shared his small room with relatives, friends, and friends of friends. His brother-in-law came to Paris when he needed an operation, and his niece came to live with him and attend a French university. He realized that his apartment had become "a kind of rooming house for acquaintances" one night when he came home late to find two "big, strong girls" asleep in his bed and a note on the table, explaining that they had just arrived from Siberia. Because a mutual friend had told them how helpful he was, they were sure he would not mind finding another place to sleep that night and coming back in the morning to help them get their papers in order, find a place to live, and enroll at the Sorbonne.[5]

An-sky complained that Paris was disappointing. The Parisians he encountered had little in common with the earnest, persecuted Jean Valjean of *Les misérables*. His complaints about Paris echoed the common critique that the glitter of the French capital concealed its inhabitants' moral decadence. He disliked much about France and the French: their fondness for suggestive song lyrics, their ignorance about Eastern Europe, even their looks. "The Italians are incomparably more attractive than the French, among whom it is very rare to find pretty, or even rarer, open and friendly, faces." The émigré community offered cold comfort. "Sadly, there are no real Russian revolutionaries from the intelligentsia here in emigration. (Not speaking of PL [Lavrov], a saintly figure)." An-sky knew he was homesick. "A hangover after someone else's feast—that's what this life is for a Russian. You sit and watch as they celebrate, they get upset, they fight, they move history forward in a way, and you don't care." He felt that the history that mattered was occurring elsewhere and he was missing out on the chance of affecting it.[6]

In spite of his complaints, An-sky was changed by Paris, where he began to move away from his politically uncompromising positions and his hard-line asceticism. He had always adapted to new surroundings, and in spite of his own resistance he adapted to Paris too, recognizing that he could not turn his back on consumer culture completely. He urged Zhitlowsky to visit, promising, "I'll take you to the Eiffel Tower and show you a *café chantant*. And the cigars here are so good—ay-ay-ay!" Paris cigars were a far step from the cheap cigarettes Chaim and Shloyme-Zanvl had smoked in the attic, but sharing them would be a way for An-sky to reinforce his connection to his old friend—and consumerism became, for him, a way to connect with people. Zhitlowsky pushed An-sky toward a new consumer experience when he asked him to buy him a bicycle (An-sky was willing to help, although he warned, "I understand absolutely nothing about this stuff"). He experimented with Parisian clothing when he found himself guiding another Siberian visitor, Avgan Dzhordziev, a Tibetan lama with shaven head and yellow robe who had come to Paris to represent his government. The lama asked An-sky what he should wear to dinner with members of the French government. An-sky assured him that his traditional costume would be appropriate, but when the lama insisted on a Western-style suit, An-sky led him to a ready-to-wear shop. Impatient as he waited for the lama to choose a suit jacket, An-sky selected a black one of about the right size from the rack and laid it across the lama's shoulders. The lama recoiled, and his translator explained that he had insulted the cleric, because in Tibet, only criminals wore black (the lama then bought a brown suit).[7]

Before he came to Paris, An-sky had been sure it was time for him and other Jews to jettison the old ways. In Liozno, he had tried to convince young Jews to abandon their parents' beliefs and behaviors and embrace enlightenment. Yet when he moved to the Donets Basin and began living among miners, he took a different view of modernity. He described traditional village life as healthier and more moral than the new mining ways, and he strove in his journalism to expose the evils of capitalism, in contrast to the peasants' way of life. In Paris, where An-sky found new interlocutors and a different kind of modernity, he was forced to reexamine his old ideas about cultural change. To reach people, he realized, he would need to accept some of the values of consumer culture.

Almost twenty-nine years old when he reached Paris, An-sky had never studied formally past his Talmud training in *heder*. Now he met Russian students, especially women and Jews frustrated by the quotas and restrictions that kept them out of university at home. He did not enroll in classes, but he began a systematic program of education in political thought, reading in Russian, German, and, soon enough, French. He read Herbert Spencer, the English philosopher whose writings established the field of sociology, and he followed socialist debates about where largely peasant Russia fit in the Marxist scheme of history: did it need to undergo industrialization and the development of a proletariat before the revolution could come, or could the peasants, inspired by their proto-socialist communal institutions, skip over that stage?[8]

He found clear answers in Karl Kautsky's *Erfurt Program,* a set of ideas adopted by the German Social Democratic Party during an 1891 congress. Kautsky, who had edited some of Marx's writings, explained the concept of "historical materialism" in simple language, stressing that history is moved by economic forces, rather than individuals' ideas or actions: "Many are the ways in which economic development may be influenced: it may be hastened and it may be retarded; its results may be made more, or less, painful; only one thing is impossible—to stop its course, or turn it back."[9] The condition of the proletariat will inevitably deteriorate, which will lead to class struggle, which will bring the ideal socialist commonwealth of the future.

The insistence of Marxist Social Democrats (SDs) that history is moving inexorably toward socialism, regardless of individual actions, irritated An-sky's friends at *Russkoe Bogatstvo.* Mikhailovsky published a series of articles critiquing the Marxists for what he saw as their self-satisfied certainty: "Marx himself was far less certain of the inexorability of the historical process than the 'Marxists' are." He lambasted the Marxists' ignorance, in-fighting, and sanguine attitude toward human suffering, and he passionately attacked their skepticism about the possibility of individual heroism. Such a philosophy, Mikhailovsky insisted, betrayed a poor grasp of reality, a willful denial of the fact that some people are "heroes" who lead, others part of the crowd that follows. An-sky and his friends agreed with Mikhailovsky that these Marxists lived in a "fantastic kingdom where the metaphysical shadows of phenomena block our view of real phenomena, with their color and smell, beauty and ugliness, meanness and greatness." For the SDs, Mikhailovsky wrote mockingly, "there are no heroes or crowds, but only equivalently necessary humans, bobbing up in a certain order from the hidden depths of history." The term *hero,* for Mikhailovsky, was not necessarily positive: he had responded to the 1881–1882 pogroms with an analysis of the destructive role of the "heroes" who led the brutal crowd. Nonetheless, in his attack on the Marxists, he insisted that ethics require that one respond to injustice, because life is not a theater where one can just observe: "They don't give out theater tickets for free, you have to pay for them, and thus in one way or another, one must participate in life." [10]

The argument between Kautsky and Mikhailovsky, between the Marxism of the German SDs and the Populist ideals upheld at *Russkoe Bogatstvo,* divided the Paris émigrés. An-sky was loyal to Mikhailovsky, Lavrov, *Russkoe Bogatstvo,* the growing Socialist Revolutionary (SR) movement, and the conviction that history does not move forward mechanically and individual acts do matter. He played on words in Russian, scornfully calling the SDs "rude Democrats" rather than "Social Democrats." Their self-certainty grated on his nerves: "I so dislike them, God forgive me, when they start to pronounce their eternal truths in the tone of Moses at Sinai." What divided An-sky's crowd from the SDs was not just ideology but style, and he scorned the SDs who had no sense of honor or dedication to transparent action. [11]

While the SDs argued that an individual's actions do not ultimately matter, An-sky followed Mikhailovsky in categorizing human actions as heroic or villainous, beautiful or ugly. When An-sky visited the Louvre, he saw aesthetics as bound up with politics. Unimpressed by the contemporary collection, he praised "The Peasants' Meal," a seventeenth-century image by the Le Nain brothers, of peasants eating in a hut. Such works, he said, "call the viewer to life, turn his face toward the most horrible side of it and force him to shudder, force him to live through a few hours of someone else's life, to feel the gnawing of his conscience." [12]

When Uspensky was in Paris in 1872 he had had a similar experience; he wrote about it in an 1885 essay, where his narrator visits the Louvre and stumbles upon the Venus de Milo. Looking at it, he feels transformed. "Until then . . . I had been like this glove, crumpled in my hand. Does it look like a human hand? No, it is just some kind of leather ball. But if I blow into it, then it starts to look like a human hand. Something I could not understand had blown into the depths of my crumpled, crippled, tortured being and straightened me out, sending a tingling feeling through my reviving body." In the mid-1880s, Uspensky used the same words to describe certain Russian radicals whose image could also transform a "crumpled, crippled, tortured being" into something fully human. He was obsessed by Vera Figner, a Populist woman involved in planning the assassination of Alexander II in March 1881. She was arrested and tried in 1884, and Uspensky sent her a message during the trial, saying that he envied her. Figner understood that "Gleb Uspensky saw in me in those minutes [of the trial] a whole, undivided person, going on a certain path without wavering or looking back, possessing something that I cherish and for which I give up everything." [13]

An-sky found the same kind of inspiration at the studio of Mark Antokolsky, a Jewish sculptor from Vilna who spent his last thirty years in

Europe. Antokolsky was close to Ilia Repin and other members of the Realist movement in Russian painting, who saw art as a tool to expose the problems of society and shock the viewer into looking for solutions. He was known for his realist figures from Russian history, literature, and the New Testament. An-sky wrote to Sinani in 1894 of his ecstatic but inarticulate reaction to Antokolsky's work. "I often become embarrassed for language—it's so weak, pale, insufficient, often false. Do you know that feeling of a prayer service? When the soul, with painful yearning, strives somewhere up high and wants to cry? Could one convey that in words?" In 1896, writing in the St. Petersburg journal *Novoe Slovo* (New Word), he described Antokolsky's statues of Mephistopheles and Baruch Spinoza. "Each one of these characters is the hero of an epic battle, in which, for the most part, the elemental force of darkness and backwardness were on one side, and bright, recently born thought on the other . . . They are a triumphant hymn to the immortal, unvanquishable spirit."[14]

The effect of paintings and statues on An-sky and Uspensky made sense for people who shared Tolstoy's ideas about the power of art. In his 1896 *What Is Art?* Tolstoy argued that effective art moves its consumer, whether or not that person wants to be moved. The reader is "infected" by art that transmits its creator's emotion: "Art is a human activity consisting in this, that one man consciously, by means of certain external signs, hands on to others feelings he has lived through, and that other people are infected by these feelings and also experience them." A person who hears a group of peasant women sing is immediately, inevitably suffused with the singers' jubilation. In the 1890s, An-sky thought that people, especially new readers, needed protection from texts that could infect them with alien values and bad ideas. He wrote to Uspensky's wife Alexsandra of his annoyance that *Russkoe Bogatstvo* had wasted space reviewing a book of fantastic tales by the symbolist Zinaida Gippius. "Just imagine if that kind of poser had dared to bring her worthless decadent affectations into literature in Dobroliubov's day! She would have really caught it! But now nothing happens. They fuss over her. And the reader reads it and flies off to the moon with her witches and fairies, where, of course, there are no hungry people, no obligation to the narod, nothing."[15] An-sky presented himself to Alexsandra as still faithful to the ideals of the Petersburg Populists.

Yet Paris was changing him. What fascinated him most was music: folk songs, street songs, cabaret songs, protest songs. In the Donets Basin, he had interpreted the miners' songs as transparent expressions of the singers' pain at the abandonment of village life for the harsh conditions of the mines. In Paris, such a view of music was impossible. On the one hand, street music was everywhere. Even if the Parisians were less ethical than Jean Valjean, they were as musical as Hugo's Gavroche, the singing urchin who dies on the barricades in 1832. When street singers put down the hat and gathered a crowd, "a living communication" began between performer and audience: "It's hard to distinguish the singer from the public." An-sky was amazed to see how suddenly a group of passers-by turned into a crowd of happy dancers, "as though they had come from a wedding." But that happy crowd and their songs might quickly turn hostile. Early in his Paris stay, An-sky heard someone singing "France for the French" through the window of his rented room. He went outside and engaged the singer in conversation. The performer was writing antiforeigner songs lately, he explained, because "there's a demand for that now— Italians, especially Jews, we can't stand them."[16] This was a kind of folk song, but it was governed by the market and it fomented hatred. An-sky's essay on it broke off abruptly in his notebook, as though the world outside his Paris window resisted his understanding.

An-sky heard the well-known street singer Aristide Bruant in Montmartre at the cabaret Le Mirliton (The Reed Pipe) and disapproved. "This newest Paris folk song, in its contents and its execution, stands very low and corresponds to the level of contemporary French life." At times, he felt that French popular song celebrated the Paris of the poor. "What a talented people," he thought, listening. "In general, the people itself is much more sympathetic and nicer than its representatives, and it is better and purer than people think." At other points, An-sky's thoughts about street songs echoed the Populist suspicion of consumer culture. What he saw as pornography, the French took with a "warm-hearted smile"; singers performed innocent-seeming songs with suggestive gestures, and the more double entendres, the more the Parisians liked it. An-sky was still as prudish as he had been as a teenager, appalled by risqué language. His discomfort bothered him and he claimed to go to "a café of the Decadents" in hopes that the "ignorance" that had prevented him from appreciating Decadence would finally leave him. But there he found most of the performances tedious and risqué, and he was happy only at the end, when a man sang "simply and with feeling."[17]

Long after he left Paris, An-sky would tell people that he was researching or writing a big work about French folk songs or political songs.[18] The project was never finished, but the ongoing attempt to master the material may have forced him to change his ideas about art and about himself. French songs made An-sky confront the contradictions between the physical desires that French culture celebrated and his vision of himself as a pure radical, to look more closely at his sadness about his rejection by Masha Reinus and his pride in being as self-denying as Chernyshevsky's

Rakhmetov. Gradually over his time in Paris, he began to accept that art and desire are connected, and that if he wanted to succeed as a writer, he would need to produce work that would sell.

From 1895, An-sky began to find literary work. The Tolstoyan publishing house Posrednik in Russia asked him to write a book on France, and he got work doing research at the Bibliothèque Nationale. At the same time, old *Russkoe Bogatstvo* colleagues asked him to contribute articles on France to a new journal, *Novoe Slovo* (New Word). He published fiction and nonfiction in legal and illegal Russian publications, describing French streets, schools and libraries, museums and art studios, and the life of émigré students. With the development of a literary career came a sense of himself as producing for a market, aware of the consumer's desires. This new identity coexisted with his commitment to serve the truth by writing about other people's suffering. Reconciling these divergent aims was hard for him, as for other Russian writers. Another Russian journalist in Paris, Nikolai Rusanov, wrote that the newspaper business transformed idealistic writers into grasping journalists who care more about making money than serving art: "Look around you at the picture of the bestial struggle in contemporary society: so many competitors for a crust of bread! . . . Few of us are heroes who can stoically endure hunger and see wives and children going hungry." An-sky agreed that regardless of one's ideals, one must produce something responding to readers' needs and publishers' demands. He explained the literary marketplace to Zhitlowsky, calling his old friend naïve for believing that writing was not, ultimately, merchandise: "For sure, if God himself or even Belinsky published a journal, you could not get in any other way than commercially: here's a product—take it. Look, it will work out. Take commissions if you want and do them, or if you don't, don't. But if you start with this 'I would have if only,' it will never end." As An-sky rebuilt his writing career after Uspensky's decline, he realized that he could not rely on personal connections. When Zhitlowsky asked him about publishing in the respected journal *Russkii Vestnik* (Russian Herald), he answered, "I have no contacts there, but I sent something in on German libraries and it was published right away." But when the famous émigré scholar Maxim Kovalevsky sent them something of An-sky's with a personal recommendation, he heard nothing for five months. "That's influence for you," he concluded ironically.[19]

In late 1895, An-sky became interested in a new literary market: the Yiddish press. After Sholem Aleichem went bankrupt in 1889 and his *Yudishe folksbibliotek* closed, I. L. (Isaac Leib) Peretz in Warsaw continued the mission of providing a home for serious Yiddish literature, publishing *Di yidishe bibliotek* (The Jewish Library) from 1891 to 1895; an anthology, *Literatur un lebn* (Literature and Life), in 1894; and an occasional periodical, *Yontev-bletlekh* (Holiday Booklets), from 1894 to 1896. The Russian government forbade Yiddish periodicals but permitted books; thus *Yontev-bletlekh,* timed to coincide with Jewish festivals, cleverly disguised a periodical as something else. Peretz was a brilliant writer and charismatic, colorful figure, the center of a group of Warsaw writers who met regularly in his apartment. He edited collections with the help of one of this group, Dovid Pinski, with whom he shared an inclination toward socialism. Peretz would become best known for his modernist folkloric stories and plays about encounters with demons and ghosts, but during this period, he published the sort of politically engaged urban sketches that An-sky admired. An-sky read one such story, "In the Cellar," in *Literatur un lebn* in 1895, and was thrilled to see that Yiddish could be the vehicle for what he deemed to be worthwhile literature.[20]

This revelation made An-sky want to write in Yiddish again, and that year he sent Zhitlowsky his Yiddish translations of two melancholy Russian poems by the early-nineteenth-century Ivan Nikitin. He offered Peretz the early novel, *History of a Family,* that he had written in Yiddish but published in Russian—only to find that now that a Yiddish outlet existed for works like his novel, a group of Warsaw writers in Peretz's circle, including, he believed, Pinski, had already had it translated back from Russian into Yiddish and published it as *The War for Life,* without An-sky's name. (Of course, it had been published originally under "Pseudonymous.") In early 1896, Peretz sent An-sky this pirated translation. When he reported the incident to Zhitlowsky, An-sky sounded unperturbed about finding his novel stolen: "Clearly, it's not some charlatan who did it, but just a person who didn't know about the existence of 'copyright.' Who cares?" His attitude was politically correct, and he quoted Lavrov as voicing the same sentiment: "It does not matter if the world knows that certain ideas were produced by Lavrov and not another; it matters that these ideas, which are useful to humanity, be diffused as widely as possible." But he may have been privately miffed, because he noted angrily that Peretz was a "scoundrel" who had neither answered nor published his submission. "That bastard, after all, he used to be a radical, he produced propaganda."[21]

An-sky did not give up on Yiddish. His short story, "The Writings," translated from Russian to Yiddish, finally came out in August 1896 in one of the *Yontev-bletlekh, Oyneg shabes* (Shabbat celebration), signed Sh. Rapoport; at that point, it seems the persona he had constructed under

"An-sky" was only meant for a Russian audience. He took a commission to write a Yiddish booklet on "Poverty and Crime" from Pinski, although he found his "self-confident tone" irritating, and he agreed to translate Vladimir Korolenko's judeophilic Russian story, "The Legend of Flora," into Yiddish for another publication. In mid-1897, he offered the first substantial novella he had written in several years, "In a Jewish Family," for publication in Yiddish, telling Zhitlowsky, "I can give a story from Jewish life, 'Chana the Cook,' seemingly just what they want in tendency and form. But they'd have to pay me in advance, since the story is written in Russian and it takes time to rework it into Yiddish. If they don't like the story, I'll return the money."[22]

An-sky, who so often judged other people's actions as beautiful or ugly, discussed his new Yiddish publications without ideological language. Instead, he referred to market forces when he speculated that the story he had to offer was "just what they want in tendency and form." Later An-sky wrote that he had never been, "God forbid, an opponent of Yiddish, seeing the language as low or unliterary. Indeed, if there had been today's 'language tendencies,' I would certainly have been a passionate Yiddishist." He had no objections to Yiddish per se and he wrote in it happily when he knew he could get his work published; his attitude toward Yiddish displays the understanding of the literary market that he developed in Paris.[23]

The more time An-sky spent in Paris, the more work he found. When Lavrov suffered a stroke in the spring of 1895 and temporarily lost his vision, he hired An-sky as his personal secretary. A slight accident with a carriage in the street injured his foot and limited him to walks with a companion. His physical decline led him to spend almost all his time in his apartment, dictating his works. For a few years in the mid-1890s, An-sky joined him, taking dictation, reading aloud, and helping with personal business. He spent hours in Lavrov's book-filled apartment, which functioned as a lending library for the émigrés. Chernov characterized An-sky's work for Lavrov as "equal to a six-year course at the highest Academy of Sciences." Contact with Lavrov affected An-sky's reading, his interests, and his opinions: he echoed Lavrov's skepticism about artistic modernism and his insistence that neither idealism nor materialism can fully explain human history. Lavrov's lectures moved his audience: one listener remembered that "his speech had a specific effect on the painful conscience of a Russian intellectual." Close connection to Lavrov may have taught An-sky something about public speaking. In 1898, he gave a lecture about Vissarion Belinsky at a student society, illustrated with the new technology of magic lantern slide projection. His lecturing grew ever more successful, ultimately even profitable, and he became attentive to other people's speaking styles.[24]

An-sky's activities make it appear that he had planned to acquire the skills and connections a revolutionary leader needed. Until around 1899, his role in revolutionary work was secondary, but that year the Tsarist secret police—which had long been aware of his activities—decided he merited a full-length entry in their detailed book-length list of individuals under investigation. That was the year Victor Chernov, already a prominent *Russkoe Bogatstvo* writer and revolutionary, arrived in Zurich to organize the publication of propaganda aimed at the Russian peasantry. In his mid twenties, Chernov was a handsome former law student who had already spent time in jail, in exile, and organizing the peasants in Tambov. His focus on peasants instead of workers made his cause unattractive to the SDs and led to conflict with the Geneva SD leader Georgy Plekhanov. Zhitlowsky's organization, Union of Russian Socialist Revolutionaries Abroad, was more sympathetic to Chernov, and An-sky vowed to help him. An-sky was delighted by the idea of producing literature for the peasants. He urged Chernov not to rely solely on Zhitlowsky's group but to reach out to Paris and London émigrés for a broad base of support that would go beyond the borders of any single party.[25]

Chernov's project was based on An-sky's favorite cause. *Russkii Rabochii*, the newspaper he typeset in his apartment in 1894, was directed at peasants as well as workers; its agitation for literacy and against cripplingly high taxes clearly had the countryside in mind. After 1894, An-sky kept thinking and writing to Zhitlowsky about the need to agitate among the peasantry. His frustration at being so far away from the forward movement of history in the Russian Empire led him to embrace Chernov's project. He told Zhitlowsky about the variety of radicals he had convinced to support Chernov's idea: "Now our circle has a socialist revolutionary, someone from People's Right [Narodnoe Pravo], a liberal, and a Populist. We'll speak to T and I think then we'll have a People's Will person. I have nothing against inviting an anarchist, a very efficient guy."[26] Perhaps most exciting for him was the awareness of his own expertise. Having written an entire book on peasants and reading, he felt qualified to take charge.

As Chernov and An-sky worked to set up the publishing venture, Lavrov, by then in his late seventies, grew weaker. He had a stroke, and An-sky asked Chernov to come to Paris to help care for the old man. On February 6 (January 25), 1900, still trying to dictate something and moving his hand to sketch something in the air, Lavrov died. An-sky wrote, "He bade me farewell in an especially touching way, put my hand to his lips, and a few hours before his death said, 'This is my command for you:

Live well. It's ending, my life has ended.'" An-sky emphasized Lavrov's unswerving dedication to his work and his ideals. "Until his last days, he never let the pen of the socialist fighter fall from his hands. He wrote brochures, he gave 'letters' and articles to all the Russian revolutionary journals, he collaborated with various French socialist journals." Lavrov wrote in his will, "If my fellow believers think they can use my death for the cause that we have served together, I give them complete liberty to do so; but if they believe that any kind of demonstration would be useless, then I ask them to abstain completely." His friends decided a demonstration would be useful and organized a public funeral. Six thousand marchers came carrying flowers; twenty-four Russian and French radicals spoke at the grave in the Montparnasse cemetery; and to no one's surprise, there were three clashes with police.[27]

Lavrov's funeral served the Russian radical cause well. The émigré leadership gathered in Paris jointly decided to found an organization to publish peasant propaganda. As Chernov recalled, "The mourning for Lavrov became the christening of our 'Agrarian-Socialist League [ASL]'; the dear departed was chosen as the invisible godfather, and his executor in relation to the League was Semyon Akimovich himself." This organization soon proved productive, and the Russian police took note. The ASL targeted not only Russian peasants but other nationalities too: a Ukrainian revolutionary, Feliks Volkhovskoi, began to translate their propaganda brochures into Ukrainian, and inspired by his example, An-sky spearheaded the publication of Yiddish propaganda.[28]

More than any other non-Jewish Russian socialist of his generation, Lavrov had been sympathetic to Jewish workers. In May 1886, he was elected president of a Jewish Workers' Society in Paris, where he gave a speech condemning anti-Semitism and praising the Jews' socialist potential, their "endurance and patience" and insistence on waiting for a "true messiah . . . a messiah of freedom and triumph." But even while he praised Jewish culture, Lavrov assumed it would not endure. In a letter to the editors of *Der veker* (The Alarm Clock), a London Yiddish socialist newspaper, Lavrov asserted that socialist propaganda in Yiddish "is necessary only for the present preparatory stage, in order to acquaint the newly-arrived Jews, who do not yet know the language of the country, with the socialist movement." Socialists should work to ensure that eventually "divisions among the workers according to language be eliminated, for this is more harmful than useful." Lavrov was opposed to nationalism and in favor of Jewish assimilation. Thus An-sky's ASL work, where he used Yiddish strictly for propaganda purposes, fit Lavrov's prescription. In fact, An-sky published not only socialist propaganda but also stories in Yiddish, and he translated poems by the not particularly

political Nikitin; he may not have mentioned these Yiddish writings to
his Russian revolutionary comrades, who would never run across them on
their own.[29]

As a Russian Jewish Populist, An-sky was not unusual. Although one
might think the Jews of the Russian Empire would see the peasants as
their enemies, particularly after the pogroms, many Jews believed that
not the peasants but the government was to blame for the violence. Chernov and Lavrov agreed that Jewish socialists should devote their energy
to the general—that is, the peasant—cause. At the same time, Chernov
found something unexpected in An-sky's peasant loyalties. An-sky's success in founding the ASL showed he was a canny organizer with excellent
logistical skills, but Chernov painted a more picturesquely Jewish image.
He noticed a contrast between An-sky's strong frame and muscular arms
and his burning eyes and tragic expression. "Something else was lacking
from this face—and suddenly I realized that if one could add a thick gray
beard, he would make a splendid rabbi! What sort of Semyon Akimovich
was this, and with that unnatural addition—An-sky! It turned out, though,
that his given name was simpler and more natural—Solomon Rappoport." An-sky could suddenly act like an adolescent, unexpectedly challenging Chernov to a wrestling match soon after they met. (Chernov
won, but An-sky got his revenge the next week by smearing Chernov's
face with butter while he was asleep.) Chernov "was not the only one to
experience the infectiousness of Semyon Akimovich's happy, mischievous
childishness when he 'went nuts.'" He saw An-sky as representing the
paradoxical nature of Jews in general. "The living incarnation of that
complex of contradictions, Semyon Akimovich, when we discussed the
purely-Russian, peasant issue that I had raised, seemingly turned into a
Russian."[30] In spite of his admiration for the heroes depicted in Antokolsky's statues, who gave themselves completely to a single cause, An-sky
had multiple attitudes and loyalties: both joking and serious, both scorning and enjoying Paris, both producing socialist revolutionary propaganda for peasants and translating sad Russian poems into Yiddish.

The sense that it might be impossible to reconcile An-sky's Jewish and
Russian sides—that there might be inevitable tension between Jews and
non-Jews, or impassable barriers to Jewish assimilation—was growing in
the 1890s. First Germany, then France and the Russian Empire saw the
growth of "modern anti-Semitism," the belief that Jews were racially different from and inherently hostile to non-Jews. Some of the Populist intelligentsia saw anti-Semitism as a distraction from legitimate radical
causes. In October 1896, An-sky read a *Russkoe Bogatstvo* article by Sergei Iuzhakov, who insisted that he and his colleagues saw anti-Semitism as

"not only dangerous and unfair, but immoral and shameful."[31] Iuzhakov knew that not all Russians agreed: though racial anti-Semitism had not reached the level in Russia that it had in Western Europe, it had convinced some Russians that neither education nor reform could eliminate the tensions between Jews and peasants.

This debate over "inherent" differences between Jews and non-Jews spilled out of the pages of intellectual journals into the newspapers and streets of France as the Dreyfus Affair unfolded. In October 1894, the young army captain Alfred Dreyfus, a wealthy French Jew from Alsace, was arrested for spying for the Germans. The evidence was weak, but he was convicted in a court-martial, degraded in January 1895, and sent to Devil's Island as a traitor. When Lieutenant Colonel Georges Picquart found evidence in 1896 that the culprit was not Dreyfus but Major Ferdinand Walsin Esterhazy and tried to reopen the case, the army attempted to silence him. The next year, Dreyfus's brother Mathieu succeeded in having the case reopened. Esterhazy was tried but acquitted in January 1898, after which the writer Emile Zola published his famous "J'Accuse," an open letter to the president of the Republic, accusing a number of individuals of allowing an innocent man to suffer in order to preserve the prestige of the French army. With Zola's article and his subsequent trial for libel, the Dreyfus Affair reached a high pitch. France was divided into Dreyfusards and anti-Dreyfusards; people throughout the world took sides, and many criticized the actions of the French government. Dreyfus was tried again, in the city of Rennes, in September 1899, and declared guilty once more, but ten days later French president Emile Loubet pardoned him.[32]

Like readers around the world, An-sky followed the Dreyfus Affair in the daily newspapers, which reported on the developments and affected their outcome. More than ever before, the press influenced politics, now by supporting the army, now by supporting Dreyfus. At first, the anti-Dreyfusard press spoke the loudest. In 1892, the year when An-sky arrived in Paris, Edouard Drumont, who had applied modern anti-Semitic ideas to France in *Jewish France* (1886), founded a newspaper, *La Libre Parole* (The Free Word), that attacked the Jewish presence in the army and in public life. As soon as Dreyfus was arrested in 1894, the captain was denounced in articles in *La Libre Parole,* in Catholic newspapers such as *La Croix* (The Cross) and *Le Pèlerin* (The Pilgrim), and in the more mainstream press as well. In September 1896, another anti-Dreyfusard newspaper, *L'Eclair* (The Lightning Bolt), leaked information about the secret document on the basis of which Dreyfus had been convicted. This revelation spurred Dreyfus's wife Lucie to write a petition to the government protesting that neither her husband nor his lawyer had been informed about that document; when her petition was printed in the newspapers, the case became a cause célèbre.[33] After the publication of Lucie's letter, Dreyfus's defenders found more sympathy in the press. In November 1897, *Le Figaro* published a denunciation of Esterhazy by Alfred's brother Mathieu Dreyfus. Most influential were the publications of Zola, who produced a pamphlet and an article in *Le Figaro* in defense of Dreyfus before publishing "J'Accuse" in a special edition of *L'Aurore* (The Dawn).

The liberal press could not claim full responsibility for rescuing Dreyfus. Indeed, the anti-Dreyfusard press had far higher circulation. Nonetheless, at key points, documents published in newspapers on each side affected public opinion and official actions well beyond the French borders. Outside of France, the press was almost uniformly pro-Dreyfus. In England, Belgium, Switzerland, the United States, and even the Russian Empire, the conviction of Zola in 1898 was seen as a blot on French honor and proof that France's vaunted civilization had lost its value. The 1899 Rennes verdict shocked the world, triggering pro-Dreyfus demonstrations in Antwerp, Milan, Naples, London, and New York; the police were called in to protect France's embassies, and newspapers called for the boycott of the Paris World's Fair planned for 1900. The outcry fueled by the international press prompted the decision to pardon Dreyfus.[34]

An-sky had "Dreyfus-fever" and read about the affair every day. When Zhitlowsky visited Paris in 1898, he and An-sky would stay up till 4 A.M. talking, but An-sky would be up by 8 A.M. to get the morning papers. Unlike other left-wing intellectuals who read only the papers that defended Dreyfus, An-sky bought anti-Dreyfusard papers too. Zhitlowsky remembered him appalled but fascinated by Henri Rochefort, who fantasized about putting poisonous spiders in walnut halves and binding them onto Dreyfus's eyes. At the same time, An-sky himself wrote reports on Paris once a week for the newspaper *Syn Otechestva* (Son of the Fatherland). His letters about the affair were impressionistic, not analytical. He felt that the Dreyfus Affair had transformed him into a biblical prophet: "If writing press reports is something like a whale, then like the prophet Jonah, I'm lying in the belly of that whale." He complained, "I'm no longer myself, but 'the Dreyfus Affair, covered in a thin layer of skin.'" He attended the trial of Zola and wrote that the guilty verdict left him with impressions he would never forget, and that the anti-Jewish demonstrations in the streets during the days after "felt like something medieval."[35]

Unlike those Jewish intellectuals (the Zionist leader Theodor Herzl being the most famous example) for whom the Dreyfus Affair was a revelation about the Christian world's true anti-Semitism, An-sky saw it as revealing more about French heroic culture than about the Jewish condition. He diagnosed it as a manifestation of the French tendency to admire physical strength and seek salvation from the army, itself a product of the French defeat in 1870: "Force, rough, wild, cruel force won; the bayonet won!" Dreyfus was convicted not, An-sky wrote, because he was Jewish, but because he was seen as an opponent of the army, the thing that mattered most for the French. An-sky saw Zola as understanding this perfectly. Because he knew French psychology so well, he was able to touch just the right "strings of the soul" to provoke "the sensitivity and expansive sympathy for suffering that probably would have awoken if the matter did not have the character we mentioned." Zola knew that the real reason for the Dreyfus Affair was "the French worship of the bayonet," and he decided "to challenge the bayonet in the name of justice, directly, openly, and harshly." An-sky saw Zola as a revolutionary, whose letter "made the same impression as throwing a bomb." Analysis of the Dreyfus Affair led An-sky to muse on public opinion and the attempt to influence it. "People calmly pass an entire ocean of tears, sorrow, and suffering without seeing or noticing. Then they stop in front of one specific case of misery and burst out with a fountain of feelings and words of pity." Zola's genius lay in his ability to conquer public indifference. "The great writer of his country came and said that word loudly and boldly to all France, to the whole world."[36]

The continuation of the Dreyfus Affair confirmed An-sky's disappointment with France. "If a revolution happens and the good king returns to his throne, I'll let you know. If Jewish pogroms begin or the Holy Inquisition is reestablished, I'll also write. . . . I await all possible filth from France." In September 1898, he told Krivenko he had hoped to take a break from the "damn Dreyfus Affair" but recognized the need to address each new development. He saw the affair as threatening France itself and ruining the prestige of the republic: "It's really difficult to express the pain in your heart when you see this prolonged agony of a great nation."[37] In 1898 and 1899, talk of the Dreyfus Affair dominated France as families, clubs, and professional associations split into Dreyfusards and anti-Dreyfusards. Dreyfus came to stand for many causes: human rights, anticlericalism, rationalism.

For An-sky too, the image of Dreyfus, still chained on Devil's Island, took on a personal meaning. In February 1899, he wrote to Zhitlowsky complaining about his work, then abruptly switched to his love life. Once again, marriage had seemed possible for a moment, and he spoke of its rejection in terms of his own ideology.

> The courthouse, lectures, newspapers, press reports. . . . I'm sitting down in
> a café at midnight to write to you. At home I wouldn't be able to get away
> from the morass of newspapers that could finally suffocate you. . . . I was
> planning to get married, with a ceremony and everything, but it didn't work
> out. "She" wanted me to be baptized, and I said to her, "But what would
> Dreyfus say?" I kissed her and it was *au revoir*—and I went off to write
> press reports.[38]

Before the Dreyfus Affair, An-sky had never seen Jewishness as heroic;
gestures affirming Jewish identity were not among those he admired for
their power to communicate clearly or move history forward. The Dreyfus Affair changed that. Zola—who interested An-sky far more than
Dreyfus himself did—had acted heroically by publicly aligning himself
with Dreyfus. In his own private life, An-sky could make the same sort of
heroic gesture by identifying with Dreyfus and refusing to be baptized,
embracing his Judaism, no matter how little he had valued it earlier.

Zhitlowsky thought the Dreyfus Affair turned An-sky, as it turned
Herzl, from a cosmopolitan internationalist into a Jewish nationalist,
newly sensitive to anti-Semitism and aware that "he is also a Jew and
'they mean me too.'" He saw An-sky as suddenly sensitive to hostility to
Jews among the French and even among other Russian émigrés, abruptly
accusing Rusanov, the author of Dreyfusard articles in *Russkoe Bogatstvo*, of anti-Semitism. Although An-sky undoubtedly did insult Rusanov,
whom he resented for a host of reasons, his letters and articles suggest he
did not identify with Dreyfus or French Jews as a whole.[39] He responded
to the Dreyfus Affair more as a writer than as a Jew. He was most gripped
by the images in the pro- and anti-Dreyfusard press and their power to
change his mood and that of the crowds in the street. His role model was
not Dreyfus but Zola.

An-sky's era had seen a fundamental change in the role of the printed
word. Before the 1880s, only a small elite, even in France, could read the
daily news, but now more and more people were reading the mass-
circulation dailies and public opinion was beginning to form, based on the
newspapers' selection and manipulation of information.[40] In the 1880s,
An-sky had been in the Donets Basin, reading to illiterate miners, living
in a largely oral society, stunned by the power of rumors to derail people's lives. He believed then that literacy could resolve people's problems
and limit the damage caused by ignorance. In Paris a few years later, as
he pored over *La libre parole,* he saw that print could be as dangerous as
rumors. At the same time, the example of Zola and the publication of
"J'Accuse" showed that print could serve his own causes. His enthusiasm
about setting up the ASL printing operation may have stemmed from his

immersion in the "morass of newspapers" around the Dreyfus Affair. The affair confirmed his belief that carefully chosen and calibrated words could affect people's feelings and actions. It supported his conviction that writing and publishing such words was a heroic act, a revolutionary "bomb" that could effectively challenge the "bayonet" of the anti-Dreyfusard French army—or the Russian government of Nicholas II.

In his fiction, though, An-sky's depiction of the power of the printed word was more nuanced and ironic. "Mendel the Turk," which he began in 1892 and published first in 1902, may bear the imprint of the Dreyfus Affair. The narrator of this story is a young "modern" Jew living in a small Belorussian town and working as a tutor. It is 1877, and all the Hasidim in town are fascinated by the ongoing Russo-Turkish War. Some believe the Russians will win, many support the Turkish side (as Jews often did), and they debate the war in synagogue every day between the afternoon and the evening prayers.[41] Mendel, a twenty-eight-year-old melamed who sides with the Turks, discovers that the narrator can teach him about the history of the conflict and, as the only person in town who gets a Russian newspaper regularly, give him up-to-date information. When the Russian army takes Plevne, Mendel is initially upset, but he takes comfort in his discovery of mystical biblical hints of the ultimate victory of the Turks.

In an early manuscript version of the story, the narrator runs into Mendel ten years later, after both of them, like An-sky himself, have come to Paris. Although at first Mendel is appalled by what seems to him the degeneracy of Parisian life (he especially dislikes the bare-breasted statue symbolizing the French republic at the Place de la République), he quickly reconciles himself to his new surroundings, takes a job in a factory, and begins to learn French. Within a year and a half, he has become fluent and stays up nights reading Marx, Ferdinand Lasalle, and Pierre Joseph Proudhon; a couple years later, the narrator learns that Mendel has moved to London and become a labor organizer and an admired orator. This ending reveals faith in the radical ideals of self-transformation. All it takes is removal from the shtetl and a thorough immersion in radical theory for Mendel to become a different person, who stands tall and commands the respect of a crowd. The narrator recognizes that Mendel has suffered to remake himself, but he has succeeded.[42] Mendel "the Turk," who saw no reason to identify with Russians, has taken up the cause of the international worker. In its later, published form, the story carried no such clear ideological message. It concluded not with Mendel's London speech, but with the narrator's departure from the shtetl, where he leaves Mendel, who forever, it seems, will continue to dream of a

Turkish victory. Whereas the early version of the story affirmed that education can remake a Jew, the 1902 published version treated Mendel's attitude to the narrator's newspaper with irony: he does not reeducate himself, but merely finds new support for his old, absurd notions.

An-sky created Mendel, who so longs to read the narrator's Russian newspaper, after his own image.[43] Mendel's Turkish sympathies are presented ironically, but his encounter with the printed word reveals traces of An-sky's own preoccupations. Having been immersed in reading and reporting about the Dreyfus Affair, he reworked this story that he had begun in 1892 about the long-ago, far-away, but similarly divisive issue of the Russo-Turkish War. One might think that as a literacy activist and propagandist, An-sky would concentrate in his story on the liberating effect of Mendel's exposure to the Russian newspaper, the way the printed word brings enlightenment and truth. Instead, the story turns on Mendel's *lack* of enlightenment, his awareness that the Russian newspaper cannot give him the whole truth, his inability to find a Turkish newspaper, and his ultimate insistence that he can attain more understanding of Russian politics by kabbalistic interpretation of biblical verses than by reading the papers.

If the Dreyfus Affair showed An-sky the power and danger of the printed word, in 1900 he encountered a different medium, the museum display. Dreyfus had been pardoned, the World's Fair was on, and the Russian Empire contributed an exhibit displaying its wealth and geographical variety. Its pavilion was so big it was housed not on the rue des Nations with the others but at the Trocadéro palace, where it added to the "Moorish" and Byzantine features of the building with architectural elements meant to evoke the southern and eastern edges of the empire (a Turkish kiosk, a pagoda). Visitors sat in a train car meant to represent the Trans-Siberian Railroad, under construction since 1891 and completed only in 1905. Painted scenes of the Caucasus, the steppes, and Siberia passed by the windows. A visitor remembered, "We crossed great rivers dotted with floating logs, traversed huge forests of pine and larch, sped through vast deserts strewn with Mongol tombs." At the end a Chinese boy served jasmine tea and shouted, "Peking!"[44]

The Russian exhibit involved cooperation between antagonistic forces: the government, determined to flaunt the empire's economic and political strength, and the radical émigré community (on whom the Russian secret police kept strict tabs) that staffed the exhibit. Potential employees without police records may have been in short supply in Paris; at any rate, An-sky credited a liberal Russian official he knew with recruiting him to work at the Russian pavilion. When the exhibit was over, An-sky hired a group of Russian students—radicals from different camps, who cheerfully called him their "exploiter"—to pack the objects up for transport back. The students used wadded-up revolutionary newspapers and propaganda pamphlets for packing material, hoping at least some of them would "fall into good hands." At first the SD and Populist students argued about whose revolutionary literature to pack, but they eventually realized there would be room for it all.[45]

The World's Fair had long-term implications for An-sky and his community. His pay was good (300 francs per month) and the job led to others. The fair spurred the creation of an international school in Paris with the goal of organizing lectures and visits to exhibitions; its president was the former prime minister, Leon Bourgeois, and An-sky worked as the secretary of the school's Russian division. In 1901, after he left Paris, it would evolve into the Russian Higher School of Social Sciences, where Lavrov's friends Mechnikov, Kovalevsky, and Chernov lectured through 1906.[46]

The birth of the Higher School of Social Sciences indicates that across the political spectrum, people were interested in distant peoples and places. The Russian government used images of Siberia and the Caucasus to show off their country's breadth and wealth, but for the leftist social scientists in An-sky's circles, the peoples at the edges of the Russian Empire (and other empires) had another significance: they were the subjects of a sociological inquiry that found a political significance in their seemingly backward communalism, which the radicals saw as proto-socialism. An-sky and his friends were intrigued by "primitive" peoples and their ways. He observed the founding of the International Institute of Sociology (by Réné Worms in 1894) and was close to Kovalevsky, who was among its founders. He had the most exposure to "primitive" groups from the east of the Russian Empire. Through Lavrov, he met Grigory Potanin, the best known Siberian and central Asian writer, explorer, and ethnographer of his time, in Paris to research connections between European literature and Eurasian epics. Potanin was a Siberian regionalist, a cultural and political radical who wanted to increase Siberian autonomy. Soon after they met, Potanin began to share An-sky's small apartment. His ethnographic enthusiasms would leave an imprint on his host.[47]

As an intimate of Potanin's, An-sky was an attentive observer of displays of distant cultures. In Bordeaux in 1900, he found himself at a seedy nightclub, where he was surprised to see what he took to be fellow subjects of the tsar: "Eskimos, men and women in their furs, sat and attentively watched the performance." He tried to speak to them in Russian, but they did not understand, nor did they respond to the obscenities of some French customers. Finally the exhibit's organizer explained that he had brought these natives of eastern Canadian Labrador, along with a few dozen American Indians, to England, Germany, Austria, and France. They had set up an entire "Eskimo village," with dogs and yurts, where the Inuits gave performances, demonstrating how they skied, hunted seals, played with balls, shied coins with whips, and so on. The entrepreneur who brought them complained that the French were less interested in his show than the Germans had been, and he confessed that the Inuits suffered terribly from the heat: two had already died, and he had sent their bodies back to Labrador. "You know," he said to An-sky, "they're like children, they don't understand what's going on around them, but they are very wise, calm, kind, and warm-hearted. They are dying out. Now there are only 3000 of them. There are only 2000 words in their language. But they have learned how to speak. But they are confusing English and French words. You see that girl over there?" He pointed at a three-year-old girl. "She is the daughter of a French officer and an Eskimo woman. A remarkably talented and intelligent child." An-sky went to the exhibit and found it disturbing. "It was hard to see all of this."[48]

When An-sky presented the Inuits as virtuous precisely by contrast with the French, he sounded like the radicals who fantasized that modern people might gain something by imitating the "primitives." Yet An-sky did not simply admire the Inuits' "naiveté," but inquired into the circumstances that brought them to Bordeaux, the difficult physical conditions under which they lived, their suffering from the heat, and pronounced it all "very poor, very pitiable, and finally offensively cruel." He noticed that the Inuits' shows did not even succeed as education: the audience was uninterested in their songs and hunting techniques. An-sky focused on the flaws of the potentially pedagogic encounter between Frenchmen and Inuits; rather than imagining that display of a primitive group could simply infuse energy and purity into a decadent Western culture, he was intrigued by the ways in which that encounter turned out to be abortive or blocked. Here as in his other writings, he was ambivalent about the dichotomy of the primitive versus the decadent, even questioning his era's certainty that French culture was degenerate. Instead of accepting the evolutionist anthropological assumptions of his time and seeing the Inuits as simply primitives whose example might enlighten a more evolved people, An-sky reacted to the Bordeaux display by imagining how the Inuits themselves were experiencing it.[49] As when he read to the peasants, he wanted to understand what the other would do and say if the ethnographer were not present.

For the rest of his life, An-sky would think about ethnographic displays and their effect. The Dreyfus Affair had left An-sky with the sense of a "morass of newspapers," a confusing set of images producing an array of effects, from heroism such as Zola's to Rochefort's grotesque hatred. He emerged with new enthusiasm and energy for his own publishing and propaganda projects. Work at the World's Fair and exposure to ethnographic displays there and elsewhere had a similar effect. Although An-sky's writings about the Inuits in Bordeaux stress that this exhibit of a precapitalist "primitive" people did not inspire viewers, he did not lose interest in ethnographic display. He worked at other such exhibits, and ten years after he left Paris, he would be making plans to collect the objects that would be housed in the museum that he would found, the first Jewish ethnographic museum in Russia.[50]

The year of the World's Fair was a time of change for An-sky. A month after Lavrov's death in early 1900, he wrote to Zhitlowsky to report the successful establishment of the ASL. He mused on the odd feeling of easily reaching a goal:

> So, great! Or it's a bit terrifying. But probably it was a bit terrifying for Caesar and Napoleon when with one blow they acquired a whole kingdom. It seems to me there's even something in the Talmud about something of this sort, about the terror of quick victories. It seems you have to throw something in the sea. But you wouldn't want a fish to bring it out again.

In the midst of this euphoria, An-sky dropped a personal bomb. "I would hug you, maybe I would cry, I am in such a terrible state. My wife has hysterics for the third day running. . . . Chaim, I am married!" He switched from Russian to Yiddish and took a darker tone: "Oy, Chaim, things are bitter and dark for me with my laughter. I'm coughing up blood when I laugh. What kind of devil could have pulled me by the tail under the wedding canopy? Do tell me!" He concluded in a lighter tone:

> Don't pay attention to my *tkhines* and *kines* [supplications and lamentations]— this will come right in the end, it will turn out to be nothing. It doesn't matter, I'll get out of it. You know the story. An ignorant man, the son of a country bumpkin, tells his father in horror the rumor that "the messiah is coming!" The father comforts him, "Ay, my son. Haman came, and we got rid of him—so we can get rid of the messiah too."[51]

By the end of the letter, An-sky had almost equated the two events he had to report. Since he arrived in Paris, he had been working to bring Socialist Revolutionary propaganda to the Russian countryside, and that goal finally seemed within reach. For much longer, he had wondered whether he would ever get married, he had pursued women who had turned him down, and now, suddenly, he had traversed the boundary dividing the normative Jewish man from the boy—he was married. Oddly, neither of these accomplishments seemed to make him happy. With his joke about the ignorant Jew who does not even know about the messiah, An-sky suggested that marriage in particular seemed to be, paradoxically, more of a Haman, the persecutor of the Jews in the Book of Esther, than a savior.

For the Russian émigrés in Paris, An-sky's marriage was a surprise. His close friends had known he was secretly in love with a Russian émigrée, Elizaveta N., but he never revealed his feelings to her, and when she became involved with the well-known Socialist Revolutionary Ilia Rubanovich, he was crushed. Suddenly, An-sky invited his friends to a party and announced that from now on, they should consider that he and a young woman, Mademoiselle Janais, a Frenchwoman brought up in Russia, were married. In less than a month, this common-law arrangement was in trouble.[52] An-sky came to Chernov in desperation and asked for help, and Chernov visited Janais and heard her complaints: she was doing all a good wife should, keeping a pleasant home and cooking tasty meals, but her new husband refused to stay home and enjoy them; instead, he kept saying he needed to write and taking his papers off to a café. Because he wouldn't tell her which café, she was sure he was seeing another woman.

Chernov calmed her by taking her to the café and showing her An-sky at work. He was feverishly writing on long strips of paper, sitting at a table with a full glass of black coffee and an empty glass of liquor; he did not look up to see his friend and his wife watching him. Chernov then explained to Janais that An-sky was like other writers who write best in public, surrounded by human voices, drinking a cup of coffee with liquor added. "The life that she so diligently and carefully arranged for her husband had, undoubtedly, many advantages—but for Semyon Akimovich to adopt it would be an entire revolution." Soon An-sky and Janais decided to separate. Chernov attributed the turn of events to An-sky's poor luck and difficulty in changing his habits. Chernov's own first wife, Anastasia Sletova, who was close to An-sky, felt he was constitutionally unsuited for marriage. He loved women, she said, and was loved by many of them, but saved his strongest feelings for other men. Chernov remembered her explaining that An-sky possessed "enormous reserves of tenderness . . . the need to cling to someone with all the force of his being." He brought this tenderness to his friendships with women, but he loved all women equally, whereas he loved some men more. "That feminine softness of his own nature makes him unconsciously, by the law of contrasts, choose some strong male figure to wind all his passionate thoughts and feelings around, as ivy winds around a strong oak tree."[53]

Sletova's interpretation of the breakup suggests she suspected that suppressed homosexual desire was at the root of An-sky's frustrations with women. Her intuition might shed light on the pattern of the awakening of a female love interest soon after the retreat of a male patron (the pursuit of Reinus after Uspensky's institutionalization; the marriage to Janais after Lavrov's death). There may indeed have been a single psychological or physiological reason why An-sky never experienced an enduring marriage, and this may have fed an anxiety and dissatisfaction with himself that lay behind his restless energy and persistent urge to efface his old self and to adopt new identities. However, asceticism and an asexual lifestyle had their own virtuous symbolism in Russian revolutionary culture. Although his friends watched him struggle with his sexuality, now speaking proudly of his solitary status, now fleeing personal emptiness for a hasty marriage, the available evidence cannot confirm any single reason for An-sky's troubled love life.

The evidence does show that the breakup with Janais in 1900 produced a very different effect from the breakup with Reinus in 1892. After Reinus rejected him, he had fled for Paris to nurse his wounds and spent several unhappy years. He wrote little in the three years after the breakup, then slowly returned to writing; he complained frequently about loneliness and difficulty working. After An-sky separated from Janais, he again left the country. In mid-1901, he went to Switzerland, where he would stay through 1905. This move had the opposite effect professionally from the move to Paris. During his Swiss years, An-sky wrote and published more than ever before, producing novels, articles, and poetry, in Russian and Yiddish. It is tempting to connect the relationship with Janais to the shift in his writing habits. Perhaps because An-sky and Janais did marry and live together before they broke up, he experienced the separation positively. Perhaps the unwanted messiah was the longed-for but ultimately unendurable condition of marriage and obligation to a single other person, so unlike a revolutionary's obligation to serve "the people."

The An-sky of 1900 was far different from the An-sky of 1892. Like the hero of *The Dybbuk*, he had been transformed by the time he spent learning far away from home. His Paris education had made him more confident and capable. When he was in his twenties, An-sky had asked Mikhailovsky how to make his life useful. Mikhailovsky never wrote back, but over the course of his time in Paris, An-sky himself had found answers. The work for which he later became known—as an activist, an

editor, a publisher, a speaker, a writer, and an organizer of aid work, ethnographic quests, and museum displays—had its roots in his Paris experience. The image of the writer as a heroic mover of history that An-sky
had derived from his reading of Mikhailovsky continued to compel him,
but over his time in Paris, his understanding of the ways in which a
writer can be a hero had changed. He had added to his fascination with
the hero the awareness that a cultural producer must be sensitive to the
market, conscious of how words or images might be interpreted and willing to modify style or message in order to reach an audience. He still
believed that art could move its audience as powerfully as the Venus de
Milo had moved Uspensky, but he recognized that, like a bicycle or a
suit, it needed to be adjusted or tailored in response to the consumer's
needs. His understanding of readers changed along with his understanding of the role of the writer in society. At the same time, the world itself
changed, and the dream of revolution that had seemed futile when he left
Russia grew more and more realistic.

Chaim Zhitlowsky and Shloyme-Zanvl Rappoport, about ages seventeen and
nineteen, Vitebsk, 1882. (GS 10:unnumbered)

Shloyme-Zanvl Rappoport and his father, Aron Rappoport, Moscow, 1884. (GS 10:unnumbered)

Shloyme-Zanvl Rappoport, Ekaterinoslav, 1888. (YIVO 121:An-sky)

An-sky's mentor, the Russian writer Gleb Uspensky, 1889. (G. I. Uspensky, PSS [Moscow, 1952], 11:unnumbered)

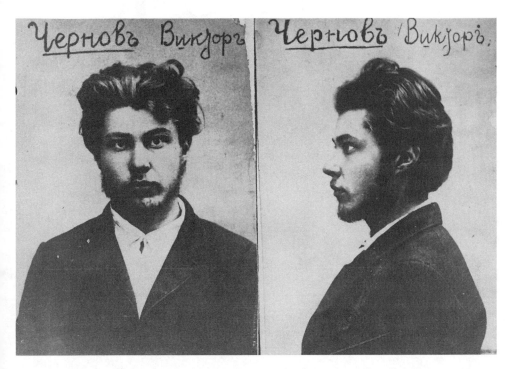

Victor Chernov, Socialist Revolutionary (SR) leader and An-sky's friend. Mug shot from the files of the Tsarist secret police in Paris. (Hoover Okhrana 100)

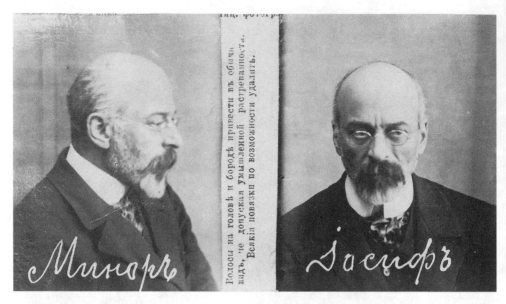

Osip Minor, SR leader and An-sky's friend. Mug shot from the files of the
Tsarist secret police in Paris. (Hoover Okhrana 100)

Boris Savinkov, SR leader and terrorist mastermind. He was Uspensky's son-in-law and An-sky's acquaintance. Mug shot from the files of the Tsarist secret police in Paris. (Hoover Okhrana 100)

Zhitlowsky and An-sky, about ages thirty-five and thirty-seven, Paris, 1900. (YIVO 121:An-sky).

Radical thinker Pyotr Lavrov on his deathbed, February 1900, painted by Ilia Mechnikov's wife the night after he died, while An-sky held a light for her. An-sky bequeathed this treasured image to the Russian writer Vladimir Korolenko. (GS 10:unnumbered)

„אים קאמבף וועסטו דיין רעכט ערווערבען.“

יעגאר סערגייעוויץ סאזאנאוו.

Egor Sazonov, the SR who assassinated Minister of the Interior Viacheslav Pleve in July 1904. As the editor of the Yiddish SR journal, *Kampf un kempfer* (The Fight and the Fighters), An-sky celebrated Sazonov as a martyr; above his picture is the SR slogan, "In struggle you will win your rights." (*Kampf un kempfer,* 3/1905, frontispiece)

CHAPTER FIVE

We Swear to Fight!

We swear to fight against the darkest power
Or valiantly to fall in battle!
      —Z. Sinanni (Rappoport), "The Oath," 1902

"THE DEVIL knows how a little boy wants freedom—that's how much I want to go to Bern," An-sky wrote in January 1901. After more than eight years in Paris, with its squabbling émigrés and endless debates over Dreyfus, An-sky yearned for the Swiss university towns where he could speak of other things. Because Russian universities had Jewish quotas and most of them excluded women, thousands of Jews and women had poured from the empire to universities in Western Europe. The University of Bern welcomed them. Vladimir Medem, a leader of the radical Jewish Labor Bund, remembered this Swiss-German town lovingly. "On the street it almost felt like being back in a Jewish shtetl, except for the absence of dirt, and for the fact that there were no old Jews about, only the young; and in vast numbers. Jewish faces, mainly female, all students, with black oilcloth portfolios under their arms." The students admired the beautiful town, with its hills; its narrow medieval streets; its clock tower whose moving figures came out at noon; its Gothic cathedral; its river, the Aare; and its distant view of the Alps. They had little to do with the Swiss, but they "maintained exceedingly close ties with one another, feeling the need to cling together. . . . Homeless, dejected, lonesome people had found a refuge for themselves."[1]

Bern was such a refuge for An-sky. Returning from Paris in 1901, he moved happily back into Zhitlowsky's orbit. In Switzerland as in their Vitebsk youth, Zhitlowsky occupied a privileged position. After over a decade abroad, he had a doctorate in philosophy and he was at the center of Russian and Jewish émigré circles; he was the leader of the "Union of Russian Socialist Revolutionaries" and the editor of their newspaper,

Russkii Rabochii. Simultaneously, he led a pro-Yiddish movement among Jewish radicals and a Yiddish publication society, the Tsayt-gayst. His wife Vera, the daughter of a Russian landowner, had made a heroic gesture by marrying a Jew abroad. She ran a cheap student cafeteria in Bern. She and Chaim welcomed An-sky to their home.[2]

There An-sky found young people who admired him, applauded his lectures, and agreed with his principles. By now in his late thirties but graying and looking older, having been the protégé of Uspensky and then Lavrov, he began to seek disciples of his own. Even though he had never had formal schooling, the students saw him as a mentor. He wrote poems that they set to music and sang; he wrote short revolutionary plays in Russian and Yiddish and directed student theatrical productions; he helped organize a reading room named in honor of Gleb Uspensky, who died in 1902, and he wrote to friends and publishers in Russia asking them to donate books. The students knew about his work among the miners and saw him as a hero of an earlier era, a link to the "Going to the People" movement of the 1870s. The authorities learned of his success in October 1903, when the double agent Evno Azef reported to the Russian police that An-sky was the center of a "big gang" of Bern radicals.[3] An-sky traveled to Zurich and Geneva, the hub of Russian émigré publishing, and he spent his summers in various mountain villages, but he returned regularly to Bern to sleep on Zhitlowsky's sofa and talk politics with the students. In Switzerland, he became a radical leader and a productive writer, and he began to see both Russian peasants and Jewish reformers as just as creative and restless as he was himself.

In the 1890s, it had seemed that the Russian authorities had quelled the revolutionary movement for good. In 1899, An-sky wrote, "I'm depressed. Russia is a wet hen," but that very year the situation began to change. In February 1899, strikes broke out at St. Petersburg University after mounted Cossacks whipped unruly students in the streets; the furor provoked more strikes and arrests around the country. Russian students in Western Europe, thrilled, declared their support. In the spring of 1901, demonstrations broke out again. In response to the arrests and beatings of students in front of Kazan Cathedral in St. Petersburg in March, An-sky signed a writers' protest letter.[4]

It seemed that events in Russia were finally playing out as An-sky and Zhitlowsky had hoped and theorized, and Zhitlowsky was becoming ever more interested in techniques of mobilizing the masses. The inheritors of the People's Will tradition defended terror, which in the Russian context meant targeted assassinations of officials held responsible for atrocities, as an essential method of mass mobilization. In an 1898 SR brochure, *Our Tasks,* Andrei Argunov (Voronovich) explained that violent acts could speak loudly and effectively: "Aside from its primary significance as a means of disorganization, terrorist activity will also serve as a means of propaganda and agitation, a form of open battle, carried out before the eyes of the entire nation, undermining the spell of state power, demonstrating the possibility of that battle, and summoning new revolutionary forces into life, along with unceasing oral and written propaganda."[5]

Although he wrote and spoke about the impact of articles and speeches, Zhitlowsky too believed that assassinations and the resulting martyrdom of the assassins inspired onlookers to join in revolution. In 1898, he argued for terror in his trademark trenchant style. He mocked anyone who thought that peaceful cultural activity within the limits of the current laws would bring socialism and freedom. "You organize a little rural library here, you open a rural school there, you lead readings among the folk, with magic lantern pictures, you organize a cultural retreat (also with magic lantern pictures)—and look, in some thirty or forty centuries, without any revolutions at all, Russia attains general well-being." This, Zhitlowsky said, was self-deception. "The socialist revolutionary . . . has long ago left behind the realm of 'magic lantern pictures,' and every step of societal life in Russia convinces him that even this modest activity cannot bear fruit under the paternal gaze of the 'tsar's eyes.' " As Zhitlowsky hoped, young radicals were moving toward illegal activities. In February 1901, the recently expelled student Pyotr Karpovich killed Nikolai Bogolepov, the Education Minister who had ordered 183 Kiev students forcibly conscripted into the army. In April 1902, the student Stepan Balmashev, a member of the SR Battle Organization, assassinated Interior Minister Dmitry Sipiagin. Like Vera Zasulich's shot at the governor-general of St. Petersburg a generation earlier, these two acts of terror galvanized public opinion in Russia and abroad, drew attention to the radical cause, and produced an upswing of support for the revolutionaries.[6]

For people such as An-sky and Zhitlowsky, even more exciting was the unrest that erupted in the countryside in the spring of 1902 in Kharkov and Poltava provinces, when peasants whose crops had failed took food from landowners and were suppressed by the army. The Social Democrats had been skeptical about the value of agitation among peasants, but the Socialist Revolutionaries had been convinced that under the right circumstances, the peasants would finally demand change. In 1902, the

SRs began to feel confident that they would see revolution in the countryside soon.[7]

Now that victory seemed more possible, the ASL redoubled its efforts. In 1900, it had begun to publish pamphlets in London. *The Next Revolutionary Task* laid out the group's beliefs: the elimination of private property, the peasants' ability to fight for socialism, and the need for socialist revolutionary propaganda in the countryside. The ASL leaders believed that a generation after serfdom, the peasants had evolved, and though it was understandable that government repression had driven some of the revolutionary intelligentsia to terror, it was time for others to focus on propaganda among peasants. In 1902, they issued more pamphlets, using a large font and simple vocabulary to reach the minimally literate peasants. *Thieves and Criminals in State Service* began in a folksy style: "Not long ago, it seems, things were quiet and smooth? And now they're yelling out everywhere, and every year they yell louder and louder. And they don't just yell, but threaten. And they don't just threaten, but act." It ended with a celebration of the revolutionary future in the form of a folk lay, a *bylina*.

> At dawn, early in the morning,
> The sun came up, the red one,
> From the great Zhiguli hills of the Volga.
> It rose in the heavens,
> It looks around with its bright glance,
> It saw free clouds in the sky,
> Free fish dance in the waves,
> And above the flowers, the blue ones,
> There's no lord, no overseer . . .
> And the bright sun looks at them
> It smiles at their freedom.[8]

The ASL ramped up pamphlet production to runs of 10,000. At a congress, ASL leaders debated whether to emphasize the nationalization of land, which interested peasants the most, or argue for agrarian terror, which could get out of hand; whether to appeal to peasants who belonged to religious sects; and whether to use more biblical or liturgical language. Chernov remembered that over the course of 1902, the ASL published 317,000 pamphlets, totaling over a million printers' signatures (units of printed pages), a milestone that An-sky celebrated as "the greatest personal holiday." Contemporaries saw ASL pamphlets as effective, well-known radicals agreed to write them, and An-sky felt "triumphant" when he learned that the SDs admired them and even distributed them (after removing the covers that indicated who had produced them).[9]

As the pamphlets came out, the Socialist Revolutionary movement consolidated and grew stronger. SR groupings had already existed underground in the Russian Empire and in emigration, where they included old Populists such as Nikolai Chaikovsky and Leonid Shishko. In 1899 and 1900, younger activists such as Chernov and Grigory Gershuni arrived in Switzerland from Russia and attempted to unify the SRs. They succeeded in establishing the Party of Socialist Revolutionaries (PSR), including first the groups in Russia, then the émigrés. An-sky and the ASL, which brought old Populists and young SRs together, had made this process possible. The ASL and the PSR merged, to An-sky's satisfaction, in the summer of 1903.[10]

An-sky retained his loyalty to the PSR through the 1917 revolutions, and he never renounced his agreement with fundamental SR principles: he believed that the Russian peasant could be moved to struggle for revolution, that history does not move mechanically along a predetermined path, and that an individual's actions can change the world. Although he would eventually step away from arguing for terror, his Swiss publications indicate that in the first years of the twentieth century he supported that plank as well. And though by 1904 he criticized the PSR leadership for their insufficient concern with the problems of the Russian Empire's Jews, he continued to be involved in PSR affairs and attend party congresses.

At the same time, he took part in cultural activities sponsored by other parties, particularly the growing Jewish parties. Although he saw Zionism as a bourgeois ideology, he associated with young Zionists who remembered him as "close to us in his soul." He was also close to the Jewish Labor Bund, a party of Jewish social democrats committed to a version of the orthodox Marxism that he abhorred. Medem remembered that An-sky "manifested the warmest sympathy toward the Bund during those years. Although formally an SR, he was no narrow partisan." The question of terror complicated his mixed loyalties, and An-sky regretted the antipathy of the Bund to the SRs' terrorist tactics. But in Bern, emotion could trump ideology. The Bundist leader John Mill recalled that An-sky and Zhitlowsky were enthusiastic for the Bund in spite of their ideological differences with its leaders: "A sympathetic, friendly atmosphere developed around the Bund. . . . Even many people opposed to the party could not keep themselves from expressing their warm feelings for the Bund."[11]

An-sky liked the Bund, and the Bund liked him. He was fluent in Yiddish, while the early Bundist leaders, who tended to be, like Medem, children of well-off families, brought up to speak only Russian, envied him for what they saw as his unmediated access to the workers. Much as public singing and recitation are at the core of Jewish liturgy, so secular poetry and song were part of Bundist meetings and demonstrations. When it was established in 1897, the Bund adopted a ritual of concluding meetings with a Yiddish song affirming party loyalty and titled "The Oath." Over the next years, Bundist leaders sought out secular Yiddish texts—songs, poems, stories—for education and agitation. They were happy to benefit from the creativity of Yiddish writers such as Peretz, who did not entirely share their principles: An-sky recalled that "few Jewish evenings occurred, Zionist or Bundist (both parties claimed Peretz as their own), without a reading from Peretz."[12]

An-sky too contributed to the Bund's repertoire without fully sharing its principles. One evening in the winter of 1901, Bundists were celebrating the twenty-fifth issue of the party's underground newspaper, *Di arbeter shtime* (The Worker's Voice), founded in 1897 in Vilna. An-sky, who had been sitting quietly in a corner, suddenly announced that he had been inspired to write a poem, and he read out, "In zaltsikn yam fun di menshlikhe trern [In the salty sea of human tears]. . . ." As Medem recalled, "We sat spellbound. . . . An-sky read with spirit and beauty. When he pronounced the closing lines: 'Long live the Jewish Labor Bund of Russia, Lithuania, and Poland,' a veritable torrent of enthusiasm welled up, and people were stirred to the point of tears." In February 1902, a London socialist Yiddish publication, *Der idisher arbeter* (The Jewish Worker), published the two poems An-sky dedicated to the Bund: "To the Bund," also known by its first line, "In the Salty Sea of Human Tears," and a new version of "The Oath."[13] Both were set to music, and they became party anthems, sung at every meeting.

As he published his Bundist songs, An-sky pondered the power of Yiddish to convey the emotions of free people. In April 1902, for the first time in almost twenty years, he wrote Zhitlowsky an entire letter in Yiddish, telling him that he had felt the urge to express himself in "our grandmother tongue" *(bobe loshn)*.

> I almost wrote "mother tongue" [*mame loshn,* a common term for Yiddish], but I realized that our mother tongue is an ugly language, a language of disgrace, a language of slaves who are embarrassed that God created them, a language covered with German mistakes so that people will think it is something else, that it is German and not, heaven forbid, the Jewish jargon. Grandmother tongue smells of *cholent* [stew usually cooked on the Sabbath], it is even missing words like "friling" [spring], "brust" [breast], and so on, but it is still a language with blood and flesh, you can cry out in it to your heart's desire, you can sing a song.[14]

An-sky defined a kind of Yiddish that was free of disgrace and capable of communicating the rebellious message of his Bundist songs. He turned away from the Yiddish used by nineteenth-century writers who grasped for legitimacy by borrowing German words and syntax; presumably, he preferred the Slavic and Hebrew/Aramaic elements of the language. And as he looked for healing in folklore, he suggested that Yiddish itself might overcome its disgrace by turning to its own folk roots, to the cholent cooked by its grandmothers.

The enduring popularity of An-sky's Bundist songs suggests that the images at the basis of his attraction to the SRs—blood and martyrdom, oaths, honor, and heroism—also appealed to Bundists. "The Oath" promises, "We swear to fight against the darkest power / Or valiantly to fall in battle!" "To the Bund" describes an abyss filled by the bloody tears of the workers and the poor and asks, "Where are the heroes, the people / Who bravely dare / To throw themselves into the abyss, into the fight?" Undoubtedly, such heroic images made better propaganda than dry restatements of Marxist dogma. They provoked the Bundist rank and file to throw themselves into the abyss, as was demonstrated three months after An-sky's poems were published. In May 1902, a Vilna Bundist, Hirsh Lekert, shot at Governor-general Viktor von Wahl after von Wahl ordered the flogging of workers who had defied a ban against demonstrating on May Day. Lekert was executed by the authorities and promptly celebrated by Bundists, in spite of the party leadership's opposition to such acts of terror. The Bund ultimately clarified its opposition to Lekert's deed, but Bundists never stopped singing An-sky's songs.[15]

That An-sky's Bundist poems could become so popular demonstrates a confluence of ideologies, styles, and moods at the beginning of the twentieth century that was the key to An-sky's success not as a revolutionary theorist, but as a creator and an organizer. This was especially apparent when he was, inevitably, contrasted with his old friend Zhitlowsky. Zhitlowsky was creative and innovative, but rarely followed through on the projects he began. He promised publishers long series of articles, but never finished them, looking to others to complete the work. Zhitlowsky was a brilliant writer and mesmerizing public speaker, but as An-sky knew, his restless intellect was at odds with the need for sustained practical work for a single cause. "Without a doubt, in conviction and deed, Zhitlowsky was a democrat—yet his character and tendencies had the stamp of a certain aristocratism. He disliked the 'crowd.' He felt uncomfortable and awkward when he was part of the majority." An-sky remembered a meeting where someone spoke up awkwardly to support Zhitlowsky's argument, and Zhitlowsky whispered to him, "We're going to win; the idiots are on our side now." An-sky shared Zhitlowsky's fascination with the techniques of mass mobilization, but where Zhitlowsky excelled in theorizing, An-sky was a master of the compelling detail. After one speech in Zurich, he was delighted that even SDs thanked him for directing their attention away from "discussions about the dialectical method, historical materialism, and other theoretical niceties, toward the living Russian village, about which we too often forget." Chernov recalled that An-sky and Zhitlowsky experienced their divided cultural identities differently: "With An-sky both his natures [Russian and Jewish] were whole, indivisible, each one its separate self. But Zhitlowsky during his life would often say: 'Two souls live in my heart and each seeks to escape the other.' "[16]

Both An-sky and Zhitlowsky were russified Jews and antideterminist SRs who believed in heroism and free will, even while both were attracted to the Bund and wrote increasingly in Yiddish. These two childhood friends became editors, writers, speakers, and productive public intellectuals, but after Bern, their different temperaments pulled them in different directions. Zhitlowsky moved to New York in 1908 and shifted his focus from Russian socialism to Yiddish culture. Where Zhitlowsky always remained a gadfly, uncomfortable in the majority, An-sky honed his skill at bringing one message to varied audiences, uniting people from disparate parties in a common practical cause. And where Zhitlowsky was celebrated in Bern and beyond as a philosopher and theorist, An-sky's reputation grew as a poet and storyteller who preferred concrete words and deeds to abstract ideologies.

An-sky loved to tell stories. He listened to other people tell stories and thought about how they worked. Sitting in cafés in Bern, Zurich, and Geneva, he wrote productively on these topics and got his work published more easily than he had for a decade, finding outlets in Russian and increasingly in the Yiddish press that was emerging from underground. He had been recounting his memories of his time in the Donets Basin among miners and peasants for a long while, but now those stories took on new meanings. In October 1902, he told Alexander Ivanchin-Pisarev, one of the *Russkoe Bogatstvo* editors, that he had begun to analyze legends and rumors in order to understand the peasants' sociopolitical views, "the existing order (how they understand and judge it); what ideal order they imagine, and . . . the ways and means they think possible to attain that order." He would use material that he had gathered in the South, as well as published sources. The book as a whole, he admitted, would be too radical to publish in Russia, but he urged Ivanchin-Pisarev to accept a single chapter, "Peasant Thought about the Land," a "ticklish" topic to print, but not an impossible one.[17]

An-sky never convinced *Russkoe Bogatstvo* to take that article, but earlier in 1902, the journal published a series of his articles: "The Folk and the Book (From Personal Observations and Impressions)" and "The Folk on the Book," the core of a later book, *The Folk and the Book: An Attempt to Characterize the Peasant Reader*. He returned there to the themes of his 1892 book on peasant literacy, but his image of popular literature was more dynamic than before. Now geographically distant from the Populists who had taken him in, he was able to present peasants in new ways, not as passive victims of oppression, needing to be shielded from outside influence, but as strong tellers of their own stories, able to respond to outside influences with tales that demonstrated their resilience. He described peasants' reactions to the texts they heard read aloud. If the stories they heard did not accord with their own beliefs, then, without contradicting them, they would tell their own stories with the opposite morals; if they agreed with the stories they heard, then they told stories of their own in the same spirit. "For me, at least, these 'incidental stories' about what had been read served as the best possible demonstration of the attitude of the peasant listeners."[18] The peasants here are active and creative: when a text is introduced that does not meet with their approval, it stimulates them to produce other texts.

The longer An-sky spent away from Russian peasants, the more optimistically he viewed them. In the 1880s, when he was living among peasants and miners, he found them fascinating and he collected their folklore, but he also wrote about the hostility and self-destructiveness he saw in the peasant rumors that fueled the migration movements. Now more and more, he insisted that the only effective way to understand peasant culture was to become invisible, to adapt, as he himself always had, to new surroundings: to observe without judging as peasants encountered new books or stories, while recording their responses and impressions. He admitted that it was "very hard, almost impossible, for the reader to keep from explaining, expressing his opinion, and correcting misunderstandings about some place, situation, type, etc." The task was complicated by the differences in culture and status between the peasants and the ethnographer: "The intellectual reader influences the listeners' level of understanding by the very process of good reading, by his personality, his presence, which prevent the peasant reader from expressing himself as freely as he is used to doing among his own people." The ethnographer needs to fight the preconceptions that influence his or her observations. "It is impossible to remember and write down the listener's every word or gesture. The reader remembers that which seems typical or interesting." Only by fighting one's own beliefs, An-sky believed, could a person collect data that are "unquestionably scientifically valid." This insistence on the creative power of the individual storyteller—and the influence of the audience—would be echoed by Russian folklorists around 1908; An-sky's consistent urge to immerse himself in the moment, to adapt to new surroundings and listen to new acquaintances with sympathy, led him to articulate views that were ahead of their time.[19]

As An-sky confronted the problem of truly understanding other people, he became increasingly convinced that intellectuals needed to recognize and respect the differences between peasant culture and their own. He knew that the notion of peasants as inherently culturally different from others ran counter to the ideas of the inherent equality that had justified the emancipation of the serfs in 1861. Liberal Russian society was gripped by "fear of any infringement of the sacred formula, 'A peasant is the same kind of human being as other people.' "[20] But An-sky argued that excessive devotion to that notion forced intellectuals to ascribe peasant difference to their backwardness and to attempt to educate peasants and make them more like the intellectuals, no matter how impractical this goal was, or how disrespectful. And in the early 1900s, An-sky was portraying peasant culture as not only different, but also creative and vibrant, a rich source of knowledge in its own right.

The shift in An-sky's ideas about peasants had many causes. Working with the ASL, he was surrounded by people who believed that Russian peasants had the creative potential to imagine a new order of things and to rebel against the regime. The spring 1902 peasant revolts in Kharkov and Poltava confirmed this notion. After his years of "university" with Lavrov, An-sky had become more aware of his own prejudices as a researcher and more respectful of his subjects, who had grown to include Western European readers as well as Russian ones. He wrote about libraries and reading in France, Holland, and Switzerland, and about adult education in other forms. He neither presented France and Switzerland as models to be emulated, nor did he agree with those who decried them as decadent or destroyed by capitalism. Rather, he portrayed the situation in each of these countries as in flux.[21]

An-sky expressed some of his new ideas about cultural change in *Pioneers,* a two-part novel about the Jewish youth of the 1870s and 1880s who were turning away from religion and embracing Russian radicalism. An-sky wrote *The First Breach* (Pervaia bresh') in 1903 and *Pioneers* (Pionery), or *The Fence-Breakers,* in 1905 and published both serially in *Voskhod.*[22] These titles suggest the invasion of a country by a band of warriors, who first make a breach into enemy territory and then send a party of pioneers. These warriors turn out to be *maskilim,* self-styled Jewish enlighteners who are fighting on two fronts: to acquire knowledge of non-Jewish languages and secular sciences and to bring that knowledge to their fellow Jews and thus reform them. In his novel, An-sky returned to new readers encountering new texts—but rather than Russian peasants, these were Jews reading Russian literature. As in his writings on the peasants, he considered whether the Jews could simply adopt Russian literary culture, or whether they had to create something new to meet their own specific needs.

The First Breach opens with Zalman Itsikovich, a young man in ill-fitting European-style clothes, entering the shtetl of Miloslavka. Like many former *yeshivabokhers* (yeshiva students), he had strayed from the Talmud and the rabbinic commentaries toward secular literature in Hebrew and Russian. After he and other freethinkers were uncovered, his yeshiva was shut down and he was forced to leave town. So he arrives in Miloslavka, much as An-sky himself had once arrived in Liozno, carrying his most precious possessions, a few maskilic books in Hebrew and a few Russian textbooks. Like An-sky in Liozno, Itsikovich seeks work as a *shrayber,* a teacher of Russian (or at least Russian handwriting). He tells the townspeople that he wants to set himself up as a teacher of Russian to girls (since girls were not traditionally obligated to spend their time studying Jewish law, they could have more free time than boys did to study non-Jewish languages—and such languages would be useful to them in commerce). In reality, Itsikovich has another goal: to spread the subversive seeds of Haskalah. As it turns out, Itsikovich had been a mediocre yeshiva student, and his grasp of secular subjects, including Russian, is limited. Nor does he have much strength of will. When the town rabbi, guessing the teacher's intentions, decides to try to bring Itsikovich back into the fold, he caves in quickly, burns most of his secular books, and dons traditional clothes again. Soon the rabbi realizes the limits of Itsikovich's intellect and loses interest in studying Talmud with him. Disheartened, Itsikovich picks up the New Testament that had been lent to him by a local Russian official and almost immediately converts to Russian Orthodoxy, ending the dream of enlightening the people and the first half of the novel.

But Itsikovich's subversive plans have not, it turns out, been entirely fruitless. The second half of *Pioneers* tells of Elye Eizerman, a teenager from Miloslavka who had borrowed Lilienblum's *Sins of Youth* from Itsikovich. Eizerman reads it and runs away to the town of M. (Vitebsk), which he finds—as he had hoped—full of enlightened Jews, from penniless ex-yeshiva students living in communes to Jewish youths who speak fluent

Russian and study in gymnasium. They take him in, start teaching him Russian, and involve him in their complex schemes and passionate debates. In the end, Eizerman heads back to Miloslavka, determined to continue the work that Itsikovich had begun and abandoned, enlightening the Jewish masses.

These two novellas abound in scenes of Jews learning to read Russian. The first ones center on Itsikovich's students in Miloslavka. In the yeshiva, Itsikovich had learned to read and write the Cyrillic alphabet, and in his grammar book he has "gotten to the verbs," which, he feels, qualifies him as a teacher. His teaching method is having students memorize texts in the target language, whether or not they understand them. He tests his method on his most promising student, Etl, who has already been reading Russian on her own. Itsikovich dictates a fable to her, and after obediently writing it down, she asks him to define some unfamiliar words in another text. Since he doesn't know those words either, he tries to justify not explaining them:

> "Those words are perfectly simple. . . . It's not hard to explain them. But what's the use? Those words are on this page, on the next page there will be others. . . ."
> "So?"
> "That's just it. You shouldn't be reading difficult books. . . ."

Eventually, Etl prevails on Itsikovich to explain just two of the words, and he tells her that "gorizont" [horizon] means "krasivaia gora" [a beautiful mountain]; his assumption that words that sound similar ("gora" and "gorizont") must have similar meanings is a typical mistake for a beginning language student. The passage is funny only if you know Russian better than Itsikovich does. An-sky addresses the novel to a reader who, like the characters themselves, is interested in the process of language learning in general. Indeed, the ex-yeshiva students in *The Pioneers*, trying to master Russian, discuss foreign language pedagogy at length. One of them defends the usefulness of learning grammar rules while another proposes a kind of contextual approach, beginning with the entire text rather than the grammatical abstraction; one looks up every unknown word in a dictionary while another figures them out from context; one student only allows himself to read Russian, while another relaxes between Russian texts by returning to the familiar Aramaic of the Talmud.[23]

Eizerman observes these approaches. First, he meets Uler, who applies the methods he once used in studying the Talmud to his favorite Russian texts, Pisarev's essays, which—foreshadowing the Social Democratic doctrine that An-sky and Zhitlowsky attacked—preached that art and philosophy were insignificant and only science and material things mattered. Uler calls the radical critic "Pisref" and resists all attempts to convince him to pronounce it as Russians normally do. Indeed, Pisarev's essays appear, in Uler's view, to have as little to do with a spoken language as the Talmud does. When asked if he understands all the words in the famous article "Pushkin and Belinsky," Uler responds scornfully:

> "The words! Who cares about the words? You just take any place in the article, whatever you want, and read a few words, one phrase, any one you want . . ."
> "Well, and what will happen?"
> "Just wait! You'll see what happens! Try!"

Uler's friend discovers that he has memorized the entire article, and next he intends to learn it "by a finger."[24] (If you say to a person who knows a text "by a finger," "I have my finger on the fourth word of the sixth line of page three," that person can tell you to what word you are pointing.) Eizerman uses a different approach to learn Russian himself, one that recalls the young Shloyme-Zanvl taking dictation in his attic room from his wealthy friend Chaim. Eizerman's teacher, Kapluner, a gymnasium student who was taught Russian from childhood, tells Eizerman that he can speak only Russian during his lesson. He begins by having his student read aloud, and when he discovers the flaws in Eizerman's pronunciation, he demotes him to an easier text. His homework is to read the story over ten times, write it out twice, and then retell it in Russian in his own words.

These scenes contrast the traditional Jewish understanding of reading, which grows out of its function as religious obligation, with modern reading habits. Itsikovich and Uler, with their emphasis on memorization, on reproducing the text physically, whether in exemplary handwriting or with the total visual recall that permits a Talmud student to know a page of Gemara "by a finger," see the Russian text as a unified material object. The goal of the reader is to assimilate that object in toto, almost literally to swallow it. Having done so, the reader can be fundamentally changed. This happens classicly with Itsikovich: having read the New Testament, he becomes a Christian, legally renouncing his old identity once and for all. In the case of Uler and the other ex-yeshivabokhers, the reader of Pisarev is converted into a fanatical adherent of Pisarev's views, a proto–Social Democrat who vehemently dismisses any literature that does not fit his materialist ideology, from Pushkin to Dostoevsky.[25]

But the ex-yeshivabokher fans of Pisarev cannot be too neatly equated with An-sky's SD opponents in Bern; their actions are governed by the kind of heroic aesthetic that motivated SR propaganda. Uler asserts that his current enlightenment is only meaningful because he once obeyed Jewish law. When Eizerman asks if Kapluner, whose maskilic father brought him up on secular sciences rather than Jewish texts, is also a maskil, Uler explains why he is not.

> "You can't call him a maskil," Uler answered with difficulty. "Of course, he is a 'modern' man, educated, knows Russian very well, has read a lot. . . . But he's still not one of us! First of all, he's an 'am-ha-arets' [a man who is not educated in the Talmud]. He barely even knows Hebrew! Well, what can you do with a person like that? What can you discuss with him? He can smoke on the Sabbath, eat pork, just like a simple peasant, but that's it! There's no heroism here, no wisdom, no Haskalah."[26]

What Uler finds beautiful is rebellion itself. Education means for him not just knowledge of the Russian classics, but the combination of that with knowledge of the Talmud; heroism means disobeying Jewish law, but only while knowing that law. Like SR terrorists, the yeshivabokhers are pioneers whose deeds are inspirational because they are transgressive.

Pisarev inspires Uler to reject an old culture, not create a new one, but the yeshivabokhers have an entirely different approach to rabbinic texts. Using the traditional exegetical genre, the *drash*, Uler offers to prove, based on any citation from the Bible, the Talmud, or the Zohar (the central kabbalistic text), that Moses was a follower of Pisarev, a "realist" who insisted on the importance of the physical world and the speciousness of spiritual beliefs. Eizerman responds with a well-known verse, "Give ear, O heavens, and I will speak; and may the earth hear the words of my mouth" (Deut. 32:1). Chaim Zhitlowsky had once invited Shloyme-Zanvl Rappoport to hear him give a bar mitzvah drash, and now, perhaps in homage to his old friend, An-sky created another such masterful manipulation of Jewish sources, which merits quotation at length. Uler stands in the middle of the room and speaks in the singsong tones of a synagogue preacher.

> "'Ai! Gi-ive ear, O heavens, I will spea-eak!' At first this whole ve-erse is incomprehensible! First of all, why would Moses suddenly decide to speak to the heavens and the earth, instead of speaking to the Jews? Second, if he had already addressed them, then why would he address the heavens directly, 'Give ear,' and to the earth he says 'may the earth hear'? Why didn't he say 'Listen, earth'? Third, why does he repeat the same thing twice, 'I will speak' and 'the words of my mouth,' when he could have said simply 'Give ear, O heavens, and may the earth hear the words of my mouth'? A-and, fourth, why did he say 'the words of my mouth,' as though it were possible to produce words from one's nose or eyes? After all, he could simply have said 'my words.' "

The listeners break in, enthralled, but Uler continues.

> "A-as you see, my brothers, this entire verse is incomprehensible and has no mea-eaning! . . . But it will become clear to us if we interpret it in the spirit of pure realism. . . . Listen, brothers! Moses did not say, 'Give ear, O heavens.' He said, "Give ear, I will speak about the heavens!' [Russian wordplay] And what are the 'heavens'? The heavens are the throne of God, his buttress, that is, the highest law of the universe. Thus, Moses said, 'Give ear, I will speak about the law of the universe. And may the earth hear'. . . . And what is 'earth'? Earth is 'khoimer,' that is, clay, material substance. On the other hand, 'earth' is dust, and dust is man, because it is said, 'dust thou art and to dust shalt thou return' [Gen. 3:19]. So, Moses is addressing man and he says 'hear, O material man, the words of . . . "fi" [my mouth].' What is 'fi'? 'Fi' are the first letters of the word 'Pisarev' [Hebrew wordplay]. In addition, 'Fi' is 90, which is the letter tsaddik, which means 'righteous man'. . . . So, my brothers! Moses says 'Listen! I will speak about the law of the universe, and may material man hear the words of the righteous man Pisarev.' "

Uler ends on a triumphant note: "I have proven to you that Moses the prophet preached realism according to Pisarev! And in recognition of my feat, may the savior come soon to Zion, and let us say 'Amen.' " Kapluner claps Uler on the back and cannot restrain his admiration. Uler, though, calls his own virtuoso performance "child's play." What would really be worth listening to, he told Kapluner, would be his engagement with the kabbalah. "Once for a whole evening I gave a drash showing on the basis of the Zohar and other kabbalistic books that there is no God. That was a drash!"[27]

The space An-sky gives to Uler's drash suggests that he was intrigued by the "pioneers'" approaches to text: their uncritical absorption of Pisarev's Russian essays contrasts sharply with their ability to retell traditional Jewish texts in their own words and even against the grain. Pisarev inspires Uler to produce a radically revisionist version of the Hebrew Bible, and the crowd's cheers show that his bilingual drash is appreciated by listeners who know both enough Hebrew and enough Russian to understand the wordplay. The Russian writer Maxim Gorky agreed: when he read *Pioneers,* he was impressed by the energy and the vitality of characters like Uler, and although he found the "artistic quality" of the novel "doubtful," he admired the "incredible tension of the will to live, which the author describes in relief and with love."[28]

When he created the sparring young Jewish characters in *Pioneers,* An-sky was working out in fiction and in a Jewish context some of the problems he had addressed in nonfiction and in a Russian context. When his ex-yeshivabokhers read Russian, they have much in common with his peasant readers who associate understanding a text with memorizing it, are primarily concerned with the moral message in a text, and are untroubled when they do not understand individual words. As exemplified by Uler learning Pisarev "by a finger," they espouse the attitude that a text is a stable, transcendent whole that can affect its reader dramatically for good or for ill, as the SRs hoped their propaganda of word and deed would do for people. By contrast, when the yeshivabokhers read traditional texts (as in Uler's drash) and when the gymasium students read Russian, they sound more like the miners and urban workers whom An-sky described in their appreciation of a text's aesthetic qualities, and they recall the peasants who react to stories they disapprove of with new stories of their own. They experience the text as flexible: one can retell it in one's own words. What is important is not so much the choice of text as the mastery of a new language. The distinction here is between a creative and a passive reader. Uler and Itsikovich are both passive readers of Russian, like the Russian peasants An-sky depicted in 1892. They absorb new texts and are "converted" by them. Eizerman, following Kapluner, is a more active or creative reader of Russian, like the Russian peasants An-sky described from 1902 to 1905. Having read the text, these readers are prepared to change it. Rather than the text converting the reader, the reader can rewrite the text. As Eizerman eventually recognized, such an attitude toward the text can be tremendously empowering. An-sky gives us Eizerman's thoughts as he does his homework:

> Retelling [the story] in Russian in his own words interested Eizerman because of its enormous difficulty, and with great effort creating "Russian sentences" that were, of course, neither "Russian" nor "sentences," he repeated in his own mind, "Good! Excellent!"[29]

An-sky suggests that, grammar aside, in some sense Eizerman may have been right: in both Russian and Jewish contexts, he was celebrating readers' creative, active responses to the written word, imagining culture as something fluid that people produce actively in response to their own changing needs and ideas. He saw both Jews and peasants as no less defiant and creative than he was. As a person who acted out new roles when he found himself in new situations, more and more he was describing both Jews and peasants as just as restless and adaptable as he was himself.

The Russian authorities had made it hard for Jews to publish newspapers and journals in Yiddish, the language of the masses, but in 1902, Minister of Internal Affairs Viacheslav Pleve gave official sanction to a single

Yiddish daily, *Der fraynd* (The Friend), to counteract the growing influence of the underground Bundist Yiddish press. The paper, which came out from 1903 till 1909 in St. Petersburg and then moved to Warsaw for four more years, had a circulation of 50,000 by 1905. The editors Shaul Ginzburg and Shabse Rapoport mixed news with fiction by writers such as Peretz, Sholem Aleichem, Abramovich, and Lilienblum. Zhitlowsky saw *Der fraynd* as a worthy outlet for his Yiddish writing, and An-sky followed him into the new sphere of the legal Russian Yiddish periodical press. He had published a few poems—revolutionary and lyrical—in 1901 and 1902 in the underground Bundist publications *Di arbeter shtime* and *Der idisher arbeter,* as well as a poem in the Odessa Zionist weekly *Der Yud* (The Jew), but no serious works. With his debut in *Der fraynd* in the spring of 1904, he began to create significant new work in Yiddish.[30]

His initial piece was the first long text he had written in Yiddish in twenty years. Entitled "Ashmedai," a *poema,* or long narrative poem, it concerned the complex relationship between the demon Ashmedai and his concubine Lilith. An-sky wrote it under the influence of Peretz, whose neo-romantic, folkloric work he had been reading with enthusiasm since 1901. One of Peretz's best-known works, "Monish," was a poema about a young Talmud genius, word of whose prowess reaches the demons Sammael and Lilith on Mount Ararat. Because the devils fear the boy's virtue will bring the Messiah and topple their throne, they decide to neutralize him. After trying various methods, Lilith succeeds in sullying his virtue by sending a beautiful girl (perhaps Lilith herself in disguise) to convince Monish to swear his love for her by God. The poem ends with the rejoicing following Monish's fall:

> Ararat goes crazy—
> one hilarious, profuse
> shrieking party in the ark,
> all Gehenna breaking loose.
>
> Ten gypsy orchestras,
> Gehenna's top musicians,
> champagne by the bucket
> while the demons do the can-can with precision. . . .
>
> Fire in her eyes,
> the queen of all that place,
> Lilith goes before, Sammael behind,
> carrying her train of Spanish lace.[31]

Peretz's rhyme and humor are virtuosic, but his plot is simple: Monish passes from virtue to sin, from pride to a fall, as Lilith neatly vanquishes her foe. The conclusion shows her the unambiguous victor, and Peretz, revealing his maskilic loyalties, is on her side, making fun of the tradition-bound Monish and enjoying his downfall.

An-sky's "Ashmedai" revisits the theme of the devil and his lover, and he heightens the folkloric effect by writing in trochaic tetrameter, the meter of the well-known Finnish folk epic, the *Kalevala,* and Henry Wadsworth Longfellow's American imitation of it, *Hiawatha,* in the originals and in translation. When he wrote about studying the peasants, An-sky spoke for methods that preserved their stories in a maximally authentic form, but when he produced his own folkloric stylization, he had no compunction about borrowing from any available source: Jewish legends and a meter associated with Finnish folk poetry and with his era's best-known example of invented American lore. Peretz's poetic form is more varied, but in narrative terms, An-sky's tale is more complex. His Lilith, the concubine of the demon Ashmedai, was a virtuous shtetl girl until Ashmedai abducted and seduced her. Following the example of "Monish," An-sky's Ashmedai sends his Lilith to the dreams of religious Jewish men, hoping to lead them astray, but the pious Linen Rebbe resists her wiles. Not only does she not make him sin, but he convinces her to return to the Jewish ways that she had abandoned. She begins to care for orphans, she confesses her identity to the Rebbe, and she resolves as penitence to spend every night in the synagogue reciting *tkhines,* women's prayers in Yiddish. Shocked at her treachery, Ashmedai asks several sorcerers for advice about punishing Lilith; they suggest that she be torn by demons into billions of pieces, given difficult, disappointing children, or transformed into a overworked medical student. Ashmedai chooses to punish her by allowing her to remain just as she is, a penitent, but with Ashmedai's "poison" still in her heart. A sorcerer explains her tragedy.

> So, Lord Ashmedai, she'll be
> An outsider in both worlds;
> Among humans, among spirits,
> Virtuous people, vicious demons,
> Far from the awful depths of Hell,
> Far from radiant Paradise.
> For the saints she'll still be Lilith,
> For the sinners—still a penitent,
> For the pious she'll be wicked,
> For the modern—a chaste lady. . . .

Alien to either side,
She will wander, languishing,
And on both sides all she'll see
Will be nasty glares and curses.
You will surely never find
Tortures, torments worse than these![32]

Lilith's punishment puts her in the same position as the new readers among Russian peasants and miners, or Uler and the other yeshivabokhers in *Pioneers:* floating between one shore and another, drawn both to the traditional world and to the secular (or diabolical) one, unable to find a stable home. Even readers who have chosen to occupy this sort of in-between space—such as An-sky himself and the Russian-Jewish students who surrounded him in Switzerland—might pity her. An-sky himself, like Lilith, inhabited various worlds and was vulnerable to seduction and persuasion from both sides. Although Chernov, who knew him in Russian, saw him as untroubled by his multiple loyalties, the poem suggests that as he moved into Yiddish publishing, he began to display—and, perhaps, to feel—the ambivalence and guilt about his bicultural status that his Zionist and Bundist friends might have expected.

As An-sky scribbled away in Swiss cafés, he and other Russian Jews in Western Europe followed the situation in the Russian Empire with horrified fascination. In February 1903, a Russian Christian boy had been found murdered (by relatives, as it turned out) in Dubossary, a town near Kishinev, the capital of Bessarabia on the southwestern edge of the empire. Two local Russian-language newspapers published accusations that he had been killed by Jews so that his blood could be used for Passover matzo. On Easter Day, April 6 (18), three days of anti-Jewish violence began in Kishinev. The dead numbered 51 and over 400 people were wounded; over 700 houses were looted or destroyed. Although these casualties would seem insignificant by comparison with later anti-Jewish violence, they outweighed those of the 1881–1882 pogroms. European and American newspapers reported on the pogrom in detail, and protests were held in New York, San Francisco, and elsewhere. The poet Semyon Frug, who usually wrote in Russian, published a Yiddish poem in *Der fraynd*, "Have Pity!" asking for material help for the victims: "Give the dead shrouds / Give the living bread."[33]

Radical writers blamed the Tsarist government that had not intervened to quell the violence. Indeed, the government was believed to have planned the pogrom, and a forged dispatch purporting that Pleve had told Bessarabian authorities not to step in was published in the *Times* of London. The Jewish Bund saw Kishinev as further proof that revolution was at hand, and its leadership proclaimed that the time had come to respond with arms: "We must answer violence with violence: no matter where it comes from. . . . Down with anti-Semitism! . . . Long live socialism!"[34]

The most influential response to Kishinev came from the Hebrew poet Chaim Nakhman Bialik. He had been sent to the city soon after the pogrom by the Union of Hebrew Writers to interview the survivors and write a report. Although he knew that in some cases the Jews had fought their attackers, in his *poema* "In the City of Slaughter," he emphasized their passivity. Jews should answer Kishinev, he wrote, with bitter words:

> Rise, to the desert flee!
> The cup of affliction thither bear with thee!
> Take thou thy soul, rend it in many a shred!
> With impotent rage, thy heart deform!
> Thy tear upon the barren boulders shed!
> And send thy bitter cry into the storm![35]

The SRs in Switzerland responded to Kishinev with a deed meant to speak louder than the bitterest cry. On July 15 (28), 1904, in an attack coordinated by the SR Battle Organization, Egor Sazonov threw a bomb at Pleve's carriage in St. Petersburg. The assassination had been planned by Azef, a double agent who had been paid by the Russian authorities to infiltrate the Battle Organization—but who, as a Jew, agreed that Pleve must be punished. Stepan Sletov recalled the moment when news of Pleve's assassination reached the SRs in Western Europe: "On every side there were shouts of joy. I can still see N. [Azef]: he was standing a little apart; he dashed a glass of water on the floor and, gnashing his teeth, shouted, 'That's for Kishinev'."[36]

The Foreign Organization of the PSR, created in 1903 to carry on the work of the ASL, was meeting in France. Neither An-sky nor Zhitlowsky was elected to the Foreign Committee, the leadership of the SRs in exile, and An-sky was annoyed. He reported on August 1, 1904, that the conference had been going poorly: "Those in the minority walked out. There were fights, it was getting close to a split. . . . Pleve came to the rescue. They had just reached a decision, everyone was fighting, frowning—suddenly, bang! Hugs, kisses, champagne, hysteria." The next day, An-sky saw a description of the event in the *Journal de Genève:* "They give a fairly detailed description of the place where those days 'there was a terrorist convention' . . . and how, learning the news, they danced all night. The devil knows what it means."[37]

Whether or not he danced at the news of Pleve's assassination, in the next few months, An-sky believed that SR terrorists were heroes and worked to convince Jews of the value of their violent acts. From November 1904 through May 1905, he edited *Kampf un kempfer* (The Fight and the Fighters), a series of Yiddish pamphlets with pictures and worshipful biographies of Sazonov, as well as Lekert, the Vilna Bundist who had shot at von Wahl; Alexsei Pokotilov, who died assembling bombs in 1904; Fruma Frumkina, a young Jewish woman who attacked a police official in 1903 while in prison; and—in an entire pamphlet—Ivan Kaliaev, who killed Grand Duke Sergei Alexandrovich in early February 1905. An unsigned article entitled "Why We Are for Terrorism" explained the platform that Zhitlowsky and other SR theorists had designed. It described the brutality of the government in great detail and called on readers to respond to it "as true citizens and not as the slaves of the holy Romanov family." The SDs may reject terror and start "clucking like a hen on an egg" when they hear of it, but, the author insisted, the SD tactic of strikes and demonstrations was only "sweet dreams and fantasies," doomed to fail when the authorities sent mounted Cossacks to trample demonstrators. Because the actions of would-be assassins such as Lekert aroused so much sympathy, they could speak to the masses. Terrorist acts were themselves a means of communication and education, teaching people "to think politically," giving voice to the voiceless by publicizing the deaths of the regime's victims. "One terrorist act changes the opinions of thousands of people about the revolutionaries and their activities more than months of oral or written propaganda." But terror could not be the party's only tactic; it must be combined with propaganda and perceived as a conflict not between two individuals but between the masses and the government.[38]

Even while An-sky must have subscribed to the idea defended in *Kampf un kempfer* that assassinations spoke louder than words, he did his best to make the words he wrote effective. He hired the Hebrew and Yiddish writer Yosef Chaim Brenner to translate articles from Russian to Yiddish; Brenner's pseudonym, Yokhanan Hakanai (Yokhanan the Fanatic) appeared on several of the issues as co-editor. An-sky was delighted with his collaborator, writing to Brenner, "In a few words, a few sentences, you express more than another in long letters." Brenner may be the Natan (or Natanchik) An-sky mentioned when he described his work on *Kampf un kempfer*: "I've definitively converted Natanchik to our faith (he's plainly declared himself an SR), and we spend three to four hours a day correcting translations for the collection. And what translations! . . . Natan and I laugh like madmen about some of the sentences. It would be a huge scandal if the collection came out in this shape. We had to translate some things over again."[39]

In March 1905, the author of "Why We Are for Terrorism" could assert confidently that this was a moment of crisis when a few assassinations could have an enormous effect. On February 10, 1904, the disastrous Russo-Japanese War had begun; by the time peace was concluded in September 1905 at the Treaty of Portsmouth, the Russian losses—to a nation the Russians had seen as inferior—had shaken the empire's confidence. By then, Russia was shuddering with political unrest. On January 9, 1905, the priest Georgy Gapon, who had run a workers' organization funded by the government and meant to draw support away from the revolutionary movements, stunned his government sponsors when he led a crowd of at least 16,000 workers and their families to the Winter Palace to present a petition to Tsar Nicholas II. Although the demonstrators were unarmed and carrying icons and portraits of the tsar, the army shot at them on the square in front of the palace. Over a hundred people were killed and several hundred wounded.[40] Casualty figures, dramatically inflated, were reported in the foreign press, and news of "Bloody Sunday" shocked the world. Within the empire, the incident set off a period of riots and strikes known as the Revolution of 1905. Father Gapon himself survived the events of January 9 and, with the help of his associate Pyotr Rutenberg, was smuggled out of the Russian Empire. He spent a short time in Switzerland, where he associated first with the SDs and then the SRs.

An-sky met Gapon at the home of his friend Boris Savinkov, the leader of the SR Fighting Organization and Uspensky's son-in-law. Gapon puzzled the Geneva émigrés when he claimed the procession to the Winter Palace was intended to put the government in an impossible situation. Savinkov was skeptical, and Gapon responded to his skepticism playfully, as if ignorant of the dangerous forces he had engaged. An-sky later saw Gapon at the home of another émigré, playing with a child's gun, and his hosts spoke of him as a child, "with the good-hearted humor with which an adult speaks of a child's mischief." In describing Gapon, An-sky repeated adjectives meaning "childish." Although he understood little of the theory behind it, Gapon spoke of SR terror in lurid language, "constantly talking about bombs, preaching mass and individual terror, and his speech was colored with choice invective against the government and expressions involving the word 'blood': 'bloodsucker,' 'comrades bound together by blood,' and so on."[41]

An-sky was intrigued by Gapon's language and its power. Fantastic reports about Gapon's activities appeared in the European press, and Gapon urged the émigrés to translate them into Russian for him. An article appeared in a Belgian newspaper about a speech that Gapon had purportedly given at a student meeting in Brussels, where he blessed the attendees with his hands before urging them to revolutionary action. The journalist reported that he spoke personally to Gapon and was impressed by his excellent French, very lightly accented. An-sky noticed that "Gapon was ecstatic about that story and long after would speak about his 'blessing of the young revolutionaries' and his 'barely noticeable accent' (he knew not a word of French)."[42]

Although he knew Gapon's fabled genius was the stuff of rumor and farce, An-sky marveled at his genuine ability to communicate. He traveled with Gapon to London, where he saw the priest walk into a store and ask uninhibitedly in Russian, "Give me a chessboard."

"Why are you speaking Russian?" An-sky intervened, shocked.

"It's fine," Gapon responded cheerfully. "They'll understand. People here are educated." He repeated the sentence in Russian, demonstrating chess-playing with his hands, and in a few minutes the storekeeper, his face glowing, brought a chessboard.[43] As An-sky saw, there was something uncanny, even magical, in the revolutionary priest's ability to communicate and convince.

Because Gapon was so famous as both a revolutionary and a priest, Jewish activists asked him to write a pamphlet condemning pogroms. Gapon agreed to do so, but asked An-sky to co-write it. So in June 1905, the assignment brought An-sky to London, where Gapon was working on his autobiography.[44] After waiting fruitlessly for Gapon to produce a draft, An-sky gave up and drafted one himself. He showed it to Gapon, who was dissatisfied and said that it was written in the wrong style and tone for an audience of workers and peasants. Gapon took it to make revisions and ended up staying up all night writing his own version.

The result, An-sky saw, was something quite distant from the usual tone of SR propaganda; it was written "in a priestly spirit and with such 'godly' expressions that it would be awkward for the Party to publish it." He was glad that it would be published with private money (though the SRs, the Bund, and other parties agreed to distribute it). It began, "Orthodox people, brothers and sisters! Listen to my true words, for your own great blessing. I will begin with a divine parable, a parable of Christ the Savior, called the parable of the good Samaritan." The Russian lines imitated folk poetry, in three-syllable meter with dactylic endings. Gapon urged his readers to be like the good Samaritan in the Gospels (Luke 10:30–37), who helps those in need with no thought of reward, rather than like the Pharisees. He emphasized that the real enemy and exploiter of the narod was not the Jews, and he condemned the tradition that depicted Jews as guilty of shedding the blood of Jesus. Those truly guilty, according to Gapon, were the tsar and his ministers, whom he described as "insatiable vampires, wastrels, traitors to the people" and "bloodsuckers, fierce carrion-crows."[45] The pamphlet used biblical imagery and Church Slavonic turns of phrase to depict the Jews as the well-meaning friends of Russia's poor and the regime as the most dangerous enemies of the peasants and the workers. Gapon, as An-sky described him, was that rare propagandist who could couch his message perfectly in terms that would move his listeners.

The storm that Gapon's demonstration had unleashed in the Russian Empire raged through the spring and summer of 1905. On October 17 (30), 1905, Nicholas II, seeing no other way to calm the disturbances, issued the October Manifesto, granting freedoms of conscience, speech, assembly, and association, and creating a parliament, the Duma, with poorly defined powers. The Russian revolutionaries in Europe, many now granted immunity from prosecution under an amnesty, wanted to return to Russia and participate in what they recognized as momentous changes. The day after the October Manifesto was issued, Gapon told An-sky that he was going back. An-sky asked him nervously, "Who are you going to Russia with?" He remembered Gapon shuddering and answering with an irritable laugh, "Who? I don't know, I don't know! I'll see once I'm there! I'll try to go with God, God . . . but if that doesn't work, I'll go with the Devil, hah-hah, the Devil! But I'll get what I want!" Those were the last words An-sky heard him say. Gapon left for St. Petersburg in early November and plunged into revolutionary politics. He entered into negotiations with Pyotr Rachkovsky, an officer in the Tsarist secret police, perhaps intending to double-cross the government again— but in March 1906, Gapon was assassinated by Pyotr Rutenberg, his erstwhile savior, acting on Azef's orders. Two years later, after Azef himself was unmasked as an agent provocateur at a party tribunal at the end of October 1908, Gapon was somewhat rehabilitated in the eyes of the SRs.[46] Thus it is not surprising that in 1909, An-sky would write a memoir describing Gapon as neither a hero (as he had appeared in January 1905) nor a villain (as he had seemed in March 1906) but rather as a tragic figure, talented but flawed, torn between the divine and the demonic. The image of a person driven to call on God and the Devil at once would inspire him when he wrote *The Dybbuk*.

In 1905, An-sky was already intrigued by Gapon's ability to mobilize the masses. The charismatic priest who set in motion the demonstration that sparked a revolution stood for the power of a single human voice to change history. But when An-sky described Gapon as just as demonic as he was heroic, he revealed some unease with the very idea of charismatic persuasion and propaganda—an unease that troubled him in Switzerland. For his remarkable productivity of 1901–1905 came out of two diametrically opposed ideologies. On the one hand, his major work—*Pioneers, The Folk and the Book*, "Ashmedai"—spoke of the impossibility of fundamentally changing another person's culture or mind. His rebellious yeshiva students, his newly literate peasants, and his Lilith all demonstrate the problems with thinking that exposure to a new idea can truly transform a person; in each case, traces of the old self remain. On the other hand, An-sky was a professional propagandist who defended the SR doctrine of propaganda of word and deed and worked to generate and circulate heroic images meant to change everyone's opinions. This inconsistency did not, it seems, bother An-sky, who had always performed different personas for different audiences. His increasing literary success, as a fiction writer, a poet, and a propagandist in two languages, meant that he was getting better at anticipating what people wanted to read. Indeed, his own malleability made him singularly unable to resolve the paradox in his work.

Throughout 1905, as he watched the stuff of the émigrés' discussions becoming reality, An-sky felt dissatisfied in spite of his literary activity and his political success. Like Gapon, he was drawn to Russia, yearning to go back and add his energy to the revolution. In May 1904, An-sky had directed a student production of a play inspired by the Kishinev pogrom, Evgeny Chirikov's *The Jews*. An-sky took the role of the old man Leizer, and a non-Jewish student, Nikolai Blinov, played Berezin, a non-Jew who is killed defending Jews. Eleven months later, in April 1905, Blinov himself was killed in the Zhitomir pogrom, defending Jews, and An-sky described him as a martyr: "Your memory, the memory of a person who gave his soul for his friends, will always be sacred to us. And with the darkness and horror that surround us, the bacchanalia of madness, shame, and hatred that has risen up . . . your bright name will be a pledge and a symbol of the future brotherhood of men and nations." It was an awkward fact that Blinov and his wife had quarreled with other SRs and been excluded from the party; he neglected to mention this in his obituary.[47]

The example of Blinov suggested that in spite of the pogroms in the empire, the revolutionary movement could realize the dream of harmony between Jews and Slavs. More than almost anywhere inside the Russian Empire, the meetings of SR leaders in emigration provided space where ethnic Russians such as Chernov, Chaikovsky, or Savinkov, and Jews such as An-sky and Zhitlowsky, Osip Minor and Mikhail Gots, could work together as equals for a common cause. But that harmony was fragile. The Yiddish writer Tsvi Hirshkan remembered a summer night in 1905 when he saw the SR leaders—including "the bears of the Russian party," Chernov, Rubanovich, Minor, An-sky—come out of a bar. The revolution seemed to be going just as they wanted; the SDs were splitting, terror was on the rise, and the disastrous war with Japan was sapping the empire's confidence. The moon shone on Lake Geneva. Suddenly An-sky called to Minor, "Hey, Osip! Come dance the Kamarinskaya [a Russian folk dance]. Quick!" The whole group of SRs formed a line and An-sky and Minor began to dance the Kamarinskaya down the quiet Geneva street— until Chernov began to laugh.

"Why are you laughing, Victor? You don't like us?" An-sky asked.

As Hirshkan recalled, Chernov replied, "Oh, Syomka, Syomka! Where, my dear, did you find this kind of Kamarinskaya? At home in Tambov we don't dance like that. . . . This is Hasidic-style, my brother, but not Russian-style, not Tambov-style . . . not at all, my brother."[48]

In late 1904 and through the summer and fall of 1905, An-sky sensed that a divide between himself and his fellow SR leaders had been opened up not by a funny-looking Kamarinskaya but by the pogroms, which inspired him to use his organizing talents for a specifically Jewish cause that transcended party divisions. In November 1904, An-sky wrote to Zhitlowsky—then accompanying the veteran SR leader Ekaterina Breshko-Breshkovskaia (known as the "Grandmother of the Russian Revolution") on a fund-raising trip to the United States—about his efforts to unify the forces of Jewish self-defense. He had created an editorial committee including one Bundist, two Zionists, two SRs, and a representative from Vozrozhdenie (Rebirth), a journal and organization founded in early 1904 that combined a commitment to revolution in Russia with a commitment to a broad-based Jewish nationalism. Already, the committee was busy producing Yiddish pamphlets urging self-defense. Meanwhile, An-sky continued to work for the PSR. In February and March 1905, he traveled to Heidelberg, Karlsruhe, Darmstadt, Halle, Dresden, Leipzig, Freiburg, Berlin, Munich, and elsewhere in Germany, fund-raising for the SRs. With the help of the socialist leader Karl Liebknecht, he met with German socialists such as August Bebel

and Karl Kautsky to complain that money that they had directed toward Russian revolutionaries had gone exclusively to the SDs, and
again, he got a sympathetic reaction. But his distance from the SR
leadership—and especially from the Geneva group of Gots, Minor, and
Chernov—was growing. He complained that the Geneva SRs did not
follow up on the contacts he had made with German socialists. And unlike the ex-SR Blinov, the Geneva group did not share his urgency about
the pogroms: "In general, I feel bad in Geneva. I feel foreign to them [the
Geneva SRs] in part (or especially) because our Genevans can't be
troubled with the Jews. Yes, brother, until there is a 'Jewish SR Party'
things will be nasty."[49]

In the spring of 1905, Gapon organized a congress to unite the revolutionary émigrés. The émigrés were skeptical about the priest and his fantasies, but nonetheless, some fifteen people—including Chernov, Breshko-
Breshkovskaia, and An-sky from the SRs, Medem from the Bund, and
Vladimir Lenin and Alexander Bogdanov from the Bolsheviks—gathered
on April 3 at Shishko's Geneva home. The Bolsheviks walked out after
Lenin picked a fight over a procedural issue. An-sky took the conference
more seriously and spoke out for Jewish autonomy and for official Jewish representation within the party, for treating the Jews as the Poles and
Caucasian peoples were treated. Other delegates—especially the representative of the Polish Socialist Party (PPS), himself a Jew—objected that
it was not clear the Jews constituted a nation at all. An-sky retorted that
"the Jews will have to speak with your future Constituent Assembly or
Seim in the language of dynamite" and stormed out.[50]

He saw the revolutionaries' "spineless position . . . toward the Jewish
question" as proof that a Jewish SR party was needed, a party that would
be able to make its own demands. "We must not forget that at the moment of revolutionary upsurge it will be possible to get rights (once they
are legal) that would have seemed utopian to demand in ordinary times
(I mean territory, if this demand is presented). It feels like among the Jews
revolutionary and socialist elements are fermenting, waiting and thirsting
for such a party so they can join it." The party he imagined would answer
their needs better than "those Marxists out of fear," the Poale Tsion (the
Jewish Social-Democratic Party or ESDRP-PZ, Marxist Zionists). It would
unite Zionists, Bundists, SRs; newspaper editors An-sky knew would
support it. "Maybe this is the 'psychological moment'—then it will be too
late." The one thing this party would need, An-sky wrote, was "its own
'Gershuni,' a person to gather it, rally it, give it a slogan and a program."
And that person, he believed, was his oldest friend, Zhitlowsky himself.
An-sky and others could do the organizing work, if only Zhitlowsky,

drawing on his archive of polemical writings, would take the leadership. "Chaim. There are people who are ready to work, ready to give themselves entirely to the new thing (and I am among them), there is the soil, but we lack the 'Word,' without which we can only talk, groan, and devour each other." As for the platform of this new party, An-sky saw it as articulating his own concerns: the defense of Jewish interests, Jewish lives, and Jewish honor, "the attitude of Jews to terror and the necessity that Jews themselves and their own organization respond to violence toward Jews." The question of territory should not be mentioned explicitly in the platform, "but the doors should be opened wide for it." (What territory he had in mind was unclear.)[51]

An-sky was one of many radicals who saw 1905 as a moment that had to be seized before it passed and who imagined that given the right grouping of people and ideas, revolutionary success was within reach. Some thought of uniting disparate groups, others of breaking off; An-sky felt both urges, criticizing his fellow SRs while seeking ways to unite with Bundists and Zionists and appealing to the territorialism that Zhitlowsky and Vozrozhdenie had advocated since 1904. Although no specifically Jewish SR party emerged, in April 1906 Zhitlowsky would return from the United States to lead an offshoot of Vozrozhdenie, the Jewish Socialist Workers' Party (SERP, also called the ES or Seimists), whose platform was close to An-sky's ideas. SERP spoke for the creation of a semigovernmental body (or "Seim") to oversee Russian Jewish culture and education, to levy taxes, coordinate emigration, and so on.[52] The SERP joined the Bund and two other new parties that combined Jewish nationalism with socialism, the Zionist Socialist Workers' Party (SS, or SSRP) and Poale Tsion.

An-sky's 1905 letters were impatient; he wanted his reader to act now, immediately, before it was too late. He himself was ready for action, ready to move. Always peripatetic, he became more so, prepared to leave Switzerland, staying in Bern only briefly, "camping out" in Baugy, a village in the Montreux region. He went to Germany, London, Geneva. "I travel so much that I don't even have an apartment," he reported as he set off to spend a month or two writing in another Swiss village. His return address was "Bern, poste restante."[53] It seems to be around this time that his constant travel and irregular diet led him to develop the hemorrhoids that would plague him for the rest of his life.

Even as the émigrés celebrated the issuing of the October Manifesto, a wave of violence began. All across the empire, the seven days after the October Manifesto saw attacks on people and property. The Black Hundreds bands, monarchist nationalists, beat up students and workers, but their primary victims were Jews, with over 3,000 killed, many more wounded, and enormous destruction of property. Some officials in the central government may have worked to coordinate the pogroms; many local authorities permitted and even abetted them. For émigré revolutionaries, the events of October heightened the sense of crisis and potential. An-sky wrote on October 24 to Arkady Gornfeld, who worked for *Russkoe Bogatstvo:* "Congratulations! . . . Unfortunately, after such congratulations, it's impossible not to put an ellipsis. And that ellipsis promises to be as long and dark as the winding Gotthard tunnel, from which you never know where you will emerge."[54] The fifteen-kilometer Gotthard rail tunnel, built through the Swiss Alps at a cost of almost 200 human lives, had been opened in 1882 to connect Göschennen with Airolo through the Gotthard massif; the metaphor gave An-sky a way to map the ferment in Russia onto his own restless travels.

Even though it was not yet clear whether he would be amnestied, An-sky decided in November 1905 to go to Russia.

> Now every day is a year, every hour a phase. In a few weeks or months of inaction you could sleep through the situation. . . . The revolution will go on in bloody paroxysms and will pull out its rights in pieces from the bloodied innards of absolutism. . . . As Jews and as SRs we must put forth two points: broad national cultural autonomy (with representation) of the Jewish nation, and *land.* Land for the ploughman, land for the Jew.

Again, he urged Zhitlowsky to come to Russia and lead a Jewish SR party. For now, furious at Chernov, Gots, and Minor (they had neglected to tell him that someone he had spoken to at length was suspected of being an agent provocateur), An-sky broke with the "Geneva group" and made plans to leave as soon as his hemorrhoids cleared up. On December 4, he wrote from Berlin. He was not afraid to go back to Russia because he was sure that this was a time fundamentally different from Kishinev, a time of fantastic potential.

> In Russian and Jewish Russia, which I can't separate, a revolution that one can't miss is under way. The situation isn't defined yet, and for that reason I must go now, in order to help it become defined. When it is defined and frozen it will be too late . . . We are living at one of the most magnificent moments in human history.[55]

As he waited for his train to Russia, An-sky wrote his will, naming Zhitlowsky and Gurevich his executors. He knew that "this might be the last letter to you, who knows?" and signed off "yours, yours till the grave." More than ever before, he used the language of blood and apocalypse.

> The Jews, perhaps, are facing the fateful dilemma of life and death. And now there must be *one* attitude, *one* goal. Either to die as a great nation, leaving for history the trace of a falling star—or to be reborn as a great nation. There is no room now for tears and sobs. We can't weaken the national energy that has reached the boiling point. Otherwise we would face the death of worms, in attics and cellars, death like the horrors of *takh v'tat* [Hebrew numerals signifying the Chmielnitsky massacres in 1648–1649], when we were trampled on like worms.

Hoping to inspire others (and perhaps himself), he spent his time in Berlin translating the "Internationale," the 1871 French revolutionary anthem, into Yiddish.[56]

But even while he imagined that this moment would change the Jewish condition once and forever, An-sky dissociated himself from that sort of messianic thinking. Although he agreed with Zhitlowsky's territorialism, he did not believe that a new territory could be attained quickly. In order to occupy a territory and live a "normal national life," the Jews would need to go through a gradual process of education.

> Until now, the Jews have have had no national-governmental institutions, but they had a binding national idea that prevented disintegration: the Talmud, messianism. We cannot replace that steel covering with another one, with Palestinian messianism or the idea of a territory. We must educate the people for national life. And then, as in a healthy organism, the people themselves will develop a longing for a territory, for a government, not an abstract but a real longing, and they themselves will begin to look for a territory.

He was full of passion, wanting to protect the Jews of Russia, to reform them, to make them over into the kind of people he needed. More than ever before, he sounded like a person who wanted to devote his energy to Jewish causes. And as he had seen the SR cause as one that united Russians and Jews, so he imagined his new Jewish cause as appealing to Christians too. He used messianic language to urge Zhitlowsky to reconcile with his estranged wife, still in Switzerland. "I have spoken a lot with Vera. She is entirely gripped by the idea of serving the Jews. . . . Reach out your hand to her, Chaim. This is a great time, a time of all-forgiveness. If Vera is guilty before you, she will atone for it by serving the Jewish people."[57]

An-sky had edited and translated worshipful biographies of terrorists and written songs and plays to glorify their deeds. Now he was using the language of revolutionary martyrdom to describe himself and his own action of crossing the frontier into the Russian Empire. He hoped that this seemingly ordinary action, performed at an extraordinary moment, would affect history, moving Russia's Jews and peasants toward some sort of redemption, and he described Zhitlowsky's reconciliation with Vera as possessing that same potential for meaning. Simultaneously, though, he revealed a skepticism about human change that had emerged in *Pioneers, The Folk and the Book,* and "Ashmedai". There he had celebrated not the heroic aesthetic of the SRs, but the gradual process of cultural evolution. Indeed, his fiction and his persona as a fiction writer reflected his own turn away from political propaganda. A reviewer praised the collection of stories he published in 1905 as Chekhovian, meaning that he treated his characters with irony and was not an ideological writer: "A moral is foreign to this author."[58]

An-sky adopted varying attitudes toward ideology and the possibility of mobilization in the texts he wrote in various genres, and he switched from one genre to another in his descriptions of his own life. Such a shift occurred after his ecstatic December 4 letter to Zhitlowsky. Once he got to the border at Verzhbolovo, he ran into trouble. In one of the many cases when an official treated him more kindly than one would expect, a police captain told him that since the old arrest warrant issued for him was still in effect, he faced a choice: to be arrested and wait in jail for the repair of the broken telegraph connection to Petersburg, after which he could find out how his case would be decided; or to return to the German border town of Eydtkuhnen and write to the police department himself from there. He chose to go west to Königsberg, and from there wrote urgently to Gornfeld at *Russkoe Bogatstvo,* pleading with him to enlist some of his other editors—Leopold Sev at *Voskhod,* or Grigory Shreider at *Syn Otechestva*—to go to the amnesty committee and ask that permission be issued for him to enter Russia without arrest. Once the paperwork came through, he asked Gornfeld to come to Verzhbolovo and send it from there to Königsberg.[59]

When he wrote to Zhitlowsky from Königsberg in late December, his style had changed completely. While he had been waiting, an uprising in Moscow had erupted and been bloodily suppressed, and gruesome reprisals were continuing. An-sky wrote mournfully that "a whole counter-revolution" had occurred in Russia, and his friends and fellow SRs had been arrested. Cooling his heels in Königsberg, he was running out of money and patience, grumbling about not being allowed to smoke in a restaurant. The fantasy of performing a grand gesture of heroism or martyrdom was forgotten. In St. Petersburg, Gornfeld did as An-sky asked, and in three weeks, he received permission to enter the Russian

Empire without arrest. He crossed the frontier at Verzhbolovo on December 31, 1905.[60] Once he arrived, he would find a different place and a different revolution from what he had imagined abroad. Over the next few years, he would come to question his own ideas about heroism, martyrdom, and the possibility that a Jew could change Russian history.

CHAPTER SIX

The Hero of Deeds and the Hero of Words

To see . . . so many dreadful things, and not to be able to call
out . . . from that alone you could go out of your mind.
      —S. An-sky on the Bialystok pogrom, 1906

A MONTH AFTER An-sky returned to Russia, he slammed his finger in a door and shattered a bone. The doctors thought about
amputation, but finally it started to heal. The shock of return
also began to diminish. He wrote in early February 1906, "It's a terrifying time in Russia now, but one can't miss it." Not all Jewish writers
shared his enthusiasm. The historian Simon Dubnov published a two-
part article in *Voskhod* in December 1905, "Lessons of the Terrible Days,"
on the pogroms that had broken out in October. In the face of death and
destruction, Dubnov urged Jews to see that both the oppressive Tsarist
government *and* the Russian masses were their enemies. Because the Russian radical parties did nothing to counter the pogroms, Dubnov concluded that the many Jews in the movement occupied an inferior position, condemned to "slavery in the revolution." Rather than fighting for
revolution in Russia, Dubnov called for Jews to devote themselves to
Jewish culture, Jewish rights, and Jewish survival—a summons to his
own program of autonomism, or Jewish self-rule within the diaspora.
Some of An-sky's revolutionary friends had similar feelings: Vera Zhitlovskaia felt that the pogroms had made Russia foreign to her and she
had become "a person without a homeland."[1]

Dubnov remembered that An-sky admitted that when he read some
parts of "Lessons of the Terrible Days" he was moved to tears, but he still
felt compelled to dispute him publicly, especially about the chapter "Slavery in the Revolution." As an SR, An-sky "felt it was his duty to defend
the honor of the Jewish revolutionaries whom I had criticized for fighting
not under the Jewish revolutionary banner and for putting class politics

above national politics." Even though An-sky had been furious at the Geneva group of SR leaders for their "spineless" reaction to the pogroms, he rejected Dubnov's claim that he and other Jewish revolutionaries were deluded—that the Russian masses were truly the Jews' enemies, and the radicals would do nothing to protect them. He responded to Dubnov in February and March 1906 in a five-part article in *Voskhod*, "Lessons of the Terrible Centuries," where he upheld revolutionary orthodoxy: those responsible for the pogroms, he said, were not the masses but the central and local authorities. He believed Bialik had voiced the right response to the violence in "In the City of Slaughter." "Instead of the cry, 'Back-wards!' away from general human culture, away from revolution, there resounded the war cry, 'Forward! To arms!' in defense of one's life, honor, and dignity." An-sky urged the Jews of the empire to heed that call and to protect Jewish communities: "We see no other solution, no other salva-tion, than the organization of broader, more systematic, and more inten-sive self-defense, which, if it can't stand up against thugs armed with state weapons and machine-guns, at least will not permit the shedding of Jewish blood and the mockery of Jewish dignity to pass entirely unpun-ished." His vision of this punishment included terrorist acts like that of Lidia Ezerskaia, who, he said, assassinated Governor Klingenberg of Mo-gilev, saying to him, "This is for the Jewish pogrom!"[2]

An-sky described the murder of Klingenberg, like the activities of Jew-ish self-defense, as unambiguous statements telling the Russian govern-ment and the world that wrongs against Jews will be avenged and Jewish honor upheld. He understood the argument that violent resistance and reprisals by Jews only made things worse for them, but he insisted that "even if the last pogroms demonstrated the . . . uselessness of self-defense, we . . . must be guided not by the lessons of these days, but those of the previous centuries, during which Jews were systematically ravaged and ruined in the most bestial way, in spite (better: because) of the fact that they did not put up any resistance to the murderers and thieves."[3] That is, the symbolic value of Jewish acts of violent resistance, as addressed to his-tory itself, outweighed their potential misinterpretation in the present.

In personal letters in the first half of 1906, An-sky spoke even more ecstatically of change. He insisted that in spite of pogroms and political reaction, this was a time of great possibilities, and Zhitlowsky should fol-low him to Russia. Experiments in political and cultural transformation that had never before been possible were now under way. "There's *life* here, you understand, the *laboratory itself*. . . . You understand the differ-ence between work in a laboratory and scholarly strolls with students." An-sky knew these experiments could turn deadly. "Of course, this is a time of revolution, there could be bloodshed tomorrow, events could force you out onto the street and you could be killed right there." For the Jews, though, the potential of the moment outweighed the danger. "Now it's not a matter of national, territorial, or socialist 'consciousness-raising,' but of rebuilding *all* of life on a new basis. This is the beginning of a new era in the history of the Jewish people."[4]

An-sky's impatience with halfway measures and his insistence that this was a time for total change reflected the fast-moving events of that year. In the wake of the October Manifesto, neither the imperial government nor the radicals wanted compromise. Even as the manifesto promised civil liberties, the December 1905 uprising in Moscow was put down brutally, with continuing government reprisals against suspected rebels. At the end of 1905 and the beginning of 1906, punitive expeditions of troops arrested, flogged, or executed rebels and burned their homes. The government succeeded in stemming mass violence, but terror continued: over 1,400 died in 1906 and 3,000 in 1907 in attacks by right-wing, left-wing, and anarchist groups. Officials, policemen, and bystanders were killed, and revolutionaries "expropriated" funds from banks. The government issued harsh new censorship laws and shut down newspapers, but radicals continued to criticize the regime.

The central topic of debate was the new legislative body, the Duma. The government had designed electoral laws that strictly limited voting in the hope that a conservative body would be elected. The radical parties, convinced the government's plan would work, boycotted the elections. Unlike the Bolsheviks and Mensheviks, the SRs did not even issue propaganda against the Duma, seeing it as a sop thrown by an evil system. Nonetheless, the population voted broadly in the elections that continued from February through July 1906, and by March, it was clear that the liberal Kadet Party was winning a plurality and the delegates elected by the peasants were much more radical than the government had anticipated.

Typically for an SR, An-sky asserted that liberals had never brought about real change in Russia. He situated his response in the broadest historical context, insisting that for four centuries, the tsars had worked to consolidate their power, using any means available. "If at critical moments the autocracy pretended it was prepared to allow 'indulgences,' then when it was out of danger it announced openly that it would defend its unlimited rights with *all* its power and by *all* means, and it carried out its plan openly."[5] The government's actions in 1906 confirmed An-sky's accusations, but the new legislators' actions showed he was wrong about liberals' willingness to compromise. On the eve of the opening of the

Duma on May 10, 1906, the tsar promulgated laws retaining enormous powers for himself, including the right to veto legislation and disband the Duma. The first Duma, dominated by liberals who saw the October Manifesto as only the first step toward a constitutional democracy that would limit the monarchy, demanded that land be redistributed to the peasants and refused to condemn terrorism. There was no common ground between the Duma and the autocracy, and the infuriated Tsar Nicholas II, who believed in the divine right of kings, dissolved it after only seventy-three days and called for new elections the next year.

In spite of the Duma's failures, the October Manifesto had succeeded in creating the new sense that the population could make political statements, and the authorities had to listen. An-sky had responded to Dubnov by affirming the belief that Jews could speak loudly through self-defense and terror. As he wrote and thought about how that might happen, Jewish causes took up more of his energy than they ever had before. He had worked in *Kampf un kempfer* to bring Jews to the SR cause, and he had described the recent Jewish past in *Pioneers,* but now he was thinking about the Jews of the present and their place in the revolutionary movements. As he spent time with the Jews he met in Russia after his return, he found himself moving away from his belief in terror; his increasing interest in Jewish culture and nonviolent politics would go hand in hand.

At noon on June 1, 1906, a pogrom began in Bialystok. As a journalist for *Der fraynd* and *Voskhod,* An-sky took the train from Petersburg on the evening of June 2, and when he arrived in Bialystok, shots were still sounding and the blood on the streets was still wet. As his train approached the city, he learned that after the murder of Police Chief Drukachev by a terrorist who was probably Jewish, the wreath brought by a Jewish delegation was angrily rejected by Officer Sheremetov, who explicitly threatened a pogrom. With the approval of the regional authorities in Grodno (who refused the Jews' request that he be replaced), Sheremetov then encouraged soldiers and citizens to kill Jews and destroy their property. The signal for the beginning of the pogrom was a staged act of terror. During a church procession, shots were heard and a bomb was thrown. "Many people saw how the policemen ran around and called out that the bombs were thrown by Jews. Immediately they heard whistles and calls, 'Beat the Jews!'" The revolutionaries of Bialystok told An-sky that while they supported terrorism in principle, they had not thrown that bomb, because they knew that "such an act would provoke the pogrom that the police wanted." A peasant eventually confessed that he had been paid to fire the shots during the procession.[6]

The pogrom raged for three days and resulted in 82 Jewish deaths, 700 injuries, and the devastation of Jewish stores. In the next weeks, rumors were rife of more pogroms in the area and some did break out (bringing the death toll to an estimated 200), although Prime Minister Pyotr Stolypin had telegraphed all the empire's governors, instructing them to prevent pogroms. Reports on the pogrom filled the press in the Russian Empire and around the world. Reporting on events day by day as they developed, newspapers for the first time illustrated accounts of the violence with solemn photographs of corpses.[7]

An-sky's Yiddish articles on Bialystok, like the photographs *Der fraynd* used to illustrate them, emphasized mourning and martyrdom. His Russian articles also questioned whether the authorities would ever respond to Jewish words. The Duma sent a delegation to investigate the Bialystok pogrom and then devoted several outraged sessions to it, and on June 8, Stolypin himself assured the delegates that the central government opposed pogroms in principle (the Duma members were not convinced). An-sky sat in the legislative hall and thought that Stolypin, who reacted impassively to even the most gruesome details of the violence, looked like a figure from a wax museum. Stolypin's silence contrasted with the pogrom survivors' need to speak of the crimes they had experienced. In Bialystok, An-sky felt as though a dam had burst, as pogrom survivors threw themselves on the journalists and begged them to listen. When he saw "that feverish thirst to have one's say," then he understood that of everything they had survived, "almost the most horrible was *silence.* To see . . . so many dreadful things, and not to be able to call out . . . to call out to a person, to a brother, to call out so that people could hear, so that everyone would know, the whole city, the whole country, the whole world—from that alone you could go out of your mind."[8] The survivors' urge to tell "the whole world" of their suffering evoked the actual transnational reach of the press where An-sky wrote, and he did his best to convey the news of their torments broadly.

As he walked through Bialystok, An-sky saw that Christians, in order to keep the *pogromshchik*s away, had drawn crosses on their doors and put icons in their windows, and he mused on the tragic irony: "It seemed that an unknown demon had summoned these visages of Christian saints to these windows, forcing them to witness the evil deeds and crimes committed on the street for two days by Christians, adherents to this religion, the religion of 'love and mercy.' . . . Could there be any darker blasphemy, any crueler mockery of these holy things?" Two weeks after Stolypin's appearance, a Duma committee submitted a report concluding that the authorities had planned the Bialystok pogrom and the police had done their best to carry it out. The Duma called for the perpetrators to be brought to justice, which for the most part did not happen. A month after the pogrom, An-sky wrote about incidents in which Bialystok Christians who had saved Jews made public statements that they had *not* done so—demonstrating that the government was promoting a new culture, with its own terrible set of ethics.[9]

An-sky described Bialystok as a place where language and communication had broken down. Sheremetov's refusal of the Jewish delegation's wreath was only the first case of a gesture that could not communicate as it was meant to; the survivors' unquenchable need to speak, Stolypin's unbreachable silence, the icons that revealed only their owners' false Christianity, all showed that the peoples of the Russian Empire no longer shared a code of meaning—if, indeed, they had ever done so. Even those gestures of violence that An-sky had insisted, in "Lessons of the Terrible Centuries," could restore Jewish honor had become ineffective. Although An-sky did not disavow terrorism in June 1906, when he unmasked the provocateurs in Bialystok, he revealed a new anxiety about the possibility of misinterpreting acts of violent resistance. He began his articles with the murder of the police chief Drukachev, most likely committed by anarchists, who had a stronghold in Bialystok and were known for killing policemen. Drukachev had in fact protected the Jews, and when he was assassinated, the Jews had sought to express their regrets, and many were angry at the anarchists.[10] However, the murder had given the regional authorities the motive and the means to engineer the pogrom. By beginning with Drukachev's death, An-sky's first Bialystok article took a step back from the arguments in favor of terrorism that he had once endorsed; it suggested that terrorism may in fact result not in justice but in a confusing cycle of violence. In the wake of Bialystok, he was unsure that words *or* violent deeds could transmit clear messages.

In November 1905, in the immediate aftermath of the October Manifesto and the pogroms, An-sky had started a novella about the revolutionary movement, calling it "In the Whirlpool." He was working on it when he went to Bialystok, and he used the novella to express some of what he saw there: some revolutionaries' intoxication with power and violence; the urge for revenge and for heroic action; the divisions among Jewish revolutionaries; the authorities' angry, disproportionate responses; and the sense of violence spinning out of control. It was hard to write about current events; in September 1906, he complained that he didn't know the current situation well enough and felt that he was "dragging each line out of the tar." Events were happening too fast for him to make

sense of them, and he was afraid that the story would end up "all plati-
tudes, one scene of life after another, with no depth, no essential logical
connection. One shouldn't write novellas in a country where the newspapers are allowed to write about shootings and pogroms." He finally completed it in October 1906 and published it in early 1907 in Russian in a
Jewish-themed miscellany, *New Breezes,* and in Yiddish installments in
Der fraynd. Like his Bundist songs, the titles drew on the metaphor of the
revolutionary masses as bodies of water: the Russian title was *On a New
Course,* literally referring to a stream; and the Yiddish was *With the
Flow: A Tale from the Jewish Revolutionary Movement.*[11]

The story is set in the town of N., apparently Vitebsk, where An-sky
was living. As it begins, we learn that Stepan Ryzhy, an unpopular policeman, has just been murdered, and for the rest of the story, everyone tries
to figure out who killed him and what the consequences will be. Both the
Jews on the street and the authorities suspect an SR is guilty. The police
search the apartments of revolutionaries during the night after the murder, find a cache of weapons and bombs, and arrest eight SRs, but it turns
out that the killer is the Bundist Gershon. Throughout the novella, everyone is waiting for the other shoe to drop, fearing that—as An-sky reported in Bialystok—the murder of a policeman would lead to a pogrom.
In the final pages, a demonstration erupts as a protest against the closing
down of the "birzhe," the park where workers gather for discussion, modeled on the park in Vitebsk where An-sky took walks as he struggled to
write. Singing An-sky's own Bundist anthem, young workers, mostly Jews,
mass. The scene ends ominously as the workers see Cossacks advancing
on them, and in the final lines, the sound of shots in the center of town
becomes audible in the outskirts, suggesting that a pogrom has started.[12]

An-sky used the novella to contrast various attitudes toward Jewish
self-defense and Jewish violence. When the young revolutionary Matvey
talks to his dying father, Eliokum the *sofer* (Torah scribe), he voices the
idea that self-defense can create heroic meaning. The father tells his son
of the Jewish self-defense fighters of Gomel, who gave their lives to defend their fellow Jews and the holy Torah. He calls them *kdoishim* (translated in a footnote as "holy ones, who died for a holy cause") and com-
pares their lives to his own. "I carried out all the commandments precisely
and strictly—and God did not grant me the great deed of hallowing His
name . . . in defense of the tablets of His law, which I wrote out my entire
life . . . He did not grant it to me! . . . And He granted it to them . . . I
wrote my entire life, but I inscribed nothing . . . in the great book. And
they . . . in one moment . . . inscribed. . . ."[13] Using the language of Jewish martyrology, Eliokum presents the deeds of the self-defense fighters as

effective acts of communication. Not only are their actions transparent to Eliokum, but they even impress God, whose judgment is represented in Jewish terms as a book where good and evil deeds are recorded.

When An-sky reveals that the policeman's murderer was Gershon, it becomes less clear that violent acts can have meaning. Gershon explains that his father was wounded and his sister was killed when policemen attacked a workers' demonstration. When he sat by her body, he felt she was saying, "Revenge." The next morning he took her gun and began to carry it around and shoot policemen whenever he could. Gershon tells another Bundist, Basya, "I have truly become foreign to myself. . . . Yesterday, I had just gone out and that policeman came toward me, and everything stirred again in my soul . . . Probably that's how it will always be, as long as the image of my sister and my father is before my eyes, until they take me and hang me."[14] He sounds like an automaton with no power over his own actions. Gershon recalls Hirsh Lekert, the young Jew who had shot at the Vilna governor-general in 1902: both are Bundist terrorists, inspired by revenge, whose actions provoke sympathy among other Bundists even though they know they should condemn them on ideological grounds. Their first names sound similar, since Hirsh could be pronounced Girsh. But compared to Lekert, An-sky's Gershon is less heroic. Lekert was celebrated for his willingness to risk his life, the logic of his choice of target (the official who had acted unjustly), and his martyrdom. That Lekert barely wounded his target lent poignancy to his image. An-sky's Gershon creates a more muddled message. Instead of assassinating a notorious man and publicly accepting blame, he shoots all the policemen he sees, without undergoing the public martyrdom that made Lekert's name a byword. While Lekert's deed said loudly that the Jewish workers' honor would be avenged, Gershon's deed is only explained in private to his Bundist colleagues, who are unimpressed.

An-sky knew that some Jews were drawn to violence by their own demons. The Bundist Basya runs into an old friend, Sender, a former Bundist and a former SR, who admits that as a Jew, he has always envied Russians for their strength and "healthy nature." Only once in his life has Sender felt strong and heroic as a Russian—when he was getting ready to throw a bomb. "I held a small box in my hand and I knew that I was the sovereign master of an enormous force, that one move of my hand would be enough to create death and destruction all around! And it seemed to me that I myself was made of steel and dynamite, and my soul felt larger and more peaceful than ever before! It was as though something that had been taken away from me had been returned." Basya is repelled, and so, presumably, was An-sky. Sender's bomb has little to do with violent

resistance as just punishment and defense of human dignity. In this novella, An-sky hinted that positions that were easy for him to endorse at
the beginning of 1906 in his debate with Dubnov seemed by the fall more
complicated and less tenable.[15] The novella shows him reevaluating his
attitude toward the place of Jews in the revolution and toward the ability
of violent acts to communicate clearly. As was so often the case for An-
sky, even while he insisted in his journalistic writing that propaganda
could communicate clear messages, in his fiction he stepped back from
that certainty, demonstrating all the ways in which people could fail to
hear each other.

Even while he questioned his faith in terror, An-sky could not imagine
not responding to what he saw as the government's crimes. "Right away,
every healthy person's whole soul should blaze up with the desire for revenge, with the passionate urge to find some kind of answer for yesterday's events, to find salvation from the repetition of these horrors." As he
participated in SR debates, he began—together with his party—to articulate a new tactic of resistance. In February 1907, as *On a New Course*
was coming out, An-sky attended an SR congress in the Finnish town of
Tamerfors, outside St. Petersburg. For the SRs, the political situation was
troubling. They had seen their cynicism about reform justified when the
tsar ordered the first Duma dissolved in July 1906, but they needed to
take a position on the elections for the second Duma and had called
an "extraordinary party council." An-sky remembered the failure of the
SRs' faith in imminent revolution. "Every one of the comrades brought a
gloomy tale of a broken organization, the drying up of revolutionary
energy among the masses, the loss of influence, demoralization, and everyone had the premonition of even darker defeats in the near future."
They nonetheless maintained an optimistic front, discussing individual
and mass terror, a general strike, speaking in the same tone as in 1904
and 1905. "No one could determine to look the sad truth boldly in the
eyes and say straight out what we all knew already: that the broken and
powerless party had lost its strength and had no more force to decree
mass terror, or even less a general strike."[16] On the second or third day of
the congress, Chernov introduced a new speaker, "Comrade Kapustin."
The gathered radicals recognized him as Grigory Gershuni, poet, revolutionary theorist, and terrorist mastermind, who had just escaped from
jail hidden in a barrel of cabbage (ergo the pseudonym, from *kapusta*,
cabbage).

A decade later, An-sky recalled the effect of Gershuni's words on the
crowd. He admitted that the revolution was lost for now, but he spoke

without despair, in words "infused with passionate faith in the ultimate victory of the revolution." Now, he insisted, it was time for the SRs to work harder than ever. "He urged his comrades not to depart from real life, not to be distracted by revolutionary phrase-mongering, and to reflect seriously on the mistakes of the past, so as not to repeat them in the future." As he spoke, the revolutionaries' mood shifted. "Under the charm of his simple and calm speech . . . everyone began to feel that from now on there was no room for self-deception or for clichéd slogans, and that it was time to turn to our difficult, critical, creative revolutionary work." Even though most SRs were skeptical that a parliament could resolve the country's problems, Gershuni asserted that the party needed to put forward candidates for the Duma and cooperate with other reformist parties in order to further their party's revolutionary goals. Although Gershuni was known as a terrorist, he argued at Tamerfors that as long as the populace hoped that the Duma could bring positive change, the PSR needed to step away from its historic support for terrorism and move toward political work instead.[17]

Gershuni used his oratorical skills to describe nonviolent work in the inspirational terms often associated with terrorism. When defending the turn to politics, Gershuni drew on the emphatic terms of religious martyrdom, saying he was "throwing himself into the fire" of debate. He highlighted the novelty of his approach, his "new word" that contrasted with "the realm of cliché and revolutionary amens." Refraining from terror, he insisted, was in itself a heroic and difficult act: "Let our hearts be hard as steel and cold as stone, and in solving problems we will let them be guided only by the voice of reason. There should be no room for the feeling of revenge."[18] An-sky portrayed Gershuni as a revolutionary who fights with words instead of guns and bombs, a hero whose words can change reality. The escaped terrorist was a charismatic leader, a poet-prophet who worked magic with "the charm of his speech."

As Gershuni urged, the SRs (like the SDs) participated in the second Duma and gained twenty seats in what turned out to be a more polarized body than before, with a very conservative right wing and an extremely radical left wing. Like its predecessor, the Duma that convened in February 1907 failed to find common ground with the tsar, and its brief tenure was marked by fights about terrorism, the honor of the army, and the idea of giving land to the peasants. An-sky watched the sessions, listened to the rumors in the halls, and noted sadly in April 1907 that the Duma was "losing life" more and more. But even as he sensed that this second Duma would soon be dissolved in its turn, he admired the spectacle of delegates stating their opinions.

The peasant deputies too speak with feverish speed, speak from the tribune, speak in the halls, speak to anyone who asks them a question, and even to those who don't.

"Why these conversations?" I heard a journalist ask the peasant deputy N. I. Pianykh, a member of the SR group. "Why these conversations? You didn't come here for conversation, but for business. You should do something, instead of talking."

"Don't worry," Pianykh answered him. "Our words are not in vain. They are needed. They will fly. They will fly far. Let them fly. They'll land where they are needed; he who needs to will hear them."

Although Pianykh was an uneducated peasant from the backwoods, he was able to deliver his message: that peasants need land, and if they are not given it, they will take it, their words "flying" on the wings that journalists such as An-sky could give them. One day, An-sky was leaving the building with other journalists and heard one of them wonder if they were seeing it for the last time. Another answered, "Sometimes it seems that this whole Duma, with its deputies and debates, its guards and ceiling, is just a mirage, nothing more."[19] The second Duma continued to meet until the tsar dissolved it in June 1907, but when An-sky described it as a mirage, he suggested that the notion that in Russia the words of people like Pianykh would be heard may have been the stuff of fantasy. At the same time, he cherished the dream of the Duma, of representative democracy, and of words that could fly where they were needed and make things happen.

When Gershuni urged the SRs at Tamerfors to embrace politics over terrorism, he set a tone that An-sky would maintain in his articles on the second Duma, though neither Gershuni nor An-sky had rejected terror definitively. Overall, the Russian public that had cheered at the high-profile assassinations of 1904 and 1905 began to turn away from terror in 1907. As left-wing radicals had assassinated Sipiagin and Grand Duke Sergei, so right-wing radicals assassinated the prominent Jewish newspaper editor G. G. Iollos, who had been a Kadet delegate to the first Duma. Nonetheless, the second Duma, like the first one, did not condemn terror as a whole. The culture of revolutionary revenge was deeply rooted in the intelligentsia. Even Dubnov, who wanted Jews to distance themselves from the Russian revolutionary cause, affirmed the communicative code of the assassinations: "I learned from the newspapers that in Petersburg a terrorist's bullet had killed Pavlov, the prosecutor of the military field trials. This was the revolutionary bullet's answer to the government's rope, 'Stolypin's necktie' tied around the necks of the revolutionaries who were hanged." Dubnov even found comprehensible the era's most notorious terrorist act, the bombing of the prime minister's dacha on Aptekarsky Island during reception hours on August 12, 1906, when thirty-two people were killed and twenty-two injured but Stolypin himself was unhurt. "The August explosion of Stolypin's dacha was an answer to the July 'explosion' of the Duma, caused by that fatal minister."[20]

As he had in Switzerland, An-sky continued to socialize with terrorists. His connections meant he sometimes knew in advance about acts of terror, including the Aptekarsky Island attack and the expropriation of Fonarny Avenue on October 14, 1906, when several terrorists from a group commanded by M. Sokolov (known as "the Bear") attacked a carriage transporting money from the St. Petersburg harbor customs office to the bank and stole over 600,000 rubles.[21] By the time they committed these crimes, Sokolov and his associates were Maximalists who had broken away from the SRs to conduct a terrorist campaign on their own. (Samuil Gurevich recalled that An-sky's friends at *Der fraynd* asked him to go to the Bear to ask for a financial grant from the expropriated money.)

But even if he did not condemn terror, An-sky's impression of its communicative value was shifting in 1906 and 1907.[22] Perhaps his views began to change when he went to Bialystok and faced the failures of terrorism. Until the end of 1905 he had been living in Europe and discussing revolutionary tactics without having to see their results on the ground. Thus while the debate with Dubnov reflected the ideology he developed in Europe, in the Bialystok articles, he confronted its contradictions and impracticality. The presentation of acts of terror in *On a New Course* as unstable acts of communication, and especially the portrait of the self-obsessed ex-SR Sender, reflect a growing skepticism about the value of violence as a response to violence in the Tsarist empire.

On the night of January 4, 1907, policemen came to An-sky's apartment in Vitebsk to arrest him. The newspapers speculated that this was "a pre-election maneuver by an administration that was nervous about An-sky's authority and influence among the Jewish population." Once there, the police systematically catalogued all the papers they found in his room, listing 42 letters, manuscripts, and periodicals, including some that looked seditious: a sixty-six-page manuscript titled "The Folk and Monarchism" and one called "In the Duma." Because they had found "a significant number of manuscripts of criminal content, brochures, and conspiratorial correspondence," the Vitebsk prosecutor's office decided on February 6 to put the writer on trial. Articles 128 and 129 of the criminal code forbade insulting the tsar and inciting the population to rebellion, orally or by means of text or image, and according to article 132, paragraph 1, those who created seditious texts or images with the intent of distributing them, even if they were never actually distributed, should be punished with not more than three years of imprisonment.[23]

An-sky spent only three weeks in the Vitebsk jail before he was released on a 500-ruble bail (provided by Samuil's brother Mikhail Gurevich). He wrote about his stay as an immersion in ethnographic fieldwork among prisoners and jailers. By trial and error, he figured out how to communicate with one of his jailers, although they were not supposed to speak with the political prisoners. While taking his exercise, he overheard a murderer claiming that there is no need to fear that your victim's ghost will come after you, and explaining his killing technique (act quickly, before your victim can react).[24] The folk belief and the violence that interested An-sky were on display in jail as outside, and the fly-on-the-wall techniques that he had perfected when studying peasants in the Donets Basin still worked.

In 1907, free on bail and awaiting trial, An-sky conducted his life as before, traveling to Tamerfors for the SR congress and publishing articles critical of the government. *A Man of the 1870s,* a revolutionary one-act play that he had written in Switzerland and published in Russia in 1906, was "arrested" and forbidden. In March 1908, when his trial was scheduled, his lawyer suggested he postpone it by writing that he had to go abroad for a month for an operation, and he did so, attaching a letter from a doctor testifying that he needed an operation for his hemorrhoids (and that he also suffered from an inflamed appendix). Although he did not, apparently, go abroad, the trial was postponed until June 9. At that point, to his own surprise and that of his Petersburg lawyer, he was cleared of the charges.[25]

He gleefully sent Zhitlowsky a newspaper article explaining how he had got off. *Severozapadnyi Golos* (Northwest Voice), a newspaper where he had connections, included the trial in its "Legal Chronicle" section and described An-sky's potentially illegal manuscripts in detail. "The Folk and Monarchism" offered "a tendentious historical survey of the governing of Russian rulers" where "the writer tries to show that the Russian peasantry does not adhere to absolutist monarchism and feels no loyalty to the tsars, and Russian society, which believes the opposite, is mistaken." An-sky argued that "due to the fruitless anticipation of a manifesto giving all the land to the peasants, a legend arose that the tsar is actually limited in his power by the aristocrats (the Senate) and simply does not know what is happening in his kingdom. 'Alongside the ignorant peasant masses, an intelligentsia formed that has already revealed itself and accepted the Socialist Revolutionary teachings with an open soul, warmly, passionately.'" The illegal manuscript, "In the Duma," ended with the line,

> Just one or two more of this sort of meetings, this sort of answers to questions, and the Kadets themselves, the most moderate of the moderates, will grasp that you can't speak in the language of parliamentary debates with these blind-from-birth idiots who want to hoodwink the revolution with bureaucratic gobbledygook. The only language that will be understood by our ministers and make them take notice is the language of a rebellious people, the language of the revolution itself.[26]

Based on these manuscripts, An-sky was accused of the intent to distribute writings fostering scorn for the ruler and inciting the population to bring down the government. Particularly suspicious was his language in "The Folk and Monarchism," where he called the tsar a "plunderer who devastates the peasantry and sucks its blood through the draft, crushing bureaucratic arbitrariness, theft, and violence." An-sky answered that he was not guilty of the charges because he did not intend to publish either manuscript: he had written "The Folk and Monarchism" as a talk for a student group in Bern, considered publishing it, and changed his mind; he wrote "In the Duma" after the Duma meeting of July 3, 1906, but decided not to publish it and put it away in his desk. Witnesses were called to testify that even though the manuscripts looked like clean copies meant for publication, they were actually rough drafts, albeit written, as was An-sky's habit, neatly and on only one side of the page. The court determined that even though the manuscripts' content was illegal, An-sky genuinely had not meant to publish them and thus was innocent.[27]

If An-sky did intend to foment scorn for the tsar and to incite the population to bring down the government—and that was undoubtedly just what he intended—then his arrest and trial helped him move toward that goal. He had tried to publish versions of "The Folk and Monarchism" since 1905.[28] With such a dangerous subject, he could only hope for his work to be published abroad and then smuggled back into the Russian Empire. But once this manuscript became the subject of a trial, it was legal for a newspaper to publicize its contents and thereby give An-sky's seditious ideas broad circulation. When he wrote of Gershuni's advice that the SRs turn away from terrorism and participate in the Duma, An-sky had presented the notion of stating one's opinion in a legal context as potentially heroic. With his own trial and the ensuing newspaper coverage, he found himself performing that heroic role, using words to create change—but he was still following the example of the Russian revolutionaries who had committed violent acts precisely in the hope of producing legal proceedings that would bring maximum publicity to their opinions.

As he anticipated his trial, An-sky turned away from revolutionary work. Although he never left the SR party or renounced his allegiance to it, he, like many of his comrades, stopped engaging in SR activity at some point in 1907. The second Duma was dissolved in June 1907 and the electoral laws revised to limit the representation of potentially rebellious groups, and the population reacted with mingled despair and indifference to Stolypin's "coup d'état." The SRs boycotted the third Duma elections. Terror and crime rose during the summer, then waned in the fall. With the autocracy back in control, many discouraged radicals left the Russian Empire. Political work was futile or dangerous, but Yiddish periodical and book publishing was developing rapidly in Warsaw, Vilna, and Kiev, and increasingly, Yiddish writers were translated into Russian. Contemporary, secular Jewish culture was becoming more visible to the Russian intelligentsia, and An-sky took note.[29]

The 1905–1907 period saw the rise of an array of Jewish parties: Zionist, socialist, and liberal. An-sky was close to many of the leaders: Zhitlowsky, now a leader of the SERP; the librarian and historian Alexander Braudo, from the Jewish National Party (ENP); the prominent liberal lawyers Maxim Vinaver and Genrikh Sliozberg from the Jewish National Group (ENG); and Dubnov, whose ideas of Jewish cultural and governmental autonomism were propagated by the Folkspartey (or Jewish National Party). An-sky wrote for Russian- and Yiddish-language Jewish publications of various political affiliations, but he did not join any of the Jewish parties. Like other radicals, he turned to "organic work," meaning community service and cultural activities. For even while the authorities had reneged on the promise of a freely elected parliament, the new freedoms of speech and assembly remained in force, and people had plunged into talk. Dubnov's daughter Sofia recalled that "the discordance was deafening. It was as if a dam had broken and verbosity engulfed the whole Petersburg intelligentsia. Political meetings were held in the huge assembly hall of the Technological Institute, gatherings were in full swing at the university, papers were read at meetings of the Philosophical-Religious Society, and in literary salons and humble dining rooms of the intelligentsia over tea, people stay up till almost dawn, resolving universal questions."[30]

In March 1907, An-sky told Zhitlowsky that he was sympathetic to the program of the SERP, but could not bring himself to join it, because he felt purely political work was a waste of energy, too much focused on "the distant problems of the future." Jewish party politics left him cold. "All these hundreds and thousands of 'victories' of one group over another, all those drum beats and joyful cries, make me feel exhausting sadness, not joy. Sometimes you get tired even of victories." He was drawn, instead, to the notion of serving the Jews by using his editorial skills. "In my soul I long for some kind of real deed, maybe a small one, but a general one in the service of my people. So I organized a publication, 'Evreiskaia Starina' [The Jewish Past]. We have the means to support it and a group of people to lead it."[31] He had always described himself as motivated by the desire to serve "the people." He did not explain what had shifted his attention from the Russian narod to the Jews, but spoke of his emotions, his joy and sadness, and the longing of his soul. When he worked on *Evreiskaia Starina*, it appears, he was reaching for the same happiness and sense of self-worth that he had pursued when he used his reading and writing skills to help the peasants.

By 1909, An-sky had joined three new Jewish cultural organizations that gave him the opportunity to use the verbal talents he had honed in his SR work: the Jewish Historical-Ethnographic Society, a Petersburg scholarly group; the Jewish Literary Society, a national coalition of literary and discussion societies that organized speeches in the provinces; and the Jewish Folk Music Society. He eventually also joined Dubnov's Folkspartey and traveled around giving speeches for it. He edited and published a stream of articles in Russian and Yiddish in the new Jewish journals in Petersburg.[32] He kept sending fiction and some nonfiction to *Der fraynd*, and he began to write for Zhitlowsky's New York journal, *Dos naye lebn* (New Life).

He had once decribed folk songs as a way for the peasants in his mother's tavern to find healing and peace. Now, as he recovered from the trauma of the failed revolution, he sought help from the same source. Increasingly, his articles focused on Jewish ethnography and folklore, and much of his fiction and poetry of this period was folkloric stylizations. He continued to take on large editorial projects, directed at a broad Russian audience, for money—his book *What Is Anarchism?* and a series of "almanacs," compilations of edifying material cheaply produced for new readers by the liberal publishing house Razum (Reason)—but more than ever, he devoted his energy to research and writing on Jewish folklore. That seemed possible in late 1907, when Samuil Shryro, a Jew who had gotten rich on oil, offered him a "grant" of 100 rubles a month. With six months' income in hand, he gathered songs, sayings, and stories from people he met in Vitebsk and read Hebrew and Yiddish collections of

Hasidic stories, Saul Ginzburg and Peysakh Marek's 1901 *Jewish Folk Songs in Russia* and then Ignats Bernshtein's 1908 *Jewish Sayings and Proverbs*. The money from Shryro dried up by April 1908, but An-sky continued to write about the material he had gathered, planning an ambitious article that synthesized his views on biblical and Talmudic folklore as well as his largely Hasidic Vitebsk material.[33]

Other Jewish intellectuals had already started gathering folklore, such as Ginzburg and Marek, Peretz, and Bernshtein (whose proverbs were first published in the 1880s). Dubnov and Peretz sang Yiddish folk songs when they gathered in the evenings, and as he began to associate with them, An-sky must have remembered the Jewish student gatherings in Bern.[34] Intellectuals saw song as a way to connect with the workers, and An-sky, who so valued human contact, may have felt that lure. But when he devoted himself to Jewish literature and ethnography, he was not turning away from his older revolutionary convictions or his loyalty to Russian intelligentsia values; this was not a conversion or a rejection of his old self. Rather, An-sky was motivated, as he had always been, by the need to find soil where he could feel that he was accomplishing something and improving people's lives. The evidence for his continuing attachment to his revolutionary ideals lies in his treatment of Jewish folklore. As he retold Jewish folktales, he transformed them into revolutionary propaganda, using them to articulate his and his party's positions on the value of the word, as opposed to the violent deed.

"Jewish Folk Art," a long article that he published in the first issue of *Perezhitoe* (January 1909), suggests that when he analyzed folklore, An-sky was also trying to explain the dramatic shift in his own activities. By linking violence with other nations and verbal art with the Jews, and arguing that the latter inevitably triumphs over the former, he hinted that his own turn from SR propaganda to Jewish writing and speaking was primarily the choice of a more effective means to continue his struggle for justice. He related dozens of Jewish folktales and argued that they showed that the Jewish imagination celebrates not people who have mastered "physical" or "material" power, but those who possess "spiritual" strength and conquer by means of "the word or the spirit." Jewish folklore empowers humans by creating "man in the image and likeness of God, having constructed a bridge between them in the form of the Torah." After retelling a famous Talmudic episode in which a group of rabbis insist that they, rather than God, can define justice on earth (Baba Metsia 59B), An-sky moved to more recent narratives about Hasidic rabbis. "Like the Talmudic sages, the heroes of modern legends do not feel obligated to obey the heavenly voice, and they deal with God simply, as an equal."[35]

He reworked one legend to show that human justice takes precedence over divine will. The theme of legal battles with God appears often in Hasidic lore. The best-known story of a rabbi who puts God on trial is associated with Levi Yitzkhak of Berdichev, a late-eighteenth-century Hasidic leader known for his compassion. He is believed to have composed a poem called "The kaddish of rebbe Levi Yitzkhak" (the *kaddish* is a central Jewish prayer praising God), or "God on Trial," in which he rebukes God for permitting an excess of Jewish suffering. Levi Yitzkhak summons God to a trial because He has demanded too much of the Jews. An-sky undoubtedly knew this text, but he based his tale of God on trial instead on a less well-known legend about Elimelekh of Lyzhansk, an eighteenth-century founder of Hasidism in Galicia, recently published in Warsaw.[36] In this legend, a king issues an evil decree; a poor man comes to rebbe Elimelekh and argues that the situation is not fair; rebbe Elimelekh encourages the man to voice his complaint and then decides to put God on trial; during the trial, Elimelekh and other rabbis determine that God is in the wrong; and after they make their decision, the decree is lifted.

By careful editing, An-sky turned this pious tale of a wonder-working rebbe into a subversive parable. The first lines of An-sky's legend make this evident. Whereas the original legend was set in Galicia, An-sky set it in Romania. Readers of the Russian-Jewish press knew that articles about anti-Semitism or anti-Jewish legislation in Romania often veiled controversial opinions about those very problems in the Russian Empire, and thus An-sky signaled that the story could be read as a commentary on the situation in Russia. The original editor, presumably with pious Hasidic readers in mind, had focused the narrative on the figure of the rebbe. In his legend, the person who brings the complaint to Elimelekh was introduced as "one honest man who feared the Lord."[37] An-sky named this character Faivel and had him, rather than Elimelekh, locate the crucial precedent that demonstrates that God is in the wrong. The rebbe (now joined by several other rebbes) reaches his conclusion after lengthy debates; the verdict must be spoken and then written before it can take effect. With this new ending, An-sky depicted the source of power not as the Hasidic rebbe himself and his privileged relationship with God, but as the words he and others speak and write. The rebbe commands this power of the word, but it can be used by another. Thus when Elimelekh in An-sky's version tells Faivel, "I give you the power of the word," the rebbe gives him access to the source of his own strength. With his adaptation of the story, An-sky created a hero who changes the world with words, and Faivel's example was meant to inspire readers to change the world as well.

An-sky's obsessive revisions of the legend of God on trial suggest that this legend had personal and political significance for him. In the first few months of 1909, he produced four versions of the tale, in Russian prose and verse and in Yiddish prose and verse. More than ever before, he translated his own work cannily, calibrating each version to appeal to a slightly different audience. He advertised the story as just one example of the kind of folkloric stylization he could produce. He admitted cheerfully that when he translated his own works from one language to another, he saw no reason to be strictly faithful. (Thus when he started translating "Ashmedai" into Russian, he found himself creating a fundamentally new text. "I translated from Yiddish only chapters one and two, and I wrote completely new versions of the remaining five chapters. I think I succeeded with the meter no worse than I did in Yiddish, and as for the content, I gave it a completely different character: a serious, naïve, religious poema.")[38]

In all his versions of the tale of God on trial, he offered his vision of Jewish verbal rebellion to readers of Russian and Yiddish, in the Russian Empire and the United States, now making it evident that he was publishing a story of his own invention, now drawing attention away from his own artifice and presenting it as genuine folklore. He conveyed the message that interested him most in the aftermath of the 1905 revolution, the message he took away from Gershuni's speech in Tamerfors and that he experienced with the newspaper reporting of his own trial in 1908: that the word could fight injustice. The rabbis who put God on trial could represent the Russian liberals and radicals who longed to put the regime, or perhaps Tsar Nicholas II himself, on trial. In 1912, a police agent heard An-sky read the Russian verse version of his tale aloud, and gave a confused summary: "It describes a protest of workers against the bourgeoisie, and it has sacrilegious places. For instance, the workers drag God to trial."[39] While the agent may not have been listening carefully, he was undoubtedly right in grasping that it hardly mattered whether the heroes of the story were workers or rabbis: they were protesting effectively, and the author wanted his audience to follow their example.

An-sky felt that the causes of Jewish resistance to oppression and Jewish cultural rebirth were linked. Like many other Russian-Jewish intellectuals, An-sky was certain that traditional Judaism would soon vanish, as urbanization, assimilation, and emigration threatened old forms of shtetl life and community. In the 1880s, An-sky had observed the disappearance of old folkways among the Russian peasants and felt regret; now, he recognized the same loss among the Jews. He yearned to rescue and rebuild Jewish life in a maximally inclusive way, appealing to both traditional and modern Jews, but he knew this task would be hard. "We have no significant cultural institutions," he had written in "Jewish Folk Art," "and our literature in all three languages (Yiddish, Hebrew, and Russian) has no underlying material soil." That he spoke in terms of the search for soil was a clue that An-sky was preparing to shift his own activity to a new realm.

In 1888, An-sky had told Zhitlowsky that if only there were soil for his activity in Jewish life, he would work on behalf of Jews rather than Russians. Finally, he could work to prepare that soil. An-sky's shift to a new mission was—like his gradual turn to writing in Yiddish in Europe—a pragmatic response to new circumstances by an artist who had grown adept at finding new audiences in a changing world. Now that SR work on behalf of the Russian narod had become impossible, he could embrace a new cause. Having begun to advocate for and participate in a new Jewish culture, An-sky insisted that it should be based on what had always compelled him: the stories and habits of the poor. He was not alone in his urge to reinvent Jewish culture. Eastern European Jewish intellectuals had been working since the turn of the century to foster what they defined as a new Jewish secular culture. Ordinary Jews had been engaging in new secular cultural practices in public and private—reading, speaking, performing, and imagining themselves in ways unconnected to older religious norms—since the 1890s, and the events of 1905 accelerated that transformation.[40] The cultural Zionist leader Ahad Haam (Asher Tsvi Hirsch Ginsberg) spoke for the renewal of Jewishness in the diaspora through the development of a Hebrew spiritual center in Palestine; Dubnov argued for national autonomy and an identity based on history; and Zhitlowsky ultimately argued for a secular Jewishness based on the Yiddish language. An-sky himself proposed folklore as the source of a strong secular Jewish identity, a choice that echoed the Russian intelligentsia's vision of the folk as providing the most authentic way to unify the nation. Once Jews read and retell the tales of their people, he insisted, they will find confirmation of the potential of their own words. Given his aspirations, it is not surprising that An-sky took stories that confirmed the awesome power of God or the *tsaddik* and edited them to emphasize the power of human speech, creating tales about the kind of heroes he thought Russian Jewish culture needed—verbal artists such as himself.

By celebrating alternatives to physical confrontation in the years immediately after 1905, An-sky was in step with the intellectual movements of his time. In the aftermath of the failed revolution, the Russian intelligentsia entered a period of self-criticism. In 1909, a group of seven writers published *Landmarks,* a volume of essays that criticized radical culture for its asceticism, its support for terrorism, its materialism, and its unwillingness to compromise, and that urged Russians to imagine a new course of action. Even as they faced the aftermath of the pogroms, Russian Jewish intellectuals wrote similarly about spirituality and nonviolent, often verbal, methods of confronting the regime.[41]

The word that An-sky celebrated had an ecstatic potential. In the Yiddish versions of the God-on-trial legends, the "power of the word" that Elimelekh grants to Faivel is translated as *hislayves,* or in Hebrew *hitlahavut,* the ideal ecstatic state of the Hasidic worshipper during prayer (from the Hebrew *lahav,* flame); it means "to be completely absorbed in prayer, to lose the self and 'strip off one's corporeal nature' . . . to burn in longing for the divine." In his Russian letters, An-sky used that Yiddish word to talk about the inspiration he needed to write. In October 1908, he told Zhitlowsky that he feared not having enough energy to produce creative work. "I really want to work with you, but I don't know if I'll have the mood, the inspiration, the hislayves, and whatever else is needed." Two months later, when he produced "The Trial" and other poems in a burst of productivity, he used this same word in his Yiddish texts.[42] What An-sky saw as the basis of the Jewish folk imagination and the source of his own energy as a writer, the power of the word, was linked to Hasidic mysticism and to the ecstatic loss of self that the believer yearns to achieve, the ecstasy that *The Dybbuk*'s Khonen achieves when the name of God is revealed to him before he dies.

Even as An-sky moved away from SR ideology in his writing, post-1905 Petersburg saw him as an SR in the company of SRs. The poet Osip Mandelstam, a friend of Sinani's son, remembered An-sky as a regular denizen of the Sinani house, where young people were indoctrinated in the ideals of glory, honor, and SR terror: "Glory was in the Central Committee, glory was in the 'fighting organization,' and feats of valor began with a novitiate as a propagandist." Sofia Dubnova recalled An-sky inviting her, around 1908, to an SR party in the Finnish suburbs of Petersburg. On the train to Terioki, "at the frequent stops noisy groups of young people tumbled into the car on their way to the party. Lively rosy-cheeked girls kissed my companion with gusto." Dubnova resisted An-sky's urging to abandon the Bund for the PSR, but enjoyed her nighttime walk with him by the Finnish Gulf.[43]

An-sky continued to identify and to be identified with the SRs even as he moved away from a belief in violent action, and he continued to celebrate the power of the word in a way that recalls SR aesthetics. He retained his

Populist faith in individuals who move history forward through their heroic deeds. Though he moved from promoting terrorism to celebrating Jewish verbal resistance, An-sky was always preoccupied by the same concern: the need to respond to oppression with answers that would be at the same time effective acts. As revolutionary work became ever more unpromising, An-sky devoted his energy to Jewish folklore, still believing that ethnography could lead to radical political change. He presented Jewish folktales as containing answers to political questions: how Jews should respond to pogroms, and how he could work for the ideals that had inspired him as an SR in Switzerland, now that he was back in his autocratic homeland. Rather than simply moving, in the wake of 1905, from supporting terrorism to rejecting it and from Russian radicalism to Jewish culture, An-sky remained fascinated by the terrorist's impulse to make a definitive statement that might counter injustice, but he gradually shifted from realist depictions of actual violent acts toward Jewish tales of resistance, which provided space for unambiguous or even magical verbal acts. He turned to Jewish culture as he came to believe that it offered him just those things he had sought in the revolutionary movement: the opportunity to see himself as heroically devoting himself to those who needed him, and the self-forgetting ecstasy he found in connections with other people.

CHAPTER SEVEN

No Common Language

And now we must create something firm in our hearts, something
that will allow us to live as a nation.
    —S. An-sky, remarks made on January 9, 1910

PREMATURELY STOOPED and gray by his mid-forties, having
lived through the failure of the 1905 revolution, An-sky was
tired. He wrote in March 1907 that he was "dreaming about a
vacation and an apartment. Especially an apartment." Having acknowledged that he wanted the bourgeois comfort of his own space, as opposed to the rooming houses and friends' couches where he usually slept,
he could admit that he was again dreaming of romance. In August 1907,
writing to Zhitlowsky, he switched from Russian into Yiddish to discuss
his love life. He had fallen in love with a much younger woman, Edia
(Esther) Glezerman, the beautiful daughter of a lamp store owner in
Vitebsk, who had been brought up in a well-to-do Jewish home and played
piano. Sinani urged An-sky not to pursue her and An-sky took his advice,
writing to Edia "as a free man would do" to break off the affair. He was
delighted when she responded by leaving Vitebsk to visit him in the Petersburg region. By December, they were planning to marry and find an
apartment in Vilna. He told Zhitlowsky, "She's out of her mind for me
and I've lost my head completely. I don't know how this will end, but for
now, I'm happy." She wrote to him, "I can't wait!" and he wrote, "My
bright child . . . It's hard for me to put into words how much I miss you,
how I want to see you, hear your voice, feel you close by, your soul, your
mood."[1]

Most of An-sky's friends thought that the match was ideologically and
practically impossible. Whether or not they knew about the astonishing
brevity of his marriage to Mademoiselle Janais, they had trouble imagining him happily married to any woman, let alone a girl expecting a comfortable, settled life. Vera Zhitlovskaia used strong language: "If it would

help, I would hold on to you until the grave to keep you from marrying that *baryshnia* [aristocratic young woman] . . . but you can't help a madman." When he mentioned his friends' doubts to his intended, she defended herself: "It's not true that I can't deny myself in petty, pathetic matters!" She insisted that she too was a radical, a visionary who dreamed of a better future: "I believe that it will be possible to burst out of these cursed chains. If you only knew how I dream about casting off from myself all this filth and becoming completely free from all this petty, everyday, really completely unnecessary and insignificant rubbish of life." Edia told An-sky that these dreams were associated for her with her passion for theater and her ambition to go on the stage: she and he shared a love for theater, music, and literature, as well as a restless urge to travel.[2]

An-sky's friends thought that Edia's pretty speeches were self-deluding nonsense. They were certain that this spoiled girl could never be a suitable companion for a self-sacrificing radical intellectual such as An-sky, but on some level, it seems, An-sky longed precisely for the comfortable provincial lifestyle of Edia's childhood home, so like the family homes of his wealthy childhood friends. When he wrote that after the failed revolution the Jewish intelligentsia had "cooled toward the workers and the movement and retreated into their own private lives," he undoubtedly had himself in mind. After a lifetime of roaming, he promised to set up housekeeping with Edia. "I'd make a cozy little nest for you, so that everything would be peaceful, joyful, bright for you, so you could rest and give yourself to your music . . . When we sit at home I'll teach you to play chess. We'll speak French and read Anatole France and Rostand [author of *Cyrano de Bergerac*] in the original. I just haven't decided what color the wallpaper in your room will be." He told Zhitlowsky the relationship had changed his life. "In the three months since the day of our second meeting my entire life has been suffused with light, warmth, tenderness, and happiness, such as I had never experienced and never expected in my life. It would be worth it to give one's life up for such happiness, to pay, if fate demanded, with years of suffering."[3]

After the couple moved to Vilna in early 1908, An-sky recognized that his life there contradicted his old ascetic ideals. "I have rented an apartment and moved from the ranks of the proletariat to those of the petty bourgeoisie." In admitting that he had left the revolutionary street for his own apartment, An-sky expressed an idea that intrigued a part of the Russian intelligentsia in the wake of the 1905 revolution. In *Landmarks,* Mikhail Gershenzon urged intellectuals to return home and face their real obligations. "A handful of revolutionaries has been going from house to house and knocking on every door: 'Everyone into the street! It's shameful to stay at home!' And everyone, the lame, the blind, and the armless, poured out into the square. . . . At home there is dirt, poverty, disorder, but the master doesn't care. He is out in public, he is saving the people—and that is easier and more entertaining than drudgery at home." When he moved to Vilna with Edia Glezerman, An-sky was experimenting with a new way of seeing his life and his work. He responded to Gershenzon's dictum that ordinary domesticity was better and healthier than radical asceticism. Indeed, the beginning of his romance with Edia coincided for him with the disappearance of a host of perhaps psychosomatic medical problems.[4]

He was also experimenting with a new way of being Jewish. Because Jewish law obligates people to have children, religious Jewish adults were (and are) almost universally married. Thus, far more than when he entered into his brief liaison with the non-Jewish Mademoiselle Janais, An-sky could be seen as striving via his marriage to the Jewish Esther Glezerman to become something resembling a traditional Jewish man.[5] As a Jewish cultural activist, the editor of Jewish journals, and a person who, more and more, was engaging in public debates where he claimed to speak for the Jews of the Russian Empire, An-sky may indeed have felt the need to make himself a more conventional member of the Jewish community.

But he felt ambivalent about the formal step of marriage. He and Edia went back and forth about going through the legal ceremony. He told Zhitlowsky they would do it, but Edia shocked her mother by revealing they might not. He told Gurevich he would do it, then was upset when his friend wrote with congratulations before it happened. Gurevich responded by suggesting gently that marriage would be a way for An-sky to demonstrate that he was a man:

> Of course, you might feel embarrassed about such a, one might say, ordinary thing as marriage. Since time immemorial, scholars say, men have gotten married, and in our times, they say, even high school students don't hesitate to do it. It would be odd if you were a person who was frightened of the risk. And if there are some land mines among the roses—my friend, we're not women, we won't snivel? Right? After all, you won't grow stupid from happiness, and from grief, if it comes to that, you won't perish.[6]

In December 1907, Edia was already complaining about An-sky's suspiciousness and jealousy, but the two were married in March 1908 in a Jewish ceremony in the Vilna apartment of Rabbi Dr. Kantor. As his friends had predicted, the relationship soon foundered. By the beginning of April, he returned to Petersburg, to live in a cheap Finnish boarding house and spend nights on his friends' couches in the city, and Edia was back at her parents' house in Vitebsk, wondering if their marriage would ultimately "work out." She hinted that she would like to have a child: "The doctor asked me in detail about our marital life. Then he said that I can't live this way and *I must have a baby*. How do you like that? . . . Oh well, the Devil with all of that!" Her tone indicated that she knew the doctor's suggestion would be ignored. For the next three years, the couple spent only a few months together each year, usually summers in Finland or Vitebsk; the rest of the year, Edia, who was diagnosed with tuberculosis in 1909, convalesced in the Swiss Alps (her parents may have helped pay). She complained of boredom and loneliness, saying in May 1910, "It's so hard that it's already three years that we are close, but we have been together so little in that time." She reported on her temperature, her weight, and how well she had slept, and she asked for money to pay for clothes and her frequent moves from one sanatorium-resort to another. She usually wrote every day, and when she did not, An-sky became angry and threatened to disappear in his turn. Whether or not this mostly long-distance marriage satisfied him, he was committed to maintaining the impression that it was going fine. He told people that he and Edia loved each other passionately.[7]

An-sky had made a desperate attempt to change his life, and he saw the Jewish communities of Russia as in need of equally dramatic transformation. Working with Jewish writers and speaking with Jews in shtetls and cities, he saw that they were preoccupied with the questions that obsessed him, about finding a balance between the personal and the political, between tradition and assimilation. His relationship with Edia was undermined by mixed signals and differing expectations. In his relationship with the new Jewish culture arising in Russia after 1905, he faced similar problems.

In 1908, when he traveled back to Chashniki, he was struck by the sense of cultural stagnation for both the young Jews emigrating *en masse* to America and those who stayed behind and tried to explain what had happened. One old man told An-sky that he understood the emigrants perfectly. "Here I am a person. How could I leave? But for today's youth, it's a different matter. They've dealt with everything. God? Where's God? What do you mean, God? There's no God! Torah? Huh, what Torah? Just tales, nothing more. There's no Torah . . . There's nothing! And when there's nothing—you can follow your nose. Isn't that how it is?" In this vitriol, An-sky saw a measure of truth: the emptying out of the shtetl was the result of the "contemporary Russian Jew's lack of cultural soil for life in Russia." The old culture was expiring and hollow, but a new one had yet to take its place: "There was nothing to live on any more."[8]

Like Zhitlowsky, Ahad Ha'am, and Dubnov, An-sky was beginning to see himself as a Jewish leader, compelled to redefine Jewishness for a post-religious era, to create or promote literature, theater, or music that could reinforce Jewish identity *and* satisfy the aesthetic and spiritual longings of a modern people. For him, the way to revitalize the culture was to seek its roots in ethnographic work. He believed he could find both the living sources of Jewishness and inspiration for how they could be adapted to modern life, transformed and made newly viable. His cultural nationalism, like Dubnov's, was based on the Jewish experience in the diaspora; by privileging living folklore over other sources, An-sky privileged the present over the past and the current home of the Jews in Russia over their former home in Palestine.

The problem of adapting Jewish culture to modern life was complicated by An-sky's distaste for the modern culture he saw in Petersburg. In September 1908, he complained bitterly about the literary scene. "The book market is completely destroyed. . . . Even pornography isn't selling any more. A month ago [Leonid] Andreev told me that they've stopped reading even him. So what do they read? Probably obscene graffiti! After [Mikhail] Kuzmin, [Anatoly] Kamensky, and [Sergei Sergeev-]Tsensky, that's all there is left to read."[9] Kuzmin was known for his 1906 novel, *Wings,* about same-sex lovers. It may be that some uncertainty about his own sexuality led An-sky to reject Kuzmin so harshly. He was consistent in his disapproval of erotic writing and of the modernism that Kuzmin, Kamensky, and Sergeev-Tsensky embraced. Just as he had been unimpressed with French Decadence in the 1890s, so An-sky disliked Russian Decadence.

Unlike when he lived in Paris, though, now An-sky was the husband of a young woman with tastes unlike his own. He had fantasized that he and his wife would read together the politically engaged writers he admired, such as the Dreyfusard Anatole France, but Edia preferred trendy fin-de-siècle literature. She read the fashionable book *Sex and Character,* published in 1903 by Otto Weininger, a convert from Judaism who associated Jewishness with femininity and decay, Christianity with masculinity and genius (he later committed suicide). She praised Dmitry Merezhkovsky's 1896–1905 trilogy, *Christ and Antichrist,* which explored spirituality against the background of European history; Merezhkovsky and his wife, the writer Zinaida Gippius, were known for their unconventional "white" (unconsummated) marriage and their ménage à trois arrangements.[10] Discussing modern literature with his wife, An-sky must have grasped the genuine appeal of its spirituality and sexuality to her generation, and his own attitude toward the literary avant-garde gradually became more nuanced than it had been in Paris.

When he first encountered literary modernism, unexpectedly, in Yiddish, a language that he had seen as a vehicle for propaganda rather than literary experimentation, he reacted negatively. In early 1908, a group of young writers in Vilna published four issues of *Literarishe monatsshriften* (Literary Monthly), a journal meant to showcase highbrow, experimental, and frankly modernist Yiddish work in the name of a Jewish cultural renaissance based exclusively in Yiddish.[11] The editors were brash, talented writers: A. Vayter (Ayzik-Meir Devinishski) was a former Bundist and a playwright; Shmuel Niger (Charny), a Socialist Zionist who would become the most powerful Yiddish literary critic of his generation; and Shmarye Gorelik, a Zionist feuilletonist. Like An-sky, they believed that they were working to promote Jewish cultural renewal, but they wanted a literary renaissance that would produce frankly highbrow literature, powerful new myths aimed at the intelligentsia rather than the masses. Their new journal included translations from Knut Hamsun and Weininger, Sholem Asch's drama *Shabtai Tsvi* and Niger's critical articles praising the writer; and erotic, impressionistic texts by Der Nister (Pinchas Kahanovich), Peretz, and others. Its slim format and decision to print belles lettres and literary criticism but no political materials linked it to the new avant-garde journals then coming out in Russian, such as *Vesy* (Libra, 1904–1909) and *Apollon* (Apollo, 1909–1917), which rejected the model of thick journals such as *Russkoe Bogatstvo*.

An-sky knew that he belonged to the generation that Niger, Vayter, and Gorelik were attacking, and he led a public debate in Vilna against the journal, its anti-Russian Yiddishism, and its announcement that literature should serve aesthetic rather than social aims. He praised many of the individual works by Peretz, Niger, and others, but he saw the journal itself as decadent, inaccessible, and "un-Jewish." He was particularly annoyed by the announcements for the journal, which, with the stridency of a manifesto, attacked the "assimilationist intelligentsia" for their rejection of Yiddish culture. By June, though, when the journal was about to fold, he tried to save it, suggesting that its editors appeal to the Petersburg Jewish intelligentsia for support.[12]

In the fall of 1908, a few months after *Literarishe monatsshriften* closed, An-sky asked a number of well-known Yiddish writers to contribute to a new publishing venture: *Evreiskii Mir* (Jewish World), a monthly journal in Russian. His goal in editing the literary section was to familiarize the Jewish public that read only Russian with "the best works of Jewish literature in all languages," including new stories and poems by Yiddish and Hebrew writers. He offered to pay 40 rubles per signature for new, never-before-published Yiddish stories: the editorial office would organize and finance the translation, and after the stories came out in Russian, the writer would be free to republish them in the original. With these conditions, he successfully recruited the best-known Yiddish writers of the time. The first issue, in January 1909, contained memoirs by Mendele Moikher Sforim, a dramatic poem by Peretz translated by An-sky himself, and a new story by Sholem Aleichem about Tevye the dairyman.[13]

He recruited many of the *Literarishe monatsshriften* writers, including Vayter, Niger, Der Nister, Asch, and Peretz. Some of them found the notion of having their Yiddish work appear first in Russian translation deeply upsetting. Der Nister explained his reaction to Niger in December 1908 when An-sky invited him to submit something new for *Evreiskii Mir*, "to release first in Russian something that was born and raised in Yiddish." He would feel "like a person bringing his only child to be baptized," but he knew that his options were limited. "I'm not even talking about money, but where can you find a place to publish in Yiddish?" Concerns such as Der Nister's were voiced in *Evreiskii Mir* itself. Gornfeld, writing in the first issue of 1909, expressed discomfort about the translation of Yiddish literature into Russian. Even while this could keep the intelligentsia informed about currents in shtetl life, and even while it made economic sense for Yiddish writers to want their work to reach a Russian audience, Gornfeld wrote, "From my perspective, the perspective of a linguistic nationalist . . . not a single significant work was created or could be created in an atmosphere of national effacement and calculated attempts to appeal in various languages."[14] But in spite of Gornfeld's qualms and his own, Der Nister sent An-sky his manuscripts; Russian occupied a privileged position relative to Yiddish, and because An-sky offered a path into Russian publication, he had to agree to his terms.

Over its two-year existence, *Evreiskii Mir* drew closer to the literary trends of early-twentieth-century Petersburg. The cover of the January 1909 issue used the serif font and style of *Russkoe Bogatstvo*, but the February 1909 issue sported a more contemporary sans-serif font, and the 1910 weekly version had an Art Nouveau style. The January–March 1910 special issue on belles lettres, which An-sky edited, resembled slim Russian literary journals such as *Vesy*: it contained stories by Mendele, Ben-Ami, Peretz, and Der Nister, criticism by Niger, and an article about Asch, along with poetry translations by Sofia Dubnova, who had just begun her literary career by publishing in *Apollon*.[15] No matter how stridently An-sky had rejected *Literarishe monatsshriften* in early 1908, when he began working as an editor a few months later, he could not dismiss trends as confidently as he once had; he recognized that both its writers and its notion of an apolitical literary journal appealed to readers.

An-sky proved to be a genial, humorous editor. Dubnova told him, "I hope to get an editorial letter from you in verse (as you see, I have secret agents who keep track of your activity)." Peretz, who was becoming increasingly friendly with An-sky, appreciated the opportunity to reach a Russian audience and published in *Evreiskii Mir* regularly. An-sky became close to many of the writers who wrote for his journal, such as Alter Kacyzne, a writer and photographer whom he was the first to publish. (Kacyzne later became well known for his photos of Jewish life in interwar Poland.) As Kacyzne moved from writing in Russian to writing in Yiddish, he moved to Warsaw and wrote to An-sky to tell him that Peretz himself was tutoring him; learning to write well in Yiddish, he remarked, actually is not easy at all. An-sky stayed close to some of the *Literarishe monatsshriften* writers, including Niger and Vayter, who themselves moved away from the fiercely aesthetic stance they had taken earlier. In 1912, after *Evreiskii Mir* folded, Niger became the editor of its successor, the Yiddish publication *Di yudishe velt* (Jewish World), now located in Vilna.[16]

But for a cohort of Yiddish writers of the younger, more militant generation, An-sky became a symbol of the resentment they felt about the subordination of Yiddish culture to Russian and a target for their anger at what they saw as assimilationism and betrayal. Gorelik described An-sky darkly as living in Vilna in early 1908 as though he were a political exile in the Siberian city of Irkutsk: he may have been an admirable person with charmingly old-fashioned Yiddish, but he was a mediocre writer, committed to outdated Russian Populist ideals, and a member of a generation that "had understood literature wrong." Alexander Mukdoyni (Kapel), a theater critic in Peretz's circle, insisted that An-sky, though a warm personality, was a "fifth-rate writer" who became popular among Jews only because he had made a career in Russian and had such strong connections to famous figures in Russian literature and culture. An-sky's fashionable wife made it hard to see him as out of step with the times, and Mukdoyni asserted that he and the rest of Peretz's circle observed signs of the dissolution of their marriage without surprise—indeed, he wrote (of a time when he was already in his thirties and An-sky only in his forties), "it was a bit embarrassing for all of us to see the stooped, elderly An-sky with such a young, still beautiful wife." Even when An-sky publicly embraced Yiddish and Jewish culture, these young men saw him as unable to overcome his own deep-rooted assimilationism.[17]

It was hard to become the sort of husband Edia had wanted, but it was easier to become the sort of Jewish writer that the new generation demanded. As he became more aware of the attitudes of men such as Niger and Vayter, An-sky began to produce the kind of story they might like to read. In June 1909, he published "Behind a Mask: The Story of an Old Maskil," in *Evreiskii Mir.* The title itself pointed to his habit of disguise. He drew again on his memories of his time in Liozno, trying to lead pious youths astray toward Haskalah and revolution, but this story was much less sympathetic than *Pioneers* toward the maskilim. The first-person narrator (named Joseph Krantz in the later Yiddish version) moves from "V." (probably Vitebsk) to the shtetl of Bobiltseve with two aims: to find tutoring work that would give him access to young people whom he could subvert, and to convince Krayne, the mother of Shekhtl, who lives there, that his friend and fellow maskil back in V. was actually studying in a yeshiva and deserved a monthly allowance. Before the narrator leaves V., Shekhtl explains how to make contact with other secret maskilim in Bobiltseve, especially their leader, Chaim-Wolf, who had succeeded in convincing the townsfolk of his piety. When the narrator arrives in Bobiltseve, he convinces Krayne of Shekhtl's diligence, and makes contact with Leivik, another secret maskil, who seems unimpressed by his plans to foment rebellion. Instead, he says he distrusts the big-city maskilim. "They want to show off their heroism, make scoffing remarks so someone can hear, play tricks, but they don't know how to work slowly and quietly. What's worse, they love to talk a lot and to write long letters about everything that ought to be kept secret, and their letters have a habit of falling into the hands of the rabbi and the head of the yeshiva."[18] Leivik helps the narrator find tutoring work, but soon he starts acting just as Leivik had predicted, sitting bareheaded in his room, smoking on the Sabbath where people might see him, dropping skeptical remarks about the rebbe revered by the local Hasidim. Even worse, Krayne visits V., where she learns the truth about her wayward son—and about the narrator. When Krayne comes back to Bobiltseve, she confronts the narrator with his lies. He admits them, but threatens that if she reveals the truth, he will order Shekhtl to be baptized. Horrified, Krayne submits—but then, in the story's last line, goes mad.

Obviously, the story critiqued the attitudes and the behaviors of the maskilim of the 1870s and 1880s, people who resembled An-sky himself when he had lived in Liozno. When he mocked the maskilic narrator, An-sky was mocking himself and his cohort of self-confident Jewish reformers; his confession that his generation had gotten so many things wrong was a public gesture of conciliation toward the generation of Niger, Vayter, and Der Nister. It contained a hint that An-sky's self-reevaluation was connected to his marriage to Edia. Bobiltseve, the name of no real shtetl, comes from the Russian word *bobyl,* a bachelor. By making fun of something like his old self, An-sky indicated that his new married self saw things differently.

The plot of "Behind a Mask" also reflected An-sky's political concerns. In December 1908, the central committee of the PSR admitted that Azef, a powerful SR leader and for a time head of the Fighting Organization, was actually a police spy and double agent: he was unmasked by Vladimir Burtsev, editor of the revolutionary historical journal *Byloe* (The Past). The news became public in January 1909, demoralizing Russian radicals and discrediting the SRs. An-sky was furious at the SR leaders. "Idiots who for six years can't tell the difference between an *agent provocateur* and a revolutionary have no right to be involved in politics." In the wake of the revelations, An-sky gave *Russkoe Bogatstvo* his warm memoirs of Father Gapon, who had been assassinated as a double agent on Azef's orders, and he showed his respect for Burtsev when he went to considerable trouble and expense to disassociate himself from Evalenko, a Yiddish publisher whom Burtsev had uncovered as a police informer.[19]

In the aftermath of the Azef affair, An-sky mused about heroism and rebellion in terms that recalled the critique of the concept of intelligentsia heroism voiced in *Landmarks.* The philosopher Sergei Bulgakov wrote there that "the heroic *intelligent* is not satisfied with the role of modest worker. . . . His dream is to be the savior of mankind, or at least of the Russian people. . . . Maximalism is an integral trait of intelligentsia heroism . . . it produces a fanaticism deaf to the voice of life."[20] Bulgakov's picture of the heroic *intelligent* captures An-sky's narrator in "Behind a Mask": his ruthlessness and his ineffectiveness, his obsession with his own heroism, his love for conspiracy, his sense of superiority, and his impatient distaste for careful detailed work. The narrator's mask slips because he genuinely despises the people he hopes to convert.

However, it would be a mistake to see "Behind a Mask" as a rejection of the Haskalah conviction that the traditional Jewish way of life needed fundamental reform. Bulgakov had imagined a better model for intelligentsia heroism: the true Christian ascetic, whose faith in God "frees him from heroic posing and pretensions," and whose attention is focused on "the recognition of personal duty and its fulfillment, and on self-control."[21] Similarly, An-sky provides an alternative model for maskilic heroism in the character Chaim-Wolf, a modest master of disguise. No more than the narrator is Chaim-Wolf truly a pious traditional Jew, but he is a more effective strategist and propagandist for secularism. While Bulgakov critiqued the revolutionary culture of the intelligentsia, he retained the revolutionaries' conviction that the Tsarist regime was morally rotten. In the same way, the An-sky of "Behind a Mask" remained convinced that certain aspects of the old way of life were wrong—but he argued for cautious, gradual reform that would not threaten Jewish continuity itself.

This reform was an alternative to conversion, whose advantages were obvious, especially to ambitious young people; by formally renouncing Judaism, they gained unimpeded entry to higher education, a range of careers, and residency in the big cities. In early 1910, An-sky published an article decrying the "epidemic of national suicide," meaning the conversion of young Jews to Eastern Orthodoxy, Protestantism, or Islam. He knew that they often saw conversion as a way to gain access to "light and knowledge," whereas they felt only a formal connection to Judaism. "For that formality, is it worth it to sacrifice one's striving for knowledge, for scholarly discipline, for the possibility of developing one's intellectual forces broadly?" But paradoxically, An-sky asserted, conversion could not produce the desired result. Although people can change their religion, they cannot change their "national" (or ethnic) identity. "The baptized Jew who has denied his own people ends up with no national identity, no vital connection to the main source of cultural creativity. . . . By striving toward a broad cultural life and spiritual creative work, people cut themselves off from their living roots and end up alone and outcast."[22] The equation of conversion with death and destruction recalled the end of "Behind a Mask." By threatening that Shekhtl will convert, the narrator achieved only a momentary, hollow victory. When he drove Krayne mad, he eliminated the very source of financial sustenance that he and Shekhtl had hoped to tap. The mother's insanity suggested the madness of conversion as a response to Jewish problems.

An-sky wrote stories that advertised his agreement with the younger generation of Jewish writers, but some of what those young men published in Yiddish upset him, for ideological and personal reasons. In the summer and fall of 1909, he became involved in a public debate about the place of Christianity and its central image, the crucifix, in the culture and ideology of the modern Jew. Zhitlowsky had recently published two stories involving the cross in his New York Yiddish journal, *Dos naye lebn* (New Life): Lamed Shapiro's "The Cross" and Sholem Asch's "On a Carnival Night."[23] Lamed (Levi Yehoshua) Shapiro was a Ukrainian Jew who had left the Russian Empire in 1905 for the United States. "The Cross," one of his many graphic pogrom stories, depicts a Jewish SR forced to watch pogromshchiks rape and kill his mother before they carve a cross on his forehead as he struggles, tied to a bedpost. After he frees himself, he rapes and murders Mina, the non-Jewish leader of his

SR cell. The story gruesomely exemplifies the rejection of SR ideals in the wake of the pogroms and the Azef revelations.

The more controversial story was not the horrifying "Cross" but the much tamer "Carnival Night." Asch was in 1909 an increasingly popular writer, celebrated for his melodramatic prose and plays. "On a Carnival Night" depicts a festival night in medieval Rome. The Jews are ritually tormented, Jesus descends from the cross to join them, and Mary and Mother Rachel sew shrouds for the Jewish martyrs. In the 1930s and 1940s, Asch would become controversial after publishing a trilogy based on the Christian Bible: *The Nazarene* (1939), on the life of Jesus; *The Apostle* (1943), on Paul; and *Mary* (1949). Although Asch himself saw the novels as an attempt to reclaim the Jewish roots of Christianity and thus of Western civilization, he was pilloried by the Yiddish press for turning his back on his people, glorifying Christianity while Jews were persecuted in Europe, and even propagandizing for conversion. "On a Carnival Night," while weaker than his Christological trilogy, visited similar themes, emerged from similar impulses, and engendered a similar controversy, though in miniature.

The debate began when Zhitlowsky published an article lauding Shapiro and Asch's stories for bringing Yiddish literature closer to non-Yiddish literature both in quality and theme; he described them as among the first Yiddish writers to confront the enormous changes in Jewish life over the past century and to raise a taboo topic: "Us and the cross!" While Zhitlowsky admired Shapiro's depiction of a modern Jew's response to Christian violence—the urge of the powerless to demonstrate their strength—he preferred Asch's story. He praised it for suggesting it was time that Jews abandon their traditional suspicion of Jesus and recognize that becoming modern Europeans with full access to the riches of European culture required reconciliation with this central Christian cultural image. "And if we are fated to put ourselves on the cultural-historical path of modern, progressive humankind—it's the same no matter where we live, in the diaspora or in our own country—we will have to take in not only their cares of today, not only their hopes for tomorrow, but also the entire contents of their past."[24] He explicitly acknowledged the most radical implication of his argument (which, he argued, was implicit in Zionist theory as well): that in a post-religious age, a modern Jewish nationalist need not be an adherent of Judaism and could perfectly well be Christian.

An-sky read the article and was appalled. He told Zhitlowsky angrily that he felt his old friend was breaking away from his own people, and he stayed up until dawn writing a response, which he insisted needed to be printed immediately. He assumed that Zhitlowsky would then print another article of his own. "Maybe you'll convince me. I don't know, maybe you're right, maybe we will go through the experiences of the German Jews after Mendelssohn, maybe we will die out completely as Jews, but we won't die simply or peacefully. We know how to fight for Jewishness." An-sky spent the bulk of his two-part article, published in the September and October issues of *Dos naye lebn,* outlining his objections to a Jewish reconciliation with Jesus. He dismissed the notion that most of Western civilization was based on Christianity, arguing that much of it was actually anti-Christian.[25] Jews already have a set of beliefs and legends about Jesus, and abandoning them would require a huge psychological shift. Rather than undergoing that change in order to appreciate Christian art such as Dante's *Inferno* or the Sistine Madonna, he insisted that Jews "must and will remain Jews, and they will never deny their Jewishness even for such treasures as Raphael and Beethoven's work." Anyway, they do not need to do so: they can admire Christian art through their own, Jewish eyes. Just as Uspensky could see the Venus de Milo as a monument of spirituality (rather than pagan materialism), so Jews can adapt Christian culture to their own needs, transforming it as they had transformed European folklore.

In his anger at Asch, An-sky accused the younger writer of the sin of which he himself had been accused, assimilationism. He adopted, for the first time, a stridently nationalist tone. He compared Jesus unfavorably with other religious leaders, such as Buddha and Confucius. Not only had more violence been committed in the name of Jesus than Buddha, but Jesus' example left much to be desired: he relied on miracles to gain followers, his teachings were inconsistent, his own faith in his ideals was imperfect (as he demonstrated with his fear when on the cross), and he promoted himself shamelessly. An-sky concluded that Jews could never honor the name of Jesus, which had been on the lips of those who perpetrated violence against Jews for millennia. "In every attempt to make peace between 'us and the cross,' the Jewish people will see only a new insult to themselves and to the hundreds of generations of martyrs and victims who have left us their tragic legacy, their faith, their trials, their unavenged blood, the tears they are still crying, and the holy name of *Jew.*"[26]

As An-sky had anticipated, Zhitlowsky then published a response. In "The Christianity Question for Educated Jews," he stepped back from some of his earlier claims, insisting he had never meant to promote conversion. Speaking in scholarly terms, he noted that humans have always felt drawn to religion and religious images. Educated Jews could no longer believe in miracles, but they could love "the poetry of religion, no matter its form," and it was the beauty of the cross, rather than the religious faith associated with it, that he promoted. Zhitlowsky retold Jewish legends that mock Jesus as a bastard, a magician, and a thief who is eternally punished in hell, cooked in a pot of excrement; every year on Christmas, traditional Jews demonstrate their scorn for Jesus by playing cards rather than studying rabbinic texts. In aesthetic terms, Zhitlowsky insisted, Christian legends about Jesus were simply more beautiful than these ugly Jewish stories.[27]

Drawing on his own 1887 book, *Thoughts about the Historical Fate of the Jews*, Zhitlowsky argued that Jesus and his teachings had emerged from the beliefs of "a communist Jewish sect, the Essenes." Jesus was really the first Jewish Socialist Revolutionary, who could have brought down the Roman Empire had he not been betrayed by "Judas-Azef." Had he himself lived at the time of Jesus, Zhitlowsky said, he would have fought with him for revolution in Jerusalem. He urged An-sky to see Jesus' teachings as emerging from their own era and to understand him as a strategist who designed revolutionary propaganda to appeal to his primitive audience, accepted the inevitable doctrinal inconsistencies, and acted confusingly because, as "the leader of an undercover organization," he saw no alternative. Instead of scorning him for his fear on the cross, one should remember his final, "more characteristic" words of mercy toward his tormenters: "Forgive them, Father, for they know not what they do" (Luke 23).[28]

Western European civilization, Zhitlowsky insisted, is simply superior to the Jewish culture of rabbinic learning, which is not worth the "rivers of Jewish blood" spilt in its defense. He insisted on his own right to try to bring Jews out of that old culture into the world of Dante, Raphael, and Bach, and he asserted that he was still a Jewish nationalist. "If An-sky believes that his view of Christ and Christianity is the Jewish, national one and mine is the goyish [non-Jewish], assimilated one, he is making a terrible mistake. I hold that the situation is *precisely the opposite*. Only a person who is not entirely free of the ideal of assimilation, only he who sees no national life force in the Jewish folk, lives in permanent fear of his poor surroundings."[29]

Zhitlowsky was explicit that his own project of cultural revival was opposed to everything in which traditional Jews believed and that he neither wanted to nor could ever co-opt the conservatives; at the same time, he insisted that An-sky, still a Populist, believed in an artificial distinction between the intelligentsia and the folk and thus did not recognize the true vitality of Jewish culture, which did *not* need to be protected from outside influences. Whereas An-sky approached Jewish culture as a repentant *intelligent*, perpetually guilty of disrespect for the simple people,

Zhitlowsky embraced his status as an intellectual and had no qualms about urging that others follow his example.

The difference between the old friends' views on the question of the cross reflected their distinctive temperaments: Zhitlowsky's love for beautifully worded, ideologically uncompromising polemics; An-sky's enduring skepticism that philosophical ideas correspond to real life. Zhitlowsky's attitudes were of a piece with his linguistic nationalism, his belief that a renewed Jewish culture could be created exclusively in a Jewish language—Yiddish—but it could embrace any content. An-sky's ideas display his own nationalism as more cultural than linguistic. Certainly, his rejection of Zhitlowsky's call for Jews to embrace Jesus is consistent with other writings where he situated present-day problems in the broadest possible historical perspective: when he wrote about the Duma, he stressed the autocracy's age-old ability to exploit the liberals, and when he wrote about the 1905 pogroms, he looked for the "lessons of the terrible centuries." He could hardly, then, imagine Jews suddenly turning their back on "hundreds of generations of martyrs and victims." His recent immersion in Jewish folk culture had renewed his Populist sense of respect for the folk and made it impossible for him to accept a vision of a renewed Jewish culture based exclusively on highbrow values and images. For An-sky, Zhitlowsky's attitude—that as an educated Jew, he knows what is best for the shtetl—must have recalled the fatal self-confidence of the narrator in "Behind a Mask."

An-sky may have taken such a strong stance against Zhitlowsky's call to reevaluate Jesus in order to compensate for his own past as a radical who had once been more interested in Russian peasants than Jews, something that he was feeling particularly apologetic about in 1909 as he interacted with the younger generation of Jewish activists. He also felt ambivalent about these young men, including Asch himself. Asch wrote regularly for *Evreiskii Mir* and other St. Petersburg Jewish publications. In late 1908, Asch had stayed in the room next to An-sky's in a hotel in the Finnish town of Terioki. An-sky published him and called him "a strong, a very strong force!" But when Asch offered "On a Carnival Night" to *Evreiskii Mir*, An-sky thrust it back angrily, telling Zhitlowsky the story was "talentless nonsense" and its author an opportunist. "You can't imagine how disgusted I am now by that literary *shnorrer* [beggar] who is ready to pray to any god you want, so long as it's fashionable and they pay." Even as An-sky rewrote his own works in answer to the changing times, he criticized Asch for doing something similar. Everything Asch wrote, An-sky said, was in response to trends—for Polish nationalism, for brothels, for the homoerotic, for anything profitable. "Now those who are satiated with pederasty and lesbianism demand Christ and Maria, of course all the *yeshivabokher*s are in a rush, but Asch has beaten them all. He's pulled out the martyrs under Trajan, he's pulled out the old Jewish martyrs of Italy, he's sacrilegiously fastened them on to Christ, and he's off to the store. Foo, it's disgusting!" Asch had everything An-sky wanted: he was prolific, admired, published, well paid, and he even had residence permission and the ability to leave Terioki for an official Petersburg address. Undoubtedly resentful, An-sky insisted that Asch's success came at the price of abandoning his ideals and serving the market—a service An-sky connected with homosexuality, something that had always upset him.[30]

An-sky's anger at Asch and his story undoubtedly stemmed from genuine ideological differences, even while it revealed his own anxiety at the ways in which he was making himself over to please the market. His anger may also have something to do with his position as the older husband of a beautiful, childless young woman. In Anton Chekhov's 1896 play *Uncle Vanya*, Elena is the beautiful, bored, piano-playing young wife of Alexander Serebriakov, an ailing retired professor; the younger men at the estate lust after her. When Edia Glezerman, by then separated from An-sky, found herself in acting school in 1911, she chose the role of Elena for her exam, perhaps because her life thus far had prepared her for it so well. An-sky's friends never concealed their doubt that he could continue to attract a woman so much younger than himself, as when Vera Zhitlovskaia asked pointedly, "Are you building a *terem* [a medieval Russian women's chamber] for your young wife? Or sitting in a *terem* yourself?"[31] In *Uncle Vanya*, Elena falls out of love with Professor Serebriakov and at the same time, she and the young people around her realize that they have lost their respect for his writings: his intellectual and sexual vitality are linked. In 1909 and 1910, when Edia Glezerman was falling out of love with An-sky, he seemed to be particularly sensitive to the suggestion that other, younger men were more in tune with the literary marketplace. Asch, who was seventeen years younger than An-sky, wrote plays about lesbians in brothels and about the seventeenth-century Jewish sectarian Shabtai Tsvi, famous for his physical beauty and his marriage to a former prostitute. This was just the kind of fashionable literature that Edia found exciting. Whether or not Edia ever met Asch at the rooming house in Terioki, the creative and romantic competition that Asch represented (regardless of his own wife and family in Warsaw) could have motivated the angry article that An-sky stayed up all night writing.

An-sky ultimately retreated from his anger and his uncompromising nationalism. After all, for An-sky's closest friends, Zhitlowsky's assertion that educated Jews needed to reconcile themselves with the central images in Christianity was convincing. Gurevich told An-sky he agreed that modern Jews were in a tragic position—yearning for spirituality, rejecting Jewish belief, but prevented "by old Jewish memory" from turning to Christianity—and he found it not at all absurd to think of religion decoupled from national identity, so that one could have "Russian Lutherans, German Buddhists, and Christian Jews." An-sky relayed Gurevich's argument dismissively, saying, "Keep in mind there's an assimilator in Samuil's soul," but at the same time, he told Zhitlowsky he had realized that there was not really an abyss between the two of them.[32]

The tone of reconciliation was audible in some of An-sky's other work. In 1909, 1910, and 1911, he was paid 700 rubles a volume to edit three 128-page collections of Russian and world literature for the popular reader, sold for only 15 kopecks. These volumes reflected the Tolstoyan idea that educated people are obligated to work for peasant literacy: Tolstoy and his followers had established a publishing house, the Intermediary (Posrednik), to produce cheap editions of selected classical stories for the new reader, and other publishers followed their lead. The articles An-sky edited spoke for the Tolstoyan virtues of tolerance and nonviolence. A reviewer noted, "The distinctive feature of these excellent little books is their humane, 'reasonable, good, eternal' content, presented in such an accessible way that it will be understood by children or a barely-literate adult reader." The theme of the 1910 collection, *For God's Truth,* was religious and philosophical leaders, shown in a Tolstoyan light as rational ethical heroes, with stories about Buddha, Confucius, Socrates, Moses, Jesus, Mohammed, Jan Hus, Galileo, and others. The essay on Jesus presents him from a perspective similar to Zhitlowsky's as a humanitarian who preached social justice. It concludes with what Zhitlowsky had identified as Jesus' most characteristic last lines from Luke 23: "Forgive them, for they know not what they do."[33] Whether An-sky was the author or only the editor of that essay, the echo of Zhitlowsky showed that the gap between the old friends was closing.

An-sky's marriage was hard to fix, but his professional life was more promising. As he experimented with a range of attitudes toward the artistic trends of his time, An-sky began to occupy a more visible position in Russian and Russian-Jewish culture, and he found more to admire in both spheres. With the new freedoms of speech and assembly, Jews organized cultural societies in the provinces as well as the capitals and invited speakers, including An-sky, to their events. An-sky loved traveling throughout the empire on his speaking tours, although (or because) the work made it even harder for him and Edia to be together. Even in the short periods they spent together, they faced tragedy. On September 12, 1909, they left the Northern Hotel in Terioki for an evening stroll. Half an hour later, they heard cries of "Fire!" and ran back to see their rooming house burning. They lost everything but what they had with them, his manuscripts, books, and archive, her clothes and jewels. Now An-sky worked harder than ever to earn money. When Edia wanted to return from Switzerland to Russia in the spring of 1910, An-sky responded that he wanted her to be completely well before she came back, and, anyway, he planned to be out of town for the first three weeks of April, giving lectures in Riga, Vitebsk, Kovno, Bialystok, Moscow, and elsewhere; she seemed to have forgotten that there was nowhere for her to stay in Petersburg ("Do I have an apartment?"). Like his own father, he preferred being out of town to being home, and the admiration of the provincial crowds gave him a kind of satisfaction that his young wife could not. He told Zhitlowsky in August 1910, "This year I earned 1,000 rubles from lectures in sixteen cities (I enjoy moral success and great pleasure), but it's a drop in the sea of my debts and expenses."[34]

The police agreed with An-sky about the significance of his lectures. For the authorities, unaccustomed to the new freedoms, it was troubling to see lecturers traveling around and speaking to crowds. The authorities shared An-sky's own belief that cultural work was also political. When *Evreiskii Mir* was established, An-sky had written to Burtsev, offering to exchange a subscription to his new journal for a subscription to his radical émigré journal *Byloe*; the Tsarist secret police in Paris, who intercepted the letter, grasped the assumption that the two publications—one a vehicle for new Jewish writing, the other a forum for attacks on the Tsarist administration—were functionally equivalent. As An-sky wrote and published fiction and poetry, the authorities tried to determine whether he was still an active revolutionary. The Petersburg police found evidence that this "so-called littérateur" served the SRs abroad as a contact in the empire, but the Paris secret police was skeptical, insisting that An-sky had abandoned SR activity.[35]

When An-sky spoke about Jewish literature in Vilna on January 14, 1910, at a Jewish literary circle (that had obtained the necessary permissions in advance), the police attended, took notes, filed a report, and maintained their surveillance to his next stop, Dvinsk. He was also followed in Minsk. On February 3, a police officer who had staked out a house in downtown Kiev noticed An-sky going in and, aware of his SR membership and the old arrest warrant, tailed him to his hotel. When An-sky left the hotel on February 5 and got in a taxi with his suitcase, blanket, and pillow, two agents, Moisei Iurshenko and Grigory Shevchenko, followed him to the train station, where they bought tickets on his train to Berdichev. Other agents followed him in Zhitomir, Lutsk, and Grodno. A Vilna police major-general filed a report at the end of the month stressing that An-sky was an important threat: he was the author of dangerous publications; he was the editor of *Evreiskii Mir*, whose slogan was "fight for the civil and national equality of the Jewish people"; and his friend, the lawyer Mikhail Kulisher, had said that he "was the first of the Jewish writers to respond to the voice of the Jewish worker and to support him in his fight for freedom." The Interior Ministry disagreed, sending telegrams to tell the Kiev and Vilna police to stop spending government money following An-sky on his lecture tours.[36]

An-sky was amused to watch the provincial police try to adapt to the new order of things. He was struck "not just by the arbitrariness, but by the senselessness and randomness of that arbitrariness in relation to something as uncomplicated as public lectures." The police prevented him from lecturing, insisted that he lecture in Russian rather than Yiddish, or forbade debates following his lectures. When a local man in G. (probably Grodno) asked why debates were forbidden, a policeman said, "You know what? Tell your lecturer to get out of here voluntarily before anything goes wrong—or I'll arrest him." Why? "Just because. I'm sick of dealing with these lectures." One policeman applauded An-sky's lecture on literature and admired his flawless Russian, but interrupted the discussion afterwards, saying to An-sky, "How could *he* [the audience member] ever fight with *you*? He can't even speak Russian." When a listener quoted the Talmud in response to something An-sky had said, the policemen was sure something illegal was happening: "That's enough! You're departing from the program. The lecture here was on literature, and suddenly you talk about the Talmud!" An-sky faced this sort of censorship too, as when a policeman accused him of departing from the program. "You should be reading a lecture, and instead, you are expressing your own thoughts." An-sky asked, "What, I'm supposed to express your thoughts?" and the policeman insisted, "Not mine or yours—you should just read the lecture."[37] The policeman was certain that from discussions of Jewish culture to the revolutionary politics of a few years earlier would be a very short step.

Whether or not they intended to rebel, the people who crowded into An-sky's provincial lectures were excited and moved. He was inundated with requests to speak, and after he returned from a talk, he got letters from young workers and shop assistants, telling him of their impressions, urging that he read their own poems and stories and give them advice. Ben-Tsion Balter, from the Jewish cultural society of the town of Soroka, wrote to An-sky, "You reign in the hearts of all Jews, especially those who love Jewish literature and art." Basking in this admiration, An-sky noticed that Jewish cultural life in the provinces was reviving. Rather than waiting for some kind of cultural direction from the capitals, shtetl Jews were demonstrating energy and initiative. "The cultural movement that has now possessed all the Jews was born and became strong in the depths of the Pale."[38] While in 1908 he had bemoaned the stagnation of Jewish life in the Pale, by 1910 he was optimistic.

Somewhat more slowly, An-sky also found things to admire in the Russian cultural life of the capital. In 1908, he had connections to one part of the polarized Russian cultural scene: the neo-realists who had gathered around the Znanie (Knowledge) publishing house and were associated with the famous radical writer Maxim Gorky. In 1908, Gorky read An-sky's *Pioneers* with some approval and noted, "This thing acquaints us with the Jews better than the tear-soaked works of Aizman and the incoherence of Iushkevich." (Aizman and Iushkevich were two Jewish writers associated with Znanie.) An-sky knew Gorky's onetime protégé, Leonid Andreev, and he recommended that Vera Zhitlovskaia send her novel to Andreev for the publishing house Shipovnik.[39]

In the ensuing years, the Petersburg literary landscape shifted. Andreev split with Gorky, and his work—especially his drama—became more modernist and mystical. A new generation of modernist poets, such as Alexander Blok and Viacheslav Ivanov, were inspired by history, Slavic lore, and folk religion. In 1908, Blok wrote "On Kulikovo Field," a cycle of poems that connected the 1905 revolution to the fourteenth-century Mongol invasion of Russia. In 1910, Andrey Bely published the novel *The Silver Dove,* about a poet who seeks redemption in the mystic rituals of a provincial sect, only to meet a terrible end. An-sky's interests in folktales and history and his conviction that a society in crisis needed to turn to its own past for inspiration were shared by those modernists whom he had always distrusted. At the same time, as he chose work to include in *Evreiskii Mir,* he found himself supporting a generation of modernist Yiddish writers.

One friendship symbolized the shift in An-sky's literary allegiances. The wife of the modernist author Fedor Sologub, Anastasia Chebotarevskaia, who was also associated with the publishing house Razum, invited An-sky to dinner in March 1910. An-sky became friendly with Chebotarevskaia and Sologub, who was already famous as the author of the 1907 novel *The Petty Demon,* about the perverse, frustrated lives of provincial schoolmasters and students. Sologub, together with Merezhkovsky and Gippius, identified with the first generation of the Russian

Symbolist movement, which since the early 1890s had promoted aestheticism and individualism over the literary utilitarianism of the Populists. Sologub and Chebotarevskaia hosted literary gatherings that drew all the fashionable writers of St. Petersburg: Sologub's old friends Merezhkovsky and Gippius, the second generation of Symbolists, such as Blok, Alexsei Remizov, and Ivanov, and other young writers, including Kuzmin, Anna Akhmatova, and Futurists such as Igor Severianin. In Sologub and Chebotarevskaia's salon in 1910, guests gathered at ten or eleven at night and stayed until four or five in the morning; true intimates were served breakfast. They ate and danced, read poems and plays, and spoke about politics and philosophy.[40] Chebotarevskaia, who carefully guarded admission to the salon, may have cultivated An-sky as an expert on Jewish questions, which she and Sologub found fascinating. Regardless of its motivation, her attention presaged a turn in An-sky's favor with the Russian literary establishment.

As An-sky's attitude toward the modernists mellowed, he saw his literary fortunes improve. In August 1910, he signed a contract for a five-volume edition of his collected works in Yiddish, to be published by an American publisher, Evalenko. After Burtsev accused Evalenko of working for the Tsarist police and An-sky terminated that contract, the project was taken up by a St. Petersburg Yiddish publisher, Ezra, with the first volume coming out as planned in 1911. At the same time, the Russian publishing house Prosviashchenie (Enlightenment) arranged to produce a five-volume edition of his works in Russian. The first volume, *The Old Foundations,* was reviewed in 1911 in *Apollon* by Kuzmin, the openly gay decadent poet whom An-sky had so despised in 1908. Kuzmin paired An-sky's book with a recent volume by Remizov, *The Pond,* and treated them both scornfully. He found An-sky's depiction of shtetl Jews saccharine and predictable: "The people are all 'stern, pious, fine-looking.' If old, they all have 'a great, carefully combed beard and thick, bushy brows, under which gazed wise, piercing eyes.' If young, then 'with delicate features and a small sharp beard, deep thoughtful black eyes, and sharp wrinkles on the brow gave the face an expression of a special seriousness.' If children, then 'frail, with a pale, nervous face and lively black eyes.'" It was over the top and might have worked better in Yiddish, but, Kuzmin admitted, he was won over by "the idyllic optimism of the writer, and some of the details of life." Mandelstam, another modernist poet, sounded the same notes in his description of An-sky. He was a character from a different era, comically out of place in the modern world: "In his single person he contained a thousand provincial rabbis. . . . Semyon Akimovich was not yet old but he had an aged grandfatherly appearance and was stooped over from the excesses of Jewishness and Populism. . . . Semyon Akimovich gave the impression of a gentle Psyche afflicted with hemorrhoids." Nonetheless, Mandelstam admitted, there was something charming about him: "People ran after him to hear his stories. The Russian-Jewish folklore of Semyon Akimovich flowed out like a thick stream of honey in marvelous unhurried stories."[41]

There were other indications of An-sky's rising fame. On December 27, 1909, the Jewish Literary Society organized a celebration of the twenty-fifth anniversary of the publication of *History of a Family*. The speeches in An-sky's honor and the readings of his works in Russian and Yiddish drew 700 writers and students, the largest crowd the society had ever seen. The speakers stressed both An-sky's radical credentials and his modernity: unlike an earlier generation of Jewish writers in Russian, who wrote primarily to acquaint Russian readers with Jewish life, An-sky wrote of the Jews' inner life and the folk life, and his work was more artistic than tendentious.[42]

An-sky felt ambivalent about the celebrations in his honor. On December 27, as the literary evening began, he stayed home. Samuil Gurevich, who had come from Riga for the occasion, left the event and came to An-sky to persuade him to attend. This reassurance by one of the privileged friends of his youth moved An-sky and he agreed to go to the celebration, where he was greeted with prolonged applause. The organizers read dozens of congratulatory telegrams from the provinces and friends read his poems and stories. Long after midnight, when the event finally ended, An-sky gave a brief response. He tried to explain why he found the jubilee so surprising, suggesting that the very idea of drawing so much attention to a single individual was not authentically Jewish; whether or not he was right, his anxiety about the event signaled his continuing allegiance to the radical notion of the writer's anonymity that he had embraced when he became "An-sky."[43] If he had yearned to erase his identity—and expressed that yearning as an inconspicuous folklorist—then his growing fame was troubling.

The evening was reported in the Russian-Jewish press and for a month similar An-sky–focused events continued in the provinces. In Petersburg itself, the celebration went on with a banquet at Mikhalevich's restaurant on January 9, 1910, organized by An-sky's colleagues at *Der fraynd* and *Evreiskii Mir* and attended by some of his old Russian radical friends as well as his Jewish colleagues. By then, An-sky had articulated his own thoughts about his jubilee, and he came to the banquet with prepared remarks in Russian that showcased his complex attitude toward Jewish culture, Russian culture, and his own place in them. His speech is worth quoting in its entirety.

> A writer has a difficult fate, but a Jewish writer has an especially difficult fate. His soul is torn; he lives on two streets, with three languages. It is a misfortune to live on this sort of "border," and that is what I have experienced. When I first stepped into literature 25 years ago I wanted to work on behalf of the oppressed, the working masses, and it seemed to me, mistakenly, that I would not find them among the Jews. I thought it was impossible to stand aside from politics, and I found no political movements among Jews. Bearing an eternal longing for Jewishness, I threw myself in all directions and left to work for another people. My life was broken, split, torn. I am not one of those lucky ones raised in their own environment, whose work is normal. I spent many years on that "border," on the boundary between the two streets—and thus I ask you, from the 25-year sum of my literary work, to cut off 16 years. But that time too, which was not dedicated to literature, was not wasted for me. I lived among the Russian folk for a long time, among their lowest strata, but I was never insulted because of my national identity, which I never tried or wanted to conceal. Living among the Russian folk, I was also befriended by Russian intelligentsia leaders and I had the rare honor of being close to people whom the Russian folk will always remember with love—and the hope lives in me that our current dark times will pass, because the Russian folk has no hatred for the Jews. Thousands of years ago, Jews lived on their own land; we have lost it. Jews created a mantle of laws and customs; we have lost that too. And now we must create something firm in our hearts, something that will allow us to live as a nation, a folk. Things are different for us now than when I wrote my first story. We have cultural, political, and literary movements. Long live the Jewish people, long live Jewish literature, long live everything good among the Jews! I believe in a better future and in the survival of the Jews![44]

The Vilna writer Moyshe Shalit, who represented a student organization at the meeting, reported these comments in full, describing the speech as a *vidui,* the confession of sins that Jews recite on Yom Kippur. For Shalit, a conservatory student who was one of only two speakers at the restaurant to give his speech in Yiddish, it must have been moving to hear this well-known Russian writer assert that he envied those who wrote in only one language, who lived in the center of a single culture rather than on the border between two. Shalit heard the speech as a renunciation of Russian culture, of the decade and a half that An-sky had spent immersed in it, and of assimilation of any kind.

When seen as a whole, though, An-sky's speech was not exactly a vidui. Although he told his friends at Mikhalevich's restaurant to cut off 16 years from the tally of his literary work, he did not want them completely to discount the period from 1884 to 1900, relatively dry years when he wrote mostly nonfiction in Russian on non-Jewish themes. Al-though he declared that his life had been "broken, split, torn," he also insisted that his years among first Russian peasants and miners, then Russian writers and revolutionaries, had been a time of friendship, privi-lege, and respect. Characteristically, he saw his life in historical perspec-tive. In the 1880s, he had worked for Russian radical causes because at that point, he did not find Jewish political movements to inspire him. Now that the situation had changed and Jewish movements had arisen, he could work on their behalf.

In order to attract the new audience he wanted, An-sky edited his own past. In the fall of 1910, he published a memoir of his months in Liozno. He had already returned half-a-dozen times to his experiences there, most recently in "Under a Mask." Now he told his story in the first per-son, in the Russian "Sins of Youth and Sins of Age," using it to suggest that he had moved away from his old maskilic beliefs to a more modern cultural nationalism. Lilienblum and his autobiography were on his mind that year; Lilienblum had died in March, and An-sky began the memoir with a paean to Lilienblum and the impact of *Sins of Youth* on An-sky's generation. "They didn't just read it but studied it piously, like a book of the bible, a symbol of our faith. The more bitterly it was persecuted by the elders, the holier it became for the youth . . . The influence of this book was simply magical. Under its influence people sometimes were reborn overnight."[45] By titling the Yiddish version of the essay simply "Sins of Youth," An-sky paid homage to Lilienblum and suggested an organic tie between himself and the Hebrew writer.

When An-sky hinted that his youth was analogous to Lilienblum's, he adopted a conceit that Lilienblum himself had used. As part of his defense of autobiography in general, Lilienblum had compared his own work to another Hebrew autobiography, Mordecai Aaron Guenzburg's *Aviezer* (1864). Because *Aviezer* tells the story of the writer's childhood and youth, Lilienblum announced that his own autobiography would start at the end of adolescence, where Guenzburg's left off, as though their lives were so similar that one description would suffice for both. This narrative de-vice created the sense of a community of Jewish radicals like the writer, all with shared experiences and goals, their lives unfolding according to a single plot.[46] The "sins" of Lilienblum's youth—committed not by Lilien-blum himself, but by the family and community who urged him to devote his mental energy to the Talmud alone, married him off young, and made it impossible for him to leave the Jewish world—were repeated in Guen-zburg's youth and in the youths of many other Jewish men.

At first glance, it seemed the conceit might work for An-sky too. Indeed, the bare outlines of the narrative of An-sky's life in Liozno echoed elements of Lilienblum's life as he retold them in *Sins of Youth*. Having started to question his faith in God, Lilienblum began writing articles advocating religious reform, and his fellow townsmen responded by branding this yeshiva teacher an unbeliever and an atheist. He was persecuted and threatened with exile to Siberia. Finally, he left his home for the more liberal city of Odessa, where he supported himself as a tutor and a clerk. There he read Pisarev and other Russian radical writers and turned into a yet more severe critic of Judaism. He began to write articles asserting that secular sciences would not be enough to resolve the problems of the Jews: their entire economic structure would have to change, and young people would have to study real crafts rather than musty tomes.

An-sky shared Lilienblum's fascination with Pisarev and practical work, and he too was branded an unbeliever and chased out of a shtetl, but more careful examination shows that An-sky's childhood was very different from Lilienblum's. An-sky could hardly complain that the "sins" that ruined Lilienblum's life had marred his own as well. Where Lilienblum had no mother (she died when he was very young) and a father who brought him up within the bonds of tradition, An-sky had an absent father and an indulgent mother; where Lilienblum read only Hebrew and Yiddish, An-sky was reading Russian novels in his teens; and where Lilienblum reserved special wrath for the institution of early marriages and criticized his family harshly for marrying him off at fourteen to a girl three years younger than he was, An-sky was unbetrothed not just at seventeen in Liozno but into his forties. As An-sky was well aware, a deep cultural gap separated him from Lilienblum. Whereas Lilienblum experienced the loss of belief in God as a trauma and spent his life searching for a faith to replace his former one, An-sky, in his voluminous writings, rarely touched on religious faith. But with his retrospective analogy between his childhood and Lilienblum's, An-sky claimed membership in a fellowship of Jewish writers that included Lilienblum.

If An-sky's implicit analogy between his own life and Lilienblum's was factually shaky, it had an ideological import that would have been clear in 1910. By the time of his death, Lilienblum was seen not as the angry narrator of *Sins of Youth,* but as the Zionist activist that he later became, the author of the 1899 *Path of Repentance,* an account of his rejection of assimilationism. Thus An-sky's "Sins of Youth" conveyed not the maskilic bitterness about the constraints of traditional Jewish life from the first part of Lilienblum's memoirs, but a move away from the Haskalah and the embrace of new possibilities for Jewish community, which are associated with the second part of Lilienblum's memoir. Certainly An-sky's "Sins of Youth" suggests cynicism about his own youthful idealism. The notion of a community that is collectively guilty and that then suffers collectively is implied in the Hebrew word that Lilienblum uses: a reader immersed in Jewish religious tradition could hardly fail to associate the *hattot* (sins) of his title with one of the central prayers of Yom Kippur, the confession in which the congregation chants in unison, *Hattanu* (we have sinned). But An-sky's "sins" were not the communal hattot to which the Jewish congregation confesses on Yom Kippur, but rather the individual sins that the Russian word of his title, *grekhi,* implies, remembering that Russian Orthodoxy knows individual but not collective confessions of sins. While the Hebrew title of Lilienblum's *Sins of Youth, Hattot Neurim,* could refer to the sins against youth of which the entire community is guilty, the Russian title of *Grekhi molodosti* would more likely mean the sins of which a single young person is guilty. Given the irony in the story about the protagonist's attempts to lure his students away from tradition, the primary sin to which the title refers may be the Christian sin of pride. Much more than his speech at Mikhalevich's restaurant, "Sins of Youth" was a public vidui, a confession of sins that was also a performance of the role of a returner, meant to lend its writer legitimacy among the Jewish cultural activists of his era.

These same impulses guided An-sky as he prepared his Russian stories for inclusion in his new "Collected Writings." He revised some of them, including "Twenty Years Old," which he had started in 1892 and published for the first time in 1905. He released a new version of it in 1911 as "Hungry," affirming the connection of the two stories by retaining the date of 1892 after the new version. In the later version, the starving hero has a Jewish name, Yosele, and a Jewish aunt in the town where he lives. He obsesses about his Jewishness, fearing that Jews and non-Jews will recognize it and judge him. Asking a Jewish shopkeeper to give him bread on credit seems impossible, because "She looks at me with sad eyes. . . . Of course she knows that I am a Jew, but she pretends that she hasn't guessed . . . and in her heart she is cursing me. . . . How could I barge in and ask her for credit? She won't just turn me down, but she'll rejoice in my sorrow . . ." When his friend's father asks whether as a Jew, he is interested in the problems of the city's poor Jews, Yosele responds in confusion. "It's strange: I never hid my Jewishness, but nonetheless, each time someone reminded me of it out loud, I inadvertently got confused and blushed, as though I had been unmasked. It wasn't that I was ashamed of my Jewish roots, but it was unpleasant when anyone reminded me of it." He knows that he could appeal to his relatives, but resists, wanting to avoid contact with the family he dismisses as "fanatics" with whom he has "nothing in common." Finally, dazed from hunger, he wanders into his Aunt Basya's house and collapses. When he wakes up, he hears the *havdalah* service that marks the end of the Sabbath and sees Basya and his Russian friends. At first he is embarrassed when his friends hear his aunt's Yiddish accent, but after he learns that his friend's father is friendly with Basya, he calls to his aunt "happily and freely," asking her for some gefilte fish.[47]

The revision made the story stronger and less derivative, though paradoxically, the changes brought it even closer to its Dostoevskian model. Religious texts are central to both *Crime and Punishment* and "Hungry." What sets Raskolnikov on the path to release from his agony is his encounter with the prostitute Sonia, who reads to him from the New Testament about the raising of Lazarus (John 11); in the final scene of the novel, when he recovers from his illness in the Siberian prison and his story of renewal and rebirth begins, he looks at his New Testament and remembers Lazarus. Yosele experiences the same kind of relief—"as after an illness" that recalls Raskolnikov's sickness—when he hears another woman's voice, his aunt singing a *tkhine*.

> Somewhere through the wall a woman's voice was singing, very quietly, in the sad, drawn-out, but soft and peaceful chant of a prayer. And suddenly I remembered: this was the prayer of the end of the Sabbath, which begins with the words, "God of Abraham, Isaac and Jacob in your glory!" Once I guessed which prayer it was, I immediately recognized Aunt Basya's voice. I was not at all startled by it; I didn't even ask myself how I had ended up here. I felt peaceful and joyful, as after an illness, and my aunt's singing seemed tender and poetic.

Aunt Basya is singing the tkhine "Got fun Avrom," a well-known song that even russified Jewish readers might recognize.[48]

By designing his story as a reworking of Dostoevsky's *Crime and Punishment*, An-sky suggested that Judaism, no less than Christianity, might cure the modern intellectual. When contrasted with the passage Sonya reads from John, though, Aunt Basya's tkhine represents a very specific facet of Judaism. What Yosele responds to is not a Hebrew prayer that might represent the normative male experience of the religion, nor a rabbinic text that might speak of the experience of elite, educated men, but rather one of the Yiddish prayers that were at the basis of women's experience of religion within the domestic sphere. The final pages of the story reinforce the power of the female, domestic aspects of Jewish life, the conversation and the food of the kitchen. An-sky's protagonist returns not to Jewish high culture and Jewish men, but to a Jewish woman and the Jewish home. Yosele's redemption is facilitated by an older woman, the mother of a family. Since Yosele's own mother is dead, his aunt stands in for her, and other female characters double this figure, such as the old Jewish woman in the shop who looks at him with "sad eyes," and An-nushka, the friend who takes in the poor children and bears the Russian name of An-sky's own mother (Annushka is a nickname for Anna). If An-sky's encounters with a new generation of Jewish cultural activists in 1908 and after motivated him to transform himself into the kind of inter-locutor they wanted, then he could do so by recasting his memories, re-writing his old stories, and reclaiming his connections to his own mother.

Even while he was willing to rewrite his old works in order to appeal to a new audience, An-sky could not accept all the younger generation's ideas. He had begun his speech at the 1910 jubilee dinner with the most compli-cated question that Jewish literature faced: in what language should it be written? A Jewish writer faces an "especially difficult fate," An-sky said, because "he lives on two streets, with three languages," which is "a misfor-tune." A few months later, An-sky was defending Jewish multilingualism. The argument about the proper language for a modern Jewish culture had heated up after the 1905 revolution. In 1908, Jewish and non-Jewish writ-ers publicly debated the role of Jews in Russian literature and the role of Russian in Jewish literature. The fashionable literary critic Kornei Chu-kovsky, a partially Jewish young man who articulated his notions about Jewish culture in conversation with his friend, the brilliant journalist and future Zionist theorist Vladimir Jabotinsky, wrote the first of a series of articles in Jewish and mainstream newspapers about whether Jewish writ-ers could ever find a home in Russian letters.[49]

Strong arguments for the importance of Yiddish were made at the First Yiddish Language Conference at the end of August and the beginning of September 1908 in Czernowitz, in what was then the far Eastern edge of the Austro-Hungarian Empire. Fourteen of the participants were from the Russian Empire, including Peretz, Asch, and Zhitlowsky, who had already moved to New York but was numbered by the participants among the "Russians." (An-sky was miffed not to have been included: he read about the conference in the papers and considered going, but decided not to "for fear of being in the position of an uninvited guest.") The attendees planned to talk about systematizing Yiddish spelling and grammar, but they ended up spending most of their time talking about how Yiddish, so often dis-missed as "not a real language," could get more respect. This meant dem-onstrating that Yiddish could be used for high-culture functions such as writing poems and serious novels—or running a scholarly conference.

The Czernowitz conference was the harbinger of further debate about Yiddish and its status for modern Jewish culture.[50]

The cultural status of Yiddish was complicated by politics. The native language of most Jews was still Yiddish, though increasingly from the 1860s through 1917, those in the Pale strove to educate their children in Russian, hiring tutors such as An-sky had been in Liozno, and a growing population of Russian-speaking Jews was appearing in the capitals. Although the authorities, especially after the ascension of Alexander III, were anxious to limit potentially subversive manifestations of non-Russian cultures, Jews had succeeded in printing secular books and periodicals in Russian, Hebrew, and Yiddish. The government began to make concessions even before 1905, permitting the 1903 appearance of the Yiddish daily *Der fraynd* in Petersburg, followed by more newspapers and public lectures in Yiddish. The Yiddish theater had been officially illegal since 1883, but the ban was relaxed in 1900, and it flourished after 1905.[51]

These shifts spurred Russian-Jewish intellectuals to weigh the possibilities offered by the increased opportunities for work in Yiddish, and the Czernowitz conference provided some terms for debate. A year and a half later, the echoes of Czernowitz were audible in St. Petersburg, where the writers of *Evreiskii Mir* renewed the argument about the proper language for modern secular Jewish culture. The beginning of the debate was an explicit continuation of Czernowitz. Though Hebraists such as Ahad Haam had insisted that Hebrew was the only appropriate language for Jewish culture and scorned Jews who wrote instead in Yiddish or Russian, contributors to *Evreiskii Mir* argued that Hebrew was accessible only to the intelligentsia, but Russian and Yiddish both could be truly national languages, in which a writer could speak to the Jews as a whole. Writing in April 1910 under the pseudonym Mathias Acher, the Yiddishist activist Nathan Birnbaum, the chief organizer at Czernowitz, decried Ahad Ha'am's Hebraism as elitist, puritanical, and out of touch with the Jewish people. What makes a work of literature truly national, he insisted, is not language but the fact that it was "created in the shining glow of the wide-awake Jewish soul, under the influence of the genuine, living Jewish collective."[52] This definition excluded Hebrew, since Birnbaum denied its connection to any genuine Jewish collective.

In July, the debate moved to newer territory, Yiddish versus Russian, when Shmuel Niger, who had been one of the editors of *Literarishe monatsshriften,* jumped into the fray. Niger pointed out the irony of the situation: the entire debate about the value of Yiddish was going on in Russian, and the defenders of Yiddish were, according to Niger, actually assimilated Jews whose vaunted love for the *mame loshn* was only "platonic" and "sterile." Writing in an urbane Russian, Niger accused his fellow Russian-speaking Yiddishists of being only "sympathizers" with the cause of Yiddish rather than dedicating their full strength to it. He called them products of "reverse Marranism" (the Marranos were Iberian Jews, forced to convert to Catholicism under the Inquisition, who continued to practice Judaism in secret), "because the historical Marranos said that they were Christians but in reality, that is, in the depths of their souls and their cellars, they were Jews, whereas our Marrano intelligentsia makes such a noise and fuss about their nationalism, but in real life they are no less 'goys' than the rest of the assimilated intelligentsia."[53] Niger was accusing these writers of being Jewish on the outside, but Russian on the inside.

An-sky joined the debate in September in an article titled "Creative Nationalism and Conversational Nationalism," accusing Yiddishist intellectuals such as Niger of doing little to combat the situation they criticized or to bring assimilating Jews back toward Jewish culture and Yiddish. With their attention to polemics rather than creative work, they were shifting attention away from substance and toward a mere "battle of tongues." An-sky criticized Niger for being so in the grip of his ideology that he had become blind to the complexity of life. In language that echoed his review of *Literarishe monatsshriften,* he called on writers such as Niger to stop unmasking assimilators and to start thinking about the educational and economic factors that had created strong connections between Jews and non-Jewish languages. The Jewish professional class had been educated through Russian schools and Russian culture, and therefore "they continue to live by means of this culture, both spiritually and materially." This was true of Yiddishists like Niger too. "We have to have the courage to admit that *all* our intelligentsia *in reality* are 'reverse Marranos,'" because "they satisfy all their practical, cultural, and higher intellectual needs not through Jewish culture, but through Russian, Polish, German, and other cultures." In order for the Jewish intelligentsia to return to Yiddish, they would first need to return to Jewish culture, and that would require "cultural soil where they could invest their powers and their knowledge." Traditional Jews truly live within a Jewish culture that possesses not only a religion but also its own science and literature, art, festivals and days of mourning, institutions, an educational system, and customs for inside and outside the home: An-sky urged secular Jews to work to create a new Jewish culture that could be equally all-encompassing and compelling, in order to fight "our 'Marranism,' our dividedness and our inconsistency."[54]

Niger responded to An-sky in the next issue by offering a new argument. He agreed that if some members of the Russian-Jewish intelligentsia knew no Yiddish (or "the jargon"), they should not be asked to use it. But for most of that intelligentsia, he asserted, though they may speak Russian and even think in Russian, their native language is not truly Russian. "A language is more than a simple conglomeration of words, a language is something organic, *animate*," and in its spirit, the language of their thoughts was Yiddish. The Russian-Jewish intelligentsia would act more beautifully if "they used Yiddish as their own native language, if they used it not only 'asleep' but also awake, and did not erect a wall between themselves and their nation." In response to Niger's second sally, the editor Iakov Saker called for a more serious sociolinguistic study of the reasons behind Jewish linguistic assimilation; Medem called for more community resources to go to support Yiddish literature and an end to compromises that allow for "all three Jewish cultures (really one culture and two assimilations) under one roof"; and An-sky, in an article titled "Assimilation from the Cradle," called for a new system of education to provide a real alternative to assimilation. Having spent so much of his youth tutoring children, he spoke with authority about early childhood education. This essay, in which he criticized upper-class Russian Jews who hire Russian peasant women to care for their children and thereby ensure that they will feel more at home with Russian traditions than Jewish ones, provoked a set of attacks on him in *Novoe Vremia* and other right-wing newspapers.[55] It also marked the end of the debate in *Evreiskii Mir*. The newspaper itself folded seven months later.

Although Niger and An-sky could articulate coherent arguments for one stance or another toward the issues raised by living between languages and cultures, they could not live consistently by these views. Even while An-sky attacked Niger in print, he wrote to him warmly. Since he had recruited Niger for *Evreiskii Mir* in 1909, in letters written first in Russian and then for the most part in Yiddish, An-sky, perhaps attempting to atone for his hostile 1908 review of *Literarishe monatsshriften*, expressed respect for the younger writer's style and judgment. He sometimes assigned Niger specific topics or suggested Yiddish writers or publications to review and at other times gave him a list of themes or asked him to propose a topic. He expressed his confidence not only in Niger's critical judgment but also in his linguistic abilities. "But write something and send it and God will bless you for writing in Russian, since from this motley crew of grave-digging traducers from Yiddish into Russian I have already contracted typhus on top of consumption, if not something worse."[56] An-sky insulted his journal's poor translators with an untranslatable play on words, replacing the Yiddish term for "translator," *iberzetser,* literally "one who carries over," with *ibershleper,* or "one who awkwardly drags over." When he expanded the expected *khevre* (literally, "comrades") into *khevre-kadishe* (burial society), An-sky indicated that these translators' incompetence brought them (and perhaps the texts they translated) close to death, a fate that he hinted he too feared when he wrote that their work had made him ill. By writing to Niger in these terms, An-sky distinguished between, on the one hand, old, moribund Jews with poor Russian, and, on the other, himself and Niger, whose mastery of Russian was connected to their vitality. Instead of bemoaning his and Niger's linguistic "divided-ness," he celebrated it as a source of strength.

When he decided to attack Niger in print, An-sky wrote to warn him.

> I'm writing a big article now about the national question where there will also be an answer to your article. I may be a bit blunt in it. But I hope you won't be offended: "If you start a fight, don't try to save your topknot." In my article I will pose the question more broadly, and among other things I'll show that you zealots are just as much Marranos on the left side as the "sympathizers," because you also live with foreign cultures.[57]

In the middle of his Yiddish letter, An-sky inserted a Russian saying, thus reaffirming the connection between himself and Niger, the perfect mastery of Russian—indeed, the Marranism—that set them apart from the "grave-digging traducers." The saying he chose was drawn not from the world of Russian high society but from the Cossacks, who are known for the topknot produced when they shave all the hair on their head except for a section on top. With this phrase, An-sky defended his decision to disagree publicly with his colleague and suggested that the two of them had something in common with Cossacks, the defenders of the Russian Empire and the Jews' traditional enemies. Even while An-sky announced that he would criticize Niger and his fellow Yiddishist "zealots" for their allegiance to non-Jewish cultures, his phrasing showed he also wanted to convince Niger that they could both rejoice in their mastery of non-Jewish vocabulary and behaviors.

No matter how much he tried to convince Niger and others that he was really a Yiddishist, An-sky remained ambivalent about choosing between Russian and Jewish cultures, as evidenced in his 1910 *Almanac for Every-one, For God's Truth.* The first section, called "Faiths are varied—God is one," had short quotations from the Hebrew and Greek Bibles, the Tal-mud, and Tolstoy himself, arguing, "One of the most important com-mandments that Christ gave to people says, 'Do not make distinctions between your own kind and others, because all people are children of a single God.'"[58] Tolstoy's point contradicted An-sky's in "Assimilation from the Cradle." An-sky had spoken for fighting assimilation, preserving the specificity of Jewish culture (albeit in new secular rather than older religious forms), while Tolstoy insisted that national or religious differences are fundamentally insignificant and should be forgotten. When An-sky designed *For God's Truth* in the spirit of Tolstoyan universalism, he stepped away from his defense of national specificity in *Evreiskii Mir.*

An-sky's inconsistency could be attributed to expediency; it may be that the articles in *Evreiskii Mir,* a publication he controlled, reflected his true beliefs, whereas he edited *Almanac for Everyone* for money and was obligated there to support the Tolstoyan views of its publishing house. However, this ignores his long-standing admiration of Tolstoy and his principles. Along with much of his generation, he was drawn to Tolstoy's idealism even while he questioned the conviction of the writer's followers that their radical asceticism made them superior to others. Tolstoy's death in 1910 triggered a vicious battle between his widow and his disciples over his inheritance. At the Moscow trial of the Tolstoyans, An-sky was repulsed by Vladimir Chertkov, the disciples' leader, but when he got to know Chertkov later, he admired his "great intellectual ability" and "spiritual force." (Chertkov, in turn, invited An-sky to give the Tolstoyans a lecture on Jewish folklore.) An-sky continued to believe with Tolstoy in the necessity for creative intellectuals to remain comprehensible to nonintellectuals. He told Niger that he strove to be a true *intelligent*: "This is the kind of intellectual that Tolstoy is. The real mark of such an intellectual (a real prophet) is that the folk understands him, follows him, appreciates him."[59] When he urged upper-class Jews, in "Assimilation from the Cradle," to make sure their children were exposed to traditional Jewish culture, he acted on the Tolstoyan inclination to value lower- over higher-class ways, traditional lore over European-style education. However, when he insisted on the need for the Jews of the Russian Empire to retain or reinvent a particular, exclusively Jewish culture, An-sky spoke for the creation of texts that would be inaccessible to the newly literate Russian reader, to whom he had devoted so many years and pages. Even while in "Assimilation from the Cradle" he argued for the preservation and recreation of a modern, secular, but exclusively Jewish culture, An-sky felt pulled in the opposite direction, toward a broad, inclusive vision of culture and to the idea that one should not make distinctions between one's own kind and others, "because," in Tolstoy's words, "all people are children of a single God."

An-sky's private life, like his writing, was unsettled by the tensions between assimilation and tradition, Russian and Yiddish. Edia ultimately grew frustrated with her marriage to a man who had more time for his cultural mission than for his wife, and she found a lover in Vitebsk, where she often stayed at her parents' house. Her husband had discouraged her from coming back to St. Petersburg in the spring of 1910, and when she returned in the winter of 1910–1911, she was pregnant. Although An-sky suspected the baby was not his, he wrote to Zhitlowsky in February 1911 reporting Edia's pregnancy as a piece of good news and sounding thrilled about becoming a parent. Three months after her return, Edia admitted that the pregnancy was the result of an "isolated incident" with a man she and An-sky called "P." An-sky soon realized, though, that she was still in contact with P., writing him letters and taking money and gifts from him. Now nearing fifty, An-sky had been diagnosed with heart problems, and Edia told P., who urged her to carry the baby to term and wrote to her about what they might do should her husband die soon. Ultimately, Edia and An-sky decided to abort the pregnancy (a legal operation for tuberculosis patients). She spent two weeks at Ligovskaia Hospital recovering from the procedure. An-sky wrote to her later that he would never forget the "Golgotha" of that time, "that torment of pretending for strangers to be a pitiable father who had decided on this difficult step to save his wife's life, and boiling in my soul that mix of hatred, suspicion, and love and pity for you, pouring out like blood, which I also had to hide." Writing in Yiddish, he reported the end of the pregnancy to Zhitlowsky in April, blaming it on a miscarriage caused by Edia's illness. He admitted that he had become fascinated by the psychology of people who die without leaving children.[60]

Both were shaken by the abortion, and Edia insisted that she wanted to change her life. An-sky urged her to study something seriously to demonstrate her moral "rebirth." But over the summer of 1911, which Edia spent, again, in Switzerland, he realized that she was still writing to P. and he began to think of asking her for a divorce. What troubled him most was the idea that his marital troubles—his inability to transform himself into a conventionally married Jewish man—might become public knowledge. "I am almost at the end of my life's road," he wrote to her.

> My life was hard, full of work. There were many stones in my path. And I went down this path without ever falling into the dirt. I am no braggart, but I can with a clean conscience say that that small name I have created for myself is as pure as a diamond. And my pure name, my pure working life are the dearest things in the world to me. I can give that name only to a person who will treasure it and guard its purity. So I ask you, as though before the face of God, can you again become my wife, to whom I could with a peaceful conscience entrust my dearest possession, the only thing I own, my unsullied name, my pure life?

Over his nearly fifty years, An-sky had succeeded in creating a public—albeit pseudonymous—self, recognized for his writing and his community work, and he valued that creation more than anything else. Edia could not give him the assurance he needed that his name would be protected. Writing to Edia at the end of August 1911, he asked for a divorce, saying that he had never believed the pregnancy was the result of an isolated incident. He promised to continue to support her for two years. She asked again for forgiveness, but he made the arrangements for a formal Jewish divorce officiated by a rabbi. In October 1911, he insisted that further explanations could not help, because the distance between them had become unbridgeable. "I am sad to see that we speak different languages."[61]

The phrasing is telling, for language had become a point of contention between husband and wife. An-sky urged Edia to work to realize her dreams of becoming an actress. As they both knew, Jewish actors who wanted to go on the Russian stage faced both legal barriers (due to the restrictions on Jews living outside the Pale) and widespread prejudice. The newly legal Yiddish theater, though, offered unparalleled possibilities—if only Edia knew Yiddish! She had reacted skeptically in May 1910 when her husband proposed that she study Yiddish: "Of course your idea about a Jewish theater is attractive to me too, but where, pray tell, could I learn Yiddish? You could hardly think this possible in Moscow?" Eventually, she changed her mind. An-sky told Niger in August 1910 that Edia had started studying Yiddish after reading Niger's article on it, presumably in *Evreiskii Mir*. The next year, in a conciliatory mood after An-sky had asked for the divorce, Edia wrote that she would become a Yiddish actress and suggested that she spend three months in a shtetl to master the language. After the divorce, Edia enrolled in an acting course in Moscow where she studied Russian and European drama. But she did not forget her promise, telling An-sky, "Word of honor, I read in Yiddish every day."[62]

When An-sky and Edia tried to repair their marriage, they found themselves discussing the same cultural and ideological questions that filled his writings. With his frank acknowledgment that as things are now, the entire Russian-Jewish intelligentsia was addicted to non-Jewish culture, he explained and excused his own dreams of living in a "bourgeois" home in Vilna with Edia, playing chess and reading French. The educational and economic factors that made the Russian-Jewish intelligentsia unable to function in Yiddish, which An-sky described sympathetically in the *Evreiskii Mir* articles, had made his wife who she was. His vision of a trilingual modern Jewish culture allowed him to imagine his Russophone wife acting in a Jewish play. When he offered to write such a play for her, she urged him (echoing Nina in Chekhov's *Seagull*) to include a love story. "There's almost no romance in anything you've written. I think that's crucial for a play. A romance makes a play more lifelike, bright, and complete."[63] The result may have been *The Dybbuk*, written first in Russian. The ideal of linguistic and cultural translatability that he defended in "Creative Nationalism and Conversational Nationalism" suggested that both Edia and their marriage were redeemable, that the Europeanized Jewish intelligentsia could eventually become producers and consumers of a new Jewish culture in their native language, Russian.

But even while An-sky argued for the possibility of creating a modern Jewish culture in Russian, he remained as ambivalent about the language question as he had always been about marriage. He told the "fanatic" Yiddishist Niger that he felt closer to him than to his fellow editor, the Russophile Saker. An-sky's attempt to reeducate his Russophone wife and transform her into a Yiddish actress reveals the fissures between his varied unrealized fantasies—one of a new life as a married member of "the petty bourgeoisie" in Vilna, another of a return to a traditional Jewishness that he associated with the Jewish "proletariat" and its language, Yiddish—and the reality of his peripatetic, solitary, multilingual, and modern urban existence. His second article in the language debate, "Assimilation from the Cradle," where he argued that upper-class Jews need to bring their children up differently, might have emerged from the same impulses that led him to urge Edia to learn Yiddish; it was a reflection on the educational process that had produced her, a Russian-speaking Jewish baryshnia, and an attempt to repair them on paper, if not in reality. An-sky and Edia had no children themselves, but with this article, An-sky tried to compensate for the traditional Jewish family life that he was unable or unwilling to lead. In the same year of 1910, he undertook other projects focusing on Jewish children, traveling through the northwest parts of the empire, where he and Edia were both born, to collect Yiddish counting rhymes and children's songs, which he eventually published; he was the first Jewish folklorist to see children's lore as a separate sphere, worthy of study.[64]

In the aftermath of the 1905 revolution, An-sky had hoped for rest and renewal. He had wanted to become a new kind of person, with an apartment, a wife, and a stronger connection to a Russian-Jewish culture that itself, he hoped, would experience a rebirth. During the years after 1908, he celebrated the rise of a new secular Jewish culture, in which he himself played an important role. He argued with friends and colleagues over the definition of that new culture; in print he defended a vision of Jewishness based on history and folklore rather than language, but in his private letters he considered the possibility that a strong secular Jewish identity might require fidelity to a single Jewish language, to Yiddish over Russian. By 1911, it was clear that An-sky would not find the kind of happiness he had once pursued. As his marriage fell apart, he found himself going back to the questions he had debated in 1909 and 1910. When he wrote about the abortion, he used Christian imagery, recognizing Edia's release from hospital as the end of "that way of the cross."[65] And when he told Zhitlowsky about the end of the pregnancy, he returned to the Yiddish of their childhood. Although for years he had included phrases and passages in Yiddish in his Russian letters to Zhitlowsky, especially when discussing his love life, it was the end of his relationship with Edia that prompted him to seek a new, linguistic intimacy with his old friend by writing whole letters regularly in Yiddish (which he would continue to do almost exclusively until his death).

An-sky's writings after the revolution of 1905 showed that the questions that troubled him most had no easy answers. He lambasted the young Yiddish modernists at *Literarishe monatsshriften* in 1908, then found himself recruiting them and trying to convince them how much he and they had in common. In his own letters he questioned the conclusions that he defended in his debates with Zhitlowsky and Niger. He rejected his own past in "Behind a Mask," "Sins of Youth," "Hungry," and his speech at Mikhalevich's restaurant—and then, in the next breath, embraced it. Most painfully, the marriage that had given him "light, warmth, tenderness, and happiness," such as he had "never experienced and never expected," did not last. Dubnov wrote with sadness of the end of An-sky's marriage. "It was joyful to think that that eternal wanderer would finally find domestic happiness, but it did not last long. Whether because of the age difference or some other reason, An-sky was soon alone again. Then he thought up his ethnographic expedition to the Pale of Settlement. . . . This gave the Jewish Populist and folklore collector moral satisfaction and, perhaps, relief from the misfortunes of his life."[66] In fact, An-sky had been thinking about the expedition since 1907 if not earlier, but Dubnov may have been right that the divorce from Edia prompted him to turn his plans into reality, to leave Petersburg, as he had so often left places where he was unhappy, and seek personal and cultural renewal elsewhere.

CHAPTER EIGHT

The Dybbuk and the Golem

It's as though I'm climbing up a tall mountain, from which I see a greater and greater area. I'm starting to see the folk, the nation, with flesh-and-blood eyes,
> —S. An-sky to Chaim Zhitlowsky, August 26, 1913

W HEN HIS PLANS for personal happiness seemed to be falling through, An-sky's thoughts turned to "the future of the Jews." After the September 1909 fire in his Finnish rooming house, he had written about his despair and his hope, both personal and communal.

> Jewishness lies in a 4000-year-old psychology and a 4000-year-old . . . culture. If we can succeed in adapting *our* culture to life we will live, if not we will suffer and run out of air until we suffocate. But no surgeon can sew someone else's head and heart on to us. . . . This last misfortune (the fire) practically cut off half my life with a knife; I'm going to have to struggle like a fish against the ice, because of money. But I'm not losing my good spirits. I want to work, and I believe in the future of the Jews.

He planned to convince the Jewish Historical Ethnographic Society (EIEO) to send him to gather folklore through the country, a project that he thought would cost 8,000 to 10,000 rubles. "If this works out, I'll willingly dedicate what remains of my life to it. It's worth it." An-sky saw his personal pain mirrored in the struggles of Jews to live in the modern world without losing their tie to Jewish culture. Since 1907 if not earlier, he had been conceiving an enormous project: organizing and fund-raising for an ethnographic expedition to collect Jewish tales, songs, and customs in the entire Pale of Settlement. He had begun this work when he got support from Samuil Shryro to collect Jewish lore in the Vitebsk area and to write "Jewish Folk Art" in 1908. Now he had decided to dedicate his life to folklore collection, which he saw as "colossally important for the creation

of Jewish culture." He contemplated writing a book about Jewish ethnography in the fall of 1910, but although he made outlines, collecting
folklore was much more inspiring to him than producing another book.[1]
He viewed an ethnographic expedition as a heroic mission, an "enormous
cultural task," whereby he personally and Jewry as a whole might break
through the ice to find happiness greater than anything he had experienced before.

   While his marriage fell apart, An-sky threw himself into his expedition
plans. In April 1911, after he told Zhitlowsky about the end of Edia's
pregnancy, he wrote, "Well, on to something happier!" and turned to his
plans for collecting folklore. He was sure it would be better to work in the
Pale of Settlement than among immigrants in the United States, as Zhitlowsky had suggested. "Something like folklore must be gathered in the
place where it was created. Once removed from its place it loses its bou-
quet, its flavor and meaning. No, you have to collect Jewish stories, songs,
and so on only there in the little shtetls, from old people who carry the
undisturbed past in themselves."[2] The process of collecting the material in
situ and the human contacts it would offer were crucial to his vision of his
task. He sought both personal redemption and national renewal. As he
worked on the expedition—interrupted by the infamous Beilis blood libel
trial—he wrote articles, stories, and finally the play, expressing the yearning to find salvation in the folklore that he was himself saving; at the same
time, *The Dybbuk* reveals doubt that folklore could really save anyone.

With increasing energy, he communicated an ethnographic vision that
wed the technology of contemporary Russian anthropology and folkloristics to a belief in traditional culture as a source of materials that could
be recombined to create inspirational art. His first audience was the readers of the 1908 "Jewish Folk Art," whom he urged to gather "the most
precious pearls of folklore" before they vanish, in order to establish an
"underlying material soil" for modern Jewish culture and literature.
Whereas earlier Jewish ethnographers had focused on the defensive task
of demonstrating that Jews are not dangerous to Christians, An-sky described a more broadly conceived ethnographic effort that would value
the collected materials for their ability to teach and inspire. He established his own credentials and vision as a collector with a series of articles based on his research in the Vitebsk region: collections of spells and
charms, folk songs, children's counting rhymes, and sayings that revealed
unusual breadth of scope. He criticized Ignats Bernshtein's 1908 collection of sayings for neglecting to situate folk texts in the culture of the
shtetl Jew, and he critiqued Noyekh Prilutski's 1911 collection of songs

for including printed material in the style of elite writers.[3] He saw songs and stories as vehicles for understanding the experiences of Jews, especially the most traditional and poorest, and for considering the history of their interactions with Christians.

He spoke about Jewish folklore at an Evening of Jewish Music, at the Russian Geographical Society, to the intellectuals who belonged to the Jewish Folk Music Society and the Jewish Historical-Ethnographic Society. With the founding of the EIEO in 1908, a fifteen-year communal effort to study the history of Russian Jews gained a public face, visible in the new journal *Evreiskaia Starina*. The members of the society—the historian Dubnov, the political activist and lawyer Maxim Vinaver, the lawyer Mikhail Kulisher, the anthropologists Lev Shternberg and Samuel Weissenberg, and An-sky himself—were liberals and radicals, and underlying their examination of Jewish history and ethnography was the conviction that the Jews of the empire faced urgent political problems. An-sky knew that the EIEO was the most logical sponsor for his expedition, and he pushed its members to agree. In December 1908, he spoke at an EIEO meeting about the urgency of a broad-ranging expedition, and in October 1909 he suggested that the society sponsor such an expedition. The EIEO members accepted this message, and An-sky's authority within the society grew in March 1910 when he was elected to its board. He gained yet more authority in 1912, when he was elected to the board of the Jewish Folk Music Society.[4]

With time, An-sky's plans grew more ambitious. In 1909, when he thought he would need 8,000 to 10,000 rubles, he had hoped merely to go by himself to collect folklore as he had done before. By 1911, when his goal was 30,000 rubles, he was hoping to mount a full-fledged modern ethnographic expedition, on the model of the expeditions that Vladimir Tan-Bogoraz and Vladimir Iokhelson had led to study the peoples of Siberia at the beginning of the century, or the expeditions that the folklorist brothers Boris and Iury Sokolov had taken to collect peasant lore in Novgorod province in 1908 and 1909, with at least two people on each team and technology such as cameras and phonographs. Bogoraz and Iokhelson had been hired for the Jesup North expedition by Franz Boas and the American Museum of Natural History; An-sky hoped to find similarly generous sponsorship and institutional legitimacy, and he wanted to produce a large quantity of material, to be published in its entirety.[5]

When he described his expedition plans, An-sky emphasized its broad scope and numbers. He wanted to visit 300 places in ten provinces. He planned to record "traditions, legends, tales, parables, songs, proverbs, by-words, sayings, riddles, the peculiarities of local dialects and so on," an all-encompassing and impressive project. He wanted to write down "customs, beliefs, charms, superstitions, remedies," to gather "historical materials relating to each location—communal record books, documents, old papers, memoirs, stories of eye-witnesses." With a museum in mind, he wanted to acquire "old books, manuscripts, documents, Jewish art objects: *mizrahim* [markers for the east wall of a home], ark curtains, carvings from pulpits, menorahs, decorated Torah scrolls, religious objects, women's old adornments, old outfits, relics, objects connected to the memory of famous people or well-known events," to photograph "types, scenes, historical places, monuments, old or famous buildings." He insisted that the beauty of the ethnographic material made it politically and culturally valuable. "If anti-Semitic theories are based on slander about the economic danger posed by Jews, then we must arm ourselves with the materials given directly by folk art, which brightly depict the face of the Jewish people, its opinions, beliefs, hopes and fears."[6] He believed that folk art would inspire modern Jewish artists to produce works that could speak to Jews and Christians alike, art that itself would defend and renew Jewish culture.

The most important person to hear his plea was a wealthy Kiev businessman, Baron Vladimir Gintsburg (or Günzburg or Guenzburg). The baron was the son of a well-known financier and philanthropist, Baron Goratsy Gintsburg, who had made a fortune in banking and gold-mining and maintained residences in Kiev, Petersburg, and Paris, where his bank had a branch. Both the Gintsburg family and the Brodskys, the baron's wife's family, were also involved in beet sugar production. The Gintsburg family belonged to the wealthiest class of Russian Jews, who had access to Russian society at its highest levels and functioned as *shtadlonim,* leaders who interceded with the government on behalf of the Jewish community. Vladimir Gintsburg attended St. Petersburg University, and the Russian writers Ivan Turgenev, Mikhail Saltykov-Shchedrin, Ivan Goncharov, and Vladimir Solovev frequented his father's Petersburg home. Baron Vladimir Gintsburg continued the family tradition of philanthropy for both Jewish and general causes: he supported a hospital, a synagogue, a library, and a girls' high school. An-sky met the baron in Kiev in early 1912 and found him "sweet, charming, with a big heart."[7] He convinced him to provide the expedition with 10,000 rubles of seed money and to help with future fund-raising.

An-sky and Gintsburg proceeded to strategize. An-sky organized meetings of Jews in large cities throughout the empire to explain the expedition goals and ask the audience to donate. He approached wealthy Jews individually, sometimes with the help of an intermediary. For instance, the baron recruited Genrikh Sliozberg, a famous lawyer who worked for his family, to raise funds for the expedition from "the Port Arthur Ginsburg" (Moisei Ginsburg, a Petersburg merchant who had supplied the Russian army at Port Arthur during the Russo-Japanese War). To show donors the tie between the expedition and the empire's Jewish elite, An-sky decided to name it after Vladimir's recently deceased father. These strategies paid off. Although An-sky did not in the end gather all the 30,000 rubles he had hoped for, he did collect 23,000, more than doubling Gintsburg's original grant and almost triple what he had dreamed of in 1909.[8]

At times, the financier Gintsburg and the radical An-sky disagreed on fund-raising techniques. An-sky considered establishing the expedition as an independent organization, whereas the baron felt that funders would rather donate to a specific, time-limited project housed within another organization. Gintsburg's financial and emotional support was consistent: in the spring of 1913 when An-sky, annoyed with people who promised to help raise money but did not follow through, threatened to call off the expedition for that year, Gintsburg wrote to insist that the project go through as planned. Threatening to call off the expedition was "a good maneuver to frighten sluggish donors, but you mustn't go so far as to commit *hara-kiri*. That's absolutely impossible. You must go at the appointed time, no matter how much money is in the bank. And you must always complete the work plans in full, not doing less for lack of money; you must do it all as planned." If it was impossible to raise enough money among the donors they had targeted, they should find other sources. This unwavering support from his primary sponsor was just what An-sky needed to hear, and he responded, "I can't express what an enormous, joyful, encouraging impression your good and heartfelt letter made on me! Of course you can see that even the faintest notion of postponing the expedition until next year was simply a tragedy for me."[9]

An-sky used some of Gintsburg's money to organize a conference in March 1912 to discuss the expedition. He invited the Hebrew poet Bialik (who, with Yeshua Hana Ravnitsky, had published a collection of Talmudic legends), telling him that he was gathering people from three categories: "1) those who have worked in Jewish ethnography, 2) those who have worked in Russian ethnography but are now ready to begin working in Jewish ethnography (no converts to Christianity), 3) those who helped organize the expedition materially." Ultimately, An-sky gathered fifteen Petersburg intellectuals, three Moscow visitors (including the folksong collector Peysakh Marek and the composer and ethnomusicologist Iuly (Yoel/Joel) Engel, and the doctor and anthropologist Weissenberg from Elizavetgrad.[10]

At the conference, An-sky described his plan as the only path to Jewish cultural renewal. "Gathering folklore is not only a scholarly task, but a national and topical one. To educate our children in a national Jewish spirit, we must give them folktales, folk songs, in short, what forms the basis of children's education for other peoples." The gathered experts were skeptical. Shternberg argued that physical anthropology, or resolving the "question of the Jewish race," was more important than folklore, and the Moscow doctor Samuil Vermel thought demographic information was more important. Weissenberg and Iokhelson asserted that folklore could never accomplish what An-sky hoped, and the historian Shaul Ginzburg, who had been An-sky's editor at *Der fraynd*, agreed: "No matter how many folktales we gather, that will not diminish the wave of conversions. Even the language of Jewish folklore is inaccessible to our children." An-sky was not discouraged by the scholars' disagreement. He reported to Gintsburg that the group had decided against gathering economic information, because it would be too great a task and too distant from ethnography.[11]

Even though they disagreed about the purpose of the expedition, the men at the conference, presumably impressed with the funds their host had raised, supported it. Dubnov, Kulisher, Sliozberg, Shternberg, Ginzburg, the editor of *Voskhod* Leopold Sev, and the historian and librarian Alexander Braudo all joined the organizational committee.[12] Some of them, such as Shternberg, provided considerable professional help. Others offered advice that An-sky could implement immediately, such as Peysakh Marek's idea that the expedition start in Volynia with the earliest Jewish settlements in the Russian Empire, dating from the fifteenth century. With this shift in plans, An-sky decided to move the home base of the expedition from Vilna to Kiev, and thus shifted focus from the Litvak Jews and the Chabad Hasidism of his own childhood to the exotic (for him) Galician Jews, with their more emotional strains of Hasidism.

Nineteenth-century ethnographers asked informants to respond to lengthy questionnaires so they could determine the geographical dispersion of folk beliefs and practices, and as early as 1907, when An-sky first told him about his dream of undertaking the expedition, Gurevich had urged him to make sure he got everyone to answer the same questions. Now that the expedition would really happen, An-sky knew he would need a questionnaire, and he recruited seven people to a commission that would develop it: Shternberg, Iokhelson, Kulisher, and Dubnov worked on general questions; Engel, Zinovy Kiselgof, and David Maggid on musicological ones. An-sky explained to Gintsburg that this questionnaire, or "Program for collecting materials on Jewish ethnography," would be a long, complex document. "In order to give you a sense, I'll say that just the word 'Synagogue' required 100 questions. The word 'Yeshiva' the same number. I begin with the 'birth of the fruit' and follow the human life until death. Death, life after death, demonology. Holidays, everyday life, abstract questions. In short, we'll have over 10,000 questions, covering all aspects of everyday life and the beliefs of the people."[13] This was a hugely ambitious and awe-inspiring mission that required hiring some Jewish history students to help with the questionnaire. An-sky's enthusiasm was boundless.

Although An-sky succeeded in attracting broad support for his expedition, the reactions he heard at the conference suggest that his fellow Jewish intellectuals did not share his faith that folklore collection could renew Jewish culture, and he was wary of relinquishing control over the expedition, reluctant for it to belong officially to the EIEO. Ultimately he gave in to Gintsburg's insistence that forming a separate organization was too much work, would require a separate bookkeeper, and would be bad for fund-raising.[14] The stationery he used during this period identified his project as the Baron Goratsy Osipovich Gintsburg Ethnographic Expedition of the Ethnography and Folklore Section of the Jewish Historical-Ethnographic Society. But his hesitation suggests that he wanted to preserve control over the project because only thus could he attain the personal and national renewal he craved.

In his 1908 "Jewish Folk Art," An-sky had complained that "there is no people that has talked about itself as much and knows itself as little as the Jews," that "for many years now there have been endless debates and passionate fights about the essence of Jewishness, folk culture, nationalism, the great spiritual heritage, the national-cultural values, and so on, but still in fact one encounters among Jews neither serious interest in Jewish culture, nor concern about its preservation and further development, nor any conscious striving to study the national worldview and the national particularities of the Jewish people." In fact, Russian-Jewish scholars had already been studying traditional Jewish culture for fifty years. Moisei Berlin had published a study of Jewish ethnography in 1861, and the lawyer Ilia Orshansky published essays about Jewish life, including folk songs, in the 1870s. In 1891, Dubnov had appealed to Russian Jews to collect and preserve Jewish legends, folk songs, community record books, and tombstone engravings for posterity, and he had

established a series of volumes to publish the results. In 1901, Saul Ginzburg and Marek had published a large collection of Yiddish folk songs.
An-sky was well aware of all these efforts, but he felt that they were too
weak, narrow, and theoretical. They had not led to the renewal of contemporary Jewish culture because they were not art meant for consumption by a healthy Jewish community, but polemics meant to defend Jews
and their way of life against attack. An-sky's aim was not at the past, but
the future.

Earlier scholars of Russian-Jewish culture, such as Berlin and Orshansky, influenced by the maskilic rejection of the irrational, saw Jewish
folklore as "primitive." They argued that rather than restrictive legislation, the imperial government should offer Jews equal rights and encour-
age them to adapt to Russian culture. Orshansky, a lawyer, was particularly concerned with the Jews' legal status. Even in his own generation,
An-sky found few allies. Dubnov agreed that collecting folklore was a "sacred task," but An-sky complained that history was the real daughter of
the EIEO, ethnography only its step-daughter. Dubnov used folk material
to produce histories of the Jews that supported his ideology of Jewish
cultural autonomism.[15] An-sky was unique in his commitment to the expedition as a way toward cultural renewal.

An-sky's conviction that folklore collection was a path to personal and
communal redemption derived from his Russian mentors, Uspensky,
Lavrov, and the Populists, who believed that educated people have an
obligation to the poor. In his *Historical Letters*, Lavrov had urged readers to repay the debt they owed the peasants by working in the countryside on their behalf, and Uspensky imagined that contact with the soil
was healing, as in the story of Mikula, beloved of Moist Mother Earth,
who gains a magic strength when he touches the ground. When An-sky
wrote of the importance of gathering folktales in their place of origin,
from "old people who carry the undisturbed past in themselves," and
when he expressed his faith that the folkloric expeditions would make
him "infinitely happy," he echoed Lavrov and Uspensky's belief that
alienated intellectuals thirst for contact with the soil. As Russian intellectuals had been doing for generations, he contrasted his own seemingly
inauthentic way of life with that of rural folk, and as he had done so often, he imagined that by finding acceptance among a new group of people he might finally find joy. His insistence that Jewish folklore was the
product of continuous and ongoing interaction with Christians reflected the broad humanist horizons that he shared with his Russian
teachers.[16] Just as he was able to reconcile his internationalist socialism
with his nationalist sympathies, so he did not, apparently, see a contra-

diction between his ecumenical view of folklore and his belief that it would provide the seeds and spirit of a specifically Jewish revival.

An-sky's ideas about folklore also resembled those of Peretz, who gathered songs and stories from Warsaw Jews and urged his followers to bring him more. Peretz used folk motifs in his own writing, and he articulated the importance of folklore for the creation of a modern Jewish culture, inspiring a generation of Jewish *zamlers,* collectors who gathered and published Yiddish folklore, editing it with increasing sophistication. An-sky's friendship with Peretz extended to some of the Polish-Yiddish folklorists, especially Pinchas Graubard.[17]

An-sky's ideas were close to the Russian folklore study of his day. Like the nineteenth-century mythological and historical schools of folklore study that saw folktales and songs as the tattered remains of old myths that required collection and reconstruction, An-sky feared the loss of Jewish tales. In his 1908 "Jewish Folk Art," he argued for the persistent preference of spiritual to physical strength in Jewish lore, and he urged readers to collect it before it disappeared. Once the expedition had begun, following current trends in Russian folkloristics, he shifted focus to legends that stemmed from specific local historical experiences. With his insistence on gathering folklore in place and his complaint that earlier collectors did not explain the significance of sayings in their context, he adopted the sociological bent of the members of the Moscow Commission on Popular Literature, who believed that oral tradition varies in response to changing conditions.[18]

The growth of "performer studies" (study of individual tale performers' choice of material, attitudes, and artistic style) in Russian folkloristics marked a philosophical turn: rather than seeing folklore as a way to access the past, it became a way to understand the present. In this spirit, at the beginning of the expedition period, An-sky saw Jewishness as a choice, not a relic, and he became interested in people who decided to embrace Jewish identity. In his 1912 Yiddish story "A goyisher kop" (A goyish mind, a blockhead), he wrote about Anastasia Stefanova, a revolutionary who sneaks into Russia from Switzerland on a false passport that assigns her a Jewish identity. When they find that the police give her trouble as a Jew, her comrades suggest that she simply convert to Christianity in order to have permission to live in St. Petersburg. She refuses, insisting that to convert for reasons of gain would be dishonorable—even for a person who was not, in fact, Jewish. The same year, An-sky wrote about the Gers, Russian peasants who had adopted Jewish practices and considered themselves Jewish; they were similar in some ways to other Russian-Christian sectarian groups, such as the Subbotniks, who followed some Old Testament practices but did not identify as rabbinic Jews. Communities of Gers existed in Tsaritsyn (Volgograd), Privolnoe, in the Caucasus, and elsewhere from the early nineteenth century. For An-sky, the Gers proved that people could be drawn to the beauty of Jewish culture. "That brief encounter with the Judaizers, which revealed the characteristic Russian traits of passionate God-seeking and thirst for heroic deeds, forced me to see Judaism as not only an ethnic but also a world-wide, general-human value."[19] In 1912, hoping to renew Jewish culture, An-sky was intrigued by the idea of people who were inspired to declare themselves Jewish. His performance-based vision of folklore made him sensitive to the ways in which non-Jews might decide to perform Jewish identity, and he collected their stories as examples of vital—if unexpected—Jewish lore. He used the language of ethnographic "salvage" to urge that people help him collect folklore, a language that must have resonated in a period that saw Jewish identity and Jews themselves under siege from emigration, assimilation, and conversion, as well as physical attacks on Jews in pogroms and legal attacks in blood libel cases. But he also presented Jewish identity as the product of choices made in the present, and as the conscious embrace of a culture that offered something attractive.

An-sky differed from his predecessors in Jewish ethnography in ideology, temperament, and methodology. Whereas Dubnov and Peretz asked their readers to bring them samples of folklore, An-sky spoke literally to a much larger audience: his readers, his listeners during his provincial lecture tours, the philanthropists whom he approached for funding, and the shtetl Jews from whom he personally gathered material. The large-scale expedition project that he imagined was made possible by speaking with many people, and the expedition itself allowed An-sky to speak with even more people. Undoubtedly, An-sky's success in 1912–1914 in organizing the ethnographic expedition can be attributed to the tactics that explained his success in 1899–1903 in organizing the Agrarian-Socialist League and its publication of revolutionary brochures for peasants: his fund-raising abilities; his attention to detail; his enthusiasm for new media technology; his perseverance; his charisma as a speaker; his belief that his project would finally improve a bad situation; his location outside the center of major party or organizational groupings; and most of all, his ability to inspire people from different backgrounds and ideologies to come together and work on a concrete task, which itself promised to bring people together.

An-sky's persona was crucial. When he organized revolutionary publishing in Paris and Switzerland, his friends had remarked on his accessibility, his childlike enthusiasm, and his warmth. An-sky knew the effect he produced, and he was well aware that it contributed to his success—that because he lacked Zhitlowsky's "aristocratism," he could be a more effective organizer. When he turned to organizing the collection of Jewish folklore, his democratic demeanor continued to serve him. Although his views of the function of Jewish folklore were similar to Peretz's, he never modeled himself on his Warsaw friend, disapproving precisely of Peretz's aristocratic stance. In 1911, he wrote of the ten days Peretz had spent in Petersburg, fund-raising for Yiddish theater and in the process offending nearly everyone who tried to help him: "The wisest of wise men, a true artist, but of a confused mind. Spoiled rotten by the Warsaw youngsters. Thinks he's a god and walks around in a big Warsaw-style cape."[20] Whereas An-sky liked to think he was performing the role of "Anonymous-sky," the intellectual as the humble servant of the folk, he criticized Peretz for playing the moody romantic artist whose difference from ordinary people is at the root of his genius.

An-sky's style mattered as much as his methodological innovation. He was the first to propose that the Jews of the Russian Empire were worthy to be studied as Russian peasants and Siberian peoples had been studied, by a team of researchers who take modern technology with them into the field over several seasons. This method does produce better data than older methods (such as gathering published data and urging provincial readers to send in more). But rather than stressing the quality of his data, An-sky justified his work by emphasizing the amount of his data—and over and over, he wrote about ethnographic fieldwork as a path to national renewal, personal transformation, and ecstatic experience.[21]

The expedition allowed An-sky to weave together the divergent strands of his life: his commitments to Jewish culture and Populist belief, his urge to act out a self-denying and heroic role in public, his need for acceptance among others and inspiration in the ecstasy of human contact. As he finally set out on the expedition at the beginning of July 1912, An-sky told Gintsburg that he worried his high expectations were unrealistic. "I am powerfully agitated, as before something large and unknown. How will it go? Will I manage to attain the trust of these poor, primitive people, from whom I myself emerged, but from whom I have traveled so far in the last years? At times I become terrified. But at the same time I have a great joyful feeling in my soul, that the most cherished dream of my entire life is beginning to be realized."[22] As he set out to the shtetls in the Kiev region, he dreamed of personally bridging the gulf that separated educated people from the masses and separated him from his own origins.

Linking his ethnographic work to the dream of his "entire life," he suggested that he was trying to return to his own childhood—his parents' poverty and discord—finally to set everything right.

An-sky feared that his subjects might not trust him and his two co-workers, the musicologist Engel and his young cousin once removed, the photographer Solomon Yudovin. Whereas An-sky's Yiddish was fluent and his beard made him look like a traditional Jew, his co-workers were clean-shaven and Engel barely spoke Yiddish. It was easy to imagine that shtetl folk would be skeptical of these outsiders who suddenly appeared with exotic recording equipment and asked people to perform for them. These fears seemed to be coming true on the first day of the expedition, July 1 (14), 1912, at the train station in the town of Ruzhin, where the team hired a wagon driver named Henekh. When they spoke with Henekh in Yiddish, he immediately identified them as big-city Jews and frustrated them by answering in the mix of Ukrainian and Russian typical of the Kiev region. Soon, though, Henokh warmed up to the visitors and spoke, in Yiddish, about himself. He told them that he used to be very poor. "Right now I have nothing but a piece of bread—but then I didn't even have that, and there were my wife and children." He sold everything he owned for a ruble and used it to go to Skvira and give an offering to the local Hasidic rebbe (the Skvirer rebbe), who responded, "Go, God will help you." He realized then that "God helped him and not me; he took my last 50 kopecks and I was even worse off. I haven't been to see that rebbe since."[23]

No longer a fervent Hasid, Henekh was still fervent about Jewish music. As Engel recalled: "Synagogue singing was his passion, and he even had a decent voice. Right away he decided that we would not set off from the station that day (although it was morning) so that we could hear the local cantor. The driver was in general an enthusiast, with the soul of an artist." Henekh was overjoyed that people had come from Petersburg to record songs in his small town and that these experts shared his own enthusiasm for liturgical music. Engel was struck by the strength of Henekh's emotions: his passion, his enthusiasm, his "ecstasy about the phonograph." He found in this wagon driver just what he had hoped Hasidism would provide: more powerful joy than modern life offered. When he spoke about Hasidic song, Engel emphasized joy: "God is in joy, the Baal Shem Tov [the eighteenth-century founder of Hasidism] taught, and all of life must be joyful because it gives us the ability to know God. . . . In prayer, you must reach *hislayves*, break away from the consciousness of an independent existence and feel united with God. One of the things that can help produce this condition is singing." Engel told the story of Reb Pinkhos of Korets, a Hasidic rebbe who sang a peasant carpenter's song because, as he told his followers, "This peasant is singing in such a way that heaven is opening up before him. You are blind and do not see it." An-sky too defined Hasidism as "a striving for the mysterious and the miraculous. . . . The Besht [the Baal Shem Tov] spoke out against rabbinic asceticism, expressed in the mortification of the flesh, and preached the ecstatically joyous contact of the human with God, as with a merciful father."[24] As they met shtetl Hasids, An-sky and Engel looked for evidence of this ecstatic joy.

As they developed a system for collecting, An-sky, Engel, and Yudovin discovered which methods worked best. They experimented with paying children 5 kopecks per song and discovered that children would make up new songs in order to get more money, and parents would be annoyed when children skipped heder to spend time with the folklorists. The team found that if they took the phonograph out on the street, it would draw such a crowd that they could not move. When he needed to go somewhere with the phonograph, Engel asked Yudovin to help distract the crowd, "to draw their attention by bringing out his big camera in the main street. The crowd was drawn to him, and I went secretly through backyards."[25]

The work of collecting was exhausting and frustrating. Vendors with objects for sale crowded the team's hotel rooms from early morning; elderly beggars came to the hotel for handouts and sometimes stayed to tell stories. Many of the shtetl folk were desperately poor: in one town, An-sky saw forty children (thirty-five boys, five girls) crowded into a heder "like herrings in a box," although the limit was officially twenty. An-sky knew what it was like to live at the edge, joking, "Not changing your shirt is hard only for the first month—as the saying goes, after that you forge an 'inner bond' with the shirt." But on the expedition he saw people living worse than he ever had. One informant was a seventy-year-old woman with no shirt, no socks, and torn shoes. To make matters more difficult, suspicious policemen wanted to know exactly what Yudovin had photographed and why.[26]

To his diary, An-sky admitted the tension between the team and the shtetl folk. Informants were uncooperative. Khaye-Gite, a "typical old lady . . . knows spells but won't recite them." Another woman started to recite a spell, then became frightened after An-sky asked to hear a word again, refused to go on, and told him to go to a drugstore if he needed a cure. People would agree to be photographed, recorded, or interviewed, then change their minds. The legends that arose about the expedition suggested that like the Tsarist policemen, shtetl folk were suspicious of the ethnographers' motives. People believed that "Baron Gintsburg is very rich, and he gives money to buy old Jewish things because he wants to be like Jesus or Mohammed, so that people will print all these things and say that he invented them all by himself. They will say that he is a god."[27]

An-sky did not report any of these difficulties to Gintsburg or Zhitlowsky, nor did he mention the bad weather that scared Bialik away from joining them. (Bialik wrote in October 1912 that he had heard that in the shtetls, "the mud is so deep you could die.") And when his co-workers described the expedition, they insisted on An-sky's charismatic ability to convince people to talk, sing, tell stories, and sell him valuable objects. Engel felt that overall, the shtetl folk, like Henekh the wagon driver, were enthusiastic about the expedition. "Whether they wore jackets, whether they had *peyes* [sidelocks] or not, people would go out of their way to help us."[28]

While the poverty An-sky recorded in his diary was real, so was the enthusiasm that Engel recalled. Between July and September 1912, the team went from Ruzhin, Pavoloch, and Skvira near Kiev to Polonnoe, Berdichev, Slavuta, and Novograd-Volynsk. After a break for the High Holidays, when the logistics of travel were difficult, the team, now reduced to An-sky and Yudovin, visited Korets, Rovno, Ostrog, Zaslav, Miropol, Ostropol, Staro-Konstantinov, Kremenets, Shepetovka, and Lutsk. Local teachers and students helped the ethnographers, and many remained in contact with An-sky and continued to gather material and send it to him. Young men and women hoping to be writers wrote to An-sky much as he had once written to Mikhailovsky and Uspensky, asking for advice about how to get published and how to live their lives. M. Zilberman from Korets wrote many times with ethnographic material he had gathered, explaining that he wanted not to be paid but to be as useful as he believed An-sky to be: "In my situation, my difficult circumstances, I can depend only on you, my friend, for the realization of my great ideals; I wish you success in your great national Jewish project."[29]

It was not only the secular shtetl intelligentsia who welcomed the ethnographers. A man named Labunsky wrote in the language of Jewish ritual that when the team was in Ruzhin, "it was like *Shabes* [the Sabbath]!" Even the religious leaders appreciated An-sky's attention. Samuel Kaufman, the rebbe of Miropol and the grandson of the famous Hasidic rebbe Shmuel Kaminker, wrote in his will that he knew the religious books he was leaving his children were valuable, because An-sky himself had offered to pay him the improbable sum of 2,000 rubles for each one. An-sky had donned a new, effective mask: his "venerable appearance, observance of the rituals, and ability to speak with the elders" helped the team gain their subjects' trust. The shtetl Jews knew that the ethnographers were outsiders from the distant capital, and they welcomed them in part for that very reason, delighted that these sophisticated people, and especially the well-known public figure An-sky, were investing time and money studying what shtetl folk knew.[30]

During the High Holidays that forced him to take a break from the field, An-sky wrote that the attempt had been a success. In twelve places, the team found more material than expected: about 300 stories, 500 to 600 songs, and 100 wordless Hasidic melodies. They had taken 400 photographs and purchased manuscripts and 200 other objects for a museum. The amount of material collected justified the collection of more material; it would make it possible to raise funds to continue the expedition.[31]

For the 1913 expedition, An-sky brought a larger team: Yudovin again to take pictures; the musicologist Kiselgof (or Kiselhof), who spoke better Yiddish than Engel, to work the phonograph; and three students from the Baron David Gintsburg School of Oriental Studies in St. Petersburg, Avrom Rekhtman, Itskhak Pikangur (or Fikangur, later Gur-Arye), and Shmuel Shraer (later Shrira). They started work on June 9, and by the end of the fall the team had visited eleven towns in Podolia and seventeen in Volynia, as well as Tetiev and Berdichev in Kiev province, and some places in the Vitebsk and Mogilev provinces, where An-sky went alone with the camera. Even more than in 1912, they found willing helpers. In July, An-sky published notices about the expedition in the new large-circulation Warsaw Yiddish newspapers *Haynt* and *Der moment,* appealing to readers to gather and send in material, and so many people wrote to ask for copies of the guidelines for gathering material that Levi Yitskhok Vaynshteyn, An-sky's secretary back in Petersburg, ran out of copies. Enthusiastic shtetl Jews wrote to report on especially beautiful wooden synagogues, to donate old yarmulkes or sell 200-year-old ritual fringes, and to ask advice about purchasing gramophones so they could record folk songs themselves.[32]

In this second season, An-sky knew what techniques would work. As he had done in his radical youth in Liozno, he established contact by joining the community in prayer. Each time his team came to a new shtetl, they would go to the shul and pray. Naturally, after the service the locals would speak with the newcomers, and the ethnographers would invite the men back to their hotel room for some whisky. There, the ethnographers could ask questions, hear detailed answers, and take notes. They collected stories about synagogue buildings, relations between Jews and Christian estate owners, local rebbes, their graves and those of others, songs and melodies, marriages and how they went wrong, and interactions between the living and the dead. They heard certain legends in many places: in twelve towns, they were shown a fenced-off place near the synagogue where a bride and groom, killed during their wedding by the Haidamaks (eighteenth-century Cossack rebels), were buried, and they heard often of how children playing on wasteland had started to dig and uncovered an entire synagogue. When he gave talks about the expedition, An-sky emphasized the connections among legends, the history of the place where they were gathered, and physical spaces such as graveyards and synagogues; he projected slides of buildings and gravestones, community record books, and synagogue ornaments.[33]

He saw Jewish folklore as varied and dynamic, containing elements of European folklore and songs and sayings in several languages. Some tales and songs were more didactic, reflecting the morals of religious leaders and focusing on the spiritual perfection of the righteous and the struggle to bring the messiah. Other texts reflected humor and skepticism toward religion. An-sky was fascinated by aspects of folk belief that were distant from normative rabbinic Judaism and close to local Slavic practices: helpful and harmful magic and folk medicine. He had begun to collect spells and charms against the evil eye in the Vitebsk region, and in 1909 published the spells of I. Azarkha, a man who had "used these charms for 50 years." Now he returned to this topic, finding traditional healers in each community and using devious strategies to transcribe their charms.[34]

The team gathered stories about movement from the world of the living to the "true world" of the dead and back. They recorded tales about people who died and then returned to life, and a legend about a man who finds himself in "Korach's land" beneath the earth and marries a woman there, only to abandon his otherworldly bride for a human woman to whom he is obligated. The team was fascinated by stories about dybbuks, dead souls that possess the bodies of the living. In one story An-sky collected, an old cantor, jealous of his successor, dies, possesses the young man, and forces him to sing the Yom Kippur service in his voice, with the old cantor's melodies.[35]

The healers' charms and the rabbis' exorcisms functioned in a world in which the word, written or spoken, possessed magical power. Music was magic as well. Reb Gokhberg, a fifty-five-year-old clarinetist whom the team recorded, told Engel that "a real Jewish musician pulls out your soul, pulls out your life. The playing goes to the end of the earth." The ethnographers studied and discussed the Hasidic attitude toward song, learning that Rebbe Shneur Zalman of Liady had said, "Song is the language of the soul and also of the ministering angels," and that songs sung with true *kavone* (intention) were a vehicle for messages from the world of the living to the "true world."[36]

What would happen to that power if the charms and melodies were collected, tabulated, studied, or displayed, as An-sky hoped to do? The question arose concerning the phonograph. The shtetl Jews had heard of phonographs, which they called "Edisons," but few had seen one function. So in one shtetl after another, the team would set up the phonograph in the study house after prayers for a demonstration. One of the team would sing a song, deliberately laughing in the middle, and then they would play the cylinder on which it had been recorded. The amazed audience realized that the performance they had just heard had really been recorded, and they admired the phonograph as "one of the seven wonders of the world." Even the rabbis liked the machine and would cheerfully delegate one and then another sweet-voiced follower to sing into it.[37]

In Korostishev, the team heard of a different response. They were welcomed in the court of the local *rebbe,* a grandson of the *tsaddik* Reb Moyshele Korostishever of the Chernobyl Hasidic dynasty. An elderly synagogue official, Reb Avrom Blokh, knew many songs, including old Chernobyl table songs, and the ethnographers were eager to record him. But when they asked, he responded with a story about Reb Motele, the current rebbe's father. A couple of decades earlier, presumably when gramophones first became commercially available in the 1890s, men had come to Korostishev with the marvelous new invention. Reb Motele had inserted the hearing tube in his ear and listened, then suddenly pulled it out and stood up, as though bitten by a snake. He turned to Blokh and said, "Avrom! Try to sing into this machine, a melody or prayer. Sing with feeling, with an outpouring of your soul, with higher holiness!" The terrified Blokh refused, and Reb Motele shook his head and said, "Help! Where can one find a great man?" Later, Reb Motele explained his words by telling another story. One day the Besht went into a prayer house and cried out, "Help, Jews! The prayer house is full of prayers, it's choking!" Pure prayers, the Besht explained, went straight to heaven, but prayers with blemishes could not rise and were stuck on earth in the study house. This, Reb Motele told Blokh, was the secret of the "Edison": the machine captured only simple words and blemished songs. He had asked Blokh to sing into the gramophone in order to test this idea, and then cried out that he needed to find a great man, because the words of a great man should rise high above this world.[38]

Reb Motele's anxiety that the phonograph could never preserve song with its true power did not seem to trouble the generation of shtetl Jews whom the ethnographers recorded. For the most part, men would come to the hotel room and be recorded singing songs. Women, hesitant to disobey the Jewish stricture against their singing in the presence of men, were more reluctant to be recorded, and they refused to go to a man's hotel room for the purpose. The team discovered that some younger women were willing to be recorded in a public location such as a school. An-sky persuaded one elderly woman in Kremenets to sing in a room with other women, while the men listened from another room—and, without her permission, recorded her.[39]

The process of collecting, whether difficult or easy, gave An-sky tremendous happiness. Pikangur remembered that after An-sky had succeeded in persuading a family to sell him a valuable old manuscript, his delight was "boundless." An-sky wrote to Zhitlowsky at the end of the summer of 1913 that the wonderful objects they had collected in Volynia alone had convinced him to organize an exhibit, as a way to generate more funding that would allow the expedition to continue. He described the collection in mystical terms. "The expedition is becoming a study of all the Jews if not something bigger. . . . It's impossible to write to you about the expedition. So many impressions—it can't be described. It's as though I am climbing up a tall mountain from which I see a greater and greater area. I'm starting to see the folk, the nation, with flesh-and-blood eyes." This was a kind of miracle; he had gained access to something not quite of this world. He moved from revelation to statistics. The team had gathered 1,000 tales and 1,500 songs, taken 1,000 photographs, and bought 400 objects for the museum, including 20 manuscripts. "The happiness I feel from this work is limitless." The ecstasy that drew An-sky to the Ukrainian Hasids was finally his.[40]

An-sky's enthusiasm about traditional Jewish culture emerged in a talk he gave in Kiev in April 1913, praising the heder. Moyshe Litvakov, a radical Yiddish critic, hated the talk and labeled An-sky a reactionary. An-sky wrote wryly of the incident to Bialik, saying Litvakov had called him "a renegade, an obscurantist and a Zionist," but he admitted that some of his own ideas were genuinely changing. He told Zhitlowsky that his work on Jewish emigration had made him "a territorialist (almost a Zionist)"; his sympathy for Zionism—or for the idea that Jewish problems might demand political solutions that would not be supplied by the non-Jewish radical parties—would grow through the next years, though he never gave up on radicalism. And he was always subject to new passions; in the spring of 1913, he admitted, "Last night at 7 P.M. I fell in love with a 23-year-old and I've already written her a fiery letter. But nothing will come of it."[41] Passions or no, An-sky retained most of his old habits of thought. Like Peretz and Martin Buber, An-sky was a neo-Hasid who drew selectively on the mystic movement's legends and beliefs, while remaining firmly anchored in the secular world.

An-sky repeatedly measured his distance from his subjects in his research methods and in his choice of objects to collect. He was willing to deceive his subjects, such as the traditional healers to whom he represented himself as a formerly rich man, now nearly blind and fallen on hard times, who needed to "borrow" a charm for his own use and have his cousin write it down. Jewish law mandates that all the parts of a corpse be buried and it forbids the living prolonged contact with the bodies of the dead, but An-sky collected just the kinds of human remains that were typically exhibited in ethnographic museums at the time. In Proskurov, the team met an old man whose finger had been chopped off when he was a child, to save him from recruitment into the Tsarist army. Families who performed this operation on their sons would save the fingers, so they could eventually be buried along with their owners, but An-sky convinced the old man to sell them his finger for the Jewish ethnographic museum. An-sky wrote proudly to Gintsburg when he acquired some even older body parts. "In one shtetl I managed to get from an old cemetery (from the time of Chmielnitsky), which was on the estate of a landlord who was digging ditches, two skulls, one of which visibly had been broken by a weapon. I myself dug this skull up from a depth of one arshin [28 in.] and pulled it out with my hands, so the break is undoubtedly old."[42]

Had the shtetl Jews realized that the ethnographers did not scruple to dig up a Jewish corpse and carry a part of it away for exhibit in a St. Petersburg museum, many of them would have been appalled. An-sky's hereditary status as a *cohen,* a member of the priestly class who is forbidden contact with corpses, would have made the deed even worse in their eyes. Every time he wanted to visit a cemetery, he would lie about this, insisting that even though most Rappoports were cohens, he was not; he had just been given his mother's last name in order to save him from the draft. But the act was consistent with the team's behavior in other circumstances. They collected many stories about graves and tombstones, especially those of Hasidic leaders. They were interested in the *kvitlekh* (notes of supplication) left at the graves of famous rebbes: the writers believed that the power of the written word was such that their pleas might reach the dead sage in the world to come, and he might intercede for them in the world of the living. The ethnographers collected kvitlekh for their museum, with no qualms about disrupting their magic.[43]

An-sky was fascinated by the magic of the shtetl folk and the ways they believed they could penetrate the border between the worlds of the living and the dead, but he did not share their beliefs. Instead of using exorcisms or kvitlekh to influence the dead to intercede in the world of the living, he had another audience in mind. By displaying what he had found in his museum—rabbinic books and photographs, kvitlekh and skulls from the time of the Chmielnitsky uprising—he believed he might work a different kind of magic by inspiring assimilated Jews to create secular Jewish art. In spite of his ecstasy at collecting, the folklore he amassed was a means to an end rather than an end in itself. As he told Zhitlowsky in 1914 in a letter praising a young artist, "We would exchange the grave of the Besht for a good Jewish Leonardo da Vinci. True?"[44] The lore and the objects that the Jews had lived by was not, ultimately, the point: the creation of a secular new culture mattered much more to him.

While An-sky and his colleagues were immersed in ethnographic work, the Russian public was also discussing Jewish customs about the living and the dead—but from a different perspective. The late nineteenth and early twentieth centuries saw the revival in Eastern Europe of the legend that Jews use Christian blood in the matzos they make at Passover. This "blood libel" about ritual murder echoes second-century pagan beliefs about early Christians and their doctrines about consuming the blood of Jesus. From the twelfth century, Christians directed this accusation of cannibalism against Jews. The first real-life blood libel case occurred then in Britain, and a version of the legend appears in "The Prioress's Tale," in Chaucer's *Canterbury Tales*.[45] The belief spread east over the following centuries, to prompt the Kishinev pogrom of 1903.

After the 1903–1906 pogroms, the legend of ritual murder continued to circulate in the Russian Empire, fostered by the ultra-nationalist organizations such as the Black Hundreds and the Union of the Russian People that had arisen during the 1905 revolution. As support for these organizations began to wane after 1907, they worked to rally members through the ritual murder legend, which provided anti-Semitic newspapers with material for accusations against Jews—and liberal newspapers occasions to refute them. In Smolensk on the eve of Passover in 1910, Black Hundreds leader Alexander Dubrovin, the editor of *Russkoe Znamia* (Russian Banner), accused Jews of murdering a Christian for ritual purposes. Solomon Gurevich, a friend of An-sky's and the editor of the local liberal paper, *Smolenskii Vestnik* (Smolensk Herald), urged An-sky to help him find a well-known Petersburg lawyer to attack Dubrovin, hoping to create as much publicity as possible. In December 1913, this case would result in a guilty verdict for Dubrovin and the other accusers.[46] By that point, though, the ruling would draw little attention: it was far less dramatic than another blood libel case that had begun in Kiev in the summer of 1911.

The events leading up to the Beilis case started on March 12, 1911, when a thirteen-year-old Christian boy, Andrei Iushchinsky, disappeared on his way to school, and his body was found with multiple stab wounds. On July 21, Mendel Beilis, a Jewish superintendent at the Zaitsev brick factory, was arrested in connection with the murder. For two years, the Kiev police department prepared a case against Beilis, accusing him of murdering Iushchinsky in order to use his blood for ritual purposes. Simultaneously, Jewish and Russian liberals prepared the case for the defense. The intelligentsia saw the Beilis affair as a media war between right-wing forces and themselves. In Gruzenberg's words, "the question of [Beilis's] acquittal became a question of national self-respect."[47] As An-sky prepared and carried out the first two seasons of the ethnographic expedition, the Beilis affair distracted him and his colleagues constantly.

The Russian writer Vladimir Korolenko, known for his defense of ethnic minorities, asked An-sky to prepare an article for *Russkoe Bogatstvo* about the Jewish folktales that had arisen in response to blood libel accusations, and he worked a week of sixteen-hour days in December 1911 to finish it. In the article, published in the first issue of 1912, An-sky reiterated that Jewish folklore testifies to the history of interaction between Jews and non-Jews. Folktales about blood libel accusations, he explained, exemplify "the optimism of folklore, which testifies to the deep faith of the folk in the victory of truth and justice"; it "requires that the libel be uncovered, the innocent freed, and the guilty punished as they deserve." He retold stories of Judah Loeb ben Betsalel of Prague, a sixteenth-century rabbi known as the Maharal, and his invention, the *Golem*. This was an enormous servant made of clay who performed superhuman feats to save the Jews from the blood libel: he prevented Christians from depositing corpses in Jewish homes, exposed those who did so, or pointed out the grave in the cemetery from which a fresh corpse had been dug up in order to sneak it into the home of an innocent Jew. As An-sky explained, these tales were a natural response to the blood libel. "Folklore depicts remarkable circumstances where the truth is revealed in an especially triumphant and indisputable form . . . The Golem possesses exactly those qualities that are needed to prevent and uncover ritual murder accusations. What deep despair must have accumulated in the soul of the people to make them invent such a Golem!"[48]

As the Beilis affair developed, An-sky and the Jews in his circles felt something like that same despair. Iona Makhover, Baron Gintsburg's secretary, wrote to An-sky in January 1912 that he had enjoyed reading his *Russkoe Bogatstvo* article and he hoped that a good lawyer would be found for "our case." As he explained, "I call it 'ours' because in reality they're accusing not just Beilis, but all the Jews." And they were. Throughout 1912 and the first half of 1913, the Kiev police worked to build the case against Beilis, even though it was clear to the prosecution as well as the defense that Iushchinsky had been murdered by a gang of thieves (including his friend's mother) to punish him for giving them away to the police. Their insistence on proceeding with this weak case made it seem that the Kiev authorities were following orders from the tsar, although in fact, the Kiev police and the monarchist groups were acting on their own initiative, fomenting Jew-hatred to strengthen their own causes.[49]

Once the trial was finally set for September 1913, five lawyers came to his defense, all working pro bono. Gruzenberg, the well known Jewish lawyer who had obtained an acquittal in the 1903 Blondes ritual murder case in Vilna, was the head of the defense team. Vasily Maklakov, whose brother Nikolai was the anti-Semitic Minister of the Interior, was a Kadet leader who later served as the ambassador to France under the Provisional Government. The oldest lawyer was the distinguished Nikolai Karabchevsky, the youngest the fiery Alexander Zarudny, and the Kiev lawyer Dmitry Grigorovich-Barsky offered local expertise. Three non-Jewish professors of Semitic languages, Ivan Troitsky of the Petersburg Spiritual Academy, Pavel Kokovtsov of the Academy of Sciences, and Alexander Glagolev of the Kiev Theological Seminary, gave expert testimony to help Beilis, and Rabbi Mazeh of Moscow spoke against the accusation that Jewish law requires consumption of blood. (Although the prosecutor found some witnesses to testify the contrary, Jewish law forbids consumption of the blood of any animal.)

An-sky too felt compelled to attend the trial. He left the ethnographic expedition in September and wrote to his editor at the Petersburg Kadet newspaper *Rech'* (Speech) to ask for a coveted journalist's entry ticket to the trial. The editor wrote back, somewhat annoyed (An-sky had not "given signs of life" lately and his request came out of the blue), and told An-sky he could share a ticket with Ia. B. Lifshits, another *Rech'* reporter who had been assigned to send regular telegrams about the highlights of the trial. Since Lifshits was writing dispatches about the legal developments, An-sky could provide longer, more impressionistic articles about the mood at the trial and in the city.[50]

Having secured a ticket, An-sky sat in the courtroom "from ten in the morning until midnight in hell." The day the jury was chosen, the city felt haunted.

> Over the wide elegant streets with their palazzi and monuments, you can see the ghosts of the terrible time of the ghetto, the underground quarters of the inquisition, tortures, bonfires. . . .
>
> And while here, in the great hall, hundreds of people, contained and outwardly cold, anxiously strain to catch every whisper of the approaching drama, elsewhere in the city, in the narrow streets of Podol and Slobodka, in old synagogues and prayer houses, tens and thousands of Jews, wrapped in prayer shawls, just as in the old days, as in the Middle Ages, chant sobbingly the prayers for forgiveness created in dark, horrible days: "Lord, take pity on us, we are persecuted, tormented, tired, as a lost sheep, pursued by predators."[51]

An-sky looked at Kiev in September 1913 and saw Prague in the sixteenth century, its Jews knowing that the blood libel accusation threatened all of them and joining in a communal prayer for miraculous salvation. As when he had worked among the miners in his twenties, the things that inspired his revolutionary and his ethnographic work, the archaic political order he feared and the archaic culture he loved, were bound up together.

Rech' did not really need An-sky's articles, but Yiddish newspaper editors were happy to publish his impressions of the trial. In his articles for *Lodzher Tageblat* (Łódź Daily), one of the most important provincial Yiddish newspapers, he explained the weakness of the prosecution and the accusations against Vera Cheberiak, one of the accusers who was revealed to be a dealer in stolen goods, perhaps a madam, and whose obvious guilt in the murder drew ever more attention throughout the trial. He was horrified by the ideas held by some witnesses for the prosecution. When he listened to Father Justin Pranaitis, a Catholic priest from Tashkent who had published pamphlets insisting that the blood libel was real, he felt that he was seeing a living relic of a terrifying medieval past.[52]

An-sky critiqued the lawyers' rhetorical talents more than their arguments. "No matter how talented they are at speaking, Beilis's lawyers lack feeling and beautiful gestures," he complained in early October. Arnold Margolin, a member of a Kiev Jewish community commission to defend Beilis, spoke well, but he could not produce that "needed word," that "cry . . . that would upend this whole horrible trial!" The first speaker to gain An-sky's complete approval was Evgeny Pavlov, a professor of surgery who gave expert testimony that a ritual murder—with the goal of producing the maximum loss of blood—had not occurred. He was the first witness truly to "give the cry of an agitated soul and a revolted conscience." The closing arguments gave An-sky more opportunities to admire the defense counsel, who were finally succeeding in defending "revolutionary honor" and "the honor of the folk"; his language showed that he saw the proceedings as a duel between the government and the people, as represented by the liberals on the defense team. Zarudny spoke with "almost a prayerful voice," then "his voice grew stronger, the note of religious ecstasy grew ever more powerful . . . . No matter what he spoke about, from his tone, firmness and perseverance, one could recognize a crystal clear idealism, a true knight of justice!" Maklakov spoke passionately, and An-sky was pleased: "Before the tribunal, at that moment, there stood not a lawyer, but an artist!"[53]

No matter how effectively the lawyers spoke, it was not clear that their words would move the jury, a majority of whom belonged to anti-Jewish organizations. An-sky looked at the jury and remembered a Yiddish folktale about the trickster Hershele of Ostropol. A rabbi listening to Hershele argue said, "You must not fear death—with your tongue, in the other world you can answer even the strictest angel." Hershele answered, "But I do fear—that I will have to answer a deaf angel." If the Kiev jury could not be moved by human words, then the efforts of the defense would come to nothing, and An-sky feared that not only Beilis but the entire Jewish people would be condemned. At the end of the trial, Beilis said, "I am tired."

> And it seemed as though these quiet, terrible words were said not
>   by Beilis but by his tormented, homeless, persecuted and
>   offended people . . .
> I am tired! . . . [54]

The Beilis trial ended ambiguously. The jury decided that although Beilis himself was innocent, ritual murder had occurred—meaning that in spite of all the evidence to the contrary, in spite of the passionate arguments of the lawyers and the expert witnesses against the blood libel, some Jews, somewhere in the Russian Empire, were guilty of killing Iushchinsky and consuming his blood. The international press, which had followed the trial closely, focused on the acquittal, but within Russia the outcome seemed less clear. Toward the end of the trial, An-sky wrote to Alexander Izmailov, a critic and editor at the Petersburg paper *Birzhevye Vedomosti* (Stock-Market Gazette), with horror. "Here the atmosphere is not at all as it was when the witnesses were being questioned. . . . The scapegoat Mendel Beilis, Pranaitis, and blood, blood, blood, in the most base combinations. You know, I won't be at all surprised if after this trial, with its nightmare of blood, some madmen who cripple children appear."[55]

What upset him most, An-sky told the Yiddish writer Yankev Dinezon, was not the blood libel trial itself but the realization that news about it was being cynically manipulated. Even some of those accusing him "knew deep in their hearts that Beilis was innocent, that Jews don't need blood, but they still spread the slander, they still poured out the slops." After the trial ended, he confessed to Bialik that it left him with bitter feelings toward the Jews as well.

> In the old days, when the Jews experienced a misfortune, an evil decree, a plague, a calumny, and so on, our grandfathers would first of all look into their own affairs: what sin has caused this to happen? . . . And now, when this sort of misfortune happens, first of all a couple dozen Yatskans jump up and start crying to the people: You're the best and the most beautiful, without a single flaw! And the whole world is guilty before you. There are a billion people who are all Jew-eaters and bloodsuckers . . . Just try, at such a moment, when the Yatskans are tickling the folk, to say the words, "let us purify ourselves . . ." There would be violence. And really, at such a moment one can't speak to the folk in that kind of language. And that might be the most tragic side of all of our troubles. From one unnecessary blood libel the people won't be injured. But the fact that the intelligentsia cannot do its duty, scream to the people, before their eyes, about their flaws, that is terrible.[56]

An-sky's comment recalled Bialik's famously bitter criticism of the victims after the Kishinev pogrom. Having immersed himself in Jewish blood libel folklore, An-sky hoped that the despair that a blood libel accusation brought would inspire heroism and salvation. When he arrived in Kiev, he was sure that Jews, wrapped in prayer shawls, were chanting prayers of repentance created in the Middle Ages. At the Beilis trial, he wanted to hear someone speak the kind of magical words that had allowed the rabbi of Prague to create the Golem, that would move the jury even if it happened to be deaf, and that would allow the truth to be revealed "in an especially triumphant and indisputable form." He and his friends had believed at the outset of the Beilis affair that "the *truth* will triumph, it *must* triumph."[57] But even Pavlov's passionate anger, Maklakov's artistry, and Zarudny's "crystal clear idealism" produced an unclear verdict. The blood libel legend was not "shut down" by Gruzenberg's clever arguments. An-sky was left with the sense of a missed opportunity, and like Bialik in his pogrom poem, he adopted the voice of a Biblical prophet who directs his anger at the Jews themselves.

The similarities between the Dreyfus and the Beilis cases were obvious to An-sky: "'State secrets,' 'secret documents,' accusing the witnesses for the defense—how this all recalls the Dreyfus trial!" But this time there was no hero like Zola to celebrate and no final sense of triumph. The medieval pattern, where a Jewish community suffers, looks inward, and then is rewarded with a miracle, had been broken. In despair, An-sky looked for someone to blame and identified the guilty parties in the media. The cynical Black Hundreds leaders used their newspapers to spread a rumor even they did not believe; and the Jewish periodical press, as represented by the most powerful man in the business, Shmuel Yankev Yatskan, the former editor of the sensationalist *Yidishes tageblat* (Jewish Daily) and the publisher of the more respectable *Dos yidishes vokhenblat* (Jewish Weekly) and the very popular *Haynt*, discouraged the Jews from making the archaic gestures of repentance that alone could bring salvation.[58]

The double-edged verdict in the Beilis case presaged more blood libel cases to come. A few months after Beilis was exonerated, in the town of Fastov outside of Kiev, the body of an adolescent boy was discovered. It was identified as the Jew Iosel Pashkov, and it appeared clear that he had been killed by Ivan Goncharuk, a Christian with an arrest record. Briefly, local authorities attempted to create a ritual murder case, arguing that the body was really that of the Christian Boris Taranenko, that Pashkov had fled to America, and that the murderer was his father. The liberal and radical press reported the case in detail. The policemen tailing An-sky and Rekhtman on a visit to Berdichev and Zhitomir in February 1914 reported disapprovingly that the writer had been in possession of "some kind of illegal journal with an article by Burtsev about the murder of a boy in the city of Fastov, Kiev province, asserting that a Jewish boy, Iosel Pashkov, had been killed." This reading material, along with An-sky's travels and meetings, looked suspicious. "Measures were taken in case Rappoport should cross the border; Radivilov and Volochinsk were informed, and measures were taken to observe his travel in the province." In fact, An-sky was researching the Fastov case for an article for *Rech'*. Ultimately, Taranenko was revealed to be alive, the case fell apart, and Goncharuk was found guilty, but An-sky's despair about the state of Russian-Jewish relations at the conclusion of the Beilis case had been proven well founded.[59]

In the midst of his agony over the blood libel trial in Kiev, An-sky drafted a play that drew on his experiences of the past few years. On January 11, 1914, he told his friend and his patron the good news. He wrote to Zhitlowsky happily, "Chaimke! I've written a play in three acts: 'The Dybbuk.' For right now I'm keeping it secret . . . from Shmuel [Gurevich]. He gave me firm advice not to write about that theme. I can't wait to read it to you. I read it to Marek and it made a strong impression." He asked Gintsburg if he would be interested in reading the text, and the baron agreed immediately, writing, "I cannot express my extreme amazement at your limitless activity."[60] An-sky would spend the rest of his life working on this play, reading it aloud and asking the audience for suggestions, revising it, translating it from Russian into Yiddish and organizing a translation into Hebrew, and trying to arrange a staging. His efforts would bear fruit only after his death, when his play would become the best-known and most often staged work of the Hebrew and Yiddish theaters.

In its final four-act version, the play tells of a young couple, Khonen and Leah, whose fathers, Hasids who follow Rebbe Azriel of Miropol, had promised them to each other in marriage before they were born. Khonen's father, Nisn, has died young and Leah's father, Sender, has grown rich and forgotten his promise. Khonen has become a yeshiva student who takes meals at the house of Leah and her father; the souls of the young people are connected by mystic bonds and they yearn for each other. In the first act, set in the shtetl of Brinnitz, Sender seeks a rich groom for his daughter, and Khonen experiments with "practical kabbalah," Jewish magic, in order to win Leah's hand. Tempted by the vision of power and gold, Khonen calls on the devil and dies. In the second act, Leah is about to marry another man. She visits the cemetery and invites her dead mother and the dead Khonen to the wedding. As she is led under the marriage canopy, she cries out to the groom in Khonen's voice, "You are not my bridegroom!" and the crowd realizes that she has been possessed by a dybbuk, the soul of Khonen. The third act is set in Rebbe Azriel's court. Sender asks the rebbe to exorcise the dybbuk, but the rebbe discovers that Khonen's father, the dead Nisn, wishes to summon Sender to a trial, and he postpones the exorcism. The fourth act begins with the trial between the living and the dead. Nisn accuses Sender of breaking his promise, causing Khonen's death and ending Nisn's line and memory. The rabbinic court, while exonerating Sender in part, determines that he must donate half his wealth to the poor and say prayers in memory of Nisn and Khonen. The rebbe then exorcises the dybbuk, but before Leah can be married, she chooses to join Khonen in death.

The first draft of the play has not been preserved, but Gintsburg's detailed reaction reveals that it contained much of the material of the later version. It was set in a shtetl. As Gintsburg wrote, "I found in it that which I sought—a bright, inspired picture of the spiritual life of the people, to the study of which you have dedicated so many years of your life. . . . *The Dybbuk* represents for me the expression in artistic, poetic, but realistic colors of all that has interested you and me so vividly over the past two or three years." The characters were presented positively—even, Gintsburg thought, too positively: "It seems to me that your attitude toward individual characters is too one-sided, and presents an apologia that is too whole and almost entirely inviolate. . . . If you rely on the description of life to create an artistic picture, then, like any instrument, life must also reveal its negative aspects." Gintsburg had the opposite reaction to the character of the tsaddik. "I do not believe in your tsaddik. Your exposition does not leave any doubts that those surrounding him are filled with belief in his supernatural power, but nothing points to honesty, sincerity, and belief. I see on his part the ability to use the condition of the minds of his flock and a desire to preserve his authority . . . a goal in pursuit of which he is prepared to do injustice to his victims, the dead."[61] Gintsburg urged An-sky to depict the tsaddik more sympathetically and to imagine that like his followers, he truly believed in his own magic. His concerns show that in his first draft, An-sky hesitated among various attitudes toward the Jewish magic that fascinated him: should he depict it from the "inside," as a part of a mystical worldview that functions throughout the play, or from the "outside," as a phenomenon to be dissected by ethnographers?

In the fall of 1915, An-sky submitted a three-act Russian version of *The Dybbuk* to the theater censor, then added a new second act (the wedding) that he wrote on the advice of theater insiders to make the play more stageable. With the exception of this new act, the 1915 text, which has survived in full, seems to closely resemble the version he showed Gintsburg.[62] It bears the imprint of his time as an ethnographer. Like each of the team's visits to a shtetl, the first three acts of the 1915 version open with old men telling stories in a synagogue or study room, hoping for a bite to eat and a drink. The 1915 version has a prologue, in which a prodigal daughter, now back with her father after having run away with a man, asks for forgiveness, and the father offers a dybbuk tale. Throughout the play, characters ask each other to explain customs or landmarks, to perform songs, dances, and rituals, and unlike the uncooperative informants about whom An-sky complained in his diary, these people are delighted to oblige. The real plot of the play is, perhaps, the plot of the ethnographic expedition itself: over and over, it dramatizes the encounter of a loquacious storyteller and an eager listener.

As the members of the ethnographic team yearned to do, the heroes of the play have ecstatic experiences. When Leah is possessed by the dybbuk and when Khonen appeals to supernatural powers, these young rebels are experimenting with the forms of altered consciousness available to Eastern European Jews. Dybbuk possession most often happened to women, perhaps because among Jews as among other peoples, possession trance allowed people who played a subordinate role the chance to escape the limits of their position. Nonpossession trance, typified in the Jewish context by conversation with an otherworldly messenger bringing supernatural enlightenment, occurred most often to male scholars who prepared themselves by the fasting and self-denial that Khonen practices.[63] When Leah speaks with Khonen's voice, and when Khonen, at the moment of his death, announces, "I see the revelation now," they transgress the boundaries of their usual selves. An-sky had rejoiced that the expedition gave him "limitless" happiness and a mystical view of Jewish life, as if from the top of a mountain. The heroes of *The Dybbuk* share this urge for experience unavailable in ordinary life, and when Leah rejects her body at the end of the play and joins Khonen in death, she appears to have gained it.

The Hebrew poet Avraham Shlonsky scornfully called the final version of the play "an ethnographic museum strewn with bits of folktales, religious rituals, etc.—all of it devoid of literary or dramatic necessity." As he edited, An-sky had pared this material down, but the play remained an ethnographic museum, a textual counterpart to the museum that he was planning in Petersburg. As though she herself were a museum visitor, Leah asks to see the embroidered curtain on the ark where the Torah scrolls are kept, and her aunt Frade tells two of the stories that the ethnographers heard repeated in many shtetls, about the synagogue that was discovered whole underground and the mound where a bride and groom killed on their wedding day were buried. The play's central theme of the dybbuk was borrowed from the many dybbuk legends that the team collected—perhaps especially from the story of the cantor who possessed the body of his successor, a dybbuk who possesses a specific person for a specific reason. The theme of a marriage gone wrong appeared in other stories the team gathered. Like the museum An-sky imagined, the play, especially in its earlier drafts, stressed display over narrative, education over catharsis, genuine artifacts over interpretation. Like the museum, it was meant to appeal not to the Jews of the shtetl but to the assimilated Jews and non-Jews of the capitals. An-sky even complained that non-Jews always understood his play better than Jews did.[64]

More than any of his other works, *The Dybbuk* succeeded in doing what An-sky had identified as the goal of the Jewish writer—to create new secular art based on tradition, a new culture that would be as compelling as the old religious culture that Jews were leaving behind. He wanted modern Jewish culture to provide the same joy that he had found among the Hasids. "A nation lives not in suffering, but in the ecstasy of the realization of its 'I,' in joyful creation, in pride in its culture, in the poetry of its daily life. Only in that. Without that, the Jewish nation would have vanished long ago. . . . One has to see the return to Jewishness not as a religious feat, not as self-denial, but as an 'entry into an inheritance,' as the acquisition of enormous wealth, on which one could live joyously and proudly."[65] With *The Dybbuk,* he was trying to produce that pride and that ecstasy. And as when he fantasized to Zhitlowsky about exchanging the grave of the Besht for a Jewish Leonardo da Vinci, he suspected that the cause of modern Jewish culture would involve dealings with the dead.

When the dybbuk takes on Leah's form, he resembles An-sky himself, who took on different forms throughout his life as he restlessly moved from one identity to another. If the adolescent Shloyme-Zanvl's anger at Chaim's comment in the bathhouse about his marriage to a rich girl stemmed from his own attraction to his friend, then the fantasy of a man who inhabits a woman's body may have expressed his own conflicted sexuality. The issues of wealth and poverty that dominated An-sky's childhood clearly resurface in his play: until he is exorcised, the dybbuk in Leah gets to live in her house and enjoy the wealthy merchant's lifestyle that he could never have as a poor yeshiva student, and his situation parallels that of Shloyme-Zanvl, whose life was so strongly affected by his friendship with Chaim and Shmuel but whose access to their family's homes on Vitebsk's Castle Street was precarious. It may be that Leah, the wealthy girl who can never be Khonen's bride, reflects An-sky's own frustrated love for Masha Reinus and the sad end of his marriage to Edia Glezerman, for the class dynamics of the play drew on those in their creator's life.[66]

The plot of the play turns on male upward mobility through marriage, which was once a common institution—at least anecdotally—among East European Jews. Wealthy men would ask the head of the local yeshiva to choose his best student to marry their daughters, and in this way poor boys could become rich. Chaim Zhitlowsky's father had made this sort of advantageous match. By the end of the nineteenth and beginning of the twentieth centuries, though, this custom was dying out, making Khonen's frustration—he knows that he deserves Leah not only because they were promised to each other, but because he is the best student in town—realistic for the yeshiva students of An-sky's own time.[67] An-sky himself, like Khonen, pursued women from wealthier families than his own, and was frustrated. As a radical, he could never admit to desiring a bride who would give him access to a comfortable life, but his play displays the tension between the radical's desire to gain credibility through asceticism and the human need for comfort and stability.

To An-sky's contemporaries, the marriage politics in the play would have been credibly radical. The social thinkers of An-sky's generation recognized marriage as a political institution. In 1884, Friedrich Engels had argued that the evolution of family structures from a matriarchal and communal system to a patriarchal and capitalist one had transformed women from respected workers into powerless slaves, the property of their husbands. His book influenced Russian anthropologists such as An-sky's friend Lev Shternberg. Exiled among the Gilyak people of Sakhalin island, Shternberg found evidence in their kinship terms that they still practiced a form of plural marriage: cousin marriage, whereby children are assigned before birth (or at their birth once it becomes clear whether they are girls or boys) to specific cross-cousins as spouses. This image represented the powerful vision of a society in which the claims of groups (or families) take precedence over the claims of individuals, and accumulated wealth has no effect on human fates. Gilyak marriage practices gave Shternberg and his readers the hope that since these communal institutions still existed, even in the most remote part of the world, it might be possible for people everywhere to return to that seemingly so much more virtuous form of life.[68]

In Paris in the 1890s, An-sky had read Engels, and he worked closely with Shternberg on the expedition. *The Dybbuk* suggests that he too was affected by the search for living examples of the communalism of the past that could give hope for the revival of communalism in the future. Specifically, the love plot, based on the promise made by Sender and Nisn that if the wife of one of them gives birth to a girl and the wife of the other gives birth to a boy, the two children will be married, shows the traces of the ideology of Engels and Shternberg. Although Eastern European Jews were known (and criticized) for betrothing children and for early marriage, betrothal of unborn children, a topic that An-sky included in his questionnaire, was rare or nonexistent.[69] By making this practice the center of his play, An-sky made his Jews like the Gilyak, as they appear in Shternberg's descriptions of the system assigning children before birth to cross-cousins as spouses. This equation made it possible to imagine the Jewish past as, like the radicals' fantasy of the primitive past, containing the germ of an ancient communalism that gives hope for a socialist future. The rebellion of Leah and Khonen expressed their potential radicalism (even if clothed in traditionalism), their yearning for an older system, the "primitive communism" of the past, rather than the capitalist system of the present, and Leah's objection to the groom chosen by her father made perfect sense in light of Engels's theories.

Just as Shternberg unwittingly distorted the marriage customs of the Gilyak in a way that suggested that the "primitive communism" in which Engels and his followers believed was still extant somewhere, so An-sky in his depictions of traditional Jewish culture made changes that brought it closer to the ideal of a precapitalist, proto-socialist society. The depiction of the capitalist Sender as a new element, in some way foreign to the shtetl, suggests that An-sky was creating a plot that allowed him to grapple with and disarm the notion of Jews as inherently capitalist and exploitative, a notion that seemingly troubled him at the close of the Beilis trial. With the depiction of traditional Jews as anticapitalist, as with the depiction of the betrothal of unborn children, An-sky selected elements of Jewish culture that fit his ideas, but not to the exclusion of elements that did not support his ideas. In the first act of the final version of the play, the men in the synagogue tell stories about Hasidic rebbes who were famous for their wealth, including Dovidl of Talne and Reb Yisroel of Ruzhin: "Reb Yisroel of Ruzhin, of blessed memory, lived like a monarch. An orchestra of twenty-four musicians played at his table and when he traveled his carriage never had less than six horses." The visiting Messenger responds, "The holy Reb Zushe of Annopol was poor all his life: he wore a peasant's blouse tied with a rope around his waist and had to beg for alms. Yet his good deeds were no less worthy than those of the rebbe of Talne or the rebbe of Ruzhin."[70] In all these cases, An-sky's characters describe real historical figures and legends that his team had heard. Although An-sky presumably preferred the ascetic Zushe of Annopol to the wealthy Yisroel of Ruzhin, and the viewer eventually realizes that the Messenger is a more reliable voice than any other in the cast, he displays the full spectrum of Hasidic tradition.

An-sky did not characterize his own work as transparently political. In a 1920 letter to Zhitlowsky, he was uncertain about who in the play could be seen as having won a moral victory. "In the end Khonen and Leah are victorious. But is the *tsaddik* in the wrong?"[71] If Khonen and Leah stood both for the primitive past and for revolution, then An-sky sounded skeptical about the redemptive value of that revolution. In spite of his own hope that folklore would save the Jews, he created a work that was not neatly ideological—that revealed doubt that the primitive past would provide a real solution.

An-sky's radicalism echoed elsewhere in his *Dybbuk*. One of the models for the figure of Khonen may have been the real-life Father Gapon.

Writing in 1909, An-sky had depicted Gapon as a person with an almost magical ability to communicate and as a reckless child, playing with forces that he could not master completely and that would ultimately destroy him. When Gapon returned to Russia in 1905 and An-sky bid him farewell, he asked the priest with whom he was going to Russia, and heard him answer that he would try to go with God, but would settle for going with the Devil. Four years after he published his recollections of Gapon, An-sky gave very similar words to Khonen. To thwart Sender, Khonen turns to practical kabbalah, a mystical system of magic names and numbers. But the kabbalah is believed to endanger its practitioners, and for that reason, it is traditionally not taught to anyone under forty. Khonen's fellow scholars remind him of this danger. In the Yiddish text of the play, Henekh asks Khonen what motivates him to fast, recite incantations, and immerse himself in the ritual bath.

> *Khonen (as if speaking to himself):* I want . . . I want to seize a clear and brilliant diamond . . . to dissolve it in tears and to draw it into my soul! I want to seize the rays of the third Temple, the third divine emanation. I want . . . *(suddenly very distraught)* Yes! There are still two barrels of gold coins that I must get for the one who can count only gold coins.
>
> *Henekh (appalled):* What are you saying? Khonen, please, be careful. You are on a dangerous course . . . what you long for cannot be acquired by holy means.
>
> *Khonen (provocatively):* And what if not by holy means? What if not by holy means?
>
> *Henekh (very frightened):* I'm afraid to listen to you! I'm afraid to be near you![72]

It is clear that Khonen will turn to the Devil for help. A few lines earlier, Khonen had told Henekh that Satan should be understood as simply another aspect of God: "We need not wage war against sin, we need only to purify it. Just as a goldsmith refines gold in a flame or a farmer threshes the chaff from the wheat, so must we cleanse sin of its dross until nothing but holiness remains. . . . Who created Satan? It was God. Satan is the opposite of God, and as one of His aspects, he contains a holy spark." Henekh is confused and frightened, and the logic behind his fear is confirmed near the end of the first act, after the scholars learn that Sender has signed a betrothal agreement promising Leah to a rich young man. Khonen is appalled, then briefly ecstatic. He exclaims, "The great twice-proclaimed name is revealed to me! I . . . see it! I . . . I . . . I have won!" and with that, he falls dead to the ground. In the 1915 Russian text of the play, Khonen's final appeal to the Devil is even more explicit. He had told Henekh that he knows the secret to his happiness relies on the correct kabbalistic interpretation of the name Leah and its numerical value of 36. Immediately before he dies, he exclaims, "The name Leah means lo ha [lo hashem, not the Name, meaning not God]. Not God, not through God."[73] In the next act, Khonen returns as the dybbuk who possesses Leah.

Khonen is like Gapon, and not only because both the kabbalist and the revolutionary priest are willing to turn to the Devil if what they want cannot be acquired through God. Although Khonen has none of Gapon's cynicism, he possesses the attributes that fascinated An-sky in Gapon, as a child playing recklessly with dangerous weapons and a master of language, whose words have a power beyond that of other people's words. When he turns to kabbalah, Khonen attempts, in a mystical Jewish mode, the same feat that Gapon had accomplished in a revolutionary context: he uses words to change the world and to fight injustice. Both men are convinced of their own power, and like Gapon, Khonen believes that he can use the forces of evil to fight evil.

In *The Dybbuk,* An-sky combined folkloric images with the concerns of the early twentieth century. His echo of Gapon points to the disturbing stories of the downfall of idealistic young men attracted to radical ideology and violent action that were published in 1909 in the wake of the Azef affair. These included Lamed Shapiro's Yiddish story "The Cross," which An-sky had discussed in the *Dos naye lebn* debates about Jewish depictions of the crucifixion, and Boris Savinkov's Russian novel *Pale Horse,* whose central character is motivated to perform his terrorist acts more by a cynical adventurism than any real faith in the revolutionary cause. The SR terrorist in these works, like An-sky's Khonen, is portrayed as a man who plays with dangerous forces of which he may at any moment lose control, a person who wields a power that he turns against others but that may soon turn against him.

The Dybbuk bears the trace of the moral rootlessness and restless impatience that linked Khonen to Gapon and both to An-sky himself. But while the play reveals the influence of An-sky's radical experiences, it itself is not propaganda for his ideas. It emerges not from An-sky's urge to mobilize the masses through effective communication, but rather from his skepticism that radical messages can truly change people and societies for the better. His Khonen tries to be the kind of defiant hero whom An-sky and the SRs had always admired, but this character's fate suggests that such heroism may, as with Gapon, destroy its bearer. An-sky had trouble portraying the rebbe as though he truly believed in his power; this problem reveals the ethnographer's real distance from his subjects. But An-sky was also unable to make Leah and Khonen, who challenge the old order of things, into positive heroes. His play lacks admirable heroes and a happy ending. Although it was based on the folk tales he had gathered, it lacks what An-sky had identified in his golem article as "the optimism of folklore, which testifies to the deep faith of the folk in the victory of truth and justice."[74]

The pessimism of *The Dybbuk* may have reflected An-sky's experiences at the Beilis trial. In Kiev, he had hoped that the fervent prayers of the Jewish community or the passionate speeches of the lawyers would produce, if not a modern-day golem, then at least "remarkable circumstances where the truth is revealed in an especially triumphant and indisputable form." The ambiguous verdict showed that this had not happened. As he mourned, An-sky wrote a play about a supernatural hero who was the opposite of the golem. Where the golem emerged out of communal grief and saved the community, the dybbuk emerged from individual crisis, and in the play, the result is the destruction of Leah and with her, as Azriel says, "a living branch . . . on the fruitful tree of the people of Israel."[75] Whereas in Kiev, An-sky had hoped that communal longing and despair might produce a miracle, the play he wrote soon after meditated on individual longing and despair and the havoc they can wreak.

The most memorable voice in the play is that of Leah herself, who cries out in Khonen's male tones at the end of the second act, the exact center of the text, "You are not my bridegroom!" Her possession might be interpreted in many ways. Scholars see possession, whether by a dybbuk in the Jewish context or by a demon in the Slavic Christian context, as a way for women, rendered silent by tradition, to claim a voice and with it authority and attention. Leah, as a traditional young woman, can express her anger at her father and her rejection of the groom he chose only in someone else's voice. An-sky himself saw the play as more realist than mystical, and he himself rejected the patriarchal assumption that fathers should decide whom their daughters marry. He told a friend that he had been inspired to write his play when he saw a teenage girl in Iarmolintsy, Podolia, devastated by her father's decision to marry her to a rich neighbor rather than the young yeshiva student she loved.[76] An-sky would certainly have been on Leah's side in her rebellion.

But audiences, as An-sky knew, tended to see the play as more mystical than realist. When the theater director Konstantin Stanislavsky read *The Dybbuk* for the Moscow Art Theater, he praised precisely its mysticism as "more original than the mysticism of [Maurice] Maeterlinck," and the Symbolist Sologub saw it as a new, "true and unique form of theatrical mystery play."[77] Within the mystical worldview of the play, Leah is not a rebel but a victim. Khonen's miraculous ability to live on after death comes at the expense of Leah's living a traditional life—and, ultimately, living at all.

It may be that An-sky was so fascinated with dybbuk stories, in which the voice lives on transgressively after the death of its owner, because they recalled his own work with the gramophone. The fantasy of conquering death was prominent in the early history of sound recording, and An-sky recorded the people of the shtetl sometimes willingly and sometimes against their will, preserving their voices so that they could be heard long after their death.[78] Motele in Korostishev had spoken for a part of Jewish tradition that did not entirely welcome such recording, for the suspicion that gramophones could preserve only flawed songs and prayers, never the true spirit of the word. To judge from his letters and notes, An-sky paid no heed to Motele's concerns or to any of the ways in which his collection of voices, kvitlekh, and body parts transgressed the norms, or even the rights, of his subjects. But it may be that some awareness of the moral uncertainty of his ethnographic work emerged in *The Dybbuk*. When Leah speaks in Khonen's voice, she and he are like the gramophone and the singer whom it records, but the process of making his voice live on after death proves fatal to both of them.

If the play, which drew so strongly on An-sky's ethnographic work, reveals some ambivalence about the expedition and its methods, it may also emerge from uncertainty about the awe that An-sky had felt toward folklore itself, in the wake of the Beilis trial. The blood libel is, after all, a bit of folklore that has traveled widely orally and in print, proving remarkably durable. As Gruzenberg noted, no legal case could put it to rest. "If talented and experienced writers have not succeeded over the course of many years in eradicating the malicious legend about the use of Christian blood by Jews, is it possible to turn ignorant and narrow-minded jurors into judges of scholarly work?" The blood libel forces scholars to realize that folklore can unleash hatred and destruction.[79] In the Russian empire, one part of the periodical press disseminated the blood libel legend, while another part attacked it. But after the Beilis trial, An-sky found himself angry not only at the Black Hundreds newspapers, but also at the "Yatskans" in the Yiddish press who refrained from criticizing the Jews for their own misdeeds. He ended his time in Kiev feeling bitter about many things, some of which had been dear to him, such as the possibility of Jewish renewal through a return to folklore. Thus *The Dybbuk* dramatizes folklore that does not cause communal redemption but questions the viability of community.

If theater could not provide communal redemption, perhaps a museum would be more successful. In the spring of 1914, as he invited his friends to read his play, An-sky worked to set up a Jewish museum. When he first planned his ethnographic expedition he had concentrated on texts, but in the field he had gradually become more interested in material culture and visual folklore. His team had collected amulets and folk prints, bought books, ritual objects, and costumes, and taken photographs. An-sky realized that a museum would be needed to display these objects. In early 1913, Moisei Ginsburg had offered the EIEO space in an almshouse he had built in Petersburg, and An-sky used it for ritual objects, costumes, and art on paper. Although it would have shocked the religious, the museum displayed the skull and a Torah scroll torn during the 1881 Kiev pogrom. It opened to journalists and special guests on April 19, 1914, with a speech by An-sky; Sholem Aleichem visited it on May 14 and gave a speech praising the idea of a Jewish museum.[80]

In the spring of 1914, An-sky planned his next summer of collecting, but postponed the start date from June 1 to July 1 in order to appeal for more funding. Reluctantly, Gintsburg agreed to furnish an extra 2,000 rubles. Other trouble lay ahead. As the threat of war grew, the police paid ever closer attention to Jews in the western border regions. In Zhitomir in March 1914, Yudovin and Rekhtman were arrested as spies and their ethnographic material confiscated. An-sky asked Shternberg for help, and he produced documents identifying the young men as employees of the imperial anthropological-ethnographic museum, after which the Zhitomir police freed them and a friend packed up their material and sent it back to Petersburg.[81]

An-sky's team worked to avoid such incidents as the summer season began. Rekhtman's travel papers, identifying him as an official representative of the EIEO, came through only on July 13, 1914. The team, which had gone to Kiev on July 1, went on to the shtetl Stupitsy. But on July 19, Russian style (August 1, European style), the Germans declared war against Russia, and travel in the western provinces of the Empire, especially by Jews, became very difficult. An-sky returned to Petersburg, now renamed Petrograd out of anti-German sentiment. At that point, the expedition was officially over, although in fact An-sky would continue to collect material throughout the war years.[82]

In Petrograd in the fall of 1914, as he listened to the news from the front, An-sky completed the ethnographic questionnaire he had been developing since 1912. In 1913, he had printed a questionnaire focusing on local history, with the kinds of questions about specific sites that produced the stories he heard about buried synagogues and bride-and-groom mounds. In 1914, he worked to finish *Man*, a more extensive volume of questions about the Jewish life cycle, with sections on birth, marriage, and death. These were not open-ended questions, but attempts to determine whether tales and beliefs familiar to the ethnographer were known in a given place. The questions about death include the following:

> 2,014: Do people believe that corpses, like living people, hear every-thing that visitors tell them when they visit their graves?
>
> 2,015: Do people believe that all corpses or only some go to pray in a synagogue at night?
>
> 2,016: Do you know any stories about two dead people involved in litigation presided over by a rabbi? . . .
>
> 2,034: Do you know any stories about a dead person's soul that finds no rest and that turns into a dybbuk and enters a living person?
>
> 2,035: What does a dybbuk normally say and shout?
>
> 2,036: Because of what sins does a dybbuk enter a person?
>
> 2,037: Does a male dybbuk enter a female and vice versa?[83]

These were not the 10,000 questions he had once imagined printing, but some 2,500—far more than any ethnographer could ask a single infor-mant at one sitting. In their large number, they share the all-encompassing view of ethnography that An-sky revealed elsewhere, the attempt to at-tain revelation through the accumulation of details. Though the expedi-tion materials were never published as planned, the questionnaire offers a hint of what that publication might have contained.

Man was published at the end of 1914, but the next planned volume, on holidays, never went to press. Even as the war began, the editors urged readers to collect folklore, insisting that the changes of the past half century in Jewish life threatened the viability of folklore. "With every old man who dies, with every fire that breaks out, with every exile we endure, we lose a piece of our past." Things of beauty were being lost.

> The old poetic legends and the songs and melodies will soon be forgotten. The ancient, beautiful synagogues are falling to ruin or are laid waste by fire and the most precious religious ornaments there are either lost or sold, often to non-Jews. The gravestones of our great and pious ancestors have sunk into the ground, their inscriptions all but rubbed out. In short, our past, sanctified by the blood and tears of so many innocent martyrs, is vanishing and will soon be forgotten.

In order to avert this tragedy, the editors explained, the questionnaire had been created to cover "every aspect of Jewish life," so that detailed information could be gathered about people's beliefs and habits. The scale of An-sky's ambition was fantastic: he believed that he would be able to preserve traditional Jewish life in its entirety, or to bring it, like the dybbuk, back from the dead. "When all of this material is collected, it will be possible to reconstruct the life of the Jewish national community in its entirety and to exhibit it in an historical context."[84]

An-sky used a newly urgent tone in describing the ethnographer's task. Whereas in 1912 he had written and spoken about the need to gather material to inspire artists to produce a secular Jewish culture to replace the religion of the past, in 1914 he put more emphasis on the need to salvage all that remained. The events of the past year had played their part. In Kiev at the Beilis trial, An-sky had seen that neither the prayers of traditional Jews nor the arguments of modern ones could put the lie to the blood libel. In spite of all An-sky and his friends could do, in spite of their newspaper articles, stories, and plays, their spoken and written words, some Christians continued to spread the rumor that Jews were cannibals. While the Russian and German armies battled over the territory of the Pale of Settlement, even more dangerous accusations would arise about Jewish treachery. As those rumors began to fly, An-sky and his colleagues urged heroic new efforts of collection and communication. An-sky had begun to plan the expedition after his own archive burned in Terioki; he wrote in *Man* of the danger of fire to wooden synagogues and the physical symbols of Jewish communal life. In August 1914, far bigger fires began to smolder.

Postcard from An-sky to Zhitlowsky with Rosh Hashanah (New Year's)
greetings, September 1908. Although no portraits of An-sky's wife Esther
Glezerman survive, her handwriting does: she wrote the note in Russian on the
top of the image, and An-sky added the Hebrew one below. (YIVO 308)

S. An-sky, c. 1910. (YIVO 121:An-sky)

Yankev Dinezon, Y. L. Peretz, An-sky, c. 1910. As An-sky became involved in Russian-Jewish and Yiddish publishing, he grew close to Dinezon and Peretz. (YIVO 121:28)

Boy with a cigarette. Photographed by Solomon Yudovin during An-sky's
1912–1914 ethnographic expedition. (Courtesy Petersburg Judaica)

Workers in a cigarette factory, Starokonstantinov. Photographed by Yudovin during the expedition. (Courtesy Petersburg Judaica)

Torah ark, Liuboml. The umbrella pulling the chandelier out of the way appears to be held by An-sky. Photographed by Yudovin during the expedition. (Courtesy Petersburg Judaica)

At the Jewish ethnographic museum in St. Petersburg, May 1914. Left to right: Abram Rekhtman, Solomon Yudovin, An-sky, Sholem Aleichem, Olga Rabinovich (his wife), M. A. Ginsburg (owner of the premises). (Courtesy Petersburg Judaica)

Zhitlowsky and An-sky, about ages forty-eight and fifty, c. 1913 or 1914. (YIVO
121:Zhitlowsky)

An-sky in the uniform
of a wartime relief
worker, 1915. (Repro-
duced from Avram
Rekhtman, *Yidishe
etnografye un folklor:
Zikhroynes vegn der
etnografisher ekspedit-
sye ongefirt fun Sh.
An-ski* [Buenos Aires,
1958], 31; Courtesy of
IWO, Buenos Aires.)

ВСЕРОССІЙСКІЙ
СОЮЗЪ ГОРОДОВЪ
помощи больнымъ и
раненымъ воинамъ.
КОМИТЕТА Ю.-З. ФРОНТА

„ 9 " декабря 1916 г.
Г. Кіевъ.

Мѣсто
печати.

ВРЕМЕННЫЙ
Форма № 2.

Дѣйствителенъ по 9 апрѣля 1917 г.
(не болѣе 4-хъ мѣсяцевъ).

Пропускъ № 12112/16678

Выданъ на основаніи приказа арміямъ Юго-Запад-
наго фронта отъ 16 іюля 1916 г. № 1176.

Кому:
Фамилія Рапопортъ
Имя и отчество Семенъ Акимовичъ

Должность (подробно) сотрудникъ в орган.
помощи насел. пострад. отъ войны.

Мѣсто постояннаго жительства Петроградъ.

Куда Въ Галицію и Буковину
или
въ какой раіонъ
(подробно)

Для какой надобности для организаціи снаб-
женія насел. пострад. отъ войны тру-
домъ и предметами ухода и пр.

Прилагаемыя правила (на оборотѣ).

На проѣздъ

Секретарь

Identification of Semyon Akimovich Rappoport as an employee of the All-
Russian Union of Cities for Aid to the Sick and War-Wounded, giving him
permission to travel in occupied Galicia and Bukovina. Issued December 9,
1916. (GS 4:121)

Roza Monoszon, 1916. (Reproduced from *Roza Nikolaevna Ettinger* [Jerusa-
lem, 1980], 74.)

"An-sky reading *The Dybbuk*," painted by Leonid Pasternak in the summer of 1918, at the Karzinkino estate of Abraham Stybel, outside Moscow. Left to right: Stybel, his wife Sofia, An-sky, unidentified poet, David Frishman. (Reproduced from Rimgaila Salys, *Leonid Pasternak: The Russian Years, 1875–1921: A Critical Study and Catalogue* [Oxford, 1999], 2:52, cf. 1:46–47; courtesy Pasternak Trust.)

A. Vayter, Yiddish writer and An-sky's friend, killed in the April 1919 Vilna pogrom. Photograph by L. Ran. (Reproduced from Henri Minczeles, *Vilna, Wilno, Vilnius: La Jérusalem de Lituanie* [Paris, 1993], unnumbered photographic insert, courtesy Henri Minczeles.)

An-sky with the members of the Vilna Troupe, Poland, 1919 or 1920. Dovid
Herman appears on the left in the top row. (YIVO 1100:46A)

Mausoleum of Peretz, Dinezon, and An-sky, Okopow Street Cemetery, Warsaw. Photograph by Hubert Hozyasz. (Reproduced from Hozyasz, *Jewish Warsaw Today* [Warsaw, 2006], 127, courtesy Hubert Hozyasz.)

"Sh. An-ski," micrography portrait by N. Kopelovitch, Vilna 1930. This image is constructed from seven of An-sky's Yiddish poems: "Mayn lid" (My Song), "Di Nakht" (Night), "Slu-ush-ai!" (Listen!), "Lid fun katorzhnikes" (Prisoners' Song), "Mayn muter" (My Mother), "Der shnayder" (The Tailor), and "Elend" (Loneliness). (YIVO 121:An-sky)

CHAPTER NINE

A Passion for Bloodshed

I hold on to the edge of the sleigh, I try to see the road through
the murky dark, and something in my heart feels terribly absurd.
Why am I slogging in the cold, the wind, and the dark on this
foreign Galician steppe, in a fur hat, with a sabre?

— Letter from S. An-sky to Roza Monoszon, January 20, 1917

O N THE FAST DAY of Tisha B'Av, which fell July 20, 1914, three
days after the Russian army mobilized against Germany and
Austria-Hungary, Simon Dubnov wrote in his diary, "My head
is spinning at the horror of the coming slaughter of peoples, the self-
destruction of Europe." Returning to the capital from a Finnish resort,
Dubnov ran into Lev Shternberg at the Abo train station, and the two
watched refugees fleeing the border regions as trains packed with soldiers
("cannon fodder," Dubnov thought) headed to the front. The soldiers
called out, "Farewell!" and Shternberg and Dubnov answered, "Good luck
on your return!" Dubnov was struck to see "the old revolutionary Shternberg, who had been a prisoner on Sakhalin, triumphantly calling to them,
'Good luck!'" On the train going back to Petrograd, Dubnov felt shame
when he read that Jews had joined in the general patriotic demonstrations, even kneeling at the base of the monument to the anti-Jewish Tsar
Alexander III and reciting the Jewish prayer for the dead. Jewish men
returned from Europe and the United States to volunteer for the Russian
army; Jewish women signed up as nurses; an estimated 500,000 Jews
served in the army, about 10 percent of the total Jewish population.[1]
Dubnov, though, was horrified at German atrocities, at Russian losses, at
the knowledge that Jewish soldiers in different armies were fighting each
other; he hoped that the reward for the Jews' support of the Russian war
effort would be the extension of their civil rights within the empire, but
he feared that things would only get worse.

Gradually and piecemeal over the next few months, Dubnov, An-sky,
and the rest of the Petrograd intelligentsia learned how much worse

things were becoming for Russian Jews and their kin in Austria-Hungary. Gurevich, returning to Russia from a trip to Germany as the war began, was jailed by the Russian authorities for three weeks. People who were used to getting letters daily from colleagues abroad felt cut off as they combed the censored wartime press and spoke with those returning from the war zone. In Minsk, which was full of refugees and wounded soldiers back from the front, people no longer tried to get information from the newspapers. As An-sky saw, "For news, people go to the station, to the trains coming from Warsaw. The city is living on rumors." At the station, he heard that the Jews, who were seen as likely to betray the Russian Empire, were being forced to leave the border region. In November, Dubnov heard that when the Jews of Skierniewice and Grodzisk were forced to walk the fifty miles to Warsaw, they appealed to the Jewish soldiers in a Russian regiment they met on the way. The soldiers cried, but they could do nothing. In a Moscow military hospital in November, An-sky found a group of ninety Jewish soldiers fresh from the trenches in the Austro-Hungarian province of Galicia, which the Russian army controlled almost entirely by December 1914. One soldier told him that on Yom Kippur, they had gone from one Galician shtetl to another. They saw smoking ruins, with a few houses still standing. Out of the entire population of the shtetls only a few men remained—two in one town, ten in another—and the soldiers gathered with them in the half-ruined synagogues. An-sky asked, "Did you try to ask them questions, to talk with them?" and the soldier answered, "I couldn't speak with them. I could only cry together with them."[2]

From the reports of Jewish refugees and soldiers, An-sky and the other Jews of Petrograd began to grasp what was occurring in Galicia. This province's ethnically mixed population of 8 million included 3.4 million Polish Roman Catholics, 3.7 million Greek Catholic (Uniate) Ruthenians (or Rusyns), and 900,000 Jews. The Ruthenians, who spoke a language close to western dialects of Ukrainian, followed the Byzantine rite with Church Slavonic liturgy but accepted the authority of the Pope. Many Galician Ruthenians were peasants who resented the wealthier Poles and Jews in their midst. "Muscophile" Ruthenian leaders welcomed the Russians in 1914, and the Russian government saw them as Russians, overlooking their distinctive language and religion. The anti-Semitic commander in chief, the tsar's uncle Grand Duke Nikolai Nikolaevich, and his chief of staff, Nikolai Ianushkevich, saw the Russian army's task as the liberation of the Ruthenians from their Polish and especially their Jewish landlords, whom he viewed as just as much the Russians' true enemies as the German and Austro-Hungarian armies. The new science of military statistics had divided population groups into those more and less likely to be loyal during wartime. If the most loyal population was ethnically homogeneous, then more diverse populations were dangerous, and Russian statisticians had been predicting since 1885 that Jews would betray the empire. The leaders of the army were convinced that both Austro-Hungarian and Russian Jews were Russia's enemies, doing all they could to bring about its defeat. That the Jews in lands to the west of the Russian Empire enjoyed full civil rights made it even more logical to expect them to resist the Russians (indeed, the Germans issued an appeal to the Russian Jews to support them for that very reason).[3]

If Galicia's fate was, as many in the Russian government hoped, to be annexed by the Russian Empire, then the Jews living there would have to accept a dramatic downward change in status. At the general headquarters of the army (the Stavka), everyone referred to Jews as *zhidy* (Yids) and felt that administering Galicia would require solving the "Jewish problem," meaning expropriating, expelling, or perhaps killing them. Ianushkevich wrote, "We will face a difficult struggle with Jewry. It would seem essential to employ for this end the possibilities granted us by martial law." He knew that war conditions allowed him to implement much more brutal methods than what would be allowed in peacetime. Rumors of Jewish treachery were repeated everywhere, and as the Russian army entered Galician towns, the soldiers, especially the Cossacks, burned, raped, and looted: their victims were disproportionately Jewish, though they also targeted Poles and Germans.[4] In order to cause panic and remove a population they believed to be dangerous, the army leaders increasingly deported Jews—at times only men of fighting age, at times everyone except men of fighting age, and at times everyone—eastward into Russia.

Even before the Jews in the capitals learned the full extent of the atrocities against civilians in the war zone, they were already organizing to help Jewish soldiers and their families. On August 18, at a meeting of the Petrograd Jewish community, Genrikh Sliozberg suggested the formation of a relief organization, and in September, the Jewish Committee to Help War Victims (EKOPO) came into existence officially; on October 2, Petrograd mayor Ivan Tolstoy signed an order giving it permission to do aid work. Although at first the Russian government funded only aid organizations that would not help Jews, Sliozberg convinced them to allocate the EKOPO funding as well. In 1915, the EKOPO unified Jewish aid committees set up elsewhere, and as a result of international fundraising, between August 1914 and June 1917 its budget totaled over 31 million rubles. Like other official Russian-Jewish organizations of the time, the EKOPO had strong ties to the relatively conservative Gintsburg family but employed a cadre of radicalized professionals such as An-sky.[5]

From late August, An-sky had been trying to get past Minsk and Kiev and into the occupied zone. He suspected that aid was needed, and he was frustrated that at first wealthy Russian Jews seemed uninterested in Galicia. He wanted to investigate the situation of the Galician Jews, gather the sorts of "facts and figures" that would convince people to help them, and combat what he was convinced was a campaign of anti-Jewish rumors calculated to provoke violence. As he knocked on Petrograd doors, trying to get permission to go to the front, the EKOPO leaders grew more sympathetic to his project. On November 20, Sliozberg and L. Bramson, the EKOPO director and secretary, officially asked An-sky to gather information in occupied Galicia about the economic situation of its Jews and establish contact with local Jewish organizations. He was a logical choice for this task, and not only because he had already decided to take it on himself. His experience during the ethnographic expedition, traveling in Volynia and Podolia, the two provinces that lay between Kiev and the Austro-Hungarian border, had made him familiar with the region. Because he and his writings were popular with the Russian intelligentsia, An-sky could count on the cooperation of the liberals who ran the official refugee aid organizations.[6] The childless, unmarried An-sky was most likely more willing to take on this dangerous assignment than other men would have been, and as a journalist, he was eager to report on the war.

In the war zone, An-sky found a landscape of terrifying rumor, apocalyptic legend, and unrelenting violence. There, like everyone he met, he struggled to tell reality from lies and friends from enemies, to understand the meaning of the war's brutality. More than ever before, An-sky wrote frankly about Russians' anti-Jewish behaviors and beliefs. Even as the Russian government limited the Jews' freedom to travel and clamped down on Yiddish publishing, he fantasized about using words to defend the Jews, whether through careful documentation of atrocities or arguing for the Zionist dream of Jews with bayonets of their own.

The day after the EKOPO leaders wrote to him, on November 21, An-sky left for Warsaw, which by then was mobbed with expelled Jews and refugees. Peretz and Dinezon, who had both been personally ruined by the war (they were grateful for the 20 rubles An-sky sent them when it broke out), were trying to help the more than 50,000 Jews who had poured into Warsaw. The Russian offensive in the North had failed, partly due to the Germans' knowledge of Russian military plans. Because the

Russian troops were poorly trained and often illiterate, they could neither master the encryption systems needed for secure wireless communication nor set up a field telephone system, so Russian military leaders
broadcast their instructions "in the clear," and German intercept teams
simply listened in and reported all the decisions of the Russian high command to their own headquarters. Russian subjects, unaware of their army's technical problems, attributed the enemy's knowledge to espionage,
and the most common villain mentioned was a Jew. Over the month An-
sky spent in Warsaw, he heard countless rumors about Jewish treachery.
A hotel maid told him that Jews call the Germans on the telephone to tell
them where to drop bombs; a Jewish nurse told him a hospital director
had refused to allow her to work there because Jews send gold to Germany; a Jew who sneezed when an airplane was flying overhead was accused of signaling to the pilot.[7]

An-sky was certain that these rumors lay behind the Russian soldiers'
cruelty to Jewish civilians, because he did not believe that Russians were
naturally cruel. In 1908, he had written in "Jewish Folk Art" that other
nations were warlike, but not the Jews. Two years later, he felt unwilling
to characterize the other nation he loved as violent. In "The Folk and
War," he claimed that folklore revealed the Russians' fundamental antipathy to war. Although "fake" soldiers' songs presented Russian soldiers as proudly fighting foes whom they despised, "real" folklore showed
that "the Russian folk muse is not inspired by war. . . . The soldier, like
the peasant, sees only war's horrors, its blood and groans, misery and
want." No matter how much effort the authorities might put into spreading propaganda, "The soldier, even in the heat of battle, is not possessed
by savage hatred of his enemy." Like Tolstoy, An-sky felt that Russian
peasants were naturally nonviolent, so aggression and hatred among
them must be the products of lies spread by an immoral government.
These ideas were still on An-sky's mind in 1914, when he republished
"The Folk and War."[8]

Now that he was in Warsaw, daily exposed to evidence of Russian soldiers' hatred of Jews, he did everything possible to explain it. He sought
to understand the source of the "fake" legends that could have perverted
them. He blamed right-wing publications such as *Novoe Vremia,* which
influenced the officers, and the Poles, who spread rumors about Jewish
disloyalty to the tsar in order to distract from their own disloyalty. Soon,
he began to hear anti-Jewish rumors from his own liberal Russian acquaintances. Victor Muizhel, a writer who had also worked for *Russkoe
Bogatstvo,* told him he had heard an old Jew was discovered carrying a
fugitive German and 2,500 silver thalers across the Dvina river. Grigory

Petrov, a radical ex-priest, told him the same story, but set on the Vistula. Within a few weeks, An-sky saw a disturbing change. "Liberals began to show indifference toward the Jewish plight. They listened more attentively to all sorts of derogatory stories and eventually began to repeat them in their private conversations and even in their articles." He was especially shaken to hear Vasily Maklakov, who had been part of the defense team at the Beilis trial, say that anti-Jewish feeling was understandable, since Jews had shot at Russian soldiers in Lvov, a story An-sky was convinced was false. "And this was how one of the finest Russian intellectuals reacted to the idiotic lies spread by certain Polish groups. What, then, could we expect from other people?"[9]

The rumors of Jewish treachery, like the blood libel, provoked a response among Jews themselves. When he wrote about blood libel folklore, An-sky had emphasized the optimism of folktales in which dangerous rumors were disproved "in an especially triumphant and indisputable form," and throughout the war, he gathered Jewish folktales created in a similar spirit, in which Poles were triumphantly revealed to be behind the espionage attributed to Jews. In one tale, the Jews of Zamość were accused of helping the Austrians, but before they could be sentenced to death, honest Russians led the judges to the house of the local Polish landowner, Count Zamojski. In his cellar, they found the true villainess, the countess, speaking with the Austrians on a hidden telephone.

As he listened to Jewish legends about magical exposure of the rumors of espionage, An-sky thought about other ways to fight what he was sure were lies. In January 1915, he, Peretz, and Dinezon appealed to Jews to collect evidence to document themselves and their traditional way of life and how it and they were being destroyed, and thus to control, if not their own fate, then its interpretation. "We must become the historians of our part in the process. We and you who are living through this now must put away for the near and distant future each sign that the historical process inscribes upon our people. Otherwise our account will be empty, and neither people nor history will owe us anything, and our name will be erased from the page on which the world records its terrible and painful process as entitlement for better times." This "Appeal to Collect Materials about the World War" spoke of its authors' despair. "Our enemies will stop at nothing: no means that won't justify the end of blackening the Jewish name." An-sky had criticized Yatskan for being too quick to defend the Jews, but now defense was imperative. In the face of the anti-Jewish rumors and the human suffering that followed in their wake, the writers insisted that Jews claim the right to describe themselves, so that at some point, if not now then in the future, truth would

counteract lie. And as people had responded to An-sky's appeal for ethnographic materials, so they answered his plea for materials about the
war. His wartime archive contained 1,371 documents: letters about "administrative exile" to Siberia for Jews who had been at German resorts
during the summer of 1914, copies of decrees and military circulars condemning Jews, documents of people who had been arrested, official letters about hostages, copies of secret police notices, denunciations, court-
martial documents, and death sentence reports. Some of the same people
who had gathered ethnographic material for him, such as the writer Lev
Aba, sent him evidence of Jewish suffering during the war.[10]

During the month An-sky spent in Warsaw, he knocked on dozens of
doors, trying to carry out his EKOPO mission and find a way into the
war zone. He wanted to be assigned to one of the official aid organizations run by the Union of Towns (VSG) and the Union of Zemtsvos (provincial administrative units) (VZS), both permitted from the beginning of
the war to care for war wounded "under the flag" of the Russian Red
Cross. Many of the leaders of these organizations were liberal Russians,
often Kadets, with whom An-sky had connections. They worked closely
with military commanders, who were grateful to them for providing soldiers with baths and clean laundry as well as medical care. One price for
cooperation with the military authorities was acquiescence in anti-Jewish
policies, and many VZS and VSG leaders agreed not to employ Jews in
the war zone.[11] An-sky took on a job for the VZS in Warsaw, hoping to
make contacts that would result in a placement in Galicia. After countless refusals, he finally found a VZS division head willing to hire him:
Igor Demidov, a Kadet Duma deputy and writer who together with his
wife ran a medical corps. He asked An-sky to escort a shipment of medicine and linens west from Moscow through Brody, where it would have
to be moved from a wide-gauge Russian train to a narrow-gauge Austrian train, to Tarnów, which lay deep in Galicia, at the edge of the territory under Russian occupation.

In January 1915, as soon as he got the assignment, An-sky rushed back
to Petrograd to share his Warsaw impressions with the EKOPO leadership. He urged that aid be directed toward making refugees self-reliant
whenever possible; two or three people should be sent to Warsaw to
oversee aid; and a Russian-language newspaper should be set up in Warsaw, presumably to counter the anti-Jewish rumors.[12] When Demidov's
shipments left Moscow for Gomel, An-sky took the train to Kiev, where
Baron Gintsburg gave him 3,000 rubles to distribute to Jews in Galicia.
He hoped to meet Demidov's shipment in Radivilov and accompany it
from there.

As An-sky set out for Galicia, the Russian army's punitive policies toward the Jews became ever more brutal. Ianushkevich ordered the mass expulsion of Jews from areas near the front, worsening the refugee crisis within Galicia and creating logistical nightmares for the Russian army itself, whose already shaky communications and supply lines began to fail completely. Evidence of the army's anti-Jewish policies was everywhere. The American journalist John Reed, traveling through Galicia in the spring of 1915, saw villages ruined, "black with fire—especially those where Jews had lived. They bore marks of wanton pillage—for there had been no battle here—doors beaten in, windows torn out, and lying all about the wreckage of mean furniture, rent clothing." As he approached the border, An-sky saw similar scenes in the Jewish market towns that belonged to the Russian Empire. At the beginning of the war, a troop of Cossacks who had been stationed outside of Radivilov for twelve years and had had good relations with the townspeople had entered the town to loot and destroy Jewish stores. An-sky learned that several hundred Jews—Russian subjects—hid from the Cossacks in the synagogue. "The Cossacks wanted to force their way in, but a Christian, it seems a watchman, came out, protected the door with his body, and reproached the Cossacks for attacking poor, defenseless people."[13]

Having arrived in Radivilov on January 16, An-sky and a lawyer traveling with him went to the train station several times a day, hoping to find Demidov's linens and medicines. After five days making inquiries, they learned the shipment had been held up between Zdolbunov (near Rovno) and Brody. They found the supplies in Ozeriany on January 21 and got them to Brody. A week later, the shipment went to Dębica, close to Tarnów. Bedded down in the open train car full of supplies, An-sky arrived in Wola Rzędzińska, a suburb of Tarnów, on January 31. It had taken fifteen days and all his diplomatic skills to move Demidov's supplies the 260 miles from Rovno to Tarnów. Even this was an achievement, given the communications disarray on the front. During this period it took fourteen hours for John Reed to travel forty-five miles: he saw "a battalion side-tracked all day without food, and further on huge dining sheds where thousands of meals were spoiling, because the men didn't come. Engines whistled impatiently for a clear track . . . One had an impression of vast forces hurled carelessly here and there, of indifference on a grand scale, of gigantic waste." In a train, Reed met officers looking for 17 million bags of flour that had somehow been lost en route between Kiev and Tarnopol.[14]

Like Reed, An-sky was frustrated by the unpredictability of travel but relished the chance to talk with other people on the move. In spite of fears about espionage, people spoke openly. During the fifteen days he spent moving Demidov's supplies, An-sky encountered soldiers; nurses; doctors he knew from their student days in Switzerland; people he had met during his ethnographic expedition; an elderly peasant from Ufa in distant Bashkiria, trying unsuccessfully to get a train car full of presents donated by his parish to the soldiers at the front; twenty-four Jewish hostages being sent in an unheated car from a Galician shtetl, neither they nor anyone else knew where; priests discussing whether the word *zhid* comes from "Judas"; an officer who spoke frankly of his fear that his soldiers would shoot him in the back; and another officer who told him that the Russian army had three enemies, "the lice, the Germans, and our own generals."[15]

Trains made it possible to pretend to be someone else. Like the characters in Tolstoy's "The Kreutzer Sonata" and Sholem Aleichem's *Railroad Stories,* An-sky listened to the tales that people seemed to tell more openly in trains than anywhere else. His work for Demidov had allowed him to enter the occupied territory; in mid-February, he came to an agreement with another liberal Russian, Prince Pavel Dolgorukov, the director of the VSG unit in Tarnów, that he would travel around Galicia to buy desperately needed shoe leather.[16] With documentation from Dolgorukov, he was able to move freely and learn about the condition of the Jews. Effectively in disguise, he became acutely sensitive to questions of identity and loyalty.

He knew that whether or not Russian Jews betrayed their country to the Germans, many of them identified with German culture. On January 20, he ran into Konstantin Rabinovich, an old friend now working as a military doctor. Rabinovich told him that a few weeks earlier, when his division was stationed in Prussia, they had seen a German officer coming toward them with a white flag and understood that he wanted to talk with them. Because Rabinovich was the only man in the division who spoke German (like most Jewish doctors, he had studied in Western Europe), he volunteered to meet the Germans. It turned out that the Germans wanted to propose an agreement: if the Russians did not fire during the German Christmas, the Germans would agree not to shoot during the Russian one. The German officer he spoke with invited him to their Christmas celebration. "We'll cover your eyes and lead you to us. You'll spend a very nice evening with us. Then we'll bring you back." Rabinovich admitted to An-sky that he had a "powerful desire" to go, but he was not permitted.[17]

Like Rabinovich, many Russian Jews felt comfortable with Germans, and everyone knew that Jews were treated better west of the border.

Dubnov wrote in November 1914 of Jewish "Germanophilia," but An-sky insisted that the rumors of Jews betraying Russia were all false. He portrayed himself as more genuinely Russian than the army itself, which misappropriated great Russian writers to demeaning purposes. In town after town in Galicia, he saw that the Russian army, having burned down the houses, had nailed up shiny metal signs, renaming the streets after Pushkin, Gogol, Lermontov. "The cynicism of naming these horribly de-formed streets after the luminaries of Russian culture had escaped the victors; they didn't realize how offensive it was to the memory of our great Russian writers. The street signs made almost the same impression as the icons that Christians put in their windows during pogroms."[18]

As he traveled around Galicia, An-sky saw horrifying scenes that he could never forget. He spent an hour one morning in a tailor's cottage in Tarnów having his overcoat mended and chatting with the tailor. At lunch, he heard a crash and discovered that the tailor's cottage had been shelled, the tailor's assistant, sister-in-law, and nephew killed. In a mili-tary clinic that afternoon, An-sky found the tailor's surviving nephew, his hands bandaged, unable to understand where he was or what had hap-pened to his mother and brother. An-sky took the abandoned child to his own room, fed him, and put him to bed, then found the boy's relatives. He too felt that life was becoming incomprehensible. "I hold on to the edge of the sleigh, I try to see the road through the murky dark, and something in my heart feels terribly absurd. Why am I slogging in the cold, the wind, and the dark on this foreign Galician steppe, in a fur hat, with a sabre?" "There's no firewood," he noted one day. "There's no sugar in town for tea, but yesterday there was a cinematographer here." And like a film, life in occupied Galicia shifted abruptly from one image to another. In the morning of February 8, 1915, he saw the desecrated synagogue of Tuchów, torn apart by Russian soldiers and used as a toilet. That evening, he heard the soldiers in Colonel Nechvolodov's regiment sing, and noted that one soldier, Khaiut, a recent convert to Christianity, "of course couldn't restrain himself from making fun of Jews."[19]

Even though he was well aware the Russian army was responsible for the Jewish devastation he saw all around him in Galicia, An-sky retained the faith of his entire life in the fundamental goodness of the Russian peasant. He could describe those Russian soldiers as "fine fellows"; he could sympathize with their fear, admire their courage, and drink toasts with the officers. He tended to see the soldiers as fundamentally innocent peasants, led astray into war, but he also listened sympathetically to the officers. He was appalled when he heard Russians repeating anti-Jewish rumors, as so often occurred on trains. At a dark moment, he imagined that all the peasants of different nationalities who had been displaced during the war would someday come together in work and pleasure— but when they "remember their neighbor, the Jew, who fought none of them, who killed none of their people, they will nevertheless unanimously agree that the 'Yid' is the one responsible for everybody's misfortune."[20] Despite this, he never assumed all Russians were anti-Jewish.

His saw the Jews he met as varied. He knew of Jewish soldiers participating in pogroms, but he also knew of Jewish soldiers helping Galician Jews and distributing aid money. One soldier, Srulik Vaysbrod, helped the Jews of Suchostaw so much that the Galician Jews began to believe that he was the prophet Elijah in disguise. But the men who were culturally closer to An-sky, the Jewish army doctors, showed, with few exceptions, "a fearful indifference to their Galician brothers . . . Some even hid their Jewish background and swallowed all the anti-Jewish lies and insults they heard." Whether he met Christians or Jews, he judged lower-class people more kindly and was suspicious of the upper class, noting that even as refugees, the formerly wealthy Galician Jews expected to be treated better than their poorer neighbors.[21]

As he interacted with Russian soldiers and fellow aid workers, An-sky was uncertain whom he could trust to seek the truth about the Galician Jews and who would believe the rumors. In June 1915, he evaluated head nurse Alexandra Kistiakovskaia, the director of the first flying detachment of the State Duma. "She is an unusually intellectual, serious, and nice woman. She worked the whole ten months tirelessly on the front lines, walked the way of the cross there and back, and now, totally exhausted, is going to rest." He urged Sologub and Chebotarevskaia to get to know her and to hear her impressions of the Galician campaign—but he could not vouch for her complete honesty. "I never spoke with her precisely about the Jews, and it's entirely possible that, as a person born into the highest aristocracy (it seems), she has been infected by anti-Semitism. But she gives the impression of a person who is too honorable and decent to lie. More than that I don't know."[22] An-sky frankly assessed Kistiakovskaia's potential to be an anti-Semite. For a lifetime, this Populist had believed that Russians were for the most part well-meaning toward Jews, and anti-Jewish violence should be blamed on governmental policy rather than popular animosity. In Galicia, he began to step back from that belief. He still associated anti-Semitism with the authorities and was convinced that if Kistiakovskaia were an anti-Semite, this would be due to her aristocratic upbringing, but his wish to know what she truly thought about Jews shows that he was becoming concerned that people he trusted might turn out to be his enemies.

Over the winter and spring of 1915, as he investigated the situation of the Galician Jews, An-sky made trips back to Petrograd and Kiev to gather money to distribute in Galicia. On a trip in mid-February, he carried a copy of a poster that had been hung in Tarnów by the military authorities. It proclaimed that Jews were traitors and therefore some had to be taken as hostages. An-sky wanted to make sure that the Jews in the capitals were informed about the dire situation in Galicia, even though he was skeptical that Jewish lobbying could soften Russian policy toward the Galician Jews. He was certain that military and civilian authorities did not believe the rumors of treachery; they were just spreading these lies cynically, to justify removing the Galician Jews' civil rights once the Russians annexed the province.

In May 1915, the army newspaper *Nash Vestnik* (Our Herald) and the government newspaper *Pravitel'stvennyi Vestnik* (Government Herald) ran articles about the "shockingly treacherous conduct" of the Jews of the Lithuanian town of Kuzhi: "The Jews had concealed German soldiers in their cellars before our troops arrived, and at a signal they set fire to Kuzhi on all sides . . . All the local inhabitants who had taken part in this terrible affair were brought before a court-martial and the ringleaders will be sent to Siberia." The story was widely circulated until three deputies of the Russian Duma went to Kuzhi to investigate. They found that Kuzhi housed only six Jewish families—all but one living in huts without cellars. The one cellar in a Jewish house could not have hidden enough German soldiers to annihilate a Russian detachment. Furthermore, the Jews had left Kuzhi the day before the Germans attacked. A booklet published by the American Jewish Committee explained that "No Jews had been tried, convicted, or executed at Kuzhi; in brief, the story was, from beginning to end, an absolute fabrication."[23] The Kuzhi case proved that the government was trying to circulate false rumors about Jews, but such stories began to encounter skepticism in Russia and abroad.

In the fall of 1914, An-sky had been disturbed to hear Russian intellectuals repeat rumors of Jewish treachery and disappointed that Russian Jews felt no solidarity with the Jews of Galicia, but over the next two years, things changed. Beginning in March 1915, as Ianushkevich's expulsion policies took effect and the prospect emerged of even greater masses of refugees pouring into Russia proper, the civilian government was horrified. In the spring and summer of 1915, public opinion turned against the army commanders and their policies. Jews and non-Jews whose views in peacetime were divided united to counter the rumors. The Labor Zionists, the Bund, and the American Jewish Committee published refutations of the Kuzhi legend. In the Duma in August 1915, the

Georgian Menshevik deputy Nikolai Chkheidze explicitly criticized the government newspaper publication of the Kuzhi slander. Russian and Jewish intellectuals continued to speak out against the anti-Jewish slanders. In March 1916, a group of Duma deputies, not only the Jewish Kadet Fridman but also Miliukov and Maklakov himself—who had once repeated the rumor about the pogrom in Lvov—sternly condemned the Department of Police for printing the rumor that Jews were causing inflation: "This document embodies the crime of stirring up one part of the population against another."[24]

While Jews in the war zone suffered more and more from the army's policy of hostage-taking and mass deportations—at the beginning of May 1915, the 200,000 Jews of Kovno and Kurland Provinces were abruptly ordered to leave their homes and move east—An-sky began to see a shift in public opinion in the capitals. When he visited Petrograd that month, he heard rumors about the treachery of Germans, generals, and the tsarina, but no more stories about Jews. An-sky had growing evidence for his belief in the decency of some of the Russian intelligentsia. As early as the fall of 1914, some Russian intellectuals had been speaking out against anti-Semitic abuses. In November 1914, Leonid Andreev had published "The First Step" in *Utro Rossii* (Morning of Russia), insisting that their maltreatment of the Jews made the Russians appear to be barbarians. "Yes, we are still barbarians . . . we are still a dark fear for Europe, an unsolvable threat to its culture, but we don't want that any more . . . The tragic Jewish love for Russia corresponds to our love for Europe, equally tragic in its faithfulness and its unrequitedness. After all, we ourselves are the *Jews of Europe, our border is that very Pale of Settlement of ours,* a distinctive Russian ghetto . . . This is our punishment, fate's revenge on Russians for the suffering of Jews!" Although An-sky sometimes criticized Andreev's violent, erotic stories and plays, he had connections with him and his family. When he was in Petrograd in February 1915, Andreev's sister had asked him to deliver money to her other brother, who was a soldier in a military hospital in Galicia. An-sky tracked Andreev's brother down and heard him tell how brutally his commander had implemented the policy of taking Jewish hostages.[25] More than some of the other Russian-Jewish writers of his generation, An-sky exemplified what Andreev called the "tragic Jewish love for Russia." In his earnest attempts to talk the Russian public out of its suspicion of the Jews, Andreev wrote from the same stance as An-sky, the same belief in the power of words.

By the end of the year, other prominent Russian intellectuals joined Andreev in criticizing the government's anti-Jewish policies. Gorky,

Sologub, and Andreev, who were often on the opposite sides of literary-political debates, came together in December to lead the Society for the Study of Jewish Life, out of which grew a league for the defense of Jews. Dubnov attended a meeting of the league in March 1915, chaired by the old revolutionary Nikolai Chaikovsky, with the elderly Vera Zasulich herself in the audience. He was impressed by the "bold" speeches Russian writers made in defense of Jews. The society was best known for publishing the 1915 *Shield*, a collection of essays by a wide array of Russian writers defending Jews.[26] In stories, poems, and articles, these writers depicted the Jews as loyal subjects of the Russian Empire, innocent children and old people, faithful soldiers and nurses; they attacked Russian anti-Semitism and the harsh treatment of the Jews in the war zone.

An-sky too defended the Jews, writing articles for *Den'* (Day) and *Rech'* (Speech) (some censored). Restrictions were imposed on the Yiddish press, and An-sky published little in Yiddish during the war. He drafted a piece in Russian that the police acquired in January 1916 and found "full of clearly improbable examples of the savagery of the Russian soldiers and the heroism of the Jews, and in general suffused with a special Jewish spirit that is hostile to Russia."[27] From 1917 through 1920, he would transform his wartime Russian diary and the many documents he gathered into a three-volume Yiddish memoir, *The Destruction of the Jews of Poland, Galicia, and Bukovina, from a 1914–1917 Diary*, published posthumously in 1921 and usually referred to as *The Destruction of Galicia*.

In much of his wartime writings, he analyzed the causes of the army's violence against Jews, dwelling on two symbolic cases: the pogroms in Brody and Lvov at the start of the war. Brody was a Galician trading town just inside the border of Austria-Hungary, five miles from the Volynian town of Radivilov, which was inside the Russian Empire and near many of the places An-sky had visited in 1913.[28] Two-thirds of the population, in 1911 numbering some 17,000, were Jews, and Brody and its seventeenth-century fortress-style synagogue figure in Jewish history: the Baal Shem Tov's wife came from there, and the nineteenth-century Broder Singers were the first troupe of traveling Yiddish singers and actors. On August 14, 1914, Cossack scouts from the Russian army entered Brody and found that the Austro-Hungarian army had fled. The Russians then shelled the town, destroying a bank. A few days later, a Cossack division returned to the town and systematically looted and burned the Jews' houses, preventing them from removing their belongings. This action was explained as punishment because, it was said, when the Russians first entered the town, a sniper had killed an officer from a hotel window; when the shooter was identified as a Jewish woman, the daughter of the hotel owner, she was killed in retaliation, along with eight other Jews.

The story of the Jewish woman shooting from the window sounded unlikely. Vladimir Grabar, an international law attaché at the Russian headquarters, wrote skeptically in his diary that the violence probably actually arose after a Russian officer made unwanted advances toward a Jewish woman. Military authorities found no evidence of the shot, nor did anyone report the murder of an officer at the time when it was alleged to have occurred. Nonetheless, after the army investigation was concluded, the story of the shot was reported by the newspaper *Russkoe Slovo* (The Russian Word). A similar set of events occurred in the nearby provincial capital of Lvov. As a witness reported, "Early one afternoon a shot was heard in the middle of the Jewish quarter of the town. Immediately shooting began all over the town. Seventeen Jews were killed, as well as two Christians, and two Jewish houses were demolished . . . Immediately after the pogrom, Jewish hostages were taken." The story of a Jewish mob shooting at Russian soldiers in Lvov was then published in the newspaper *Prikarpatskaia Rus'* (Carpathian Rus).[29]

When An-sky reworked his wartime writings into a book, he framed it with the pogroms of Brody and Lvov, and throughout the book, he returned obsessively to the single shot that seemingly triggered them. As he accompanied Demidov's supplies through Brody, he interviewed pogrom survivors. As with the Bialystok pogrom that he had investigated in 1906, he concluded that this was violence planned by the authorities, then triggered deliberately by a provocateur. He thought the authorities invented the story of the girl shooting from the window to justify the Brody pogrom, because at the time people were not yet accustomed to the army's savagery; they then deliberately spread similar legends about girls shooting from windows before other Galician pogroms.[30]

During the next months, An-sky discussed the Brody and Lvov pogroms with the people he met. He was relieved to hear Demidov dismiss the rumors, saying, "I know very well what it means when in almost every town a Jewish girl shoots from a window at a Russian soldier, and she just happens to be in a building with wealthy stores and apartments."[31] An-sky's fascination with the explanations for these two pogroms may have resulted from the powerful impression made by the ruins of Brody, the first Galician town he saw. It may also have resulted from his conviction, as a folklorist, that recurring legends are especially significant. These pogroms and the legends about them became a litmus test for him, a way for him to distinguish those Russians such as Maklakov, who had been led astray by wartime propaganda, from those such as Demidov, who were still able to tell truth from falsehood—a way to distinguish his own friends from the foes of the Jews.

Like Isaac Babel, who wrote about his travels through that same landscape in 1920 with a Cossack division of the Red Army, An-sky was a Jew able to pass as a non-Jew, to his great logistical benefit and psychological discomfort. Like all the employees of the Zemtsvo union, he wore a khaki military uniform. As Sliozberg remembered, "Tall but stooped, with a calm, good-humored expression, An-sky took on the appearance of a Russian officer." The impression that he was a Russian officer and not a Jew meant that he often heard his Russian interlocutors express anti-Semitic feelings. Sometimes he decided to continue "passing" in order to understand better what was going on, though he wrote that this decision made him feel "dejected and insulted as if I'd robbed someone," but he periodically spoke out. He told an elderly professor in a train, "You spread rumors; you're a gossipmonger!" An-sky's exploration of his feelings in his wartime memoir gave the book unexpected power. As the historian Yankev Shatzky acknowledged in a 1921 review, the strengths of *The Destruction of Galicia* were its depictions of the attitudes of Russians toward Jews and its illumination of the complex feelings of its author, "the subjective attitude of a Jewish *intelligent.*"[32]

Compared to his wartime diaries and letters, An-sky's published memoir imposed narrative order on the author's ambivalent identification with both the victims of violence and their oppressors. The memoir made its author sound less sympathetic to the Russian army than he had been in his diary, and more appalled by the atrocities against Jews. Even while he toned down his sympathy for the Russians, though, the material he chose to publish highlighted the similarities between Galician Jews and Russian Christians. Although he spent time debunking anti-Jewish rumors, he also wrote about the rumormongers and their motivations, presenting the rumors now as propaganda spread for a specific purpose, now as folklore arising naturally from specific circumstances. He emphasized the sincerity of people who told him fantastic anti-Jewish rumors, such as a Russian physician who explained that the Beilis trial had been secretly controlled by the Hasidic rebbe of Sadagora. An-sky had no doubt that "this old, educated Russian intellectual truly believed that crazy legend."[33]

Some of the legends that most intrigued An-sky were apocalyptic, that is, concerned with the revelation of secret symbols (the Greek term *apocalypse* literally means "lifting of the veil"). Wartime violence made sense to the people he met when they could see it as part of a larger story culminating in the end of time and the beginning of a better world. The first apocalypses were written by Jews in the sixth century B.C.E. (in conjunction with the capture of Jerusalem in 587), and the canonical book of Revelation in the Greek Bible itself may have been written by an author who thought of himself as Jewish and lived before Jesus. Both Jews and Christians continued to write apocalypses into the medieval period. An-sky had been fascinated by Jewish apocalypticism long before the war: since 1911, he had been tinkering with "Ten Signs of the Messiah," a reworking of the seventh-century apocalypse *The Book of Zerubbabel* (Sefer Zerubavel); he translated two Biblical apocalypses, Ezekiel 34 and Isaiah 6, into Russian; and in December 1914 he wrote "The Book of Signs (A Jewish Apocalypse)."[34]

In the war zone, he found apocalyptic motifs in many of the stories he heard. The ethnographer who traveled through the Pale seeking meaning in stories and artifacts saw in the war zone another area of inquiry into human nature and society. Most common were stories of concealment and revelation: Russian and Polish stories about Jews who concealed gold inside empty coffins and slaughtered geese and hid Germans in bags; Jewish lore imagining Polish or German spies hidden in cellars or dressed up as Jews, or poisoned oats hidden in a granary. Jews and Russians alike told stories of the unmasking and punishment of evildoers, whether those were Poles who wanted to shift blame onto Jews, or generals or members of the tsar's family who were revealed as traitors.

Some stories were explicitly messianic. In Chorostków, a cantor told An-sky tales about the coming of the Messiah. In one of his stories, after Rebbe Yisroel of Ruzhin was arrested, one of his followers hoped that his sufferings were a symbol that the messianic age was about to begin. When the rebbe was freed, this Hasid mourned: "I was certain that our rabbi was the Messiah. When he was arrested, I was so happy and I thought that the birthpangs of the messiah [the period of human suffering believed to precede the messianic era] were about to start. And I pleaded, 'Let the blister burst! Let it burst!' But the blister hasn't burst. The Messiah hasn't come. The rebbe was set free, and now we're right back where we started. So how can I be happy?" For this Hasid, human suffering seemed comprehensible if it was imagined as part of a sequence of events leading to a messianic age. A Russian Old Believer coachman told An-sky a prophecy, predicting that after the war, there would be famine, and then "a year with very rich crops, but when they examine the grain, they will see that each kernel consists half of blood and half of sand, and then the other half of the human race will perish." Although he heard this legend in Moscow in November 1916, An-sky inserted it anachronistically in his memoir, during a discussion of the mood in Petrograd in May 1915.[35] As a rule, though, he portrayed folklore as developing at a specific time in response to specific phenomena, following the folkloristic school that had shaped his way of seeing.

An-sky told of an encounter with an educated man who also hoped that the destruction of war might bring forth a new and better life. On a train in late January 1915, soon after he entered Galicia, he met "a young officer with an intelligent face" who explained that he had once led a life of casual violence and self-indulgence, but after he happened to read Tolstoy's pamphlet *What Do I Believe In?* he became an entirely different person, nonviolent and vegetarian. Himself influenced by Tolstoy's nonviolence, An-sky challenged the officer:

> "And yet you go to war, and you kill people," I said.
>   He sat a while with a downcast head. At last he murmured with deep conviction: "War is a different matter. This war will renew the world; it will cleanse mankind of its dirt. For such a goal one can make the supreme sacrifice."[36]

Soon after this encounter An-sky met Demidov and his wife Ekaterina ("a very intelligent, educated, cheerful, active, pink-cheeked woman, absolutely the wrong thing for mysticism. But she is an occultist, a theosophist"). Like most of the volunteers in their unit, the couple were aristocrats with a Tolstoyan urge to imitate and serve the poor and the peasants: "All these titled men and women behaved very simply . . . eating the same food as the rank and file with the same wooden spoons." The mystical, philo-Semitic Demidov "repeated almost word for word" what the Tolstoyan officer had said on the train, and again, An-sky reacted skeptically. "I've been in the thick of the war for three months now, and I've seen a lot of soldiers. I've seen men who have looked death in the face, soldiers who have killed and been wounded. But I haven't seen anyone who has been renewed. . . . No, Igor Platonovich, bloodshed won't bring any renewal of mankind." Demidov heard him out silently, then asked, "How can you prove that bloodshed is a sin and not a supreme act of heroism?" An-sky wrote, "The war's ability to 'cleanse mankind' and 'renew the human soul' was evident in the pogroms and atrocities that occurred. When I met people from the army and the welfare organizations, I could see how even they had grown more savage with each passing day and were losing their moral foundations."[37]

An-sky distanced himself from the willingness to view the bloodshed of war as having an inherent value for individuals or for humankind. He defined himself as the lone sane voice in a landscape of madness and violence, one who refuses to let any kind of philosophical fantasy distract him from the reality of human suffering. But at the same time, with his usual desire to understand people's behavior, he wrote,

> I noticed that officers who had fought in battles and had met the enemy face-to-face looked and behaved with a mystical serenity. They spoke softly, slowly, never grew excited. They seemed to have grasped a great truth that made them calm. I wondered if this was the renewal Demidov had talked about. Later, I reached a different conclusion. Perhaps the passion for bloodshed has stayed with man since his animal beginnings. Perhaps blood keeps him calm, while the lack of it makes him nervous, so he unconsciously tries to appease his passion for it. Perhaps people who have shed blood are so tranquil because they have sated their need. I was shocked by the idea, but the more officers I met who had actually fought, the more I was convinced it had merit.[38]

Bloodshed might have some deeper legitimacy—not because it could save the world, but because it could respond to a physical human need.

An-sky admitted later that he himself felt some of the need for bloodshed that he saw in the soldiers. When he entered Czernowitz, which had barely been touched by the war, he felt oddly dissatisfied. "I experienced a strange and horrible sensation: I caught myself *longing* for the burned, mutilated homes and stores. Instinctively, my eyes looked for them. And the houses with windows, the open stores, the calm streets—all this everyday life struck me as abnormal! Later on, I learned that veterans of battle, who have seen corpses, maimed bodies, and rivers of blood, yearn for these things. Ordinary life seems pale and abnormal to them without the cannon, without the shrieks . . ."[39] His own reaction helped him empathize with soldiers who had been immersed in the sights and sounds of war.

A similar moment arose later in the war in Chorostków, when An-sky met Lipo Shvager, the owner of a bookstore specializing in old Jewish books and manuscripts, which had been destroyed in a pogrom. Shvager was a follower and a relative of the rebbe of Kopyczyńce, and he told An-sky that when the rebbe, vacationing in Hamburg, heard the Russians were invading Galicia, he asked Shvager to go back to Kopyczyńce to rescue two precious old documents, a letter written by the Baal Shem Tov and another signed by him. Shvager got to Kopyczyńce, found the letters, buried them inside a metal case deep in the rebbe's basement wall, and fled. A few months later, he returned to Kopyczyńce, dug up the box, and found that the letters were intact, but mysteriously, the writing had vanished from the Baal Shem's letter. Shvager showed the letters to An-sky and said, "They say that the letters vanished because of the damp and they could be restored chemically. But we Hasids have a different view . . . a different view." Looking at the letter, An-sky wrote, "I remembered the shard of the Ten Commandments that I found in the profaned and shattered synagogue in Dębica. All that was left on the fragment were the words 'kill' and 'commit adultery.' The two symbolic facts fused into the phrase 'Shattered tablets and flying letters.' These two symbols, 'shattered tablets' and 'flying letters,' exemplified the life of the Galician Jews."[40]

When An-sky argued with Demidov, he had insisted that this war would not cleanse mankind, but then he conceded that it might reveal a terrible truth about humans' need for bloodshed. When he heard Lipo Shvager's tale, he understood that for the Hasidim of Kopyczyńce, the "flying letters" from the Baal Shem's letter recalled an episode from the Talmud. In Avodah Zara 18a, the Romans punished the second-century teacher Rabbi Haninah ben Teradion by setting him and the Torah scroll from which he had been teaching on fire, and he said that he saw the writing on the scroll flying up to heaven. If the writing of the Besht had similarly flown away from its hiding place in the Kopyczyńce rebbe's basement, then the miracle revealed a mystic connection between the Torah, the Besht's writing, and the Hasidim who had been privileged to witness it. It linked the Galician Jews to Rabbi Haninah ben Teradion and made their martyrdom part of the Jewish vision of history in which cycles of oppression culminate in the coming of the messiah. For An-sky, the vanished letters were also a powerful symbol—but rather than testifying to the sanctity of the Besht and the Hasidic hope for messianic redemption, they were a tragically appropriate metaphor to describe the Jewish refugees who surrounded him in Galicia. "All these living corpses trudged past me not as 'broken tablets' but as tablets from which 'the letters had flown away.' These people had lost the supreme sanctity of human dignity."[41] After his encounters with Shvager and Demidov, An-sky adapted their apocalyptic tales. Rather than distinguishing between the apocalyptic lore of Russians and Jews, he presents them as similarly fascinating but flawed and himself as the interpreter who can find the meaning that had eluded the tellers themselves. While the tellers believed that their stories demonstrated that violence could lead toward renewal and utopia, An-sky insisted that the tales inspired by war showed the true fragility of human civilization and the moral chaos that lay just beneath it.

By the spring of 1915, the Jewish aid effort was truly under way, with funds raised in the Russian Empire and abroad for the tormented Jews of Galicia. In Galicia, An-sky was no longer primarily gathering information but working with local communities to set up committees to distribute money. Soon, though, the tide of war began to shift. On May 2 (Western style), between Tarnów and Gorlice, Austrian and German forces joined to attack the poorly built Russian trenches. They created a gap in the Russian defenses, and men poured through and seized Tarnów.[42] With this defeat, the communications problems that An-sky saw when he accompanied Demidov's supplies became evident to everyone as the Russian army began to relinquish Galicia. The reversal culminated in the Great Retreat, when the army, fearing encirclement, moved east and by September gave up almost all the Austro-Hungarian territory it had won.

In retreat, the army continued to expel Austro-Hungarian and Russian Jews. After sporadic episodes of forcible expulsion from the front zone in the fall of 1914, the Stavka had succeeded in brutally displacing 100,000 men, women, and children from the Warsaw region in late January and 150,000 from the Kurland province in May. As deportees clogged the roads and railroads, civilian authorities in both the regions from where the Jews had originated and those to which they were moved frantically protested that expulsion was economically ruinous. Hundreds of thousands of Jews were moved into the increasingly small area of the Pale of Settlement that was beyond the war zone, and it became evident that the Pale itself—the concept that the Jews of the empire were forbidden to move out of their historic territory and into the interior—would have to be abandoned. Thus in May and June, the army shifted from expelling entire Jewish communities to taking hostages from each one, with the understanding that if the Jews in their hometowns proved treacherous to Russians, then the hostages would be executed. They arrested what is estimated as tens of thousands of rabbis and community leaders. During the summer of 1915, many of the hostages were sent under guard to prisons in internal Russian provinces; later, hostages were notified that they had been selected for punishment in the event of treachery but allowed to remain in their communities.

The shifting policies of expulsion and hostage-taking, in the disarray of retreat, allowed for enormous abuse. Cossacks started pogroms, killing, raping, and torturing Jews in their homes, and expelled ones they found on the road. Those Jewish stores that had survived the Russian conquest were looted and burned during the retreat. Military authorities demanded bribes in exchange for ensuring the safety of a community or the liberty of individuals; using the hostage policy to legitimize extortion, they arrested wealthy Jews and threatened to kill them unless their families paid ransom.[43]

The EKOPO knew that once the Russians were gone, the Jews remaining in Galicia would get aid from the Austrian government and the Jews of Vienna. In anticipation, An-sky told the community leaders in Lvov in early June that they should pay back what the EKOPO had given them. Subtracting the amount needed to keep soup kitchens, day-care centers, and schools running until the end of the month, the Lvov committee agreed to return the money, although it had already been changed into coins for distribution to individuals. An-sky received a forty-pound carton with 20,000 rubles in small change to bring back to Kiev. He bid an anxious farewell to the people he had worked with in Lvov. The entire aid committee was on the list of hostages that the Russians intended to bring with them during the retreat, so they planned to go into hiding. On June 6, An-sky hitched a ride with a VZS division from Bessarabia, which had its own train going to Brody. In Brody, he and a few of the nurses got off the train for a moment. When they returned, it was gone—sent, they eventually learned, to Dubno. An-sky caught the first train to Dubno, where he found his train car and the carton of money, astonishingly untouched.[44]

For the next two months, An-sky tried to alleviate the sufferings of the Jews in the war zone. He offered to safeguard valuable ritual objects. He collected stories that were evidently about himself: "a Jewish officer was stopping passersby, questioning them in Yiddish. He would treat them to tea, give candy to the children, and hand out money." Every night, he saw the fires of burning towns in the distance. He saw the traces of the pogrom in Sokal, and in Krystynopol, a fire near the Jewish cemetery lit up hundreds of gravestones, the glowing Hebrew letters reflecting the flames. "It was an extraordinary spectacle, as if generations—centuries—of Jews had returned from the past to the mystical moonlit night, to gaze with fiery eyes at the horrors closing in on their shtetl." The next day, he went into Krystynopol and found a pogrom in process; in a few stores, he was able to stop it, pulling one Cossack out by his ear and threatening to shoot him. To his frustration, community leaders asked him for money to pay bribes; whenever possible, he refused. In late July, he drove to Kiev, passing camps of starving refugees, to attend a conference of aid organizations. Mikhail Kishkin, the vice chairman of the Zemtsvo alliance, invited him to address the conference. "When I said *Jew,* they all glared at me as if I had used a forbidden word," he wrote.[45] The conference was willing to set up food centers in towns with Jewish expellees, but otherwise resisted aiding the Jews in any way that would distinguish them from other refugees, and it would not call for the elimination of the Pale. The episode exposed the tension between even these liberals and Jewish activists.

For about a week, starting July 30, An-sky accompanied his aid division east, ahead of the retreating army, from Brest-Litovsk through Kobrin and Pinsk to Gomel. The entire population of Brest, Jews and Christians, was being evacuated, adding to the refugees on the road; the Jews traveled on foot because they were rarely allowed on trains. In Kobrin, An-sky found the synagogue packed with hungry refugees, the healthy and the cholera patients lying together, including a pair of newborn twins whose father had vanished and whose mother had died of cholera. He did what he could, commandeering train cars to bring 128 of the homeless as far as Gomel, feeding them (as well as some Christian refugees) along the way, and arranging the funeral of a man who died en route. He brought 4,000 pounds of bread back to Kobrin, where he distributed it to the refugees (and the famished soldiers he met at the train station), but in spite of his efforts, he could not get a wet nurse for the twins, and both died.[46]

In the chaos, An-sky saw authority breaking down, even as the tsar took over from his uncle as commander-in-chief in August. The officers distrusted their soldiers; An-sky met a dying soldier whose commander had had him flogged after he complained of illness. Officers and doctors were voicing revolutionary feelings, not caring who was listening. Coins had vanished, and everyone suspected Jews of hoarding them. The masses of Jews expelled to central Russia had made the Pale impossible to enforce, and it was finally abolished in August, but Jews were still barred from the capitals, and An-sky and Dubnov found it no easier to get permission to live in Petrograd. All but two provinces of Galicia (Tarnopol and part of Czortków) were back under Austrian rule, and it seemed that those too would soon fall. The first invasion of Galicia was over. An-sky left the war zone, having felt the intoxication of bloodshed and seen the horrifying brutality of the lives of the Russian soldiers and the Austro-Hungarian Jews.

He could not forget what he had seen in the war zone, although from September 1915 through December 1916, he went back to the projects he had left unfinished when the war began. Baron Gintsburg had urged him to bring his ethnographic work to a good stopping point, "to end at a period, not a comma," and he did his best.[47] Still without residency permission, he returned to Petrograd and moved to the site of the EIEO ethnographic museum, Moisei Ginsburg's almshouse on Vasilevsky Island.

The writer Mark Rivesman found him living in a messy room there, "lying on something that barely resembled a bed," sleeping late "like a real Bohemian," still working on *The Dybbuk*. Roza Monoszon, a 21-year-old student whom An-sky had befriended in the winter of 1915 when she was volunteering at the EKOPO offices, urged him to take walks and leave his smoky room, with its "big desk covered with books, papers, countless cigarette butts, an eternal glass of tea," the child of the museum guard often playing on the floor. He lived there, she noticed, as he lived everywhere, as if he were camping. He worked on the museum with the manager of the archive, Salvian Goldshtein, and the archivist, Isaac Lurie, arranging 1,000 objects, collected during the expedition and during his travels in Galicia, among the showcases. He hoped to publish his expedition materials, with separate volumes for stories and legends, music, visual art, and photographs. Kiselgof was transcribing the musical materials and Yudovin organizing the visual materials, but the work did not move forward until late 1916, when An-sky got funding and began to prepare the volume of visual art.[48]

He spent time reading *The Dybbuk* aloud, asking audiences for suggestions, revising it, and talking about it whenever he had the chance. On October 5, 1915, he read it at Vladimir Jabotinsky's house and wrote in his diary, "It seems they liked it. V. R. Kugel said it's not right for the stage. It's a literary, not a theatrical work." Between 1915 and 1917, he read it in Petrograd at the homes of Vinaver and the oil magnate Savely Poliak, in Odessa at Mendele's home, in Kiev during a conference of Jewish communities, and in Moscow at the home of Hillel Zlatopolsky. He read it in Russian and in Yiddish, to mixed and often critical responses.[49]

He wanted the play to be staged, and even before he left for the war zone, he had been writing about it to acquaintances in the theater world. He wanted it to be produced in Russian; the strict wartime censorship would have made a Yiddish production impossible. The task was difficult. The literary critic Semyon Vengerov told him that to write a play, you need talent, but to get it staged, you need to be a genius. He focused on the Moscow Art Theater, whose directors, Konstantin Stanislavsky and Vladimir Nemirovich-Danchenko, were known for their sympathy to Jews. In the fall of 1914, the director Leopold Sulerzhitsky read the play for the Art Theater and made suggestions. In September 1915, Sulerzhitsky found it improved, though the love between Leah and Khonen still needed to be made clearer and the trial between the living and the dead needed to be more realistic. At the same time, An-sky worked on getting the play past the censor. After negotiations with Baron Drizen, director of the theater censorship office in Petrograd (who asked An-sky to distinguish dybbuk possession more obviously from the possession scenes in the Gospels), the play was permitted in October 1915. Suler-zhitsky encouraged An-sky to write an additional act, the wedding, inserted after act one, and in November, the censor approved it. In December 1915, Stanislavsky himself agreed to read the play and make suggestions. After months of revisions, An-sky wrote in November 1916 that Stanislavsky was almost satisfied and particularly liked the addition of the Messenger. The Art Theater board voted unanimously to stage the play; it would go into rehearsals as soon as Zinaida Gippius's *Green Ring* was done. In Moscow, An-sky took Monoszon to dinner with the Art Theater director Sushkevich; Iuly Engel, who was working on the music for the play; the famous actor Mikhail Chekhov, who would play the tsaddik; and Grigory Khmara, the only Jew in the cast, who was assigned the role of Khonen.[50]

On those Petrograd evenings when he was not reading his play out loud, An-sky raised funds for a new Jewish cause. He was still wearing his uniform, which made him appear less Jewish and communicated his continuing preoccupation with the war. Dubnov observed that An-sky, having "seen his fill of horror," had been "infected by the romanticism of Jabotinsky."[51] He meant the Jewish Legion, an idea dreamed up by Vladimir Jabotinsky, a Russian Jew, a brilliant writer in many languages, a fiery orator, and a militant Zionist who would become known in 1925 as the founder of Revisionist Zionism (the insistence that a Jewish state be established on both sides of the Jordan River). Jabotinsky was in Bordeaux in September 1914 when he learned that the Ottoman Empire had joined the Central Powers in the World War and aligned itself against England and Russia. He realized that this move would result in Turkey's defeat, which could pave the way for the Jews to take Palestine. In November, he began to write about raising a corps of Jewish volunteers to fight for England in Palestine. When the Turks expelled 12,000 Jews from Palestine and sent them to Alexandria, Jabotinsky found in them a pool of potential fighters. He set about meeting with government officials and Jewish leaders, hoping to convince the British to accept his plan and to raise money and manpower among the Jews of Europe and the United States. He spent the summer of 1915 in Russia, where he found the Zionists mostly opposed to his idea.

Jabotinsky had been in touch with An-sky since the spring of 1914, when he had invited him to a meeting about setting up a Jewish university in Palestine, but it was probably in the summer of 1915 that An-sky decided to help raise money for the Jewish Legion. In fund-raising speeches, he insisted that people "will grow used to the concept that

Jews can go out with weapons in their hands to defend their national rights." An-sky's enthusiasm about the Jewish Legion was startling, since he had never been a Zionist. In 1901, in "To the Bund," he had denounced Zionism in typically radical terms as a bourgeois ideology, meant to isolate the Jews from the forward movement of human history: "The rich men's children, the maskilim and rabbis / They call the Jew to Zion / [This is] An old song of our enemies: / 'A ghetto for the eternal Yid!' " His ideas had changed, and since 1905, he had noticed that he was growing more sympathetic to Zionism, becoming less certain that the radical parties would resolve the problems of Russia's Jews. The spectacle of Jewish suffering in Galicia showed him that a solution was needed on an international scale, and the overwhelming evidence of Russian hostility to Jews in the war zone—no matter how insistently he attributed it to governmental rumormongering—must have shaken his belief that the liberation of Russia would mean the liberation of the Jews. He articulated none of this in his diaries and letters, though. He was apparently unconcerned in 1915 with the philosophical implications of imagining Palestine as a reclaimed homeland for diaspora Jews, nor did it trouble him that his own diaspora-centered Jewish cultural nationalism might be at odds with Jabotinsky's political work for a Jewish future in Palestine. Whatever negative implications Zionism had once had for him were not associated with the Jewish Legion.[52] Instead, he wrote proudly in his diary about the powerful effect of his own words as he described Jews with weapons in their hands.

Although An-sky's enthusiasm about Zionism was new, his attitudes speak more strongly of consistency than change. Just as he had called in 1905 for a transparent, meaningful response to the pogroms, so in 1915 the image of Jewish self-defense motivated his response to Jabotinsky's plan. An-sky consistently used the language of beauty and emotion to talk about Zionist politics. He called the donation of money by Shryro a "truly beautiful gesture," and as he recorded audiences' responses to his own speeches, he suggested that supporting the Jewish Legion required not confrontation between the abstract idea of socialist internationalism and the abstract idea of nationalism but rather the embrace of an image of Jews defending their rights.[53] Whereas the Zionism he condemned in 1901 was not an action that would be visible to the eyes of the world but a retreat from action, the Zionism he defended in 1915 was an emergence from the ghetto onto the world stage. This attention to the communicative effectiveness of one ideology versus another was typical of him. In 1908, when he shifted his attention from radical propaganda to Jewish cultural work, he wrote about the ways in which the word could be stronger than the violent deed, and in 1915, he depicted Jabotinskian Zionism as offering the potential of inspiring sympathy.

This focus on the visual appeal of the legion was consistent with Jabotinsky's own writing. Throughout his career, Jabotinsky was impelled by the urge to make traditional East European Jews over completely: to create a new, indisputably masculine Jewish soldier, who knew nothing of ghetto ways. This gentleman soldier would display attributes apparent to the observer: pride, discipline, generosity.[54] Both An-sky and Jabotinsky presented the deeds of the Jewish Legion as symbols with only one meaning that would be immediately apparent to all—that Jews were fighters. They both believed that such gestures could move human hearts and thereby change the course of history. They knew that the Jewish Legion would have seemed especially attractive to wartime audiences. Unlike the Jews of Galicia, tormented by Cossacks and pleading for money to ransom hostages, the Jews of the legion would be unbowed and self-sufficient. Jabotinsky's ideas made it possible to imagine Jews who would *make sense* to viewers, who would, like the Russian soldiers An-sky admired, be able to communicate their "boldness and bravery and strength." In the Russian Empire of 1915, when Jews were seen as acting dangerously and incomprehensibly, pretending to be loyal subjects while secretly sending messages to the Germans, there was something compelling, for Jabotinsky as for An-sky, in the notion of Jews acting in a transparent way, fighting for Palestine in the Jewish Legion in full view of the world, claiming the right to say how they would be understood.

An-sky's enthusiasm for the Jewish Legion distanced him from some of his fellow Jewish leaders but brought him closer to Russian writers, such as some of the members of the Russian Society for the Study of Jewish Life, the philo-Semitic organization led by Andreev, Sologub, and Gorky. Much of the Russian Jewish intelligentsia was irritated by the patronizing tone and philanthropic zeal of this organization. An-sky, though, welcomed their efforts and tried to help. He found common ground with the society in the Jewish Legion. Jabotinsky wrote to Gorky in August 1915 to ask for his help in bringing the legion to the attention of Russian society, and he promised that An-sky would visit Gorky to explain the plan in more detail. At their meeting, Gorky explained that he was no Zionist. As a Marxist, he was opposed to nationalism, even welcoming the entry of Bulgaria into the war against Russia, as a demonstration of the folly of Pan-Slavism. Nonetheless, Gorky liked the idea of the legion and was willing to help Jabotinsky by writing to European writers about

it. In 1916, the society published the memoirs of Colonel John Henry
Patterson about his service in the Jewish Legion. Gorky's support for the
legion indicated that it could appeal to non-Jewish radicals. An-sky's and
Jabotinsky's Zionism, based on the idea of Jewish pride, was a vision of
Jewish renewal that made sense to non-Jews.[55]

In December 1915, An-sky went to the First All-Russian Congress of
Folk Theater Activists in Moscow and spoke about the wartime ban on
Yiddish theater: "If that barrier was already absurd and unfair, then it is
especially incomprehensible and scandalous now, during the war, when
the other nationalities of Russia have experienced at least a few concessions in the area of culture." A Moscow police agent took notes as An-
sky linked theater to radicalism and pacifism, welcoming "the loud
speeches of a young populism, urging not that people create a theater for
the folk, but that people go to the folk and rouse it to create new things
of value," and rejoicing that "the congress gathered during the war and
this shows that cultural development is more valuable to the people than
bloody slaughter."[56]

He saw connections among folk theater, the war, and the Jewish Legion. During the first year of the war, the waves of refugees and their
physical needs had occupied everyone's minds. Now, the intelligentsia
was more concerned with the cultural needs of the displaced people and
with its own cultural needs. "Neither in the capitals nor in the provinces
have theaters ever been so full, never have people demanded new books
as strongly." People did not want to hear about the war, and writers were
not yet able to write about it, but people were strongly attracted to messianic tales—and the promise of renewal. "In the fact that the Jewish
people has not given up on its dream [of its own country], in the fact that
this dream can be traced like a red thread through its religion, culture,
legends—in all that there is something to which we must pay attention."[57] An-sky understood that during the war, people wanted a new
vision of the future, and his attention was drawn by the Zionist dream,
with its ancient roots, and Jabotinsky's attempt to produce it on the
world stage.

In spite of his political passions, An-sky could not stay at the center of
events. In June 1916, the Kiev aid committee asked him urgently to return to Galicia, writing, "The question of organizing aid cannot be postponed." And yet An-sky had to postpone it. He had been diagnosed
with diabetes, and he went to recover in Essentuki, a resort near Stav-
ropol frequented by Gorky, Stanislavsky, and Konstantin Balmont.
Friends joked that with the high cost of sugar during the war, it was

better to avoid it anyway. Even as he neared his fifty-third birthday and faced his own physical frailty, he fell in love, once more, with a much younger woman: Roza Monoszon, the student he had met in the winter of 1915. A few months after their first meeting, An-sky ran into her on a tram and invited her to a reading of *The Dybbuk* at the home of Savely Poliak. After that the two met at her home and at his messy room on Vasilevsky Island; they went for walks around the city and talked. He began to write her letters about his experiences and emotions, including his feelings about their relationship. "In my play an old beggar woman exclaims, 'I haven't danced for forty years.' I could say, 'For a good ten or fifteen years, I haven't written letters,' except for business ones. Now I want to write to you. But I write with an awkward sense, as though feeling my way . . . Then again, perhaps that is for the best."[58]

More than with his earlier passions, this time An-sky sounded conscious of those elements of his own character that made him unable to settle down. He wrote to Monoszon about his need for company and for solitude. "I went to the theater; I spent the whole day by myself. On these rare days I feel elevated, better. The soft sadness of loneliness merges with a special feeling of concentration and reconciliation. . . ."[59] Before meeting Monoszon, An-sky had described his life of travel and self-denial either as a tragedy or as a virtuous political statement, an affirmation that he did not belong to the majority of people who care only about themselves and their families, but to the minority that could truly serve humanity. In his letters to Monoszon, he described himself differently, admitting that although he sometimes yearned for a domestic nest, he also craved solitude and travel.

In early December 1916, he told Monoszon about visiting his sister and her children and grandchildren. "They began to feed me, to look over my clothes, they found dozens of flaws and sighed over them. I immediately learned all the tiniest details about my sister's family, about each person individually, about the relatives, people we knew in the shtetl. I was enveloped in a kind of soft feather-bed of small-town philistinism." It felt good, he admitted: he enjoyed gossiping, remembering his childhood, spending a few hours playing cards. Back on the train, he wondered about his own distance from that kind of domestic life. "How much sincere, true, deeply human poetry there is in those 'petit bourgeois ways,' where people live spiritually huddled up next to each other. And what right do I and those like me have to scorn that petit bourgeois life, to turn proudly away, as though from something low?" But these thoughts were fleeting: "In the morning, when I woke up, we were approaching Kiev and

I forgot all these thoughts and feelings and was myself again." What An-sky really needed, he knew, was travel itself.

> I love time on long trips. The feverish commotion of business, worries, and small errands suddenly breaks off, and you're alone with yourself, as though you meet yourself after a long absence, and imperceptibly, the intimate work of the soul begins. You experience a kind of renewal of life. You just need one day of that kind of solitude and silent contemplation to feel reborn and enlightened. They say that doctors advise even healthy people from time to time not to eat for an entire day so that their bodies rest and the ac-cumulated fat burns up. For the same reason, but from the perspective of the soul, one should sometimes spend at least one entire day alone and silent.[60]

More than An-sky's previous loves—for Masha Reinus, for Mademoi-selle Janais, for Edia Glezerman—his love for Roza Monoszon seemed to satisfy him. To judge by his surviving letters, he appreciated their episto-lary friendship and the inspiration she gave him to write, but he never suggested marrying her. As he grew older, he voiced regret that he had never had children: he wrote to Monoszon about playing with the chil-dren of friends and told her he had fantasized that if he could have saved the infant twins he had found among the Brest-Litovsk refugees, he would have adopted them.[61] At the same time, his letters to Monoszon show him letting go of some of the frustration he had always felt about his soli-tary status.

In May 1916, the Russian forces under General Brusilov attacked again, occupying much of Bukovina and taking back a portion of Galicia, in-cluding Brody. The Russian government was determined to avoid the mistakes of the first invasion: to reject a liberationist agenda, to maintain order rather than encouraging violence against groups of the Galician population, to establish clear lines of command, and to take responsibil-ity for the well-being of the people in the occupied territory. The deporta-tion policy was almost abandoned: in contrast to the 100,000 people deported from Galicia during the first occupation, only 393 families were deported during the second.[62]

Under the new Russian administration, Jews had less to fear from the arbitrary cruelty of soldiers, but they remained impoverished. The 100,000 Galician Jews who had stayed on Russian territory throughout the war were crowded into Tarnopol and a section of Czortków Prov-inces. Many of them were expellees who had no way of earning a living; they had been supported by Russian Jewish funding. An army doctor, F. E. Lander, and S. Homelsky from Kiev had set up committees in each town and ensured that money was distributed regularly, "not the haphazard kind of contributions I and others had handed out randomly," An-sky wrote, "but systematic assistance that saved many hundreds, even thousands, of Jewish souls from starvation."[63] The regular funding from Kiev and Petrograd that Lander and Homelsky had relied on was drying up, even as new demands emerged. Thus the Kiev Jewish Relief Committee asked An-sky to return to Galicia and rethink the aid effort to make the best use of available money and help the Galician Jews become self-sufficient. After his health improved, in December 1916, he returned to the occupied area and plunged back into the sea of bloody images and apocalyptic stories, which heightened his painful need to protect the Jews and his anger at the Tsarist government.

The landscape he traveled was still marred by traces of pogroms. In Bukovina, he saw the burnt remains of Jewish houses, scraps of torn-up Torah scrolls on synagogue floors, icons still marking Christian windows. In the rebbe's court in Sadagora, outside Czernowitz, the large synagogue had been turned into a medical ward, and An-sky was sickened to see an icon placed inside the Torah ark. He saw it as "a dreadful profaning . . . a degrading of both religions. The savage hand of a brutal soldier had punished God and man." The people were also degraded. The Russian army had closed the schools, and Jewish children in the Tarnopol region had been on the streets for eighteen months or more. Large groups of refugees had been transferred to towns that could not absorb them: the 4,000 Jews from Podwołoczyska and Husiatyn had been settled in Skałat, whose local Jewish population was only 1,000, and four or five homeless families were living in each room. The crowding and the famine brought epidemics, and the months of living on aid had transformed the Galician Jews. Whereas their sufferings during the first invasion had a quality of "epic tragedy," now, An-sky saw, "people had grown accustomed to constant hunger, to rags, to lining up for hours at the food centers. They roamed about, neglected, silent, despondent, indifferent to their dreadful situation."[64] The spiritual decline was evident in Suchostaw, where the Russians had torn up a beautiful old wooden synagogue and used it as a toilet; An-sky was distraught to see that even though the pogrom had been months ago, none of the local Jews had cleaned up the synagogue.

An-sky told Monoszon that it was painful constantly to hear requests for help and embarrassing to burst in on refugees in terrible conditions. In Skałat, An-sky woke up to find petitioners waiting in his hotel room. A short Jew with "ugly piercing eyes" urged him to tell the Kiev committee to do everything possible to bring the Podwołoczyska refugees back home—but to expect that the Skałat Jews, who were living off the money that came into town because of the refugees, would try to prevent them from leaving. His words showed that even though towns such as Skałat, where refugees were resettled, benefited economically, there were tensions between locals and refugees, exacerbated by the crowded conditions. An-sky was disgusted to see the Galician and Bukovina Jews squabble, especially when they involved local non-Jewish authorities in their intrigues. He was happy when, for the first time, a refugee "demanded rather than pleaded" in his appeal for additional wood and milk to help him care for his wife and newborn baby.[65] This man had the dignity that An-sky found so tragically missing among the refugees.

In spite of the disturbing scenes he saw, An-sky was able to find inspiring sights in Galicia and Bukovina. His young driver took evident joy in racing his sleigh over the sun-lit snow near Czortków. An-sky admired the driver and the hare and fox that he passed, and felt for a moment that ecstasy that he had sought on his ethnographic trips: "My heart sang that I was alive, that I was present in this glorious moment, and I felt a deep rapport with the boundless, incomprehensible life of the cosmos."[66] In Śniatyń, his landlady was a twenty-eight-year-old Jewish woman who had been expelled from her village in the late stages of pregnancy. She had walked thirty miles to Czortków with her four older children, given birth, and survived typhus. Back in Śniatyń, she was supporting her children by baking bread and renting out a room. An-sky marveled at her energy and vitality. He took care to record other good signs: a priest who protected the property of expelled Jews, a Russian commander who respected his Jewish soldiers' religion, a Russian soldier who wrote a tender letter to a Jewish child. The optimism underlying his account of tolerant Christians and Jews rebuilding their lives supported the recommendation he made to the Kiev committee: that as much effort and funding as possible be directed toward bringing the refugees back to their homes and reviving those communities.

In February 1917, An-sky was preoccupied with the approach of Passover in the occupied area. The Jews needed flour to bake matzos so they could eat during the holiday, but Fyodor Trepov, the anti-Jewish military governor-general for the occupied region, refused to permit flour shipments to far-flung settlements. So on February 28, 1917, An-sky went to Brusilov, who was known for his fair treatment of Jews, and the transport was permitted. He noticed that the personnel at headquarters were agitated, but only later realized that they must have known of the revolution that had already begun in Petrograd. Once he heard the news, An-sky yearned to go to Petrograd himself, to "the center, where tremendous historical events were playing out," but he knew he would first have to bring money for Passover supplies to several distant Jewish villages.[67] Traveling on freight trains, wagons, and trucks, he delivered the money as quickly as possible so that he could go to join, at last, in the revolution for which he had been waiting so long.

All Flesh Is Grass

I will look for the lost, and I will bring back the strayed; I will
bandage the injured, and I will sustain the weak; and the fat and
healthy ones I will destroy.

    —Ezekiel 34:16 (translated by An-sky into Russian)

A N-SKY ARRIVED in Czernowitz on March 1, 1917. The next
day, an army doctor he'd once met ran up to him, waving a
document he had gotten from military headquarters and calling
out, "Mazl tov! Mazl tov! Do you see this?"

"What is it?" An-sky asked.

"It's what Russia has been waiting for for three hundred years! Nicholas has stepped down! He's renounced the throne!"[1]

After two weeks of strikes and demonstrations in hungry Petrograd,
sailors at the naval base of Kronshtadt had mutinied and killed their
commander and fifty officers, and soldiers had fought policemen in the
streets. Tsar Nicholas II admitted he had lost power on March 2 when he
abdicated in favor of his brother, the Grand Duke Michael, but Michael
declined the throne. The liberal Kadets in the Duma formed a provisional
government and called for a Constituent Assembly, a parliament elected
through universal suffrage. Until elections could be held, the Provisional
Government took control of the country, in uneasy cooperation with a
more radical socialist organization, the Soviet (Council) of Workers' and
Soldiers' Deputies. Socialist Revolutionary soldiers in the Petrograd Soviet wrote up "Order Number One," declaring that soldiers no longer
had to salute their officers when not on duty, and officers were forbidden
to be rude to their soldiers.[2]

The news reached the provinces gradually. *Kievskaia Mysl'* finally
printed Nicholas's and Michael's abdication announcements, but either
the editors or the censors still suppressed part of the news, erasing the word
soldiers from the name of the Soviet of Workers' and Soldiers' Deputies.

Elsewhere in the world newspaper editors were thrilled to capitalize on their readers' desire to hear about the sudden fall of the Romanov dynasty. A friend of An-sky's in Brooklyn saw extra editions coming out every hour, reporting on the revolution. "All New York is mad with joy," he wrote. "The streets are full of people, political meetings, speeches, demonstrations, singing. . . . There are touching scenes, people meet and kiss and cry. Oh, Semyon Akimovich! Is it really true?" For An-sky's friends, the revolution sounded like a dream come true. The Russian offi-cers and soldiers he met seemed to agree, but the Austro-Hungarian Jews in the occupied zone worried that the revolution would make Rus-sia stronger, and they asked An-sky, "What's happening now? Will we have peace soon?" An-sky was sure that the change would bring a patri-otic fervor that would drag out the war, but he didn't want to disappoint the local Jews by telling them.[3] He saw that the fresh leadership was cre-ating new hopes that could not all be realized. Soon his own lifelong hopes for revolution would be realized—and then destroyed.

Many officials were reluctant to change their behavior just because the newspapers had printed the Romanovs' abdication announcements. A week after the abdications, An-sky went back to Governor-General Trepov out of curiosity, wanting to see how he would respond to a new request to authorize local Jewish relief committees, but he found the atmosphere in the office unchanged. When Trepov said no, An-sky saw his answer as "a bite from a dying snake that wanted us to feel its power for just one more day." An-sky wanted to protect Russia from that snake, and for the first time in his life, he could bring his concerns straight to his country's leaders. After a lifetime in the opposition, he was suddenly an insider of not one but all the groups jostling for power in March 1917: the Socialist Revolutionaries who controlled the Soviets were his friends from Swit-zerland and his work in the movement; the Kadets who dominated the Provisional Government were people he had worked with on cultural projects since he had returned to the empire and now in the wartime aid organizations; and his editors and fellow journalists from Jewish and mainstream publications were suddenly heading government organiza-tions. For everyone who mattered in Petrograd in the spring of 1917, An-sky's lifetime of writing, editing, and speaking, his aid work, and his association with Uspensky and Lavrov defined him as an authoritative public intellectual. The leaders of the Provisional Government—Prince Georgy Lvov, Pavel Miliukov, and Alexander Kerensky, now prime min-ister, minister of foreign affairs, and minister of justice, respectively— were An-sky's friends, his "own people." He decided to go to Petrograd as soon as possible to report on the situation in Bukovina and Galicia, to urge them to institute new policies in the war zone and replace Trepov.[4]

He arrived in Kiev in mid-March, where he turned in the accounts from his aid work. At a meeting of political prisoners just back from Siberia, he was touched by the speakers' idealism, but heard "such impracticality and helplessness" that he was "terrified not only for them but for the country they now ruled." The Socialist Revolutionary Party, finally legal, was dominated by moderate leaders such as An-sky who had remained in Russia after the 1905 revolution; they now organized conferences, elected committees, founded their own legal newspapers, and welcomed a wave of new recruits. At a meeting of 2,000 SRs in Kiev, An-sky announced that the revolutionary battle had only begun; it was time to mobilize to fight the enemies of the revolution. (He also proposed, to great applause, that Lavrov be reinterred in Russia.) Before he left for the Petrograd train, he heard a speaker just back from the front voice the biggest problem facing the new government.

> When I was traveling here I felt that at the door of my house I would see my mother, triumphant with joy. And I found my house covered in flowers, but no joy—because inside was a dead body. That dead body is the war. As long as it goes on, as long as guns resound and every day brings hundreds and thousands of victims, there is no place for celebration and triumph. We must organize all our festivals of freedom later, after the nightmare of war is over.[5]

In spite of his belief that the revolution would raise enthusiasm for the war, An-sky reported in *Delo Naroda* (The People's Cause) on the increasing urgency of calls to end it.

Continuing north from Kiev, An-sky reached Petrograd in time to feel the thrill of revolution in the capital. On March 23, 184 of the victims of the February clashes were buried ceremonially on the Field of Mars in the city center. A million people marched solemnly through the enormous field, singing revolutionary anthems; in a sign that the revolution meant to change Russians' everyday habits and beliefs, the church was absent. Sofia Dubnova spotted An-sky's gray curls among the nearby marchers as she approached the stands. He left his column and an elderly woman marching next to Dubnova whispered to her, "Let's make room for the gray-haired man." "An-sky and I held hands like children," Dubnova remembered, "walking into the March wind in a crowd of strangers who felt so close to us. The wind blowing 'through the whole world' seemed then like a herald of spring."[6]

An-sky was part of the crowd in March, but soon he became part of the new administration. By the end of the month he had work that required him to enter the State Duma regularly, and from then on, as a figure trusted by the various governmental factions, he accumulated new responsibilities constantly. In May, the Provisional Government sent him back to Galicia to collect information; in July, Chernov, now agriculture minister, asked him to travel to Romania to study land reforms; that month, he became a lecturer for the regional military education committee. In the spring and summer of 1917, the SRs dominated urban politics: cities elected SR mayors, and the SRs controlled the city dumas. Petrograd was no exception, and on August 20, An-sky was elected to the new Petrograd City Duma, where he worked with the new mayor, Grigory Shreider, who had once been his editor at *Syn Otechestva*. He represented the City Duma on committees to set up new legislation for archives and to determine the revolutionary government's attitude toward Judaism. At the same time, he published in *Delo Naroda, Volia Naroda* (The People's Freedom), and a new Petrograd Yiddish newspaper, *Unzer togblat* (Our Daily); the Yiddish press, hushed since 1914, was suddenly free.[7]

What An-sky saw in Petrograd made him worry about his friends' ability to govern. When he had approached Miliukov to explain what was happening in Galicia and Bukovina, he found him sympathetic but powerless. Miliukov succeeded in replacing Trepov with a more tolerant administrator, the Ukrainian socialist historian Dmitry Doroshenko, and Doroshenko put Dr. Lander, who had worked with An-sky distributing aid, in charge of Jewish affairs in Galicia. However, the Provisional Government postponed taking other action, and its lack of control was painfully evident: Doroshenko's orders about the Jews were disobeyed or ignored; local authorities refused to allow Jewish hostages to return to their homes; and officers rejected Lander's authority, continuing to let soldiers destroy Jewish homes and kill Jews. Lander himself barely survived a pogrom in Tarnopol.[8]

An-sky watched the country wait impatiently for the Constituent Assembly: elections had been postponed until the war ended, then scheduled for November 12. "A people that has just thrown off the chains of Egyptian slavery and headed for the Promised Land is gathered at the foot of Mount Sinai, while the great Chosen One and Leader has gone to its peak to bring down the Law and Commandments for generations and millennia. The crowd of men, women, and children awaits the word that would make them a great nation, 'a kingdom of priests and a holy nation' (Ex. 19:6)." But while they waited, their discontent grew.[9]

They were particularly unhappy about the war. Most of the leaders of the Provisional Government understood that Russia was tired of war, but they disagreed about an exit strategy. The Allies pressured the Provisional

Government to launch a new offensive on the Eastern Front, and the liberals who dominated the government felt loyal to France and Britain, feared jeopardizing the financial support they received from the Allies, and opposed a separate peace in principle. The soldiers disagreed. In late April, when Miliukov's note to the Allies promising Russia would stay in the war became public, he was forced to resign. The Left SRs and Mensheviks, although they rejected concessions to the enemy, pushed for the negotiation of an immediate peace. As everyone debated, the war continued, and support grew for the Bolsheviks, who had opposed the war from the beginning, and whose leadership was now returning to Russia (Lenin's sealed train car arrived from Switzerland on April 3).[10]

In the spring of 1917, An-sky stood firmly with the Kadets and the right wing of the SRs for staying in the war. He saw the Bolshevik call for a separate peace as shameful. No matter how badly the war was going, he asserted at a May 1917 SR congress that it would be dishonorable for Russia to abandon France and Britain. Russian revolutionaries needed to remember that France had sheltered them and inspired them with the idea of the rights of man. If Russia turns its back on France, Britain, and Belgium, he argued, the people of these nations would see it as "a knife in the back," and they would never want to join with Russians again. "The International will be reestablished, Germany, Austria, and France will be in it, and only Russia won't. That's where we'll get by means of a passive separate peace." Other SRs mocked those who thought like An-sky as Russian nationalists, "social-chauvinists," and "social-patriots." An-sky objected that derogatory nicknames were a dishonorable SD tactic, but he worried that it hardly mattered what he said: the reputation of his fraction was so low that no one listened.[11]

When he sat in his hotel room late at night, after five days of debates from 10 A.M. until midnight, An-sky felt uncertain of his own loyalties and frightened about the future. He wrote to Monoszon that he was no longer sure he even belonged at the congress. Everyone else there was "true to their oath and ready to sacrifice their own lives and those of all Russia for the victory and the purity of the Party's principles. I understand them well because I sometimes catch myself hypnotized in the same way. After all, we're at a congress of the Party, what's brought us together is not the interests of the country but the program of the Party." But for An-sky, the SR party did not matter as much as the fate of the country. "Russia is going downhill. And the most horrible thing is the feeling that there's nothing one can do about it."[12]

In June, Kerensky acquiesced to the Allies' demand that Russia mount a new offensive, even though General Lavr Kornilov and Boris Savinkov (now assistant minister of war) told him the soldiers were exhausted and demoralized. An-sky remembered Kerensky insisting with "inhuman energy" and optimism on going ahead. At Stanislavsky's request, An-sky asked Kerensky if some of the most important actors of the Moscow Art Theater could be excused from the draft, and Kerensky told him to tell Stanislavsky not to worry, because the current offensive was certain to end the war immediately with a Russian victory and the actors would never be called up. The offensive, which began in mid-June, brought victories at first and an optimistic attitude in Petrograd—accompanied, An-sky noted worriedly, with talk of pogroms. Within three weeks, though, the Russian army retreated in panic, finally giving up Galicia and Bukovina, but punishing the Jews of Kalusz, Sudilkov, and Tarnopol bloodily as they passed through.[13]

As the army retreated, the first coalition cabinet of the Provisional Government fell apart and mass demonstrations began in Petrograd. During the July Days—July 3 and 4, 1917—after the Bolsheviks called for power to be transferred to the Soviets, armed soldiers and sailors surrounded the Tauride Palace where the Provisional Government and the Executive Committee of the Soviet of Workers' and Peoples' Deputies were housed, refusing to let anyone leave the building. Chernov telegraphed from inside that the situation was serious, and An-sky and two other SRs decided to go to him. Finally one taxi driver agreed to take them for the enormous sum of 25 rubles. The whole way there, he kept making the sign of the cross over his horse. Ever the ethnographer, An-sky asked why he didn't make the sign of the cross over himself as well, and he explained, "I'm not afraid—I've come from the war." At the Tauride Palace, An-sky watched the Bolsheviks provoke Chernov into addressing the demonstrators and then seize him. An-sky grabbed a sailor who had taken hold of Chernov, then felt himself pulled by the neck from behind by another sailor. By the time An-sky was free, Chernov had been placed in a car. An-sky went into the palace to report his arrest. Soon the Bolshevik Lev Trotsky (Bronshteyn) appeared and instructed the sailors—"a bit theatrically," An-sky noted—to free Chernov.[14]

The brief July uprising, which caught the Bolsheviks by surprise, revealed that they were almost ready to act against the Provisional Government, and it confirmed An-sky's anger at Bolshevism. The Bolsheviks dirty everything they touch, he wrote, like Peredonov, the antihero of Sologub's novel *The Petty Demon,* who spat on the walls of his house. The reaction on the right provoked by the July Days made An-sky even more concerned about the future of the revolution. The far right wing of the SRs looked ready to renounce socialism, so An-sky joined a fraction led by Nikolai Avksentiev, minister of internal affairs from July to September. Starting in August, An-sky began to attack those on the right who insisted that "in order to save Russia . . . we must sacrifice both freedom and the revolution." He warned liberals that to join the antirevolutionary forces would be tantamount to joining the *oprichniks,* the hated secret police of the sixteenth-century Tsar Ivan the Terrible.[15]

When he looked back on his revolutionary experiences, An-sky would attribute the gradual collapse of the Provisional Government not to the Bolsheviks, the right-wing opposition, or the war, but to the weakness of the PSR itself. "All Russia was following our party blindly. No great men emerged who could stand above the events." He mourned the lack of leadership among the SRs, describing Kerensky as "hysterical, sick with megalomania," and Chernov as obsessive, hypnotized by Kerensky, and degenerating over the course of the revolution. As the words of the Provisional Government leaders grew less effective, An-sky returned to the notion of propaganda of the violent deed—a shift produced not by an ideological crisis but by his ongoing concern with communication. The people he would have preferred to see at the head of the Provisional Government were those who had become famous for their terrorist acts a decade earlier: "the only strong man, Savinkov," who had masterminded the assassinations of Pleve and Grand Duke Sergei, and Maria Spiridonova, known for her assassination of a Tambov district official and the scandal around her accusations that she was abused after being arrested. An-sky thought of her as "really a great figure," but unfortunately she was aligned with the Left SRs, who would split from the party officially in November 1917.[16]

In the summer of 1917, An-sky was feeling nostalgic for the terrorist era of the PSR. He dedicated a poem, "The Revolt of Revolts: A Psalm," to "the bright memory of Egor Sazonov," the young SR who had killed Pleve in 1904. In archaic Russian imagery from the biblical prophets, he spoke in the voice of "Stinking Lazar," a wounded martyr symbolizing the revolution itself. Lazar scourges his neighbors who "cast the yoke of slavery from their necks," then began to "multiply their lands and increase their wealth," without freeing their own slaves. Now, he prophesies, a new battle will sweep away the wealth of his neighbors, "built on blood and tears." Lazar prepares to fight "the giants of the earth," armed only with "the rebellious Word."

> I cast my Word into the world . . . and the sons of man, drunk with the wine of amazement, stopped in astonishment . . . Who has been slain? I, who raised the revolt of revolts, or the world, with its putrefying wounds of injustice? . . . The last Judgment of the sons of man is underway.[17]

As the revolution faced threats from right and left, An-sky remembered the glory days of the PSR in 1904 and 1905, when it had seemed that a single act or a single word could begin a revolt that would change the world. Stinking Lazar, like Sazonov, Savinkov, and Spiridonova, stood for the possibility of heroically communicating a moral message. As the months wore on after February, that possibility seemed increasingly distant, but An-sky kept seeking it.

The PSR leaders, threatened by pressure from the Bolsheviks and from the left wing of the party, which urged immediate withdrawal from the war and the division of gentry lands among the peasants, filled their lists of candidates for the Constituent Assembly with moderate figures. An-sky was proposed as a representative from Mogilev, a Belorussian city on the Dnepr about 100 miles from Vitebsk, whose population, in 1909 numbering some 54,000, was over half Jewish. The assignment was important, since the Mogilev peasant soviets, influenced by the Left SRs, had already begun to divide up the land. On an October 1917 visit to campaign in the city, An-sky must have spoken for the ideas of the center of his party, but he found himself attracted to its radical wing. He was disappointed by the young urban SR organizers he met there, who seemed as single-minded and naïve as the men of the 1860s, but when he addressed a meeting of the more left-leaning local peasants and soldiers, he saw the revolutionary spirit he wanted. "It was evident that for these listeners, the word was action, it was taken as a clear indication of how to act."[18] In Mogilev as in "The Revolt of Revolts," An-sky was compelled by the heroic image of words that can change the world.

After the 1905 revolution, when SR work became impossible and many leaders left the Russian Empire, An-sky had elected to stay and plunge into Jewish cultural work instead; now he had to find a way to combine his radical Russian politics with his Jewish activity. He could not please all his Jewish friends with his solutions: Dubnov criticized him, seeing him as influenced first by the excitement of the revolution and then by "the nightmare of Bolshevism and its antipode, black Poland" to shift "simultaneously from the Folkspartey to the Zionists and from Kadetism to his old friends, the SRs." Regardless of his sympathies, as he devoted his time in 1917 to SR and government work, his Zionism moved into the background. In May 1917, he did attend the Seventh All-Russian Zionist Congress, a landmark gathering in Petrograd that testified to the huge support for Zionism among the Jews of Russia, and he even appeared to some Russian Zionists to be a logical leader for their movement, but he was committed to the PSR. While he liked Jabotinsky's vision of the honorable

Jewish soldier, his Zionism was limited: he wrote with enthusiasm about the Balfour Declaration in November 1917, but he also said that year about Zionist groups, "After all, these are purely bourgeois parties—and there's no point talking about them." He had little time in 1917 for ordinary Russian Zionists.[19]

He did have time to write about the pogroms, and he recognized the terrible truth that the new revolutionary army, like the Tsarist army before it, perpetrated anti-Jewish violence in Galicia—but he continued to believe that Russian anti-Jewish behavior was an aberration that would pass. He wrote in mid-July that while it was a tragic necessity that Russia stay in the war, it was time to acknowledge the "nightmare of shame and madness" that had accompanied the first Russian campaign in Galicia: the burnt houses, the executions without trial, the rapes. He urged his readers to visit his new Jewish museum in Petrograd, where they could see evidence of Russian atrocities in the shoes and tobacco pouches the soldiers had made out of the parchment of stolen Torah scrolls. When he condemned the pogrom in Tarnopol, he spoke not just of the Jewish victims but of the shame that the violence could bring on the revolutionary army.[20]

An-sky also had time to imagine how Jewish life could improve in revolutionary Russia. He joined an SR committee working on nationalities questions and, once more, he urged the creation of an autonomous Jewish SR party (to the annoyance of some other Jewish SRs). He argued that with the exception of Poland and Finland, it would be a mistake for the ethnic groups of the former Russian Empire to form their own countries; for political and economic reasons, they should remain united but enjoy cultural and some administrative autonomy. While they could collectively support defense, post offices, and higher education, each group should run its own elementary schools, hospitals, and tax collection system. Protecting the rights of landless peoples such as Jews was crucial.[21]

The Jews in the new revolutionary Russia would finally have cultural autonomy, allowing them to do what An-sky had always hoped they could: make art that would appeal broadly. With that hope in mind, he fit his own cultural projects into his busy schedule of political work. He told Monoszon in May, "I organized in Kiev and Moscow a subscription to the album of Jewish antiquities, which is now almost fully funded. I dealt with Galician matters. I wrote and am finishing the program of the 'League of national-socialist unity.' I worked on SR party business here and in Moscow. I sold the book about Galicia that I haven't written yet. I sold the right to translate my stories into Hebrew. And I did other things too." In spite of his frenetic pace, An-sky must have found cultural work a welcome escape from the endless political battles. Culture itself could offer neutral ground. At a Jewish conference in Kiev, a scandal was about to erupt when a rabbi from Berdichev proposed that everyone stand to honor the Torah, but the Bundists remained sitting. An-sky pointed out that the Torah was "not only a religious symbol, but the symbol of the Jews' ancient culture," in whose honor he proposed standing, and at that, the Bundists rose.[22]

In the window between the February revolution and the Bolshevik seizure of power, Jewish publishing flourished in Yiddish, Hebrew, and Russian. An-sky was eager to release the materials from his expedition, which he expected would fill forty volumes and cost 30,000 rubles to print. In December 1916, he hoped to raise money for the entire series in Moscow and Kiev. The next spring, he was focusing on funding not the entire publication but a single high-quality album with reproductions of graphic art; he gathered subscriptions in advance from individuals who promised to pay a percentage of the cost. Over the next year, he edited the album, which would feature the illustrated covers of community record books, plates from a fourteenth-century Spanish *haggadah* (Passover prayer book) he had borrowed from Bialik, some seventeenth- and eighteenth-century Italian marriage contracts, nineteenth-century eastern Ukrainian folk prints on biblical themes, and nineteenth-century *mizrahim* and pages from kabbalistic books. He commissioned essays from the art connoisseur I. Eliashev (Baal Makhshoves), the art historian Maximilian Syrkin, and the critic Abram Efros.[23]

As Hebrew publishing in Russia grew and diversified, An-sky, who was always eager to take advantage of new publishing opportunities and who still embraced Jewish literary multilingualism, wanted to see his work printed in that language. The Hebrew publishing world was delighted to recruit him: the publisher Avraham Stybel and the editor David Frishman invited him to eat in a fancy restaurant on Petrograd's Nevsky Prospect, where An-sky, defending his credibility as an ascetic revolutionary, insisted on ordering just soup and bread and paying for himself.[24] Before February, he could never have legally published a book denouncing the Russian occupation policies in Galicia and Bukovina; now he could arrange for *The Destruction of Galicia* to come out with Stybel's press in Hebrew translation.

Even before February, An-sky had asked Bialik to find someone to translate *The Dybbuk* into Hebrew, hoping that his friend himself would do the job. He got the chance to make that happen one evening in Moscow, probably in November 1916. The actor Menachem Gnesin remembered An-sky reading his play aloud at the home of Hillel Zlatopolsky, a wealthy industrialist and Zionist philanthropist who funded Hebrew schools, publishing ventures, and the new Hebrew theater where Gnesin hoped to work, the Habima. Zlatopolsky had invited a group of Jewish writers and young actors and fed them dinner before they heard An-sky read. The only light shone on a table by An-sky's chair; some listeners found room on the couch and others sat on the carpet. In the darkness, the writer's voice sounded otherworldly, and Gnesin felt that An-sky, like a Hasidic rebbe or like the Messenger in his play, was able to transmit the mystical charm of Hasidism and kabbalah. After the reading ended, An-sky did not hear the criticism that he was used to, the complaints that his play was too Symbolist, too folkloric, or too literary for the stage. Everyone was silent until Zlatopolsky himself quietly began to sing "Mipne mah" (Wherefore?), the Hasidic melody that opens and closes the play, and all the listeners joined in. The song drew to a close, and Zlatopolsky took An-sky's hand and led him from the room. He returned a few minutes later and announced that he had purchased the play from An-sky, on two conditions: that Bialik would agree to translate it into Hebrew, and that the new Habima theater would agree to perform it.[25]

As Gnesin recalled, it was An-sky who demanded Bialik's translation, while Zlatopolsky insisted that even though the Habima was only at the planning stages at that point, it would come into existence and should perform the play. An-sky's goal was to convince the most admired Hebrew poet of his age to translate his play, and he was clever to enlist Zlatopolsky, one of the most powerful men in the nascent world of Hebrew secular publishing, as the champion of his cause. Zlatopolsky asked Shmuel Chernovits, an important Hebrew writer and editor, to convey his request that Bialik do the translation. Chernovits stressed to Bialik that the play would be the foundation stone of the Habima and that it was important that the new theater be based on the best Hebrew possible, that of the "premier stylist of our generation." In one of the few letters he ever wrote in his own rusty Hebrew, An-sky too pleaded with Bialik. "I must add my request to the request of our friends, and of the house of Hillel [Zlatopolsky] among them, that you yourself translate my play. It will be a festival and a joy for me to see 'The Dybbuk' in the language of our soul. And the festival and the joy will be multiplied a hundredfold if the translation will be by your hand. Answer, my friend!"[26]

Zlatopolsky, Chernovits, and An-sky knew they needed to pull out all the stops to persuade Bialik, because his dislike of the play was public knowledge; it reflected the belief he shared with his mentor, Ahad Haam, that secular Jews should build a new high culture based on a carefully refined distillation of the textual tradition available to the Hebrew-literate elite, not on the habits of the Yiddish-speaking masses. After An-sky read the play to a Jewish audience in Kiev, Bialik compared him to a garbage collector who "collects scraps of folklore and pieces them together." Folklore is different from "a work of national art," he argued, because "a truly great work of national art is like flesh and blood, while folklore is like fingernails and hair. They are part of the body too, and pulling them out causes pain and sorrow, but when they're trimmed it doesn't hurt. On the contrary . . . they need to be clipped from time to time." As he reminded An-sky, it was a Jewish custom to burn nail clippings instead of throwing them into the garbage; a person who threw his clippings into the garbage would have to retrieve them or risk going to the "world of oblivion" after his death. He said, "Your imagination is like a product of this world of oblivion, An-sky! You worked for the *goyim* your whole life, and at the end of your life, when you were half dead, you came to us Jews and you were sentenced to wander among the garbage dumps and gather folklore. *The Dybbuk* came out of what you gathered." It may be that Bialik came to regret his harsh public criticism of An-sky and agreed to do the work to rescue their friendship; regardless of his motivations, An-sky, Chernovits, and Zlatopolsky were correct in their guess that he could be persuaded to translate *The Dybbuk*. When he wrote of his decision, An-sky was thrilled. In February 1917, as revolution erupted in Petrograd, *Evreiskaia Nedelia* (Jewish Week) announced officially that Bialik had agreed to translate the play for Habima.[27]

Having given in, Bialik, who was going through a period of literary "silence," decided to use the translation to fulfill another obligation: to submit something to Frishman for the first issue of a new Hebrew literary magazine, *Hatekufah* (The Era). The creation of a Hebrew language for the stage was challenging, given that the language had not been spoken in secular contexts for almost two millennia, and Bialik took the job seriously. As he wrote, he asked David Vardi, future lead actor of Habima, to read scenes out loud to hear how his words would sound on stage, and when he turned the manuscript in to Frishman in July 1917, he explained that he had chosen "the literary language of the pious, so that it would be comfortable to hear and, it seems, comprehensible to a wagon driver. That's the right thing for a folk drama, considering both content and stage performance." When the characters in An-sky's play expressed the feelings of sadness and ecstasy that suffused Bialik's lyrical verse, Bialik used the language he had developed in his own work, filling the translation with echoes of his poetry. His translation drew on both Russian and Yiddish versions of An-sky's play, and a number of small differences separate it from the Yiddish version published in 1919. An-sky, whose own translations tended to depart from the originals, was delighted with the result. He wrote to Bialik when it came out in *Hatekufah*, "What can I tell you? When I read the translation alone at night, I cried tears of joy. The whole play is wonderfully refined and poetic, improved, transformed into music. . . . Thank you from the depths of my heart, my dear."[28] An-sky's days were full of writing and revolutionary politics, from within the government when his party was in the ascendency and from the increasingly dangerous margin as the SRs lost their position, but he could find time at night to admire his friend's artistry.

By the time he saw Habima actors rehearsing it, Bialik could agree that the translation had succeeded; he told his wife that he found the play "just wonderful!" An-sky himself was much less interested in the performance of his play in Hebrew than he had been in the translation of the text. His own Jabotinskian Zionism was focused on the production of grand gestures that would be visible to the world at large, and the notion of staging a play in Hebrew probably felt like an elite venture for a limited audience. When he pleaded with Bialik to translate *The Dybbuk,* he did not mention the plans for a Habima production; that his own play would ultimately reach a Hebrew audience and become the cornerstone of modern Hebrew drama would have surprised him. Even as he negotiated the Hebrew translation with Bialik, he was trying to ensure the play would be performed in Russian. But in the spring of 1918, he learned that the directors of the Moscow Art Theater, who had promised to produce *The Dybbuk* that season, had decided to move it to the next year's repertoire. Sushkevich, almost in tears, told An-sky that everyone loved the play, but the company felt that it required "the kind of effort that we can't make now, with our shattered nerves," and that it was "terribly heavy and threatening," unappealing to theatergoers looking for entertainment and distraction. An-sky wrote to Monoszon, "It's sad, but I couldn't respond." As an afterthought, he mentioned that rehearsals were due to begin at the Habima.[29]

On October 25, 1917, An-sky returned from Mogilev to Petrograd and found no taxis at the Tsarsko-Selsky station—because, people told him, the Bolsheviks were shooting in the streets. He made his way to the City Duma past speeding cars full of armed soldiers and sailors. Another Duma deputy, Saker, with whom An-sky had once debated Jewish language politics at *Evreiskii Mir,* asked him why the Provisional Government had not put down the Bolsheviks at once, and was startled by An-sky's response: "What if there are no loyal soldiers left?" At 6 P.M., the deputies heard that the Bolsheviks had surrounded the Winter Palace, where the Provisional Government ministers were meeting. They debated going to the Palace to save the ministers, or at least to demonstrate their disapproval of the Bolsheviks. Over the next hours, they became increasingly nervous about confronting the Bolsheviks, but they did their best not to sound frightened, giving speeches that were "very revolutionary," An-sky thought, "but without the needed inner fire." At 1 A.M., he went with some 300 City Duma deputies in the light rain, led by the white-bearded Mayor Shreider with a lantern. They had gone less than a block down Nevsky Prospect when they were stopped by a patrol of Bolshevik sailors. John Reed watched a group of burly sailors confronting the older, unarmed deputies in their formal dress. When Shreider asked finally, "Will you shoot us? What will you do?" one sailor said, "We will spank you! And if necessary we will shoot you too." An-sky heard the news as it made its way down the procession: the Bolsheviks were willing to shoot. The deputies discussed their options, then turned around and went back to the Duma, "all feeling," An-sky remembered, "that the heroic act we had intended to carry out had turned into a stupid farce."[30]

That evening, Mensheviks and Right SRs protested the assault on the Provisional Government by withdrawing from the Congress of Soviets, thus inadvertently clearing the way for the Bolsheviks to rule alone. Later that night, the Bolsheviks arrested the Provisional Government ministers (with the exception of Kerensky, who had left to try to round up some loyal troops). The next day, those opposed to one-party Bolshevik rule in Russia coalesced into the All-Russian Committee for the Salvation of the Motherland and the Revolution, an organization formed by the Petrograd City Duma. An-sky found himself at the center of anti-Bolshevik resistance, where people were working to record atrocities, issue bulletins, and prevent the Bolsheviks from expropriating all the money in the banks. In the short term, the Bolsheviks left the City Duma alone, fearing that dissolving it would disrupt the city's provisioning. On October 29, Vikzhel, the All-Russian Executive Committee of Railroad Workers, insisted that the Bolsheviks try to avoid civil war by negotiating with the other socialist parties to form a coalition, and the Bolsheviks—aware that the railroad workers had the power to shut down communications and nervous about resistance to their coup in Moscow and elsewhere—agreed. An-sky and another SR were chosen to represent the City Duma.[31]

The meeting in the Vikzhel office was called for 8 P.M. that night, but before the representatives left the City Duma, they asked the leaders of the SRs and the Mensheviks if they wanted to add anyone to the delegation. By the time the leaders decided not to, it was 4 A.M. Once they reached the Vikzhel conference, they found themselves negotiating with prominent revolutionaries, including the moderate Bolsheviks Lev Kamenev (Rozenfeld) and David Riazanov (Goldendakh), Fedor Dan and Mark Liber from the Mensheviks, and An-sky's friend Iuly Martov (Tsederbaum) from the Menshevik Internationalist faction.[32] An-sky knew many of them from his years in emigration. Kamenev, who was known for his good relations with his opponents (and his later advocacy for Jews fleeing the Soviet Union), was "a cold man of few words, with cold, clever, gray eyes," famous in Switzerland for his strictly conspiratorial habits. Martov, who spoke quickly and nervously, was "a Jewish type, a hairsplitter," and Riazanov "a Jewish type, a quick learner," seen in Paris as a party theoretician with encyclopedic knowledge who rarely spoke in public. He and An-sky had met and gossiped a month earlier; Riazanov had criticized Iury Steklov (Nakhamkes), another Jewish revolutionary, for converting to Christianity, and admitted that he missed the academic calm of Western Europe.

For once, An-sky's personal connections did not help him find common ground with his interlocutors. Riazanov, who had always been so calm, sounded "hysterical," overwhelmed by emotion and unable to listen. Later, Kamenev told An-sky that Riazanov was unnerved by his experience defending the right wing of the Bolshevik party. The SRs and Mensheviks made demands the Bolsheviks were unlikely to accept: the release of the ministers, armistice for Kerensky's troops, and a new government that would include Kerensky and exclude Lenin. An-sky remembered only that he offered what he thought was a reasonable compromise on behalf of the City Duma, and that Riazanov responded furiously. The meeting adjourned at 8 A.M. and another one was called for 6 P.M. that night. Soon after the second meeting finally started at midnight, fifty workers burst in. Their leader asked the gathered men why they had not yet reached a compromise that would avert civil war. "We demand that you put an end to this turmoil. If not, we will deal with you ourselves!" Riazanov responded with another hysterical speech, accusing the SRs and the Mensheviks of unwillingness to compromise, An-sky defended the moderates, and the workers, confused and angry, left. As news came in about Kerensky's failures at the front, the Bolsheviks' negotiating position grew stronger. An-sky recalled that the conference finally reached agreement on an armistice for the troops outside Petrograd itself, and he and another man were selected to bring the news to the front.[33]

At 2 A.M., the two men went from the Vikzhel conference to the Bolshevik headquarters at the Smolny Institute to get official military permission to go to the front. They found the building lively, all the rooms lit up. In the entrance, An-sky saw another old acquaintance, Vladimir

Bonch-Bruevich, a Tolstoyan writer and ethnographer who had recently joined the Bolsheviks and started avoiding An-sky. He looked startled to see An-sky and his comrade at the Smolny, but told the soldier at the door that they should be let in and brought them to the military head-quarters, a room full of evidence of a recent meeting: the floor was cov-ered with cigarette mouthpieces and torn newspaper. Three young men in military clothes sat at a table with a teapot, some pieces of black bread, and glasses full of cigarette stubs. When An-sky explained his mission to one of the men and said he needed to see the commander, the man looked at him ironically and told him that it was impossible—and that the armi-stice no longer mattered, since Kerensky's troops were surrounded and he was about to be captured. Depressed, An-sky left the Smolny. The next morning, Kerensky's defeat was confirmed. An-sky reported to the City Duma, where Shreider concluded that the Vikzhel conference must have been a Bolshevik ruse to waste time. Abraham Coralnik, a young SR for whom An-sky seemed a man of an earlier era—too soft, too lyrical, too scholarly for the harsh twentieth century—saw his account of the work-ers barging into the Vikzhel conference as a sign that Bolsheviks had won. "He was tired and looked old, older than I have ever seen him, a broken man. He read about the failure of his mission in a singsong voice, almost as if he were praying, enveloping the assembly in a feeling of doom. We realized that everything was lost."[34]

Even the indefatigable An-sky admitted that he no longer believed the Vikzhel negotiations were worthwhile. After two sleepless nights he was exhausted, and he refused to return to the conference. Of course, the Vikzhel conference was far from his first experience of long nighttime meetings. He had been happy in the émigré colonies where the students got together every evening to argue, and in his revisions of the "God on Trial" legend, he had transformed Bern into folklore, imagining that a group of passionate debaters could change the world for the better by forcing God himself to hear them. In March 1917, he had thought that he was finally in a position to make the government listen, to use his con-nections to Kadets and SRs to make his voice heard, but in October, he saw how effectively the new government shut him down: at the Vikzhel conference and the Smolny Institute, the Bolsheviks did not want to hear his words.

The Vikzhel talks broke down a few days later, and gradually, the Bol-sheviks worked to neutralize the City Duma. They dissolved it three weeks after their coup, but the deputies kept meeting in secret. They took Shreider's car away and put out an order for his arrest, but he hid. An-sky remembered that even then, the deputies remained optimistic, hoping that when the Constituent Assembly met, the Bolsheviks would have to back down. And in spite of the October coup, the Constituent Assembly elections took place as planned, starting November 12. The SRs won a plurality, with 38 percent of the total vote: one of their delegates was An-sky himself, representing Mogilev. The Ukrainian SRs got 12 percent, the Kadets 5 percent, the Mensheviks 3 percent. The Bolsheviks received 24 percent and immediately declared the elections illegitimate. They postponed the convocation of the Assembly, which was due to open in Petrograd on November 28. That day, forty-five of the delegates, Shreider at their head, got through the Bolshevik pickets outside the Tauride Palace and proceeded to elect leaders. The next day the Bolsheviks surrounded the palace with troops. Lenin argued that the fact of Soviet power made the "bourgeois-democratic" Assembly irrelevant, and it should be abolished. The Bolsheviks and the Left SRs supported him.[35]

Meanwhile, An-sky kept writing as though the Bolshevik leaders, many of whom had once been part of the warm, predominantly Jewish, Russian émigré communities in Switzerland, would finally pay attention to him. Trotsky gave a speech in December attacking the Constituent Assembly, and An-sky responded with an article recalling the beginning of the century. Trotsky was known then as a good orator, but criticized for twisting his opponent's words and taking them out of context. Someone answered him with a joke.

> "One day a holy elder who had performed great miracles gave in to temptation and sat down to play cards with two monks. Suddenly the holy elder turned out to have four aces. The monks exchanged glances. In a little while, the holy elder again had four aces. The monks started to fidget but stayed quiet. But when the holy elder got four aces for the third time, one of the monks couldn't stand it, jumped up, and cried, 'Holy father! Please, no miracles! We're playing for money!'"
>
> Trotsky's opponent ended, "Comrade Trotsky, please, no miracles. We're playing for money."
>
> Now Mr. Trotsky is playing not for money but for "great blood," but he continues his "miracles" as before. . . .[36]

Interested as always in the magic of words, An-sky drew attention not just to the Bolsheviks' perfidy but to their terrifyingly effective propaganda. By describing Trotsky's distortion of his opponents' words and the Bolsheviks' surprise attacks as the "miracles" of a cardsharp monk, An-sky transformed the October coup into a bit of folklore, something he could, perhaps, collect, analyze, and control.

Of course, he could not. On January 5, 1918, at 4 P.M., the Constituent Assembly finally opened. A crowd had marched and demonstrated in support of it earlier that day, and the Bolsheviks had shot at them from the rooftops with machine-guns. Bolshevik troops stood at the back of the assembly hall, shouting abuse as the SR delegates tried to speak. The Bolshevik delegates proposed a measure; when it was rejected, they declared the Assembly to be in the hands of counterrevolutionaries and left the hall. The Left SRs supported them. The Bolsheviks let Chernov and the other SRs make speeches for a few hours, then told them the meeting had ended. At 4:40 A.M. on the 6th, the Tauride Palace was locked up. When the delegates returned the next day, they learned that the Assembly had been dissolved.[37] An-sky's career as an elected official was over.

Having denied their opponents the forum of the Constituent Assembly, the Bolsheviks reinstituted censorship and made it difficult to voice criticism. There were 4,000 periodicals published in Russia in 1917, but only 2,800 after the Bolshevik takeover in 1918. The heirs of the Social Democrats, whom Mikhailovsky had mocked for their refusal to see that a single human voice could sway the course of history, acknowledged, in a sense, that he may have been right when they closed the journal he had edited, halfway through the year: the fall 1918 issue of *Russkoe Bogatstvo* was prepared, but forbidden to be printed.[38] A numb An-sky watched despairingly as the Bolsheviks, men and women with whom he had once been friendly, shut him and his friends down more effectively than the Tsarist authorities ever had.

It became increasingly dangerous for An-sky, as a prominent SR, to be in Petrograd. In March, he spent thirty-two hours traveling to Moscow in an unheated train car. He found a mood of quiet decay, "but it's easier to breathe here than in Petrograd: some newspapers come out, even with announcements, there's no shooting on the street, although there's so much robbery that hardly anyone goes out after 9:00 at night." Prices were high, but goods were available. "Conversations everywhere on the same topic, all suffused with the anger of impotence and the pessimism of the doomed." Even in Moscow, though, the Bolsheviks were catching up with the SRs, and a few weeks later, An-sky told Monoszon that he felt like a dying man, impatient with people who try to sustain the illusion that he might live. He apologized for his bitter letters. "Not everyone has the luck to have someone close to him, someone to whom he can cry out, 'I am so lonely!' " He was seeing the political causes for which he had worked his whole life breaking down and being destroyed one by one. There seemed to be no way out. "It all gradually turns into hopelessness, at times to revulsion. . . . Every day there is some new vileness, big or small, that already has lost its power to touch or trouble us. They closed

Russkie Vedomosti 'forever,' they sentenced the 'counterrevolutionary' Martov, they destroyed the SR club, and so on. It doesn't even register anymore."[39] Throughout his career as a writer and speaker, An-sky had responded to what he saw with powerful emotions: his writing was motivated by his feelings of sympathy, outrage, enthusiasm, ecstasy. Now, as the Bolsheviks shut down opposition and solidified their power, he lost access to the Russian intelligentsia with whom he had shared concerns and visions and whose community had given his life meaning. Without that audience, he felt his emotions go still.

An-sky continued to oppose the Bolsheviks as much as he could. He sheltered Chernov when he was pursued by the Cheka, the Bolsheviks' powerful, nearly autonomous secret police organization. On April 10, 1918, a Bolshevik commissar, a former ritual slaughterer also named Rapoport, seized the Jewish Historical-Ethnographic Society's museum on Vasilevsky Island in Petrograd and sent Dubnov a letter explaining that he was merely protecting the collections, in response to rumors that they were being stolen. Dubnov argued, then passed the problem on to An-sky, who came back from Moscow to find the museum and his own room sealed. He tore the seal from his room, went to the commissar, and demanded that he prosecute the alleged museum thieves; otherwise, he threatened to have Rapoport himself prosecuted as a liar and a rumor-monger. The stunned Rapoport took the seals off the museum, returned the keys, and promised to publish an announcement that the accusation of theft was a misunderstanding and the rumormongers would be prosecuted. Even so, An-sky was worried that the Bolsheviks would try again to co-opt his invaluable work.[40]

As he fought the Bolsheviks' fabricated rumors about the museum, he worked to oppose the much more dangerous rumors circulating about Jews. An-sky heard people blaming the Jews in general for the Bolshevik abuses. Even among the intelligentsia, people were saying that the Jews had plotted to ruin the country that had always treated them so badly. When asked to prove it, they would list well-known Jewish Bolshevik leaders. "What about Trotsky? And Steklov? And Zinovev? And Kamenev?" An-sky remembered the anti-Jewish slanders of the past few years—the blood libel accusation against Beilis and the wartime stories of Jewish espionage—and saw a similar pattern of rumors spread deliberately. As before, he fought them with his own writing. In July 1918, he pointed out that there were Jewish leaders in all the revolutionary parties, and those among the Bolsheviks did not represent Russian Jews as a whole. He fumed: "With the exception of one or two of them, they are distinguished by the way they broke off from everything Jewish, rejected their origin and their tribe, their nationality, changing their religion and their name. And these very renegades and turncoats are imagined as representing a people, acting at its will!"[41]

An-sky urged his readers to abandon the mentality behind these rumors. The intelligentsia and the prerevolutionary government had believed that the Russian people were weak, and thus they feared other peoples, including the Jews. The only way to save the Russian people, they thought, would be to protect it from the "encroachment of stronger and more cultured nationalities." An-sky pointed out the flaws in this reasoning. "It is time to put an end to this kind of nationalism that almost destroyed the Russian state. It is time to stop blaming outside influence for everything. It is time to realize once and for all that the narod can save itself only by becoming stronger, not by sealing itself off from every breeze blowing from outside."[42] When An-sky defended Jews, he argued that those who blamed them for Bolshevik behavior were traitors to the Russian people. The insistence that the Russians were victims was a dangerous myth. He wanted to rescue the Jews from the vengeful anger of people who blamed them for the Bolsheviks' misdeeds, but he spoke in the language of Russian honor.

While he wrote newspaper articles and pamphlets to stave off violence against Jews, An-sky returned in his fiction to the vision of his people's destruction. In March 1918, he told Monoszon that he was writing "a big Jewish folktale." In 1916, he had started "The Tower in Rome: A Fearsome and Wonderful Story of an Enchanted Tower with Four Gates, of an Iron Crown, and of Blades of Grass that Did Not Wither." He completed it in Russian in Petrograd in April 1918 and dedicated it to Sologub; he dedicated a Yiddish version to Peretz.[43] When compared to the apocalyptic writings he had been producing since 1911—"Ten Signs of the Messiah," the "Book of Signs," the translations from Ezekiel and Isaiah, the tales collected in *Destruction of Galicia,* and the recent "Revolt of Revolts"—"The Tower in Rome" was farther from ethnographic collage and closer to a sustained single narrative.

The longest of An-sky's apocalyptic fantasies, "The Tower in Rome" is also his most enigmatic text. A Roman emperor imagines he has correctly decoded a series of magic signs and understood that if he can kill all the Jews, he will rule the earth. His story begins when he enters an enchanted tower containing mysterious scenes, symbols, and creatures, including hands that reach eternally out of a pool of blood and dead people who come back to life. He tells his astrologers that if they cannot interpret what he has seen, they will die, and the oldest one reveals that the tower's symbols refer to an earlier Roman emperor, Nero. Nero wished to don the iron crown of Emperor Nimrod and rule the earth, but it was too heavy to lift. A mysterious tablet instructed him to lure the kings of the seventy nations of the world to Rome to try to lift the crown, but the effort failed because the Jews did not come. The sorcerers of Egypt told him to assemble a group of Jews to reach out for the crown, but instead of reaching out, they prayed for the coming of the messiah. Ultimately a magical severed Jewish head told him that he could solve his problem by killing the Jews and eliminating them from the roster of nations, if he only plucked the blades of grass containing their lives—but he failed again. Finally, Nero himself perished in his attempt to destroy the Jews. After he finishes his tale, the astrologer tells the emperor that if he unbinds the bundles of grass that contain the Jews' lives, he will kill them and he can take the iron crown himself. When he tries this, though, the emperor is destroyed by a fearsome two-headed calf, and his death triggers the arrival of the messiah.

Like the people he had met in the war zone, An-sky used ancient apocalyptic imagery to make sense of his own trauma. The story's central metaphor, that humans are as fragile as grass, is from second Isaiah: "All flesh is grass, all its goodness like flowers of the field: grass withers, flowers fade when the breath of the Lord blows on them" (Isaiah 40:6–8). This biblical image was already linked to twentieth-century Jewish bloodshed, for Bialik had used it in his famous pogrom poem, "In the City of Slaughter" ("The people is plucked grass; can grass grow again?"). An-sky borrowed much of his plot from *The Book of Zerubbabel*, which was written in the context of seventh-century wars that—like World War I—were accompanied by renewed Jewish messianism and Jewish violence.[44] It relates the visions of Zerubbabel ben Shaltiel, governor of Judah, who hears an angel foretell a millennium of destruction and idol worship, the reign of the son of Satan, the resurrection of the dead, earthquakes, war, and the arrival of the messiah. Like "Tower in Rome," the *Sefer Zerubavel* describes first the triumph of an antimessiah and then his downfall and the ascension of a true messiah.

Like other Russian and Jewish writers of his violent era, An-sky was drawn to apocalyptic literary models, but whereas ancient apocalypses contain signs that are interpreted to reveal the future, in his tale, the astrologer, the magicians, and all the mysterious scenes and symbols only lead the emperors astray and destroy them.[45] Against the background of ancient texts, An-sky's story stands out as an example of the failure of revelation to give succor. An-sky adopted a similar attitude here toward apocalyptic legend as in *Destruction of Galicia,* in which he retold the apocalyptic stories of Russians and Jews, but expressed doubt about the ways in which the people he met found meaning in destruction. Even while he rejected their reasoning, he offered apocalyptic interpretations of his own, finding a different kind of meaning in the bloodshed, one pointing not toward salvation but toward the terrible frailty of civilization. As he watched the Bolsheviks arrest his friends, An-sky must have wondered whether the bloodshed he was witnessing would lead to anything better in the long run—and he must have feared it would not. By structuring "Tower in Rome" around the false information given to the emperors, An-sky—even while he concluded his legend with the appearance of the messiah—suggested that the belief that one could find redemptive meaning in violence was wrong.

For contemporary readers, An-sky's story, like all the apocalyptic fiction published at this time, would have felt like an exploration of the fantasy of messianic redemption in response to real violence on a mass scale. Dubnov too was thinking apocalyptically; he predicted in June 1917 that Russia was entering an era of famine, brutalization, and slaughter, and on January 7, 1918, the day after the Constituent Assembly was closed, he noted glumly, "Blood, hunger, cold, darkness—these are the signs of the new year."[46] Jewish readers during the terrible years after 1917 would have seen "Tower in Rome" as recasting the horrifying visual impressions of the pogroms—the real severed heads and pools of blood—in mystical terms. The Jews in An-sky's story refuse to join the other nations in reaching for the iron crown of power; they care more for religious duty than world politics. Like the Jews An-sky depicted in his 1918 articles (and unlike the Jews among the Bolsheviks), they are only observers and victims of the power struggles going on around them. The story of the Roman emperors who try to destroy the Jews but end up destroying only themselves sounded like a metaphor for the destruction of the Russian emperor, Nicholas II (who would be murdered on July 4, 1918). By depicting the death of Nero as followed by the death of another Roman emperor, An-sky suggested that just as the Tsarist rulers had tried to destroy the Jews and ultimately destroyed themselves, so the new Bolshevik rulers, the false redeemers whose hostility to everything An-sky had worked for was exemplified by the other Rapoport's attempt to seize the Jewish museum in Petrograd, would be destroyed in their turn.

Bad as things seemed to An-sky in the spring of 1918, they would get worse. In June, he returned to Moscow to find his room requisitioned and a Bolshevik housed in it. He heard about more and more arrests and executions without trial. By August, the repressions, the hunger, and the terrifying rumors had increased and many of his friends had fled. He kept working, though, editing his album of Jewish antiquities, putting together an article for *Russkoe Bogatstvo* on political songs in revolutionary France (never published), and continuing to write *Destruction of Galicia,* which had "grown into a significant work requiring many months of concentrated effort." The first volume had been finished since April; he planned three more. He was not the only artist still at work in hungry, nervous Moscow: Jewish cultural life continued, and he was drawn into it. He attended the All-Russian Congress of Jewish Communities, a landmark, largely Zionist gathering. The director of the series "Cheap Jewish Library" died, and An-sky was asked to take his place. On August 25, he gave the opening address at an exhibit of Jewish painters and sculptors.[47]

Soon he would not be able to risk such public appearances. On August 30, as Lenin returned from giving a political speech at the Mikhelson factory in the outskirts of Moscow, he was shot three times. The would-be assassin was Fanny Kaplan, an anarchist who had become an SR but who insisted she was acting not on party orders but on her own. Though critically hurt, Lenin survived. For the Bolsheviks, Kaplan's shot was proof that rings of enemies wanted to destroy the new regime. The assassination attempt triggered the intensification of the Red Terror: the Cheka arrested, tortured, and murdered SRs, the bourgeoisie, officers, and anybody else they wanted.[48]

An-sky had held out in Moscow through the summer even as Bolshevik newspapers called for punishment of SRs, but now arrest could come at any moment. So many SRs had been arrested so quickly that he could not find out who had escaped and who had been shot. His friends from his Jewish cultural work were among the thousands of "bourgeois" arrested and held as hostages, Gurevich among them. An-sky left the city to hide out with friends in a town near Moscow where he had stayed briefly the month before. Then, he had been startled by the difference from the city: there were swans on the lake, peacocks in the park, so much bread at dinner that there were leftovers for the dogs, "as though I were on Mars," he thought, not in 1918 Russia. In September, his friends' house came back to Earth, with general searches by the police. An-sky knew that he had to leave. He abandoned everything: the Russian text of *The Dybbuk,* the diaries that he was transforming into *Destruction of Galicia,* the proofs for the *Album of Jewish Antiquities,* and, back in Petrograd, the forty volumes' worth of materials collected during the ethnographic expedition. He feared that the road south to Kiev was too dangerous, so for six days he took trains north and west, through Pskov and Dvinsk to Vilna, at that point controlled by the Germans, where old friends met him and convinced him to stay. "Here there is a densely Jewish atmosphere. That it's smothering and lifeless, that I have no one here to whom I am really close—I suppose this fits my present mood. So for a while at least, until I get my work materials from Moscow, I'll stay here."[49]

An-sky's stopping point was one of the most important centers of East European Jewish culture. Vilna (now Vilnius), a medieval city that had been the capital of Lithuania and then a provincial Polish center, housed by the end of the nineteenth century 100,000 Jews, constituting some 40 percent of the city's population. It was a center for rationalistic, anti-Hasidic rabbinic scholarship, maskilic writing, Hebrew and Yiddish publishing, Zionism, and Jewish socialist movements. Because it had a critical mass of Yiddish speakers and a few influential writers and publishers committed to highbrow, modern Yiddish literature, Vilna was known as the "capital of Yiddish."[50] This city and its writers were uniquely prepared to welcome An-sky as a Jewish cultural figure.

The war had brought waves of Jewish refugees to the city, and like others, An-sky arrived sick and exhausted; he spent his first days in a clinic. Within a few weeks, he moved out into a room of his own, filled it with books, notebooks, and cigarette papers, and decorated it with his portrait of Lavrov (presumably sent, along with his wartime diaries, from Moscow). As he worked on his own writing, he became intoxicated by the Jewish cultural and political developments around him. As in Bern and on the ethnographic expedition, he was living in close quarters with people, mostly younger than himself, who listened to him and admired him, asked his advice and invited him to give speeches. He had provided some of the Yiddish writers of Vilna an avenue into Russian publication when he edited *Evreiskii Mir* almost ten years earlier, and many of them were happy to welcome him back to the city, remembering his connections and respecting the glow of Populist heroism that he still emanated. He had arrived in Vilna feeling numb, but his emotions reawoke as he became friends with Zionists and Socialists, Hebraists and Yiddishists, doctors and playwrights. He felt especially close to two younger men, both former editors of *Literarishe monatsshriften:* Vayter, who had returned five years earlier from exile in Siberia, and Niger, who had also fled Moscow. His Warsaw friends too felt closer than before: in October 1918, he contacted Dinezon for the first time since the war had separated them in 1915, feeling drawn to him "as a brother to a brotherly heart." In November, An-sky told a new young woman friend, Liubov Libovits, that he had "plunged into community affairs" and promised to give three lectures in the next week alone. "It's a bit too much," he insisted, sound-ing pleased.[51]

As an outsider to the party politics dividing Vilna Jews, he was able to bring them together to form new organizations: a Vilna Jewish Historical-Ethnographic Society, a democratically elected community authority (the *kehillah*), a branch of EKOPO for the Vilna region, a culture league, a journalists' society. The *kehillah* was the most urgent task, because the Vilna Jews wanted to hold elections before the Germans left the city and the Poles and Russians began to fight over it. Already in November 1918, An-sky joined them at the organizational meetings. With so many fac-tions, discussions were heated. Moyshe Shalit, the tireless Yiddish writer and editor then in his early thirties, was the general secretary of the ke-hillah. He recalled the organizing committee's fear over even opening the question of election posters for discussion: should they be just in Yiddish, or also in Hebrew? An-sky, off lecturing in Bialystok, wrote to Shalit to urge that the presidium make the decision rather than permitting debate. He added a postscript: "Here [in Bialystok] posters were printed in both languages." The Vilna committee took his hint, printed posters in both languages, and avoided a crisis. An-sky knew well how touchy these in-tellectuals could be and worked hard to control the emotional aftermath of their meetings. After giving a strongly worded speech at one meeting, he wrote to Shalit, "[Tsemach] Shabad told me that you have the impres-sion that I was attacking you. I swear by Moses our Teacher and Marx together that I had nothing in mind against you at all." His phrasing was typical of his catholic approach. He told those on the right that the revo-lution had made the elections possible, and he reminded the left that the orthodox masses had preserved Jewish culture. With his encouragement, the new kehillah came into being, including Zionists, Bundists, the Or-thodox, and artisans. Until it split (with the departure of the left), it was held together in part by An-sky's example.[52]

His "favorite child," according to Khaykl Lunski, the librarian at the city's Strashun Library, was not the fractious kehillah but the Jewish Historical-Ethnographic Society. Its founding meeting took place in Feb-ruary 1919 in the Aristocratic Club, which Jews had not even been al-lowed to enter during the Tsarist years. This society took the place of the Petersburg Historical-Ethnographic Society in An-sky's heart; whenever he found an opportunity, he raised money for it and sent objects for its museum. Another cause close to his heart was the Vilna branch of the EKOPO, organized also in February 1919. His experience in Galicia and Bukovina gave him the authority to insist that homeless refugees be treated with utmost care and respect; he even told the city's many amateur ethnographers not to trouble the refugees with questions about folklore. He worked for the EKOPO, traveling around the region and investigating the refugees' condition.[53]

Even in Vilna, surrounded by Bundists and Zionists, An-sky stayed loyal to the embattled SRs, joining the local Right SR club and supporting it financially. In late February 1919, he was scheduled to give a speech there in memory of Kaliaev, the assassin of Grand Duke Sergei. The posters were up to advertise it, but the Bolsheviks (who by then had conquered the city) canceled the talk, sealed the club's door, and refused to let him enter. An-sky explained to his Jewish community friends that the ideology of the SRs was compatible with Zionism, because the SRs recognized the power of nationalism and did not insist on excluding the bourgeoisie from their vision of the revolutionary future. When Shalit came to An-sky's room one evening, he found a group of young people discussing a new party that An-sky hoped to found, which would combine socialism and nationalism, bringing together everything that he found attractive about Socialist Revolutionary ideals with everything that drew him to Jabotinsky's Zionism.[54]

Though An-sky was still making plans for a more beautiful revolution, he was unable to escape the brutal reality of the Bolshevik revolution and its aftermath. When the Germans left Vilna at the end of 1918 and everyone expected the Bolsheviks to take the city, he remembered his fear in Moscow and considered fleeing. The Red Army entered on January 5, 1919. An-sky was not arrested, but he watched the city's new masters bring inflation, shortages, and terror. In mid-March, three high school teachers came to him with an unexpected request. The Bolsheviks had arrested eight local men, charged them with forgery, and sentenced them to death, a much harsher punishment than the Tsarist authorities would have imposed for the crime. One of the condemned men was Stotsky, a talented local engraver known to be in desperate financial straits. Stotsky's wife had asked the teachers to plead with the Bolsheviks to free her husband, and they had decided to enlist An-sky to play the role of the *shtadln,* the Jew who, in nineteenth-century Russia, acted as intermediary between the Jewish community and the gentile authorities. As an SR who had no dealing with the Bolsheviks, An-sky was surprised by the teachers' confidence, but he decided that it would be wrong to refuse the mission. With only a day before the sentences were due to be carried out, he set out to plead for the counterfeiters' lives.[55]

He went from one Bolshevik leader to another, going up their chain of command, then took his upstairs neighbor, the physician, editor, and community leader Tsemach Shabad, along to meet with Mickiewicz-Kapsiukas, the chair of the local committee of commissars. He found a friendly, tired-looking man with the face of a worker, who reminded him that they had met twice before: twenty years earlier in Bern and more recently at the Petrograd City Duma, to which both of them had belonged. An-sky told him, "We're so far apart from each other now that we almost speak different languages. But there are still words and concepts that we both understand. One of them is 'human life.' Don't shed blood. It won't strengthen your position or give glory to your program." Shabad found An-sky's speech powerful and authoritative, "as though Mickiewicz-Kapsiukas were the accused and An-sky the chastising prophet." Mickiewicz-Kapsiukas admitted that he himself had been displeased when he heard about the death sentences that morning from the newspaper. He agreed to look into the matter and signed an order postponing the executions. Later, An-sky learned that only two of the men were executed. The other six, including Stotsky, were put in prison and released a few months later by the city's next rulers, the Poles who captured Vilna between April 16 and 21, 1919.[56]

The Polish victory brought a pogrom, the first episode of mass anti-Jewish violence in the city since the seventeenth century. Polish soldiers looted Jewish houses and synagogues, beat Jews, arrested hundreds, and killed some sixty-five. When An-sky and Shabad peeked out of the window at the fighting in the street, Polish soldiers shot at them, missing them but hitting an inside wall. Polish legionnaires broke into the apartment shared by Vayter, Niger, and Leib Yaffe (who had once edited An-sky's contributions to a Russian Zionist literary journal, *Safrut*). They accused Vayter of being a Bolshevik (he was not) and shot him immediately. An-sky and other friends buried Vayter while the battle still continued, feeling too stunned to give speeches. Niger and Yaffe were arrested and taken to a military camp near Lida. Once again An-sky and Shabad acted as *shtadns*, visiting Josef Pilsudski, the head of the Polish army, to plead for the two writers. With the intervention of the American ambassador (alerted by Niger's brother, Borukh Charny-Vladek, a prominent U.S. newspaperman and socialist), they were released and left soon afterward for New York.[57]

That fall, An-sky found words for his own reaction to Vayter's death: in an article he titled "Mute Despair," he brought together Vayter's play, *The Mute*, its author's fate, and the anti-Jewish violence by then raging in Ukraine. Once, he said, Jews felt that no one would listen to them, and they responded to the Crusades with mute gestures of mass suicide. Recently, Jews have grown closer to other nations and begun to believe that they should call out to them when they are in trouble—but the horrific pogroms of 1919 were giving the lie to that hope, turning the silent figures of Yiddish modernist literature (from Peretz's story "Bontshe the Silent" to Vayter's play) and the silenced Vayter himself into tragic emblems of Jewish reality.[58]

Even before Vilna's bloody April Days, An-sky's health had worsened. He still suffered from diabetes, his legs hurt from gout, and the chest pains he had had for a decade were getting worse. His friend Dr. Jakub Wygodzki diagnosed him with arteriosclerosis and angina pectoris. It was hard to work in Vilna, but he kept going to meetings, helping resolve the problems caused by the pogrom. Vayter's death haunted him, and the memory of the violence he had seen made him feel more ill. In mid-June, he left Vilna for Otwock, a resort near Warsaw, and entered a clinic. It was good to see his Warsaw friends again, especially Dinezon, Kacyzne, and the Zionist writer and editor Yitzkhok Grinboym, but there was no escaping the news of death. In the winter of 1919, Tsitron had been surprised to see An-sky equally saddened by the death of Yehuda Shimilevich, a young Communist agitator in Vilna shot by Polish legionnaires, and Nokhum-Moshe Sirkin, a Zionist, a trilingual writer, and a political leader in Kiev. His old friend Peretz had died in 1915 at age sixty-two; 100,000 people had attended his funeral, and a monument, the *ohel Peretz,* was erected over his grave. In August 1919, Dinezon, also in his sixties, died in Warsaw and was buried next to Peretz, and An-sky gave a speech at his *shloshim,* the ceremony marking thirty days since his death.[59]

While he mourned these individual deaths, the newspapers reported on death on a much larger, nearly unthinkable scale. Between 1917 and 1921, civil war, terror, famine, and disease caused an estimated 10 million deaths in the former Russian Empire. And as the Yiddish newspapers where An-sky worked related in gruesome detail, between 1918 and 1921, the armies fighting in the Civil War, particularly the anti-Bolshevik forces, inflicted a series of brutal pogroms on Jews in Ukraine and Belarus. Estimates of the number of Jewish deaths reached 250,000, with many more wounded, raped, orphaned, and impoverished. This wave of pogroms, carried out systematically by soldiers, continued the process and the behaviors that An-sky had observed in Galicia and Bukovina, but at a far more deadly magnitude.[60]

An-sky wrote angry articles about these genocidal pogroms, and he discussed them in the early winter of 1920 with two of his old SR friends, Savinkov and Chaikovsky. Both men had fought the Bolsheviks with Anton Denikin's White Army. Frustrated with the Whites, they were returning to Russia, hoping to raise a new army to fight the Bolsheviks and institute a democratic regime; they had come to Warsaw to discuss their ideas with the Polish government. Chaikovsky told An-sky that he saw the pogroms as regrettable but inevitable, and he denied that White Army leaders, in particular Denikin, were responsible. An-sky pointed out that if it was inevitable that Russian armies fighting in Ukraine would systematically kill Jews, then it was impossible to explain why the Red Army did not do so, but Chaikovsky insisted (incorrectly) that the Red Army was as guilty as the Whites. Later, Chaikovsky wrote to An-sky to reiterate that the only way to ensure the safety of the Jews would be for them to have their own state. An-sky was upset to see that even these educated men to whom he had once been close were apathetic about the immense tragedy of Jewish suffering.[61] His acknowledgment in Warsaw in 1920 that the Red Army—the Bolsheviks from whom he had so recently fled—was acting better than the allies of his old SR friends, and his insistence that pogroms were not inevitable, showed the limits of his loyalties both to the PSR and to Zionism. He retained his conviction that Russian anti-Semitism was not inevitable, that Jews could build a future in Russia, and he was willing to admire even his own mortal enemies when he saw that they were making that possible.

Unlike Savinkov and Chaikovsky, An-sky had no intention of looking for battle, but the war that had come to him in Vilna in 1919 threatened to follow him to Warsaw as well. In August 1920, the Bolsheviks pursued the Polish army almost to Warsaw. An-sky left the clinic in Otwock a day before the Bolsheviks entered the town; they fought a battle there, then retreated. An-sky stayed in Warsaw and continued work on the project that had occupied him since he left Vilna: ensuring the future of his writings. Since the spring of 1919, he had been drafting a will. He gave his executors (Zhitlowsky and Gurevich, or if they were unavailable, Shabad, Grinboym, and Kacyzne) detailed instructions. "I strongly desire that everything I have written of more or less enduring value be published as my collected works in Hebrew and Yiddish. If I do not complete this during my life, I ask my friends H. N. Bialik and S. Niger to take on the editorial work and to make sure that my desire is fulfilled." He asked Monoszon to go to the former Imperial Library in Petersburg and copy his old articles from newspapers and journals, so that the editors of his collected works would have the broadest possible selection to choose from. Assuming that his letters would be published as well, he requested that they be edited carefully, so as to remove "intimate feelings and anything that might hurt or offend the people mentioned."[62]

The task envisioned was enormous, but if limited to the project of a Yiddish collected works, it was doable. His longest work, *The Destruction of*

Galicia, was written in Yiddish, and *On a New Course, The Dybbuk,* and his one-act plays had already been translated. While he was still in Vilna, he had begun to translate the rest of his Russian stories and articles, publishing them as he went, mostly in the Warsaw newspaper *Moment.* He had signed a contract for his collected works in Yiddish and prepared the first volumes. At the same time, he tried to bring other projects to fruition. He still wanted to have *The Dybbuk* staged. Now that he had left Russia, he focused on a Yiddish production, negotiating with the talented young Vilna Troupe and urging Zhitlowsky to organize a New York performance. He finished *Destruction of Galicia* in February 1920—and feeling tired, he wrote to Zhitlowsky in Russian, for the first time after nine years of writing faithfully in Yiddish, to tell him the news. But since the Stybel press, where he had agreed to publish it in Hebrew before printing it in Yiddish or Russian, was behind Soviet lines, he worried about the fate of that project and tried to release the memoirs serially in a newspaper.[63]

No matter how sick he felt, he remained alert to the possibility of reaching new audiences with his work—and not only traditional readers. In October 1920, he explained to Zhitlowsky why he thought a New York Yiddish newspaper would want *Destruction of Galicia.* "A few months ago people here were filming [human] types and scenes from Jewish life, to show Americans their relatives and countrymen. My book is also a kind of *moving pictures* [in English], with descriptions of 200 cities and shtetls in Poland, Galicia, and Bukovina, saying what happened there and mentioning hundreds of local Jews." He feared for the fate of the ethnographic collections he had left in Petrograd and did his best to ensure they would reach museum audiences, explaining which objects had been left where for safekeeping. He left half of his money to his sisters and his cousin Yudovin, and half to three Jewish ethnographic societies, in Petrograd, in Vilna, and "an analogous institution for ethnography or archeology in Jerusalem (or somewhere else in Palestine)." He asked these establishments to publish the materials he had gathered, and if there was money left, to use it to purchase new materials for Jewish museums. He left his deathbed picture of Lavrov to Korolenko, asking him to give it to "some revolutionary museum."[64] An-sky may have lost his access to the Russian intelligentsia, but he was eager to see his work reach new audiences, whether as texts, performances, or museum displays, in Europe, New York, or Palestine, in Jewish and European languages.

At the same time, he was imagining his life itself as an object to be displayed. He saw death not as "the negation of life but its conclusion."

He wrote: "Death does not affect life, but gives it a full and completed form, the final line, the final period of a work of literature. If something is insanely frightening, it's not death but time in its ongoing endlessness. It destroys everything, wears days and centuries into dust, separates, narrows, diminishes, gnaws away, until it turns everything into nothingness." As he faced death in Warsaw, he did his best to prevent his efforts from turning into nothingness, working to impose a "full and completed form" on his life, to write a final line and to publicize it as broadly as possible. Even as he republished his old stories and articles, he told people to study his biography, not his writings, as though his actions were able to communicate more clearly than his words. Soon after leaving Vilna, he sounded more reconciled about the limits of what he had written and done, writing to Zhitlowsky that he was not afraid of death. "When I reflect on it, I have no complaints against God or man. I could have lived more wisely, more happily, more productively. But then again, I have no reason to be ashamed of my life or to repent. . . . God gave me a present when he gave me luck and dreams. They may be good or bad, but I've written 14 or 15 volumes. Now my dream is to publish them all in Yiddish or Hebrew. Well, there's a short accounting of my life."[65]

An-sky wanted the end of his life and his death itself to look as admirable to those who saw them as Lavrov's death in 1900 had looked to him. In what he suspected were his last months, he tried harder than ever before to follow a code of honorable behavior. He had been writing to Zhitlowsky and Niger in New York about his financial problems, asking them to sell his manuscripts, organize the production of his plays, and make the newspaper *Tog-Varhayt* (The Day–The Truth) pay the money they owed him. His friends responded, and An-sky began to receive money from the United States, cabled to various publishing ventures in Warsaw. He was delighted by the "golden rain" but annoyed when an American Jew left 25 dollars for him in Warsaw without any explanation. "Americans are so used to subsidizing us, but usually one should ask." If it was alms, then he wanted to return it to the donor. "I've categorically refused charity."[66]

An-sky produced new works as well as translating his old ones, returning to the themes that had always motivated him: in May 1920 he wrote a Yiddish poem, "The New Song," his most explicitly Zionist text, an anthem in the style of "The Oath," and in September 1920 he wrote "Father and Son," an article about an SR martyr, in the spirit of the terrorist biographies he had once printed in *kampf un kempfer*. He thought about honor and vengeance as he sat on the train from Warsaw to Otwock. When a rabbi sitting next to him leaned out of the window, soldiers chased after the train, yelling that they wanted to pull his beard. An-sky quickly traded places with the rabbi, then wrote an article insisting that Jews needed to respond to anti-Semites by refusing to accept insults—but when he reread his own words, he felt abashed. He knew he had been able to take the rabbi's place safely not because he was any braver than he, but because he was not recognizable as a Jew. "And if I am, in a way, in a privileged position, do I have the right to give advice to those who wear beards, to call them to perform heroic deeds?" Perhaps it was time for secular Jews to wear beards as a sign of solidarity. Mikhailovsky had said, "If they whip the peasant, they should whip me too!" but if hooligans began to bother strong Jews, then they would learn that anti-Semitism had a price.[67] In Warsaw, An-sky was still using the style of SR heroics to speak of Jewish cultural renewal.

Continuing his ethnographic work in spite of his own physical frailty was itself a mark of honor. After the Bolsheviks chased him away from Otwock, An-sky found a small room in Warsaw and filled it with books and notebooks. At 9 P.M. on November 7, 1920, he ran an organizational meeting for a new Jewish ethnographic society. He was sad, having just learned of the death of Peysakh Marek, and he looked pale, but Shabad, who attended the meeting, was struck by his energy. Someone asked whether collecting folklore was really the best use of resources, given the difficulties of Jewish life. In response, An-sky told a joke that, like so much of his work, combined Russian and Jewish sensibilities. A peasant is eating a pretzel while he is being whipped. Someone asks him how he can eat in spite of the pain. He answers, "So if I get whipped all day, I shouldn't eat?" An-sky asked, "So if the pogroms and the war last years more, will we stop caring about our historical treasures?"[68] The anecdote shows An-sky still thinking like a Populist. Even as Jewish blood flowed in the shtetls of Ukraine, he asked his Jewish listeners to defy oppression and seek self-renewal by identifying with Slavic peasants.

The next day, November 8, An-sky spent writing at the small table in his Warsaw room, remembering back to Paris in the 1890s. He finished "We Shed No Blood," a memoir about the most unusual Siberian visitors that Potanin had sent his way: the Tibetan lama Avgan Dzhordziev and his Buryat translator Buda Rabdanov. As An-sky, Dzhordziev, and Rabdanov strolled the Paris streets, their conversation had turned to the law. When the lama asked An-sky how criminals were treated "by you" (meaning outside of Tibet), An-sky, ever the social scientist, launched into a disquisition on Western criminal law, concluding with a description of the guillotine. The lama's response, as relayed by Rabdanov, surprised him:

"Khamba-lama is very surprised that you shed human blood!"

I must admit that I was a bit embarrassed. The whole time, in my interactions with the lama, I had been feeling like the representative of a higher culture, and now suddenly this question. This half-savage Asian cannot understand how we shed human blood. I began to explain to the lama that a great movement against capital punishment was arising in Europe; this barbaric punishment was already gone in several countries and one could hope that soon it would also be eliminated in France. But my speech made no impression on the lama, and again, through Rabdanov, he repeated, "Khamba-lama is very surprised that you shed human blood."

It occurred to me to ask the lama a question. "And so what you do in Tibet with serious criminals?"

Buda Rabdanov relayed my question. The lama straightened up and spoke proudly.

Buda Rabdanov, who always imitated the lama's motions, then straightened up and said proudly, "Khamba-lama says, 'In Tibet we shed no human blood! Where we live, they are strangled!'"[69]

With its trick ending, the memoir displayed An-sky at his most ironic. He had spent a lifetime among utopian ideologues; he had devoted his energy and talent to spreading the notion that some day, come the revolution, a more virtuous life would be possible. Now, everything that he had believed in was in jeopardy. The power of the word had been co-opted by the anti-Semitic Whites, the pogroms made Jewish-Slavic coexistence hard to imagine, and the Bolsheviks had stolen the revolution. The tormented Jewish bodies he had seen in Galicia haunted his last major work, "The Tower in Rome." As he faced death in Warsaw, he continued to write in the heroic mode—but he moderated his admiration for heroism and utopia with warnings that the lure of a better future after the revolution might be a fantasy. An-sky's contemporaries probably read "We Shed No Blood" as a hint directed east, not toward Tibet but toward the Bolshevik regime that, in spite of its utopian claims, was drenching Russia in blood. In a larger sense, though, his caution about Bolshevism was a caution about utopia, the compromises that people make to achieve it, and the degree to which clever packaging can convince people of anything.[70] Throughout his career, An-sky had moved between revolutionary propaganda and ironic prose. At the end of his life, he acknowledged the limits of the dream of radical change that had motivated him for so long.

In spite of everything that had happened, though, he kept writing, speaking, organizing ethnographic collections, doing the work that made him feel his life was useful. Also on November 8, he wrote three letters, in each one happily reporting the founding of the new Warsaw Jewish historical-ethnographic society. He used a Yiddish formula for biblical figures when he told Lunski that he was feeling well. "My health is much better, but I'm no Samson the Hero." He had spent his life trying to be a hero, as self-sacrificing and inspirational as Samson, but now, in spite of the energy he was still bringing to Jewish cultural work, his old ambition was fading. And the sense of improvement in his health was deceptive. At 7:30 P.M. that evening, at age fifty-seven, An-sky died suddenly of a heart attack.[71]

An-sky had requested in his will that no speeches be read at his funeral. "One of my friends should say the kaddish, and a brief biography should be read—just the facts of how I lived my life." Having been denied the chance to speak, his friends made up for it with visual display and performance. Funerals in this era were mass events, occasions for political statements on a grand scale. An-sky's funeral was a parade of thousands. Jewish writers including Medem and Kacyzne carried the coffin. They were followed by delegations from writers' and artists' unions, the *Moment* editorial office, and the Vilna Troupe. All the delegations carried banners: "To our comrade Sh. An-sky," "From Vilna to An-sky, from the journalists' union to its founder, from the artists' union to its friend." The Vilna Troupe's banner read, "On the path between two worlds, a last greeting to Sh. An-sky." One banner said, "From the Jewish Folksong to the Great Jewish Folk Soul." Following them was a hearse, then a group of friends including two Bundists, Sofia Dubnova and Medem's wife Gina, carrying a banner from Simon Dubnov. The political delegations that came next included, as Shabad noticed, a startling combination of unions and parties, Socialists and Zionists of every stripe, "black-and-red and black-and-white mourning banners intertwined." Last were the schoolchildren in the upper grades from Jewish primary schools.[72] He was buried in the Warsaw Jewish cemetery under the *ohel Peretz,* the monument where Peretz and Dinezon already lay. Over his life, An-sky had adapted to one environment after another, finding friends and followers in different places. The outpouring of emotion at his funeral was a sign that he had succeeded again, that the Jews of Vilna and Warsaw accepted him in the guise in which he had come to them, as a Jewish activist, even a "great Jewish folk soul." If this restless soul could have seen his own funeral, he might have been satisfied at last.

Epilogue

I**T IS REMARKABLE** how many of the projects that An-sky left unfinished were in fact completed and how many of the complex requests he made in his will were carried out. *The Dybbuk,* never performed in his lifetime, was staged in Yiddish in Warsaw by the Vilna Troupe as a commemoration to its author on December 9, 1920, his *shloshim,* under Dovid Herman, the director An-sky had preferred. To everyone's surprise, the production was a raging success that played for years and established the company's reputation. Two years later in Moscow, the Habima studio premiered a Hebrew production of the play, under the direction of Evgeny Vakhtangov. Again, the play was an unexpected success, attracting audiences who did not even understand the language. It became the company's signature piece during its international tours and after its 1926 move to Palestine. These initial productions were followed by films, operas, ballets, and stage versions in many languages. Kacyzne finished An-sky's incomplete play *Day and Night. Destruction of Galicia* was published in full in Yiddish in 1921 and in Hebrew in 1929, in fact by Stybel, after its move to Berlin. Zhitlowsky edited the Yiddish *Collected Writings* that An-sky had described in his will and published them, in fifteen volumes, in the 1920s.[1]

As an SR, An-sky was forgotten in Bolshevik Russia, but once the Soviet Union began to fall apart, scholars, translators, and curators set to work again finishing his projects and bringing him, like the dybbuk, back from the dead. Objects and photographs from the expeditions, unearthed in the St. Petersburg ethnographic museum, were featured in a 1992 exhibit and published in catalogs. An-sky had brought his album of Jewish graphic art near completion before he had to abandon it in the fall of 1918, never returning Bialik's haggadah; the plates from the project were found and published in 1994 and again in 2001 along with the article by Efros. The original musical recordings from the expeditions, on wax cylinders, were discovered in Kiev and cataloged, and some of them began to be released on compact discs after 1997. A cache of expedition photographs, found in 2001 in a St. Petersburg apartment, was displayed and then published. His ethnographic questionnaire, translated into Russian by a new generation of Jewish ethnographers, was used when they returned to the places he had visited. An-sky found audiences outside Russia as well: starting in 1992, English translations of many of his major works appeared.[2]

An-sky constructed his literary and public personas over the course of his life in terms drawn from folklore, and after his death, friends and scholars completed this work as well. His favorite folk hero was the rabbi who argues with God; until the end of his life, he too tried to use the written and spoken word to end injustice, offering first one argument, then another.[3] Most often, as when he denounced anti-Jewish rumors, his efforts were in vain. Only occasionally, as when he pleaded with the Vilna Bolsheviks for the lives of the counterfeiters, could he thwart an evil decree.

The prophet Elijah offered a different folkloric persona. Eastern European Jews believed that any traveler may be Elijah in disguise, bringing news or gifts to reward those who treat him well. As Elijah moves from the "true world" to the human world, so An-sky moved between worlds in disguise. Accepted equally among traditional Jews, radicals, and the Russian liberal intelligentsia, Galician Jews and the Russian soldiers whom they feared, he too revealed his identity only when he chose. The solitary life that he treated sometimes as a marker of revolutionary purity and sometimes as a personal tragedy signaled his otherworldly status. With the success of *The Dybbuk*, people began to compare An-sky to the Messenger, a variant of Elijah, and to see him as bringing news and gifts from the "true world" of the past, making visible a vanished way of life. This persona accounted for the wave of interest in An-sky since the 1990s, as he and his writings seemed to offer a view back into the prerevolutionary Jewish world.[4]

Post-Soviet scholars' and artists' enthusiasm for An-sky has transformed him into yet another folkloric hero. He endured so many failures: unrequited loves, lost manuscripts, a lifelong allegiance to a doomed political party. The writings of even his closest friends reveal gentle scorn for his talents and amused condescension for the emotions that an amateur event such as the soldiers' concert produced in him. Like Ivan the Fool, the bumbling youngest son of Russian fairytales, An-sky did everything wrong—only, in the end, to be revealed as having done everything right. He, not his cleverer brothers, was granted the kingdom and the princess.[5] An-sky transformed his emotions into art that could speak to audiences that he himself had never seen. His need to be all things to all people, which led him to revise his identity and his writings so tirelessly, allowed him to communicate more broadly than anyone would have suspected.

An-sky gave himself passionately to causes that appeared mutually exclusive: Russian peasants and Hasidic Jews; Kadets and SRs; internationalist socialism and Jewish nationalism; Jabotinskian Zionism and the revival of Jewish life in the Russian Empire; literary careers in Russian, Yiddish, and even Hebrew. His contemporaries, amazed by the variety of his contacts, imagined him—with his famous ability to win anyone over—as a conduit into lives they could not access on their own. Through him, they hoped to penetrate the worlds of the peasants and miners of the Donets Basin, the Hasids of Volynia and Podolia, the leaders of Russian publishing in Petersburg, and even the Bolshevik commissars. They saw this restless traveler as something like a train window, whose transparency could reveal any number of striking views.

Both An-sky and others sometimes imposed a narrative framework on his multiple commitments by making his biography a tale of return. When he went south and worked among peasants and miners, he was acting out the Russian Populist script of the penitent intellectual who goes to the countryside to repay his debt to the narod. When he began to publish in Yiddish, to edit Jewish-themed journals, to lead his ethnographic expedition, and finally to aid the embattled Jews of Galicia, he was acting out the Jewish nationalist script of the repentant assimilator who realizes that his true loyalties lie with his own people. An-sky recognized the power of these narratives of return and used both of them frequently, in spite of all the evidence that he rarely abandoned his earlier convictions for newer ones, and that his periodic attempts to actually live like someone other than the itinerant cosmopolitan he really was were, like his marriages, halfhearted and short-lived. The "Going to the People" movement in the summer of 1874 revealed the barriers keeping students and peasants apart; similar barriers stood between An-sky and all the Russian and Jewish objects of his ethnographic gaze.

Much of An-sky's career can be seen as an attempt to break down these barriers. As an SR propagandist, a Zionist speaker, and a Jewish community organizer, he inspired audiences with visions of revolution and renewal that would unite traditional people and intellectuals. In his editing, writing, and speaking on literature and folklore, he worked to help the folk and the intelligentsia (both Russian and Jewish) understand each other and thereby to bring them closer step by step. In his ethnographic expedition, he tried to return to the folk through the ecstatic modes of Jewish mysticism. Only in his best writing did he acknowledge the contradictions at the heart of the fantasy of reconciliation. Most of his writing was, as everyone knew, rushed, stylistically flat, badly edited, written in cafés and published piecemeal in newspapers, but in works such as "Mendel the Turk," *Pioneers,* "Ashmedai," *On a New Course,* "Tower in Rome," *The Dybbuk,* and his memoirs, including *Destruction of Galicia,* he powerfully described people who—like Chekhov's characters—ultimately fail to perform heroic roles, to communicate, or even to understand themselves. With its lack of resolution, his literary work displayed the contradictions in the notion of return that was so central to his own literary persona.

In all his endeavors, An-sky retained certain abiding concerns. He always wanted to communicate with as broad an audience as possible, to find "soil" for his activity, where he could be sure that his words would have an impact. He saw the objects of his inquiry from the outside, in historical perspective, and himself as mediator—between urban readers and peasants, or Russians and Jews. He published enthusiastically, wherever he could, in whatever languages were available. If he could reach more readers by translating his work into Yiddish (or Hebrew), or by republishing old works in new forms, or by publishing in several newspapers simultaneously, he did so. When he got access to new media—photography, magic lantern pictures, drama, museum exhibits—he experimented eagerly. His propagandist's urge to reach as many people as possible governed his Jewish nationalism, driven by the desire to create a new Jewish culture that would make sense and appeal broadly. His frankly heroic aesthetics also distinguished him. He believed that people wanted to be inspired by those whose willingness to challenge injustice was worthy of imitation. At the same time, he grappled with the limitations of propaganda and of the heroic gesture, wondering how to know whether a message had reached its audience, and how to recognize a real hero.

People are motivated, An-sky thought, more by emotional attraction than ideological conviction. His own actions and beliefs, in their bewildering variety, show the truth of his insight, and his inconsistency opens a window onto the intellectual life of an era when people's choices were less consistent than we customarily imagine. Even while he was typical of his age, though, An-sky was also anomalous. He saw his contemporaries, as he titled one of his volumes, "From the Side," as a Jew observing Russians and as a wanderer observing the settled lives of others.[6] His emotional pattern of fervor and flight kept him on the move, allowing him to assume new identities in response to new circumstances, to intuit the desires of new interlocutors and speak in the voice they wanted to hear. No matter how eagerly they listened, though, he was never completely satisfied; he always sought the reassurance he could find in new patrons, friends, protégés, publishers, and ethnographic subjects, in the grateful beneficiaries of his aid work, and in the admiration of bigger and bigger crowds. His frustrated passions, like those of his hero Khonen, pushed him to assume new forms, and in those forms his voice could live on after his death.

Archives and Abbreviations

Archives

Where possible, archival citations are abbreviated as *collection number:description number (opis'):unit number, page number,* or as *collection number:unit number, page number.*

Bet Bialik	Bet Bialik archives, Tel Aviv
GARF	State Archive of the Russian Federation (Police Department Collection), Moscow
Hoover	Hoover Institution Archives (Nikolaevsky and Paris Okhrana Collections), Stanford, Calif.
IR NBUV	Vernadsky National Library of Ukraine Manuscript Division (Jewish Section), Kiev
IRLI	Institute of Russian Literature, or Pushkin House, St. Petersburg
JNUL	Jewish National and University Libraries (Shvadron Collection), Jerusalem
RGALI	Russian State Archive of Literature and Art, Moscow
RGIA	Russian State History Archive, St. Petersburg
RNB	Russian National Library (Manuscript Division), St. Petersburg
TsGIAU	Central State Historical Archive of Ukraine, Kiev
YIVO	YIVO Institute for Jewish Research, New York

Other Abbreviations

I refer to the subject as Rappoport when citing his correspondence, An-ski for his Yiddish writings, and An-sky for his Russian writings.

Bialik   Rappoport's correspondence with Chaim Nakhman Bialik, unless indicated otherwise cited from M. Ungerfeld, "Tsum hundertstn geboyrn-tog fun Sh. Anski (Sh. Rapoport)," *Goldene keyt* (1964) 48.

DF   *Der fraynd*

Diary 1   Sh. Rappoport, Diary, 1/1–3/8/1915, RGALI 2583:1:5.

Diary 2   Sh. Rappoport, Diary, 9/9–10/10/1915, RGALI 2583:1:6.

Dinezon   Rappoport's correspondence with Yankev Dinezon, unless indicated otherwise cited from *Fun Yankev Dinezon's arkhiv: Briv fun idishe shriftshteler tsu Yankev Dinezon,* ed. Sh. Rozenfeld (Warsaw, 1921).

DNL   *Dos naye leben*

DOW   S. Ansky, *The Dybbuk and Other Writings,* ed. David Roskies (New York, 1992).

EE   *Evreiskaia entsiklopediia* (St. Petersburg, 1906–1913).

EM   *Evreiskii Mir*

EO   *Evreiskoe Obozrenie*

ES   *Evreiskaia Starina*

Gintsburg   Rappoport's correspondence with Vladimir Gintsburg, cited from *Arkhivna spadshchina Semena An-s'kogo u fondakh natsional'noi biblioteki Ukrainy imeni V. I. Vernads'kogo,* ed. Irina Serheyeva (Kiev, 2006).

GS   Sh. An-ski, *Gezamelte shriftn in fuftsen bender* (New York, 1920s) (bibliographic records list it as 1920, 1928, 1922–1925, and 1925–1929).

Gurevich   Chaim Zhitlowsky, "Sh. Z. Anski in der kharakteristike fun zayn fraynd, Shmuel Gurevich," typescript at YIVO 208.

IR   Manuscript Division

IYP   Index to Yiddish Periodicals, http://yiddish-periodicals.huji.ac.il/.

LT   *Lodzher tageblat*

M   Letters from Rappoport to Roza Monoszon, unless indicated otherwise cited from *Roza Nikolaevna Ettinger* (Jerusalem, 1980) and *Novyi Zhurnal* (1967) 87, 89.

N   S. Ansky, *The Enemy at His Pleasure: A Journey through the Jewish Pale of Settlement During World War I,* ed. and trans. Joachim Neugroschel (New York, 2002).

Pogroms   *Pogroms: Anti-Jewish Violence in Modern Russian History,* ed. John Klier and Shlomo Lambroza (New York, 1992).

PP   Jonathan Frankel, *Prophecy and Politics: Socialism, Nationalism, and the Russian Jews, 1862–1917* (New York, 1981).

PSS   *Polnoe sobranie sochinenii*

RB   *Russkoe Bogatstvo*

RO   Manuscript Division

SAA   Semyon Akimovich An-sky or Sh. An-ski (for published materials)

SAR   Shloyme-Zanvl Aronovich Rappoport (for archival materials)

SS   S. A. An-sky, *Sobranie sochinenii* (St. Petersburg, c. 1911–1913).

Uspensky   Rappoport's letters to Gleb Uspensky, cited from IRLI 3.

Worlds   *The Worlds of S. An-sky: A Russian Jewish Intellectual at the Turn of the Century,* ed. Gabriella Safran and Steven J. Zipperstein (Stanford, Calif., 2006).

YE   *The YIVO Encyclopedia of Jewish Life in Eastern Europe* (New Haven, Conn., 2008).

Z   Letters from Rappoport to Zhitlowsky, all at YIVO 208; some published as "Briv fun Sh. An-ski tsu Chaim Zhitlovski," ed. Mikhail Krutikov, *YIVO-Bleter* 2 (1992); one published as "'One of the most magnificent moments in human history': S. An-sky's Return to Russia in December 1905," ed. Gabriella Safran and Irina Denischenko, in *Sankirtos: Studies in Russian and Eastern European Literature, Society and Culture: In Honor of Tomas Venclova,* ed. Robert Bird, Lazar Fleishman, and Fedor Poljakov (Frankfurt am Main, 2008).

ZFML   Chaim Zhitlowsky, *Zikhroynes fun mayn lebn* (New York, 1935).

Notes

Prologue

1. For my opening gambit, and for much else, I am indebted to Steven J. Zipperstein. See "Introduction: An-sky and the Guises of Modern Jewish Culture," in *Worlds*, 1.
2. Diary 1, 2/7–2/8/1915; GS 4:187, 190.
3. Diary 1, 2/8/1915.
4. GS 4:190–191.
5. The evidence from An-sky supports the conclusions of recent historians and theorists of anthropology that the geographically contiguous Russian empire, with its centuries-long history of ethnic encounters and its anthropology developed in part by radical intellectuals exiled to the peripheries, created ethnographic traditions distinct from those of Western Europe. An-sky's descriptions of others in particular had a radically self-effacing tenor, more apparent in his literacy work and his wartime aid work than his more conventional ethnographic work in Ukraine. See James Clifford, *The Predicament of Culture: Twentieth-Century Ethnography, Literature, and Art* (Cambridge, Mass., 1988); *Writing Culture: The Poetics and Politics of Ethnography*, ed. Clifford and George Marcus (Berkeley, 1986); Johannes Fabian, *Time and the Other: How Anthropology Makes Its Object* (New York, 1983); Francine Hirsch, *Empire of Nations: Ethnographic Knowledge and the Making of the Soviet Union* (Ithaca, 2005); Dana Prescott Howell, *The Development of Soviet Folkloristics* (New York, 1992); Sergei Kan, *Lev Shternberg: Anthropologist, Russian Socialist, Jewish Activist* (Lincoln, Nebr., 2009); Barbara Kirshenblatt-Gimblett, *Destination Culture: Tourists, Museums, and Heritage* (Berkeley, 1998); Nathaniel Knight, *Constructing the Science of Nationality: Ethnography in Mid-Nineteenth-Century Russia* (Columbia PhD Dissertation, 1994); Marina Mogil'ner, *Homo imperii: Istoriia fizicheskoi antropologii v Rossii*

(Moscow, 2008); Yuri Slezkine, *Arctic Mirrors: Russia and the Small Peoples of the North* (Ithaca, 1994); Nikolai Ssorin-Chaikov, "Political Fieldwork, Ethnographic Exile, and State Theory: Peasant Socialism and Anthropology in Late-Nineteenth-Century Russia," *A New History of Anthropology*, ed. Henrika Kuklick (Malden, Mass., 2008); George Stocking, *Victorian Anthropology* (New York, 1987). An-sky's concerns anticipated those of today's aid workers and activists: he believed in the power of language to liberate, though he knew words served oppressors as well; he wanted to be a hero, but feared self-deception; he was painfully aware of his own limitations, and succeeded best when he took satisfaction in individual encounters. See James Dawes, *That the World May Know: Bearing Witness to Atrocity* (Cambridge, Mass., 2007), 119.

6. Cited in F. Shargorodskaia, "O nasledii An-skogo," ES (1924) 11:306; P. Ia. Chaadaev, PSS (Moscow, 1991) 1:323–324.

7. "Zaveshchanie An-skogo," ES (1924) 11:312–313. I urge those interested in more detailed textual analysis to read the literary-critical articles I have published elsewhere: "An-sky in Liozno: 'Sins of Youth' and the Archival Diary," in *Violence and Jewish Daily Life in the East European Borderlands: Essays in Honor of John D. Klier*, ed. Eugene Avrutin and Harriet Murav (Brighton, forthcoming); "'Reverse Marranism,' Translatability, and the Theory and Practice of Secular Jewish Culture in Russian," in *Jewish Literatures and Cultures: Context and Intertext*, ed. Anita Norich and Yaron Eliav (Providence, 2008); "Revolutionary Rabbis: Hasidic Legend and the Hero of Words," in *Sacred Stories: Religion and Spirituality in Modern Russia*, ed. Mark D. Steinberg and Heather J. Coleman (Bloomington, Ind., 2007); "'The Trace of a Falling Sun': S. An-sky on Zionism and Apocalypse," in *The Russian Word in the Land of Israel, the Jewish Word in Russia*, vol. 17, *Jews and Slavs*, ed. Vladimir Khazan and Wolf Moskovich (Jerusalem, 2007); "Jews as Siberian Natives: Primitivism and S. An-sky's *Dybbuk*," *Modernity/Modernism* (11/2006); "An-sky in 1892: The Jew and the Petersburg Myth," in *Worlds*; "Zrelishche krovoprolitia: S. An-skii na granitsakh," in *Mirovoi krizis 1914–1920 godov i sud'ba vostochnoevropeiskogo evreistva*, ed. Oleg Budnitsky (Moscow, 2005); "S. An-sky and Father Gapon: On the Russian Revolutionary Origins of *The Dybbuk*," in *Word, Music, History: A Festschrift for Caryl Emerson*, ed. Gabriella Safran, Lazar Fleishman, and Michael Wachtel (Stanford, 2005); "Dancing with Death and Salvaging Jewish Culture in *Austeria* and *The Dybbuk*," *Slavic Review* (Winter 2000) 59:4.

8. Shmuel Rozhansky, ed., *Sh. An-ski: Oysgeklibene shriftn* (Buenos Aires, 1964), 18; Sylvie Anne Goldberg, "Paradigmatic Times: An-sky's Two Worlds," in *Worlds*, 45; cf. Yankev Shatzky, "S. An-ski der meshulekh fun folklor," *Jewish Book Annual* (1950–1951), 9.

1. A Bad Influence

1. Arkady Podlipsky, *Evrei v Vitebske* (Vitebsk, 2004), 19; Moshe Zhitlovski, "Beveit horai," in *Vitebsk*, ed. Barukh Karu (Tel Aviv, 1957), 147; on the

Vitebsk bathhouse, Bella Chagall, *Burning Lights* (New York, 1946), 25–39; Z 4/28(5/10)/1891.

2. Dan Miron, "The Literary Image of the Shtetl," *The Image of the Shtetl and Other Studies of Modern Jewish Literary Imagination* (Syracuse, N.Y., 2000), 38; B. Chagall.

3. "Vitebsk," EE 5:640–647; ZFML 1:152; Benjamin Harshav, *Marc Chagall and His Times: A Documentary Narrative* (Stanford, Calif., 2004), 26ff; Podlipsky, 14; Chagall, "Chagall's First Autobiography," in Harshav, 87.

4. Podlipsky, 38; Fanni Shvartsman, *Moia sud'ba: Vospominaniia* (Paris, 1964), 19; M. Zhitlovski, 147, 154; ZFML 1:153; Aleksandra Shatskikh, *Vitebsk: The Life of Art,* trans. Katherine Foshko Tsan (New Haven, Conn., 2007), 3, 251.

5. B. Chagall, chap. 1; "Chashniki," EE 15:814; ChaeRan Y. Freeze, *Jewish Marriage and Divorce in Imperial Russia* (Hanover, 2002), 242; M. Zhitlovski, 151.

6. ZFML 1:18, 1:249, 2:18–19; SAR to Gleb Uspensky, 5/2/1888.

7. Citations refer to SAA, "V 'Omute,' " SS 5:3, 5:31; adapted from "In the Tavern," trans. Robert Szulkin, in DOW.

8. SS 5:43–44; DOW 64–65; "Ptichka," http://xbase.ru/guestbook/index.php ?login=bird5; "Papiroska," http:/www.ark.ru/ins/zapoved/another/rus13.html. The song ends "korol' chervenyi," but Aksinia sings "krytl' chyvychainyi."

9. ZFML 1:237–241, 2:18; Z 10/17/1887; Samuil Gurevich to SAR, 6/30/1910, IR IFO NBUV 339:389; Maria-Mariasa Zeveleva Reinus was born in 1866, per *Alfavitnyi ukazatel' k rozysknomu spisku i tsirkuliaram departamenta politsii, 2 July 1900* (St. Petersburg, 1900), Hoover Okhrana XIIId(1):158:5.

10. ZFML 1:187–190; Shvartsman, 18, 25; Z 10/17/1887; Arkady Zel'tser, *Evrei sovetskoi provintsii: Vitebsk i mestechki, 1917–1941* (Moscow, 2006), 9, 277; "Delo . . . po nabliudeniiu za formal'nym doznaniem o meshch. Shliome Rappoport, ob. po 132 st., 1/26/1907," GARF 102(DP):7:102:82, 3.

11. ZFML 1:142, 240; M. L. Lilienblum, *Ktavim otobiografiim* (Jerusalem, 1970), 1; David Frishman, "Moyshe Leyb Lilienblum," *Ale verk* (New York, 1938) 4:43.

12. Victor Hugo, *Oeuvres complètes* (Paris, 1985), Roman 2:982; ZFML 1:151–152, 205; SAA, "Evreiskoe narodnoe tvorchestvo," *Perezhitoe* (1908) 1:276.

13. D. Pisarev, "Bazarov," PSS (Moscow, 2000) 3:201; Dmitry Pisarev, "Bazarov," in Ivan Turgenev, *Fathers and Sons,* trans. Michael Katz (New York, 1996), 197, 218.

14. ZFML 1:17ff.

15. ZFML 2:20; Z 6/16/1888.

16. ZFML 1:14–16, 25, 250–252, 2:19; he wrote this play between 1879 and 1883, when Yiddish theater was legal. David Fishman, "The Politics of Yiddish in Tsarist Russia," *The Rise of Modern Yiddish Culture* (Pittsburgh, 2005); John Klier, "Exit, Pursued by a Bear: Russian Administrators and the Ban on Yiddish Theater in Imperial Russia," in *Yiddish Theater: New Approaches,* ed. Joel Berkowitz (Oxford, 2003), 159–174.

17. ZFML 1:254, 255, 2:19.

18. ZFML 1:249; Aron and Chana may have been divorced; on Jewish divorce, see Freeze; SAR, "Brat gvira," "Zadacha," "Lavochka," IR IFO NBUV 339:54, 59, 61; Psevdonim, "Istoriia odnogo semeistva," *Voskhod* (1884), nos. 9–12.

19. SAA, "V evreiskoi sem'e," RB (1900) 6:125–163; SAA, "Khane di kekhin," GS 7:7–58; SAA, "V meshchanskoi sem'e," SS 1:117, 118; Freeze, 158, 161, 232–234.

20. He later repaired his relationship with Chaim's father. ZFML 1:240; Z 6/16/1888, 1899 (Otkladyval ia pisat' tebe), 1899 (stationery of Grande taverne du crocodile).

21. Gurevich, 15.

22. ZFML 1:139–142, 2:20; Israel-Ze'ev Volfson, "Yidishe institutsies un tsionistishe bavegung," in *Vitebsk amol: Geshikhte, zikhroynes, khurbn,* ed. H. A. Abramson (New York, 1956), 106–107, 129–130; EE 5:645.

23. SAA, "Mendel Turok," SS 1; GS 7; DOW 101, 102.

24. On Chabad in Shloyme-Zanvl's youth, Aaron Wertheim, *Law and Custom in Hasidism,* trans. Shmuel Himelstein (Hoboken, N.J., 1992), 340–341; Avrum M. Ehrlich, *Leadership in the HaBaD Movement: A Critical Evaluation of HaBaD Leadership, History, and Succession* (Northvale, N.J., 2000), 211–235.

25. Harshav, 22, 23–24, makes these arguments about Chagall; on Mekler, see Jackie Wullschlager, *Chagall: A Biography* (New York, 2008).

26. SAR, "Dnevnik melameda," IR IFO NBUV 339:73, 15ob, 16ob; "Liozno," EE 10:316.

27. "Dnevnik melameda," 10, 10ob. See Safran, "An-sky in Liozno;" a section of the diary is published as "Fun Sh. An-skis togbukh," ed. Mikhail Krutikov, *Forverts* (5/27/2005), 12.

28. "Dnevnik melameda," 11, 11ob.

29. Ibid., 11ob–12.

30. P. Marek, "Bor'ba dvukh vospitanii, iz istorii prosviashcheniia evreev v Rossii (1864–1873)," *Perezhitoe* 1:125; "Dnevnik melameda," 12ob.

31. SAA, "Grekhi iunosti i grekhi starosti," EM (1910) 10–11; "Grekhi iunosti," SS 2; "Khatos neurim," GS 10; SS 2:247; DOW 70, 71, 73.

32. Hans Rogger, "Conclusion and Overview," *Pogroms,* 328; Erich Haberer, in "Cosmopolitanism, Antisemitism, and Populism: A Reappraisal of the Russian and Jewish Response to the Pogroms of 1881–1882," *Pogroms,* 125, argues that by 1884 it was in bad taste to welcome pogroms; cf. I. Michael Aronson, "The Anti-Jewish Pogroms in Russia in 1881," and Moshe Mishkinsky, "Black Repartition and the Pogroms of 1881–1882," *Pogroms;* "Iz Gor'kovskoi biografii: Pis'ma k Volkhovskomu i Zhitlovskomu," in *Materialy po istorii russkoi i sovetskoi kul'tury iz arkhiva Guverovskogo Instituta,* ed. Lazar Fleishman (Stanford, Calif., 1992) 5:124.

33. Leon Simon, *Moses Leib Lilienblum* (Cambridge, 1912); DOW 73, 74.

34. *Vitebsk amol,* 226; Gurevich, 5.

35. Z. Reyzen, "Sh. An-ski (biografishe notitsn)," *Lebn* (12/1920) 7–8:44; ZFML 1:32; Rudolf Rocker, *In shturem* (London, 1952), 39.

36. Gurevich, 21, 22; ZFML 1:25–26; "Istoriia odnogo semeistva," 9:136, 10:7, 10:11–12; SAA, "Pasynki," SS 1.
37. "Istoriia odnogo semeistva," 11:68.
38. Arkady Shul'man, "Gleb Uspenskii iz Talmud-Tory," *Mishpokhe* (1999) 5:41; S. Tsinberg, "K iubileiu S. A. An-skogo," EM (1/8/1910) 1:60; Alyssa Quint, "'Yiddish Literature for the Masses?' A Reconsideration of Who Read What in Jewish Eastern Europe," *AJS Review* (2005) 29:1:79, 81, 82–83; she cites Shomer, *Di zisene frau oder dos farkoyfte kind: eyn vundersheyner roman* (Vilne, 1882), cited in Meyer-Isser Pines, *Di geshikhte fun der yudisher literatur bizn yor 1890* (Warsaw, 1911).
39. ZFML 1:33.
40. SAR to Gurevich, 12/16/1883 (filed at YIVO with Z); EE 12:144.

2. To the Salt Mines

1. Lazarev, "Zadachi i tseli russko-evreiskoi literatury," *Voskhod* (1885) 6:11.
2. Chana Rappoport was dead by 1885. Moyshe Shalit, "Naye protim vegn Sh. An-ski," *Literarishe bleter* 340:838. Rappoport's 1884 story concludes, "Oh, mother! If you could only rise from the grave and see what has become of us!" (SAR, "Lavochka," IR IFO NBUV 339:39). His niece Anna, presumably named after Chana, was seventeen or eighteen in 1902, thus born in 1885 or 1886; if Chana died in 1884, then she was probably the first grandchild born after her death. "Prestupnaia propaganda rabochim i rasprostranenie sredi nikh prestupnykh vosstanii na Orlovskoi gubernii," GARF 102(DP):00(1898): N5:42B, 46; ZFML 1:36.
3. *Vitebsk amol*, 249; Shalit, "Naye protim," 839.
4. David Weinberg, *Between Tradition and Modernity: Haim Zhitlowski, Simon Dubnow, Ahad Ha-Am, and the Shaping of Modern Jewish Identity* (New York, 1996), 89–90. Zhitlowsky discusses the Tula relatives, ZFML 1:269–271; EE 15:44.
5. ZFML 1:40; Cathy Frierson, *Peasant Icons: Representations of Rural People in Nineteenth-Century Russia* (New York, 1993); Jeffrey Burds, *Peasant Dreams and Market Politics: Labor Migration and the Russian Village, 1861– 1905* (Pittsburgh, Penn., 1998).
6. Richard Pipes, "*Narodnichestvo*: A Semantic Inquiry," *Slavic Review* (September 1964), 450N40, 458; ZFML 1:13; A. Walicki, *The Controversy over Capitalism: Studies in the Social Philosophy of the Russian Populists* (Oxford, 1969); Richard Wortman, *The Crisis of Russian Populism* (London, 1967); Daniel Field, "Peasants and Propagandists in the Russian Movement to the People of 1874," *Journal of Modern History* (September 1987), 59.
7. PP 259; Z 6/16/1888; ZFML 1:39; Norman Naimark, *Terrorists and Social Democrats: The Russian Revolutionary Movement under Alexander III* (Cambridge, Mass., 1983), 5, 47.
8. Naimark, *Terrorists*, 39.
9. Hans Rogger, *Jewish Policies and Right-Wing Politics in Imperial Russia* (Berkeley, Calif., 1986), 6–7, chap. 5.

10. I. Michael Aronson, "The Anti-Jewish Pogroms," 46; Iu. Gessen, "Graf N. P. Ignat'ev i 'Vremennye pravila' o evreiakh 3 maia 1882 goda," *Pravo* (1908) 30:1632, cited in Rogger, 135–136; Moshe Mishkinsky, "'Black Repartition,'" 64; PP 99; Erich Haberer, "Cosmopolitanism, Antisemitism and Populism: A Reappraisal of the Russian and Jewish Response to the Pogroms of 1881–1882," in *Pogroms,* 103, 124.

11. Mikhailovsky, PSS (SPB, 1909) 3:692, cited in James Billington, *Mikhailovsky and Russian Populism* (Oxford, 1958), 95; Walicki, 77.

12. G. I. Uspensky, "Vlast' zemli," PSS 8:25, 27; SAA, *Ocherki narodnoi literatury* (St. Petersburg, 1894), 143–144; Linda J. Ivanits, *Russian Folk Belief* (New York, 1989), 15.

13. ZFML 40–41.

14. On 3/16/1885 he was at Izium station, Donetsk province; on 3/31/1885, at Lozovaia-Pavlovsk station. SAR, Yiddish story, Five-act play, IR IFO NBUV 339:62, 66. Charters Wynn, *Workers, Strikes, and Pogroms: The Donbass-Dnepr Bend in Late Imperial Russia, 1870–1905* (Princeton, N.J., 1992), 59–62, 112.

15. Z 11/9/1886, 10/17/1887, 6/16/1888.

16. SAR, "Na solianoi kopi," IR IFO NBUV 339:87, 2, 3; Anton Chekhov, "Perekati-pole," PSS (Moscow, 1974) 6:263.

17. "Na solianoi kopi," 12–13, 14–15, 16–17, 25.

18. SAA, "In zalts-grobn," pt. 2, *Grininke boymelakh* (1/1920) 3:92. This is Ansky's only extant publication on his work in the mill.

19. Gleb Ivanovich Uspensky, "Novye narodnye stishki," *Russkie Vedomosti* (4/23/1889), no. 110, reprinted in G. I. Uspensky, SS (Moscow, 1957) 8:562–564; S. Vid'bin, "Temnaia sila," IRLI 313:4:59; N. I. Prutskov, "V poiskakh putei v budushchee," in *Voprosy metodologii istoriko-literaturnykh issledovanii,* ed. Prutskov (Leningrad, 1981), 220.

20. SAA, "Ocherk kamennougol'noi promyshlennosti na iuge Rossii," RB (1892) 11:1–2, esp. 2:9–11; Aleksandr Fenin, *Coal and Politics in Late Imperial Russia: Memoirs of a Russian Mining Engineer,* trans. Alexandre Fediaevsky, ed. Susan McCaffrey (DeKalb, Ill., 1990), 52; Wynn, 57, 89–93.

21. SAA, "Ocherk kamennougol'noi," 1:9, 18, 2:10–11.

22. SAA, *Di ershte shvalb,* GS 12:19; trans. from Roskies, "The Maskil as Folk Hero," *Prooftexts: A Journal of Jewish Literary History* (5/1990) 10, 2:225.

23. See Willard Sunderland, "Peasants Pioneering: Russian Peasant Settlers Describe Colonization and the Eastern Frontier, 1880s–1910s," *Journal of Social History* (2001) 34, 4:895–922; S. Vid'bin, "Na novye zemli," *Trud: Vestnik literatury i nauki* (1–2/1890), 35.

24. "Na novye zemli," 35–36; cf. Aleksandr L'vov, "Emigratsiia iudeistvuiushchikh v Palestinu," in *Evreiskii muzei,* ed. V. A. Dymshits and V. E. Kel'ner (St. Petersburg, 2004).

25. "Na novye zemli," 37–38, 39, 40–41, 43–44, 46, 158; cf. Burds, 117.

26. "Na novye zemli," 157.

27. Z 11/9/1886; SAA, *Narod i kniga: Opyt kharakteristiki narodnogo chitatelia* (Moscow, 1913), 65–66; Howell, 19.

28. Ben Eklof, *Russian Peasant Schools: Officialdom, Village Culture, and Popular Pedagogy, 1864–1914* (Berkeley, Calif., 1986); Jeffrey Brooks, *When Russia Learned to Read: Literacy and Popular Culture, 1861–1917* (Princeton, N.J., 1985), 295–356.
29. Z 11/9/1886, 4/7/1888; cf. Uspensky to SAR, 5/3/1889, PSS 9:556, 738; ZFML 1:43–52; *Ocherki narodnoi literatury*, 8.
30. Ibid., 37, 38.
31. Ibid., 149.
32. Z 11/9/1886; L. N. Tolstoi, PSS (Moscow, 1957) 23:39–40.
33. Z 7/13/1888; V. M. Chernov, *V Partii Sotsialistov-Revoliutsionerov. Vospominaniia o vos'mi liderakh*, ed. A. P. Novikov and K. Khuser (St. Petersburg, 2007), 118–119; Roza Ettinger, *Roza Nikolaevna Ettinger* (Jerusalem, 1980), 11.
34. ZFML 51; Z 6/16/1888; PP 267–268.
35. Z 6/16/1888.
36. SAA, "Dozhd'," SS 5:186–187.
37. *Five Sisters: Women against the Tsar,* ed. Barbara Engel and Clifford Rosenthal (New York, 1974), 71, 109, 211; Brooks, 347; ZFML 1:39, 52.
38. SAR to Uspensky, 1/9/1889, in Uspensky, PSS 14:664; "Delo D. P. o meshchanine Shleme Aronov. Rappoporte," GARF 102(DP)1902: 782(724/907):1, 2, 3; GARF 102(DP):3(1890):328, 2ob., 18–20.
39. "Delo D. P. o meshchanine Shleme Aronov. Rappoporte," 6, 4, 18; Naimark, *Terrorists*, 28, 188, 200–201.
40. ZFML 1:52–53.
41. Z 8/29/1889.
42. Z 6/16/1888.
43. Z 11/9/1886, 10/17/1887; SAR to Uspensky 5/2/1888.
44. SAR to Mikhailovsky, 10/19/1887, IRLI 181:1:578, 1–4.
45. SAR to Uspensky, 4/1888, cited in N. V. Alekseeva, "G. I. Uspenskii, russkaia narodnaia pesnia i ee sobirateli," *Uchenye zapiski LGU, seriia filologicheskikh nauk* (Leningrad, 1949) 16:208–209.
46. Uspensky to SAR, 5/26/1888, 4/18/188, PSS 14:133, 121.
47. SAR to Uspensky, 6/11/1888.
48. Z 6/16/1888; Henrietta Mondry, in "Gleb Ivanovich Uspensky," in *Russian Literature in the Age of Realism/Dictionary of Literary Biography,* ed. Alyssa Dinega Gillespie (Detroit, Mich., 2003), 277, identifies it as schizophrenia; O. Aptekman, *Gleb Ivanovich Uspenskii* (Moscow, 1922), 89–91; Uspensky, PSS 14:181, 264, 372; G. I. Uspensky, "Novye narodnye pesni (Iz derevenskikh zametok)," *Russkii Vestnik* (4/23/1889) 110, republished as "Novye narodnye stishki (Iz derevenskikh zametok)," SS 8; Uspensky apologized on 6/9/1889, PSS 14:313; Uspensky to SAR, 12/9/1889, PSS 9:605, 606; Vid'bin, "Na novye zemli"; he tried "Nikolai Vitebinsky" in 1885; SAR, Five-act play, IR IFO NBUV 339:66; Alekseeva, 205N1.
49. Z 11/9/1886; Benjamin Nathans, *Beyond the Pale: The Jewish Encounter with Late Imperial Russia* (Berkeley, Calif., 2002), chap. 2; Z 8/31/1891.

3. A Revolutionary Has No Name

1. SAA to the editors of RB, "Iubilei 'Russkogo Bogatstva' v 1918 godu," ed. K. Shmidt, *Minuvshee* (1986) 1:304; ZFML 58.
2. F. M. Dostoevsky, PSS (Petrozavodsk, 2005) 6:10.
3. Written in 1890. SAR to Uspensky, 4/26/1891; Chernov, *V Partii*, 123–124.
4. Aleksei Shilov, "'Katekhizis revoliutsionera' (k istorii 'nechaevskogo dela')," *Bor'ba klassov: Istoricheskii zhurnal* (1924) 1–2:268.
5. V. G. Dmitriev, *Skryvshie svoe imia: Iz istorii psevdonimov i anonimov* (Moscow, 1970), 27, 36, 37, 38, 55, 106.
6. Ibid., 150; *Novoe Vremia*, 1/22/1910, cited in Moyshe Shalit, "Sh. An-ski loyt zayn bukh fun di tsaytungs-oysshnitn," *Fun noentn over* (Warsaw), 1 (1937), 232N.
7. Uspensky to V. A. Gol'tsev [1889], cited in Alekseeva, 195; SAR to Uspensky, 4/16/1888.
8. "An-sky Sh.," in Zalmen Reyzen, *Leksikon fun der yidisher literatur, prese un filologie* (Vilna, 1928) 1:129; ZFML 69; SAA, "Ocherk kamennougol'noi," 2:9–11; SAA, "Pokhmel'e," RB (1892) 3; SAA, "Ocherki narodnoi literatury," RB (1892) 7–10; I cite from SAA, *Ocherki narodnoi literatury* (St. Petersburg, 1894); presumably "Na torgakh," SS 5.
9. SAR to Uspensky, 2/27/1892.
10. SAA, *Rasskazy* (St. Petersburg, 1905), 271; DOW 87 (translated from a later version).
11. ZFML 57; Chernov, *V partii*, 122; S. O. Minor, "Semen Akimovich Rappoport (S. An-skii)," *Volia Rossii* (Prague) (11/17/1920) 55:4.
12. SAR to Uspensky, 4/16, 5/2/1888, IRLI 313:3:254, 6, 4, 7, 13.
13. SAR to Uspenskaia, 12/21/1898, n.d., IRLI 313:7:90, 9ob, 23ob.
14. V. E. Cheshikhin-Vetrinsky, *Gleb Ivanovich Uspenskii: Biograficheskii ocherk* (Moscow, 1929), cited in Frierson 3; Frierson, 89–100; Wortman, 61–100; Vladimir Korolenko, "O Glebe Ivanoviche Uspenskom," *Otoshedshie* (St. Petersburg, 1908), 13–14; I. N. Kubikov, *Gleb Uspensky* (Moscow, 1925), 105. Cf. Henrietta Mondry, *Pisateli-narodniki i evrei* (St. Petersburg, 2005).
15. "Vlagaet persty svoi" (in Slavonic in first person: "vlozhu persta moego"). Chernov, *V partii*, 122.
16. For a detailed analysis, see Safran, "An-ski in 1892."
17. Nathans, *Beyond the Pale,* esp. 104–107.
18. Z. Sinanni, "Di shvue" and "Tsum Bund," *Der idisher arbeter* (2/1902) 13 (14 inside); Sinani, *Di Untertenige* (Geneva, 1904); *Kampf un kempfer* (March 1905) 3, ed. Z. Sinan and Yokhanan Hakanai (Brenner), and *Kampf un kempfer* (1905), 4, ed. Sinanni and Hakanai. S. Sinani, "Na konspirativnoi kvartire," Hoover, Nicolaevsky, ser. 54, 88–32, 1; DOW xvii.
19. Z. Reyzen, "Sh. An-ski (biografishe notitsen)," 43N2; Ettinger, 12; Roskies, "S. Ansky and the Paradigm of Return," *The Uses of Tradition: Jewish Continuity in the Modern Era,* ed. Jack Wertheimer (New York, 1992).

20. Cf. Fedor Tiutchev, "Sviataia noch' na nebosklon vzoshla" (1848–1850).

21. Mikhail Krutikov, "The Russian Jew as a Modern Hero: Identity Construction in An-sky's Writings," in *Worlds*.

22. Dan Miron, *A Traveler Disguised: The Rise of Modern Yiddish Fiction in the Nineteenth Century* (Syracuse, N.Y., 1996), and *Sholem Aleykhem: Person, Persona, Presence* (New York, 1972).

23. Boris Sinani to Sergei Krivenko, 6/27/1892, RNB RO 1029:95, 1; Nikita I. Prutskov, *Gleb Uspensky* (New York, 1972), 16.

24. "Delo departamenta politsii o meshchanine Shleme-Aronov Rappoport," GARF 102(DP):00(1906):1:782, 32 (7/4/1894); S. Tsinberg, "An-skii," EE 2:617; Reyzen, *Leksikon*, 130; ZFML 1:71–72.

25. Z 10/2/1892; ZFML 1:90–91.

26. SAR to Glezerman, n.d., IR IFO NBUV 339:980.

4. A Propagandist's Education

1. The letter *Ia in Ianvar'* in *Russkii Rabochii* 1 is upside down, confirming that An-sky was a bad typesetter. Reyzen, "Sh. An-ski (biografishe notitsen)," 48; Rudolf Rocker, *In shturem*, 39; Z 12/16(4)/1892, 3/1/1893, 4/17/1893, 11/7/1893, 5/1894, 5/21/1894, 1/5(17)/1895.

2. "Stolitsa mira," IR IFO NBUV 339:86, 3.

3. Nancy L. Green, *The Pletzl of Paris: Jewish Immigrant Workers in the Belle Epoque* (New York, 1986), 33; Eugen Weber, *France, Fin de Siècle* (Cambridge, 1986); Friedrich Kittler, *Gramophone, Film, Typewriter*, trans. Geoffrey Winthrop-Young and Michael Wutz (Stanford, Calif., 1986); David Harvey, *Paris, Capital of Modernity* (New York, 2003).

4. "Kovenskaia guberniia: Agenturnye svedeniia," GARF 102(DP):00(1911): 9:34, B35857; "Delo D. P. o meshch. Shleme Aronov. Rappoport," GARF 102(DP)(1902):782, 724/907, 5, 8.

5. Charles Rappoport, "The Life of a Revolutionary Émigré," *YIVO Annual of Jewish Social Science* (1951) 6:218; Z 1/23/1900, 11/1/1895, 7/2/1897 GS 10:113.

6. SAA, Paris notebook, "Putevye zametki: Italiia," IR IFO NBUV 339:85, 67ob–71; 339:55, 2, 15; Z 9/9/1893; SAR to Uspenskaia, 1/8/1896 (12/27/1895), IRLI 313:7:90, 1; cf. N. K. Mikhailovsky to N. S. Rusanov, June–July 1898, "'Zadacha nasha trudnaia': Perepiska N. S. Rusanova. 1898–1907 gg.," ed. O. S. Kashchavtseva, *Istoricheskii arkhiv* (1998) 2:14.

7. Z [1894/1895?] (Absoliutnoe molchanie), 4[3?]/22/1899; GS 10:117–118.

8. Dmitrij A. Gutnow, "L'école russe des hautes études sociales de Paris (1901–1906)," *Cahiers du Monde Russe* (4–9/2002) 43/2–3, 380, 385; Z 9/9/1893, 10/24/1896.

9. Z 1/29/1893[1894?]; Karl Kautsky, *The Class Struggle (Erfurt Program)*, trans. William E. Bohn (Chicago, 1910), 92.

10. N. Mikhailovsky, "Literatura i zhizn'," RB (1894) 1:101, 111, 114, 120.

11. Z 5/26/1895, 7/27/1895; Gutnow, 385.

12. SAA, Paris notebook, 22.

13. G. I. Uspensky, "Vypriamila," PSS (Leningrad 1953) 10:1:262–263; Viken-tii Veresaev (Smidovich), *Vospominaniia* (Moscow, 1946), 406–409; Henrietta Mondry, "With Short Cropped Hair: Gleb Uspensky's Struggle against Biological Determinism," *Russian Review* (7/2004), 63; Lynn Patyk, *"The Double-Edged Sword of Word and Deed"*: Revolutionary Terrorism and Russian Literary Culture (Stanford University, PhD Dissertation, 2006).

14. SAR to "B.N.," IR IFO NBUV 339:56, 31, 31ob; SAA, "V masterskoi Antokol'skogo," *Novoe Slovo* (11/1896) 2:2, cited from SS 5:274.

15. Mikhailovsky shared some of Tolstoy's ideas about art. Leo N. Tolstoy, *What Is Art?* trans. Almyer Maude (New York, 1985), 51, 135; Walicki, 63–66; Nikolai K. Mikhailovsky, *Dostoevsky: A Cruel Talent,* trans. Spenser Cadmus (Ann Arbor, Mich., 1978), 28–29, first published in *Otechestvennye Zapiski* (1882), 9–10; SAR to Uspenskaia, n.d. (address rue St. Jacques), IRLI 313:7:90, 32.

16. SAA, "Ulichnaia pesnia," IR IFO NBUV 339:26; Paris notebook, 23ob.

17. SAA, Paris notebook, 28, 28ob, 29, 30, 33, 44, 67, 70ob; Z 7/27/1895.

18. Z 7/27/1895; Paris notebook, 47, 49ob, 58, 59; M 8/15(2)/1918.

19. Z 1/17(5)/1895, 7/14(2)/1895, 11/25/1895, n.d. (Pozdravliaiu ia tebia, doro-goi, s novym godom. . . .); SAA, "Ulichnaia pesnia," "Zhizn' i mytarstva pari-zhskogo rabochego," "Ulitsa v pesne," SAA to the editor of *Russkie Vedomosti,* 2/1894, IR IFO NBUV 339:26, 52, 69, 80; SAR to Krivenko, 3/11(2/28)/1896, 6/29(17)/1898, RGALI 2137:1:192, 2, 9; "Delo D. P. o meshch. Shleme Aronov. Rappoport," GARF 102(DP)(1902):782, 724/907, 5, 8; N. K. Kuprin (N. S. Rusanov), "Frantsuzskaia pressa," *Ocherki sovremennoi Frantsii* (St. Peters-burg, 1904), 340, first published RB 1896.

20. Ruth Wisse, *I. L. Peretz and the Making of Modern Jewish Culture* (Seattle, 1991), 40–42; Reyzen, "Sh. An-ski," 48; SAA, "Yitzkhok Leybush Peretz," GS 2:151.

21. Z 11/25/1895, 1/10/1896, 5/21/1896; SAA, "Der keyver," GS 8:148; Reyzen, "Sh. An-ski," 48, 49; PP 261. I am grateful to David Roskies for explaining that this testifies to a shift in Yiddish literary fashion; S. A., "Pierre Lavroff," *Le Mouvement Socialiste* (2/15/1900) 28:197; cf. GS 2:153.

22. Sh. Rapoport, "Di ksovim," *Oyneg Shabes* (8/23/1896); Z 9/5/1896, 7/2/1897, 9/1(7)/1897; SAR to Pinski (1896–1898), YIVO 204:84; PP 271.

23. GS 2:151; Fishman, "The Politics of Yiddish in Tsarist Russia"; Sarah Abraveya Stein, *Making Jews Modern: The Yiddish and Ladino Press in the Russian and Ottoman Empires* (Bloomington, Ind., 2004), chap. 1.

24. Philip Pomper, *Peter Lavrov and the Russian Revolutionary Movement* (Chi-cago, 1972), 223; on An-sky helping Lavrov's family, "Delo o Marii Negreskul" (1/1903), GARF 102(DP):7; J. Tchernoff, *Dans le creuset des civilisations* (Paris, 1937) 2:35; Chernov, *V partii,* 131; SAA, "Idealizm i materializm v istorii," *Novoe Slovo* (1/1896 and 3/1896) 4, 6; SAA, "P. L. Lavrov," GS 10:70; SAR to Uspenskaia, 4/11/1898, IRLI 313:7:90, 6; SAR to Pinski, 7/10/1897.

25. *Spisok lits rozyskivaemykh po delam Departamenta Politsii* (St. Peters-burg, 1899), 601–602, Hoover Okhrana XIIId(1):157:4; Chernov, *V partii,* 126.

26. *Russkii Rabochii* (1/1894) 1, insert 1; Z 2/17/1897, n.d. (Na vashi pis'ma nado bylo otvechat' podrobno).

27. Chernov, *V partii*, 130; Z 2/7/1900; [SAA], "Poslednie dni P. L. Lavrova," *Pamiati Petra Lavrova* (Geneva, 6/1900); S. A., "Pierre Lavroff," pt. 2, 284; Pomper, 224–225.

28. Chernov, *V partii*, 130, 140; "O gosudarstvennom prestupnike Nikolae Karloviche Pauli, April 1903 g.," GARF 102(DP):00; this must be the *Kampf un kempfer* series.

29. Peter Lavrov, "Peter Lavrov and the Jewish Workers," in E. Tcherikower, "Peter Lavrov and the Jewish Socialist Émigrés," *YIVO Annual of Jewish Social Studies* (1952) 7:142, 143; cf. Green, *Pletzl*, 97; Lavrov, "The Jewish Question and Socialism," in Tcherikower, 145; Chernov, *V partii*, 137.

30. Jews were 13.5 percent of the members of the Socialist Revolutionary (SR) Party but 4.0 percent of the population of the empire, and among party leadership the percentage of Jews was even higher. Maureen Perrie, "The Social Composition and Structure of the Socialist Revolutionary Party before 1917," *Soviet Studies* (10/1972) 24:2, 236; Haberer, 275; Chernov, *V partii*, 113–114, 115, 125.

31. Z 10/24/1896; S. N. Iuzhakov, "Dnevnik zhurnalista," RB (1896) 8:157.

32. Jean-Denis Bredin, *The Affair: The Case of Alfred Dreyfus*, trans. Jeffrey Mehlman (New York, 1986).

33. Ibid., 79, 163–169, 517.

34. Ibid., 272, 430, 518, citing Maurice Baumont, *Aux sources de l'affaire* (Paris, 1959), 194ff; see Richard Mandell, *Paris 1900: The Great World's Fair* (Toronto, 1967).

35. ZFML 1:103; Tchernoff 3:26; Z 2/27/1898, 11/9/1898, 6/7/1898; SAR, "Ekhidnye ulovki," IR IFO NBUV 190:79, 1.

36. SAA, "Perekhodnyi moment v zhizn' sovremennoi Frantsii," *Sibir'* (1898) 9:2–3, 4.

37. Z 2/27/1898, 6/7/1898; SAR to Krivenko, 9/23(11)/1898, RGALI 2137:1:192, 11–11ob.

38. Z 2/3/1899.

39. An-sky may have been jealous of Rusanov, who wrote about Paris for *Russkoe Bogatstvo*. ZFML 1:110, 111–112; Chernov, *V partii*, 134–135; Rusanov, *V emigratsii* (Moscow, 1929), 225–227; Rusanov, *Iz moikh vospominanii* (Berlin, 1923), 294.

40. Weber, 240.

41. SAA, "Mendel Turok," *Knizhki Voskhoda* (12/1902) 22; GS 7; I cite from SS 1; Charles Rappoport, 207.

42. SAA, "Rasskaz iz zhizni russkikh evreev v Parizhe," IR IFO NBUV 339:90, 10, 25, 45, 50.

43. ZFML 1:108–109.

44. Paul Morand, *1900 A.D.*, trans. Romilly Fedden (New York, 1931), 103; Mandell, 79.

45. SAA, "Ekht frantseyzish," GS 10:55; M. M. Rozenboym, *Erinerungen fun a sotsialist-revoliutsioner* (New York, 1924), 156.

46. Z 3/9/1900; S. Brus, "Internatsional'naia shkola," *Iuzhnoe Obozrenie* (9/4/1900) 1249:2; Dmitrii Gutnov, *Russkaia vysshaia shkola obshchestvennykh nauk v Parizhe (1901–1906 gg.)* (Moscow, 2004).

47. Ssorin-Chaikov; SAA, Paris notebook, 10; GS 10:112–113.

48. SAR, "Putevye zametki," IR IFO NBUV 339:92, 12ob–14ob.

49. See Elazar Barkan and Ronald Bush, "Introduction," *Prehistories of the Future: The Primitivist Project and the Culture of Modernism* (Stanford, Calif., 1995), 14; SAA, "Vyrozhdaetsia-li sovremennaia Frantsiia?," *Obrazovanie* (4–5/1903) 12:4–5; SAA, "Idealizm i materializm v istorii"; see Kan, 85.

50. He worked at a Rouen exhibit and was offered work at a Glasgow one. Z 1/6/1901.

51. Z 3/9/1900.

52. The name is given in Cyrillic as Zhane; I have guessed at the French spelling. The marriage was not registered in any Paris district. Research by Claire le Foll, 2004.

53. Chernov, *V partii*, 144, 149.

5. We Swear to Fight!

1. Z 1/6/1901; Vladimir Medem, *The Life and Soul of a Legendary Jewish Socialist*, trans. Samuel Portnoy (New York, 1979), 217, 219.

2. Manfred Hildermeier, *The Russian Socialist Revolutionary Party Before the First World War* (New York, 2000), 37; PP 267, 270–287; Tony Michels, *A Fire in Their Hearts: Yiddish Socialists in New York* (Cambridge, 2005), 125–178; Chernov, *V partii*, 99–100. Hoover lists her as Vera Zhitlovskaia-Obukhova.

3. SAA, "Zhertva vecherniaia: Pamiati Nikolaia Ivanovicha Blinova," SS 4; SAA, *Na konspirativnoi kvartire* (St. Petersburg, 1906); SAA, *Semidesiatnik* (St. Petersburg, 1906); SAA, *Otets i syn (bytovye stseny v odnom deistvii)*, SS 4; S. Sinani, *Na konspirativnoi kvartire* and *Starik*, Hoover, Nicolaevsky, ser. 54, 88–32 and 88–33; Sinani, *Di untertenige: a drame in eyn akt* (Geneva, 1904). Zhitlowsky and SAR, representing Bern Russian student colony, to Uspenskaia, 3/1/1903, IRLI 313:7:90, 15; SAR to Ivanchin-Pisarev, 2/3/1903, IRLI 114:2:379, 3ob; A. Kaufman, "Khoze yehudi yashish," *Heavar* (1964) 11:55; Minor, 4; Ivan [Evno Azef] to L. A. Rataev, 10/24/1903, *Pis'ma Azefa, 1893–1917* (Moscow, 1994), 93.

4. Z [1899] (rue des Handriettes), 5/7/1899; Samuel Kassow, *Students, Professors, and the State in Tsarist Russia* (Berkeley, Calif., 1989); SAR to Mariia Petrovna, 3/18/1901, IRLI 114:3:52.

5. PP 271; O. V. Budnitsky, *Terrorizm v rossiiskom osvoboditel'nom dvizhenii: Ideologiia, etika, psikhologiia—Vtoraia polovina XIX–nachalo XX vv* (Moscow, 2000), 112–116; S. Grigorovich [Kh. Zhitlovsky], "Sotsialdemokraty i Sotsialisty-revoliutsionery," afterword to [A. A. Argunov], *Nashi zadachi: Osnovnye polozheniia programmy Soiuza Sotsialistov-Revoliutsionerov* (London, 1900), 62.

6. S. Grigorovich [Kh. Zhitlovsky], *Sotsializm i bor'ba za politicheskuiu svobodu: Istoriko-kriticheskii ocherk* (London, 1898), 11–12, 52–66; Norman Naimark, "Terrorism and the Fall of Imperial Russia," *Terrorism and Political Violence* (1990) 2:2, 185; Anna Geifman, *Thou Shalt Kill: Revolutionary Terrorism in Russia, 1894–1917* (Princeton, N.J., 1993), 18.

7. Hildermeier, 48.

8. [N. Chaikovsky], *Ocherednoi vopros revoliutsionnogo dela* (1900); Hildermeier, 39; L. Shishko, *Golod i samoderzhavie, ili, po ch'ei vine golodaet russkii narod* (1902); *Skazanie o nespravedlivom tsare i kak on v razum voshel i kakoi sovet liudiam dal* (1902); L. Shishko, *Rasskazy o russkoi istorii. Chast' pervaia i vtoraia* (1902); Sergei Nekrasov, *Vory i razboiniki na kazennoi sluzhbe* (1902); *Doloi politsiiu!* (1902); *Volia tsarskaia i volia narodnaia* (1902); Nekrasov, *Vory i razboiniki*, 3, 29. The poem has the dactylic endings characteristic of the bylina.

9. *Pervyi s"ezd agrarno-sotsialisticheskoi ligi* (1902); V. M. Chernov, *Pered burei* (Moscow, 1993), 125, 156. See the figures on the back cover of *K krest'ianskomu voprosu (obzor tekushchei literatury)* (n.d.).

10. Hildermeier, 38, 46–47N58; Chernov, *Pered burei*, 155.

11. Kaufman, 55; Sh. L. Tsitron, *Dray literarishe doyres: Zikhroynes vegn yidishe shriftshteler* (Warsaw, 1920), 75; Medem, 240; John Mill, *Pionern un boyer: Memuarn* (New York, 1949) 2:23.

12. David Fishman, *The Rise of Modern Yiddish Culture*, 50; Henry J. Tobias, *The Jewish Bund in Russia from Its Origins to 1905* (Stanford, Calif., 1972), 44–45; GS 110:54.

13. Medem, 239; "Di shvue" and "Tsum Bund," *Der idisher arbeter* (2/1902) 13 (14):113, 140.

14. Z alef April taf taf kuf bet. Numerically, these Hebrew letters equal 902, and the context suggests 4/1/1902. Hebrew letters are never used for dates in the Gregorian calendar; this oddity indicates An-sky had not written a letter in Yiddish for a long time.

15. Tobias, 152; Geifman, 102–103; Leizer Janklewicz, "Bundism and Terrorism," *Shmate* (1/1982) 1:4:16–17, 21.

16. Chernov, *V partii*, 100–101; SAA, "Chaim Zhitlovski (als mensh un gezelshaftlikher tuer)," GS 10:196; SAR to Uspenskaia, 12/30 (n.d.), IRLI 313:7:90, 27; Chernov, *Yidishe tuer*, 197, cited in PP 287. The line is from Goethe's *Faust*.

17. Z 6/25/1904; SAR to A. I. Ivanchin-Pisarev, 10/11/1902, IRLI 114:2:379, 1–2.

18. SAA, "Narod i kniga (iz lichnykh nabliudenii i vpechatlenii)," RB (6–8/1902); SAA, *Narod i kniga: Opyt kharakteristiki narodnogo chitatelia* (Moscow, 1913), 106–107.

19. SAA, "Narodnyi chitatel', kak osobyi sotsial'no-psikhologicheskii tip," *Russkaia Shkola* (2–3/1905) 3:152–153; Howell, 13–34.

20. "Narodnyi chitatel'," 2:112.

21. See *Narod i kniga*; SAA, "Narodnye biblioteki Parizha," *Novoe Slovo* (1/1897) 2:4; SAA, "Kul'turnoe dvizhenie na pochve vneshrkol'nogo obrazovaniia vo Frantsii," *Zhurnal dlia Vsekh* (2–3/1902), 7–8; SAA, "Zemledel'cheskoe obrazovanie vo Frantsii," *Russkaia Shkola* (3/1903) 4; SAA, "Narodnye biblioteki v Gollandii," *Russkaia Shkola* (12/1903) 12; see Johannes Fabian, *Time and the Other*.

22. "Pervaia bresh'" and "Pionery," SS 2–3; "Pionern," GS 12–13; I quote the more complete Russian text.

23. SS 2:23, 84, 100, 101, 3:62–64.

24. Z 5/17/1905; SS 3:22, 24, 25.

25. Jeffrey Veidlinger, *Jewish Public Culture in the Late Russian Empire* (Bloomington, Ind., 2009), 67–77; SS 3:41.

26. SS 3:30.

27. SS 3:216–218.

28. Gorky to K. P. Piatnitsky, 7(20)/3/1908, M. Gor'kii, PSS (Moscow, 2000), 6:198–199; cf. Eliz. Abr., "Literaturnaia letopis'," *Evreiskaia zhizn'* (1907) 1; Roskies, in "The Maskil as Folk Hero," sees it as An-sky's attempt to "provide the incipient Jewish youth movements with a myth of origins" (231).

29. *Narod i kniga*, 84, 106 and passim, 168–169, 170–176; SS 3:177.

30. The exceptions were two Yiddish weeklies, *Kol mevaser* (Odessa, 1862–1871) and *Dos yudishes folksblat* (Petersburg, 1882–1890); Fishman, 24, 13; Nathan Cohen, "The Yiddish Press and Yiddish Literature: A Fertile But Complex Relationship," *Modern Judaism* 28:152–153; on *Der fraynd* see Tsitron, *Dray literarishe doyres*, 81; SAA, "Dos elnt," *Der yud* (11/21/1901) 46; SAA, "Der Keyver iz fartik . . . ," *Der idisher arbeter* (1901) 12; SAA, "Tsum Bund," *Di arbeter shtime* (1/1902) 26; "Tsum Bund" and "Di shvue," *Der idisher arbeter* (1902) 14; Nikolai Nekrasov, "Di muters," trans. SAA, DF (3/17[30]1904) 63; SAA, "Viglid," DF (4/11[24]/1904) 81; SAA, "Di luft is klor . . . ," DF (3/28[4/10]1904) 69; Ivan Nikitin, "Der keyver," DF (9/7[20]1905) 198.

31. SAA, "Ashmedai," DF (9/16[29]/1904) 210 through 11/19(12/2)/1904 263; GS 8; SAA, "Angel smerti (Iz poemy 'Asmodei')," EM (11–12/1909); SAA, "V tsarstve mraka (Iz poemy 'Asmodei')," EM (1–3/1910); Reyzen, "Sh. An-ski," 50; I cite from Yitskhok Leybush Peretz, "Monish," trans. Seymour Levitan, in *The Penguin Book of Modern Yiddish Verse*, ed. Irving Howe, Ruth Wisse, and Khone Shmeruk (New York, 1987), 80–81.

32. GS 8:76; I cite from *The Dybbuk and the Yiddish Imagination: A Haunted Reader*, ed. and trans. Joachim Neugroschel (Syracuse, N.Y., 2000), 358–359.

33. Edward H. Judge, *Easter in Kishinev: Anatomy of a Pogrom* (New York: 1992), 72–73, 84–91. Sh. Frug, "Hot rakhmones," *Ale shriftn* (New York, 1910) 1:4, cited DF (4/1903) 82:1.

34. Central committee of the Bund, Proclamation, in *The Literature of Destruction: Jewish Responses to Catastrophe*, ed. David G. Roskies (Philadelphia, 1988), 156.

35. H. N. Bialik, *Kol shire* (Tel Aviv, 1960), 366; cited from H. N. Bialik, "In the City of Slaughter," trans. A. M. Klein, in *Literature of Destruction*, 168.

36. Cited in Naimark, "Terrorism and the Fall," 185.

37. Hildermeier, 111; Z 8/1/1904.

38. *Kampf un kempfer* (London, 11/1904) 1; *Kampf un kempfer* (n.p., n.d.); *Kampf un kempfer*, pt. 3, Z. Sinan and Yokhanan Hakanai (London, 3/1905); *Kampf un kempfer*, Z. Sinanni and Yokhanan Hakanai (n.p., 1905); see Yitskhak Bakon, *Brener hatsair* (Israel, 1975). Most of the articles are translations from the SR newspaper, *Revoliutsionnaia Rossiia*; see Claudia Verhoeven, *The Odd Man Karakozov: Imperial Russia, Modernity, and the*

Birth of Terrorism (Ithaca, N.Y., 2009); "Varum shteyen mir farn teroristishn kampf," *Kampf un kempfer* (London, 3/1905), 27–39.

39. SAR to Brenner, 11/20/1905, cited in Bakon 2:194; Bakon 2:192; Z 11/24/1904. On his SR affiliation, see Bakon 2:183–197; Jonathan Frankel, "Yosef Chaim Brenner, the 'Half-Intelligentsia,' and Russian-Jewish Politics, 1899–1908," in *Culture Front: Representing Jews in Eastern Europe,* ed. Benjamin Nathans and Gabriella Safran (Philadelphia, 2008).

40. Walter Sablinsky, *The Road to Bloody Sunday: Father Gapon and the St. Petersburg Massacre of 1905* (Princeton, N.J., 1976), 263–268.

41. Boris Savinkov, *Memoirs of a Terrorist,* trans. Joseph Shapeln (New York, 1931), 124; SAA, "Moe znakomstvo s G. Gaponom," SS 5:331–333, 334, 338; A. S., "Iz zagranichnykh vstrech," RB (1909) 1:173–196; SAA, "Der ershter onzoger fun der rusisher revolutsie," *Moment* (9/22/1920) 241, (10/29/1920) 247, (11/5/1920) 253.

42. SS 5:347N1.

43. SS 5:359–360.

44. Z 7/3/1905, 9/1/1905; Georgii Gapon and Petr Rutenberg, *Istoriia moei zhizni: Ubiistvo Gapona* (Khar'kov, 1994).

45. Z 9/1/1905; SS 5:352, 353; Gapon, *Poslanie k russkomu krest'ianskomu i rabochemu narodu* (n.p., 1905), 6, 15–16, 21–22.

46. SS 5:357; Untitled note, *Byloe* (7–8/1909) 11–12:121.

47. SAA, "Fel'eton: Nikolai Ivanovich," *Voskhod* (5/26/1905) 21:48, revised as "Zhertva vecherniaia"; Z [1904] (Moe pis'mo ot 17/V).

48. Tsvi Hirshkan, "Der rusish-yidisher yid (Sh. A. Anski)," *Unter eyn dakh* (Warsaw, 1931), 73–74.

49. Z 11/24/1904, [1904] (Moe pis'mo ot 17/V), 5/17/1905; PP 280–283.

50. Medem, 330–333; Sablinsky, 297.

51. Z 8/18/1905.

52. Michels, 135.

53. Z [Sept 04], 11/24/1904, [1904] (Moe pis'mo ot 17/V), 7/3/1905, 8/15/1905, 8/18/1905.

54. Abraham Ascher, *The Revolution of 1905* (Stanford, Calif., 1988) 1:255, 257-262; Shlomo Lambroza, "The Pogroms of 1903–1906," in *Pogroms;* SAR to Gornfel'd, 11/6(10/24)1905, RNB OR 211:912.

55. Z 11/3/1905, 12/4/1905.

56. The text appears at YIVO 208:1491; see *Dos Oyfkumen/The Upward Flight,* in *Worlds,* 24.

57. Z 12/4/1905.

58. E. Bronshtein, "Bytopisateli evreiskoi massy: S. A. An-skii," *Knizhki Voskhoda* (10/1905), 109, 110. The 1905 "Mendel Turok" criticizes the melameds' "fatalism and narrow nationalism," language An-sky eliminated from later versions. SAA, *Rasskazy* (St. Petersburg, 1905), 326.

59. SAR to Gornfel'd, 12/8/1905, RNB OR 211:912.

60. Z 12/23/1905; "Delo ... po nabliudeniiu za formal'nym doznaniem o meshch. Shliome Rappoport (26.I.07)," GARF 102(DP)7:102:82, 3.

6. The Hero of Deeds and the Hero of Words

1. Z 2/3/1906, 2/16/1906 (Sent to Vera in Switzerland, who added a postscript before sending it to Chaim in New York); S. M. Dubnov, "Uroki strashnykh dnei," *Voskhod* (12/1/1905) 25:47–48:1–10 (5, 6 cited), (12/16/1905) 49–50:1–12; SAA, "Uroki strashnykh vekov," *Voskhod* (2/23/1906) 26:8:6–9, (3/2/1906) 9:11–16, (3/9/1906) 10:5–13, (3/16/1906) 11:9–15, (3/30/1906) 13:9–14.

2. S. M. Dubnov, *Kniga zhizni: Materialy dlia istorii moego vremeni—Vospominaniia i razmyshleniia* (St. Petersburg, 1998), 275; SAA, "Uroki," 8:8, 9:15, 10:8, 11:14.

3. Geifman, 35, 104, 105; SAA, "Uroki," 11:14.

4. Z 5/19(26)/1906.

5. SAA, "Liberal'naia zemshchina v svoei bor'be s biurokratiei," *Sovremennost'* (3/1906) 1:14 (2d pagination).

6. SAA, "Varfolomeevskie dni v Belastoke," *Voskhod* (6/10/1906) 26:23:5, 9, 18; SAA, "Fel'eton: Iz pogromnykh vpechatlenii," *Voskhod* (6/24/1906) 26:25:48–56; SAA, "Di bialistoker shkhite," DF (6/6[19]/1906) 124, (6/8[21]/1906) 125, (6/9[22]/1906) 126; Abraham Ascher, *The Revolution of 1905* (Stanford, Calif., 1992) 2:150.

7. Ascher 2:149; Stein, *Making Jews Modern,* 113–119.

8. Stein, 117; SAA, "V gosudarstvennoi dume," *Mysl'* (6/23/1906) 4:2; SAA, " 'Ne strashnoe,' " *Mysl'* (6/24/1906) 5:1.

9. " 'Ne Strashnoe' " Ascher 2:150–154; SAA, "Pogromnaia moral'," *Mysl'* (7/2/1906) 12:1.

10. Geifman, 132; PP 153.

11. Z 11/3/1905, 9/6/1906, 9/15[28]/1906; "V novom rusle," *Novye veianiia: Pervyi evreiskii sbornik* (Moscow, 1907); SS 4; "In shtrom," DF, 1/3[16]/1907; GS 9; see Jonathan Frankel, " 'Youth in Revolt': An-sky's 'In shtrom' and the Instant Fictionalization of 1905," in *Worlds.*

12. Mikhail Krutikov, *Yiddish Fiction and the Crisis of Modernity, 1905–1914* (Stanford, Calif., 2001), 79; SS 4:136, 198–199, 210; Z 9/15[28]/1906.

13. SS 4:88, 89.

14. SS 4:163–164.

15. SS 4:170–172; see Frankel, "Youth."

16. SAA, "Pogromnaia filosofiia g. Zhabotinskogo," *Voskhod* (6/17/1906) 26:24:14; Hildermeier, 140–168; SAA, "Zavet," *Volia Naroda* (6/4/1917) 31:1.

17. "Zavet"; "Protokoly vtorogo (ekstrennogo) s"ezda sotsialistov-revoliutsionerov (12–15.02.1907 g.)," "Chetvertoe zasedanie (13 fevralia, vecherom s 4 ch. dnia do 12 ch. nochi)," *Partiia Sotsialistov-revoliutsionerov: Dokumenty i materialy* (Moscow, 1996) 1:524–534; Hildermeier, 165–166; Christopher Rice, *Russian Workers and the Socialist-Revolutionary Party through the Revolution of 1905–1907* (London, 1988), 179.

18. Hildermeier, 43. An-sky translated Gershuni's revolutionary poem into Yiddish. G. Gershuni, *Razrushennyi mol (Fantaziia)* (Berlin, 1906); SAA, "Der tsushmeterter yam-tsoym," GS 8:135–144; "Protokoly," 524, 525, 534.

19. Z 5/1/1907; SAA, "V gosudarstvennoi dume," *Narodnoe znamie* (4/19/1907) 1:4, 5.
20. Naimark, "Terrorism and the Fall," 171; Dubnov, *Kniga zhizni*, 279, 285.
21. Gurevich, 6; Geifman, 81.
22. Ettinger, 20.
23. "Arest pisatelia," *Vek* (1/12/1907) 8:5, citing *Smolenskii Vestnik*, edited by An-sky's friend Solomon Gurevich; "Delo po nabliudeniiu za formal'nym doznaniem o meshch. Shliome Rappoport, ob. po 132 st. 26.1.07," GARF 102(DP)7:102:82, 17; *Novoe ugolovnoe ulozhenie, vysochaishe utverzhden-noe 22 marta 1903 goda: Izdanie neoffitsial'noe* (St. Petersburg, 1903), 70–74.
24. SAA, "Za vysokoi stenoi (ocherk)," SS 5; SAA, "Hinter a shtumer vand," GS 11; SAA, "Hinter der hoykher vant (a fragment)," DNL 7/1909.
25. On *Semidesiatnik* and *Na konspirativnoi kvartire*, see RGIA 776:34:21, no. 12247, 264 (12/11/1907), 23, no. 11271, 85 (8/28/1912); on the Vitebsk prosecutor's knowledge of this, "Delo po nabliudeniiu . . . 26.1.07," 10, 11, 14; Moisei Gol'dshtein to SAR, 3/13/1908, IR IFO NBUV 339:343; Z 7/15(28)/1908.
26. *Severozapadnyi Golos* advertised in *Evreiskii Mir*, and An-sky got mail there. Z 12/25(1/8)/1908; "Sudebnaia khronika. Sostavlenie rukopisei, kak prestuplenie," *Severozapadnyi Golos* (7/1/1908) 781:5.
27. Ibid.
28. Z 5/17/1905, 5/19(26)1906.
29. Gennady Estraykh, *In Harness: Yiddish Writers' Romance with Communism* (Syracuse, N.Y., 2005), 18–26.
30. Christoph Gassenschmidt, *Jewish Liberal Politics in Tsarist Russia, 1900–14: The Modernization of Russian Jewry* (London, 1995), 45, 71; John Klier, "The Jews," in *Critical Companion to the Russian Revolution, 1914–1921*, ed. Edward Acton, Vladimir Iu. Cherniaev, and William G. Rosenberg (Indianapolis, Ind., 1997), 694; Sofiia Dubnova-Erlikh, *Khleb i matsa: Vospominaniia, stikhi raznykh let* (St. Petersburg, 1994), 126.
31. Z 3/7/1907.
32. Izaly Zemtsovsky, "The Musical Strands of An-sky's Texts and Contexts," in *Worlds*; M. Beizer, *Evrei v Peterburge* (Jerusalem, 1990), 300–310; Dubnov, *Kniga zhizni*, 145; Z 1/21/1908; *Evreiskaia Starina* (1909–1918); *Perezhitoe* (1908–1913); *Evereiskii Mir* or *Evreiskoe Obozrenie* (1909–1911), replaced in 1912 by the Yiddish *Di yudishe velt*, to which he also contributed; Cohen, 56.
33. An-sky's folklore articles: "Bibliografiia: Ignats Bernshtein, 'Evreiskie poslovitsy i pogovorki' . . . ," EM 2/1909; "Der grund-motiv fun dem yidishen folks-shafn," DNL 3/1909; "Iz legend o Mstislavskom dele," *Perezhitoe* (1910); "Narodnye detskie pesni," ES (7–9/1910) 2:3; "Evreiskaia narodnaia pesnia," EM (3/18/1911) 11; "Chad-gadio," EM (3/31/1911) 13; "Ritual'nye navety v evreiskom narodnom tvorchestve," RB (1/1912) 1; GS 15. His articles on travel: "Provintsiia: Voprosy dnia: Paradoksy zhizni i smerti," EM (1/8/1910) 1; "Sredi iudeistvuiushchikh. Iz putevykh zametok," SS 4; "In der Peysakh-nakht," DNL 10/1910; "Kto? (Iz paskhal'nykh misterii)," EM (4/24/1911); "Paskhal'nye misteriia," (1910) SS 4. His folkloric stylizations:

"Ad," (1909) SS 1; "Meshochek muki (narodnaia legenda)," (1909) SS 1; "Nad chem rydaet on. . . . ," EM (3/1909); "Legenda (Iz D. Ainhorna)," EM (4/1909); "Angel smerti (Iz poemy 'Asmodei')," EM (11–12/1909); "V tsarstve mraka (Iz poemy 'Asmodei')," EM (1–3/1910); "Der gehinem," *DNL* (11/1910). Other large publications: SAA, *Chto takoe anarkhizm?* (St. Petersburg, 1907); *Vsiudu zhizn': Sbornik rasskazov i stikhotvorenii,* ed. SAA (St. Petersburg, 1909); *Za pravdu bozhiiu: Sbornik rasskazov i stikhotvorenii,* 2, ed. SAA (St. Petersburg, 1910); *Smekh i slezy: Sbornik rasskazov i stikhotvorenii s risunkami,* 1, ed. SAA and Stellin, 5 (St. Petersburg, n.d.); on his desire to do ethnography, Z 8/31/1908.

34. Itzik Nakhmen Gottesman, *Defining the Yiddish Nation: The Jewish Folklorists of Poland* (Detroit, Mich., 2003), xx.

35. SAA, "Evreiskoe narodnoe tvorchestvo," *Perezhitoe* (1908), 298, 300.

36. Louis Newman, ed., *The Hasidic Anthology: Tales and Teachings of the Hasidim* (New York, 1934), 56–59; Samuel Dresner, *The World of a Hasidic Master: Levi Yitzkhak of Berdichev* (Northvale, N.J., 1994), 86–87; "Dem berdichever rovs kaddish," *Treasury of Jewish Culture in Ukraine* (Kiev, 1997); "Chasidic Chant," *Paul Robeson, Live at Carnegie Hall* (New York, 1985); Shelomoh Gavriel ben Mordekhai Zeev, *Sefer hitgalut hatsadikim: vesipurim moraim, umafli pelaim* (Warsaw, 1901, 1905); I cite from Shlomo Gabriel Rozental, *Hitgalut hatsadikim: Tifereth hatsadikim,* ed. Gedalyah Nigal (Jerusalem, 1996), 81–83; E. S. Raize, *Evreiskie narodnye skazki: Predaniia, bylichki, rasskazy, anekdoty,* ed. Valerii Dymshits (St. Petersburg, 1999).

37. Rozental, 81.

38. SAA, "Sud (Skazanie)," EM (1/1909); SS 1; SAA, "A Din-toyre mit got," GS 1:147–158; SAA, "Evreiskoe narodnoe tvorchestvo," SAA, "A Din toyre," DNL (2/1909), 142–146; SAA, "A Din-toyre (A khsidishe folks-mayse)," DF 3/16(29)/1909; see Tony Kushner and Joachim Neugroschel, *A Dybbuk and Other Tales of the Supernatural* (New York, 1998), 160; for a detailed analysis, see Safran, "Revolutionary Rabbis"; Z 1/7(20)/1909.

39. "Vilenskaia guberniia: Agenturnye svedeniia," GARF 102(DP)1912:6–11-b, 2384/913.

40. Kenneth B. Moss, *Jewish Renaissance in the Russian Revolution* (Cambridge, Mass., 2009), 8; Veidlinger.

41. Brian Horowitz, "Spiritual and Physical Strength in An-sky's Literary Imagination," in *Worlds.*

42. Louis Jacobs, *Hasidic Prayer* (New York, 1973), 93ff; Z 10/17(30)/1908; "A Din-toyre mit got," 152.

43. O. E. Mandelstam, "Shum vremeni," SS, ed. G. P. Struve and B. A. Filipova (Moscow, 1991) 2:97; trans. from *Noise of Time,* 108; Dubnova, *Khleb i matsa,* 146.

7. No Common Language

1. Z 3/7/1907, 8/10(23)/1907, 12/25/1907(1/8/1908); Glezerman to SAR, 10/12/1907, IR IFO NBUV 339:1032; SAR to Glezerman, 12/27/1907, IR IFO NBUV 339:967.

2. Zhitlovskaia to SAR, 2/2/1908, IR IFO NBUV 339:782; Glezerman to SAR, n.d., IR IFO NBUV 339:1268.

3. SAA, "Zhit' nechem," SS 4:254–255; SAR to Glezerman, n.d., IR IFO NBUV 339:981; Z, n.d. (Chto zhe ot tebia tak i ne budet pis'ma?).

4. SAR to Gornfel'd, 2/4/1908, RNB OR 211:912; M. Gershenzon, "Tvorcheskoe samosoznanie," *Vekhi: Sbornik statei o russkoi intelligentsii* (Sverdlovsk, 1991), 78; Z 9/4/1907, n.d. (Chto zhe ot tebia. . . .).

5. Yohanan Petrovsky-Shtern, " 'We Are Too Late': An-sky and the Paradigm of No Return," in *Worlds,* 87.

6. Z 12/25/1907(1/8/1908); Glezerman to SAR, 10/22/1907, IR IFO NBUV 339:1038; Gurevich to SAR, 12/12/1907, IR IFO NBUV 339:303.

7. Glezerman to SAR, 12/21/1907, 4/3/1908, 4/8/1908, 5/2/1910, IR IFO NBUV 339:1042, 1043, 1047, 1168; Khaikl Lunski, "A halb yor zikhroynes," 20; SAR to Glezerman, n.d., IR IFO NBUV 339:980; Z n.d. (Ikh hob zikh aropgeyen fun zinen), 4/29(16)/[1909?], 8/10/1910.

8. "Zhit' nechem," 257, 265.

9. Z 9/6(19)/1908.

10. Glezerman to SAR, 2/17/1910, IR IFO NBUV 339:1302.

11. Kenneth Moss, "Jewish Culture Between Renaissance and Decadence: *Di Literarishe Monatsshriften* and Its Critical Reception," *Jewish Social Studies* (Fall 2001) 8:1:160.

12. Moss, 169–170, 178, N46; SAA, "A nayer yudisher zhurnal ('Literarishe monatsshriften,' Ershtes bukh, Februar 1908)," *Di shtime: Zamelbukh* (1908) 2:190–192.

13. The journal ran monthly through 1909. The first eighteen issues of its weekly newspaper version came out as *Evreiskii Mir* 1/8–5/6/1910, as *Evreiskoe Obozrenie* 5–8/1910, and as *Evreiskii Mir* 9/10/1910–4/30/1911; U. G. Ivask, *Evreiskaia periodicheskaia pechat' v Rossii* (Tallinn, 1935), 56–66; SAR to Dinezon, 11/20/1908; SAR to Ben-Ami (Mark Iakovlevich Rabinovich), 11/27/1908, cited in Laura Sal'mon, *Glas iz pustyni: Ben-Ami: Istoriia zabytogo pisatelia* (St. Petersburg, 2002), 100–101; Mendele-Moikher-Sforim, "Istoriia odnoi zhizni (vospominaniia pisatelia)," I. L. Peretz, " 'Na pokaiannoi tsepi': Dramaticheskaia poema v trekh chastiakh," and Sholem-Aleikhem, "Tev'e-molochnik uezzhaet v Palestinu," EM (1/1909).

14. Front cover, trimonthly supplement to EM 1 (1–3/1910); Der Nister to Niger, 12/13/1908, "Igrotav shel Der Nister al Shmuel Niger," ed. Avraham Novershtern, *Khuliot* (Winter 1993) 1:179; A. Gornfel'd, "Zhargonnaia literatura na russkom knizhnom rynke," EM (1/1909) 1:74.

15. Listed as "Pri blizhaishem uchastii S. A. An-skogo," EM (1–3/1910) 1; S. D-va, "Iz Bialika: Stikhotvorenie," EM (3/1909).

16. Dubnova to SAR, n.d., IR IFO NBUV 339:435; Dinezon to SAR, 7/8/1910, asked how Peretz could publish in Russian, in Shalit, "Naye protim vegn I. L. Peretz: Loyt di materialn fun An-ski-arkiv," *Literarishe bleter* (4/24/1929) 6:17–18:332; Yitzkhok Niborski, "Alter-Sholem Kacyzne," YE 1:839–841; Kacyzne to SAR, 2/23/1910, 4/1913, in Shalit, "Naye protim vegn I. L. Peretz," 330; Moss, "Jewish Culture," 182.

17. Shmarye Gorelik, *Eseyen* (Los Angeles, 1947), 336–339; A. Mukdoyni, *I. L. Peretz un dos yidishe teater* (New York, 1949), 252–253; Tsvi Hirshkan, "Der rusish-yidisher yid," 73–74; Hirshkan's correspondence with SAR is at IR IFO NBUV 339:1013–1025; Hirshkan to SAR, 4/30/1910, cited in Shalit, "Naye protim vegn I. L. Peretz," 330.
18. Z 6/31(7/13)/1909; SAA, "Pod maskoi (rasskaz starogo maskila)," EM (6/1909); "Pod maskoi," SS 2:73, 85; cf. DOW 125, 135.
19. Z 2/[1909?] (Ochen' obradovalo menia tvoe pis'mo); SAA, "Iz zagranichnykh vstrech," RB 1/1909; Z 8/10/1910, 9/5/1910, 10/25(11/7)1910, 2/24/1911; Zhitlowsky, "Sh. An-ski un der provokator Evalenko," *Moment* (12/9/1910) 17:4; Hoover Okhrana XIIIf:14.
20. Sergei Bulgakov, "Geroizm i podvizhnichestvo," *Vekhi*, 40–41.
21. Ibid., 49.
22. *Jewish Apostasy in the Modern World,* ed. Todd Endelman (New York, 1987); SAA, "Voprosy dnia: Paradoksy zhizni i smerti," EM (1/8/1910) 1:18, 19, 20.
23. L. Shapiro, "Der Tseylem," DNL (5/1909) 6; Sholem Asch, "In a karnaval nakht," DNL (6/1909) 7.
24. Chaim Zhitlowsky, "Sholem Ash's 'In a karnaval nakht' un L. Shapiro's 'Der tseylem'," DNL (6/1909) 7:413, 416. The article continues in (7/1909) 8.
25. Z 7 or 8/1909 (EM stationery); SAA, "Di tseylem frage: An entfer Dr. Kh. Zhitlovski," DNL (9/1909) 11:613, (11/1909) 12.
26. Ibid., 11:614–615, 12:665, 666, 671.
27. Chaim Zhitlowsky, "Di kristentum-shayle far gebildete idn (an entfer herrn Shmi un An-ski)," DNL (10/1909) 11, continued in (11/1909) 12; citations from 11:623, 629, 631; see Matthew Hoffman, *From Rebel to Rabbi: Reclaiming Jesus and the Making of Modern Jewish Culture* (Stanford, Calif., 2007), 4–5; Michael Wex, *Born to Kvetch: Yiddish Language and Culture in All of Its Moods* (New York, 2005), 18–23.
28. Zhitlowsky, *Mysli ob istoricheskikh sud'bakh evreistva* (Moscow, 1887); Zhitlowsky, "Di kristentum-shayle," 12:731, 735, 738, 741.
29. Ibid., 743, 745.
30. Hoffman, 81; Z, n.d. (Neskol'ko dnei tomu nazad poluchil tvoe serdechnoe pis'mo), 6/31(7/13)/1909; "Di tseylem frage," 11:616.
31. Glezerman to SAR, 12/6/1911, IR IFO NBUV 339:1240; Zhitlovskaia to SAR, 12/22/1907, IR IFO NBUV 339:760.
32. Gurevich to SAR, 8/12/1909, IR IFO NBUV 339:385; Z, n.d., [9/1909] (Tvoe pis'mo menia gluboko-gluboko obradovalo).
33. Z 8/10/1910; Brooks, *When Russia Learned to Read*; Iu. Sergeev, "Almanakhi dlia vsekh," *Novyi Zhurnal dlia Vsekh* (12/1912) 12:133; "Iisus Khristos," *Za pravdu bozhiiu: Sbornik rasskazov i stikhotvorenii,* ed. SAA (St. Petersburg, 1910), 46.
34. Glezerman to SAR, 4/8–4/16/1910, IR IFO NBUV 339:1160–1166; SAR to Glezerman 3/16/1910, 3/21/1910, and n.d., IR IFO NBUV 339:969, 970, 982; Z 8/10/1910.
35. Captain's assistant, Foreign Agency, to director of Police Department, 9(22)/2/1909, Hoover Okhrana XVIId:197:1A, outgoing 107/1909; Internal

Ministry to director of Foreign Agency, 9/25/1912, Hoover Okhrana XVIb(3):191:7, incoming 1504/1912; Foreign Agency to director of Police Department, 11/10(23)/1912, Hoover Okhrana XIIIb(1):123:1H, outgoing 1475/1912.

36. "Delo po nabliudeniiu za pisatelem Rappoport Sh. A . . . 3–5.II.1910," TsGIAU 275:2069, 1747.

37. SAA, "Novye pobegi," SS 4:271–273.

38. IR IFO NBUV 339:116, 141, 180, 245, 457, 891; Ben-Tsion Balter to SAR, 2/17/1910, IR IFO NBUV 339:866; "Novye pobegi," 268.

39. Gorky to K. P. Piatnitsky, 3/7(20)/1908, PSS (Moscow, 2000) 6:198; Z 9/6(19)/1908.

40. SAR to Chebotarevakaia, 3/17/1910, IRLI 289:5:225; Igor Severianin, "Salon Sologuba," Daugava (1989) 7:86–88.

41. Z 8/10/1910, 2/24/1911; SAA, Gezamelte shriftn (St. Petersburg, 1911); SAA, Sobranie sochinenii (St. Petersburg, c1911-1933); M. Kuzmin, "Zametki o russkoi belletristike," Apollon (1911) 9:74; Mandelstam, "Shum vremeni," 95, cited from Noise of Time, 106.

42. "Tsu Anski's yubileum," DF 12/27/1909(1/9/1910); "Sh. An-ski's yubileum," DF 12/30/1909(1/12/1910); I. Ch., "Otchety o zasedaniiakh: Chestvovanie S. A. An-skogo," EM (1/8/1910) 1.

43. I. Ch., "Otchety o zasedaniiakh"; Gurevich, 19.

44. Shalit, "Sh. An-ski loyt zayn bukh fun di tsaytungs-oysshnitn," 1:230, 231; cf. G., "Banket v chest' S. A. An-skogo," Novyi Voskhod (1910) 2:23–24, including a photo that shows V. Vorontsov (V.V.).

45. "Grekhi iunosti," 243.

46. Moshe Leib Lilienblum, "Hatot-neurim," Ktavim otobiografiim (Jerusalem, 1970) 1:95; Alan Mintz, "Banished from Their Father's Table": Loss of Faith and Hebrew Autobiography (Bloomington, Ind., 1989), 29.

47. First published as SAA, "V dvadtsat' let (ocherk)," in Rasskazy (St. Petersburg, 1905); cited from "Golodnyi," SS 3:234, 245, 236, 237–238, 259.

48. "Golodnyi," 257; Noyekh Prylutski had published "Got fun Avrom" in Yidishe folkslider (Warsaw, 1910–1911) 1:15–19. In ES (1911), 591, An-sky criticized Prylutski for confusing printed tkhines with genuine folklore, and Prylutski responded in "Polemik: A tshuve eynem a retsenzent," Noyekh Prilutskis zamelbikher far yidishen folklor, filologye, un kulturgeshikhte (Warsaw, 1912) 1:154–166; cf. Chava Weissler, Voices of the Matriarchs: Listening to the Prayers of Early Modern Jewish Women (Boston, 1998), 209–210N28.

49. See Chukovskii i Zhabotinskii: Istoriia vzaimootnoshenii v tekstakh i kommentariiakh, ed. Evgeniia Ivanova (Moscow, 2005).

50. Joshua Fishman, Yiddish: Turning to Life (Philadelphia, 1991), 262; Z 8/23(9/5)/1908; Robert King, "The Czernowitz Conference in Retrospect," Politics of Yiddish: Studies in Language, Literature, and Society, Winter Studies in Yiddish 4, ed. Dov-Ber Kerler (Walnut Creek, Calif., 1998); Emanuel Goldsmith, Architects of Yiddishism and the Beginning of the Twentieth Century (Cranbury, N.J., 1976); Di ershte yidishe shprakh-konferents: Barikhtn,

dokumentn un opklangen fun der Tshernovitser konferents, 1908, ed. Max Weinreich, Zalmen Reyzen, and Chaim Broyde (Vilna, 1931); Joshua Fishman, *Ideology, Society, and Language: The Odyssey of Nathan Birnbaum* (Ann Arbor, Mich., 1987).

51. See Steven Rappoport, *Jewish Education and Jewish Culture in the Russian Empire, 1880–1914* (Stanford University, PhD Dissertation, 2000); Fishman, "The Politics of Yiddish"; Klier, " 'Exit, Pursued by a Bear.' "
52. Eremiia N-sky, "K voprosu o iazyke," EM (4/15/1910) 15 and 16. N-sky et al. were responding to Ahad Haam, "Riv leshonot," *Hashiloakh* 2/1910; see Acher, "K sporu o iazykakh," EM (4/29/1910) 17:16N1; EM 18:11; Mathias Acher, "K sporu o iazykakh (Vozrazhenie Akhad-Gaamu)," EM (4/29/1910, 5/6/1910) 17; "Evreiskii iazyk i ego kritik," EO (5/26/1910, 6/3/1910) 1, 2. Presumably, the series is a Russian translation of Nathan Birnbaum's German article, "Zum Sprachenstreit: Eine Entgegnung an Achad Haam," in his *Ausgewählte Schriften zur jüdischen Frage,* 2: 52–74 (Czernowitz, 1910), cited in Fishman, *Ideology, Society, and Language,* 37; EO 19:13–14.
53. S. Niger, "O 'sochuvstvuiushchikh,' " EO (7/8/1910) 7:8, 9; SAR to Niger, 8/9/1910, YIVO 360:57.
54. SAA, "Natsionalizm tvorcheskii i natsionalizm razgovornyi," EM (9/10/1910) 19–20:14, 16, 17, 18.
55. S. Niger, "Eshche o 'sochuvstvuiushchikh'," EM (9/16/1910) 21:4–5; Ia. Saker, "Otvet na predydushchuiu stat'iu," EM (9/16/1910) 21; V. Medem, "Pis'ma bez adresa," EM (10/7/1910) 23–24:14; SAA, "Kolybel'naia assimiliatsiia," EM (10/7/1910) 23–24; *Novoe Vremia,* 1/22/1910, cited in Shalit, "Sh. An-ski loyt zayn bukh fun di tsaytungs-oysshnitn," 232N.
56. SAR to Niger, 2/1/1909, YIVO 360:57. I thank Zachary Baker for this wording.
57. SAR to Niger, 8/9/1910.
58. *Za pravdu bozhiiu: Velikie osnovateli religii—Bortsy za svobodu very i mysli,* ed. SAA (St. Petersburg, 1910), 5; cf. SAR to Dinezon, 3/15/1912; for more detail see Safran, " 'Reverse Marranism,' " 189–191.
59. M 12/4/1916; SAR to Niger, 8/28/1909.
60. Z 2/24/1911, 4/11[24? 27?]/1911; SAR to Glezerman, n.d., IR IFO NBUV 339:983.
61. SAR to Glezerman, n.d., 8/22/1911, 10/12/1911, IR IFO NBUV 339:983, 973, 978.
62. Viktoriia Levitina, *Russkii teatr i evrei* (Jerusalem, 1988), 151–204; Glezerman to SAR, postmark 5/1/1910, 9/24/1911, 10/24/1912, IR IFO NBUV 339:1167, 1128, 1180; SAR to Niger, 8/9/1910.
63. Glezerman to SAR, 5/7/1912, IR IFO NBUV 339:1247.
64. SAA, "Narodnye detskie pesni," ES (1910) 3.
65. Glezerman to SAR, n.d., IR IFO NBUV 339:983.
66. Z, n.d. (Chto zhe ot tebia tak i ne budet pis'ma); Dubnov, *Kniga zhizni,* 311.

8. The Dybbuk and the Golem

1. Gurevich to SAR, 8/30/1907, IR IFO NBUV 339:388; Z 12/17(30)/1909, n.d. (Tvoe pis'mo menia gluboko-gluboko obradovalo), 8/10/1910. The outline of the book appears in Shargorodskaia, "O nasledii."
2. Z 4/11(27)/1911.
3. "Evreiskoe narodnoe tvorchestvo," 276; SAA, "Zagovory ot durnogo glaza, boleznei i neschastnykh sluchaev sredi evreev severo-zapadnogo kraia," ES (1909) 1; "O evreiskoi narodnoi pesne," "Narodnye detskie pesni," and "Pogovorka," EE 12; SAA, "Bibliografiia: Ignats Bernshtein," 74; review of Prilutski, ES (1911) 4:591–594; Itzik Gottesman, *Defining the Yiddish Nation: The Jewish Folklorists of Poland* (Detroit, 2003), 39–43.
4. "Doklad o evreiskom fol'klore," *Novyi Voskhod* (5/11/1912) 19; SAA, "Evreiskaia narodnaia pesnia"; Jeffrey Veidlinger, "The Historical and Ethnographic Construction of Russian Jewry," *Ab Imperio* (4/2003), 166–169; Veniamin Lukin, "Ot narodnichestva k narodu: S. An-skii—etnograf vostochno-evropeiskogo evreistva," in *Evrei v Rossii: Istoriia i kul'tura—sbornik nauchnykh trudov,* ed. D. A. Eliashevich (St. Petersburg, 1995), 128–129, citing EIEO minutes of 12/3/1908 and 10/11/1909, TsGIAP 2129:1:54, 4, 34; Irina Sergeeva, "Etnograficheskie ekspeditsii Semena An-skogo v dokumentakh," *Paralleli: Russko-evreiskii istoriko-literaturnyi i bibliograficheskii al'manakh* (2003) 2–3:113.
5. Lukin, "'An Academy Where Folklore Will Be Studied': An-sky and the Jewish Museum," in *Worlds,* 289; Stanley Freed, Ruth Freed, Laila Williamson, "Capitalist Philanthropy and Russian Revolutionaries: The Jesup North Pacific Expedition (1897–1902)," *American Anthropologist,* new ser. (3/1988) 90:1; *Drawing Shadows to Stone: The Photography of the Jesup North Pacific Expedition, 1897–1902,* ed. Laurel Kendall et al. (New York, 1997); SAR to Niger, 3/1/1913; B. M. and Ju. M. Sokolov, "In Search of Folktales and Songs (from Travel Impressions)," in *The Study of Russian Folklore,* ed. and trans. Felix J. Oinas and Stephen Soudakoff (Paris, 1975); SAR to Niger, 3/25/1913.
6. Undated document from private archive, cited in Sergeeva, "'Khozhdenie v evreiskii narod': Etnograficheskie ekspeditsii Semena An-skogo v dokumentakh," *Ab Imperio* (4/2004), 401–402; Sergeeva and A. Kantsedikas, *Al'bom evreiskoi khudozhestvennoi stariny Semena An-skogo* (Moscow, 2001).
7. G. B. Sliozberg, *Dela minuvshikh dnei: Zapiski russkogo evreia* (Paris, 1934) 3:332–333; Diary 1, 1/14/1915.
8. SAR to Bialik, 2/26/1912; SAR to Gintsburg, 1/20(2/2)1912; Gintsburg to SAR, 1/27(2/9)1912; SAA, "Pis'mo v redaktsiiu (o rabotakh Etnograficheskoi ekspeditsii)," 5/7/1915, ES 8:2; Yaukev Shatzky, "Sh. An-ski der folklorist," *Vitebsk amol,* 270.
9. Gintsburg to SAR, 5/30(6/12)1912, 5/29(6/11)/1913; SAR to Gintsburg, n.d., refers to 6/6(19).
10. SAR to Bialik, 2/26/1912; SAR to Dinezon, 3/4/1912; SAR to Gintsburg, 4/13(26)/1912.

11. On Weissenberg, John Efron, *Defenders of the Race: Jewish Doctors and Race Science in Fin-de-siècle Europe* (New Haven, Conn., 1994); Lukin, "Ot narodnichestva," 132, cites "Fragment protokola soveshchaniia evreiskikh uchenykh po organizatsii Evreiskoi etnograficheskoi ekspeditsii ot 24–25.03.1912," Central Archive of the History of the Jewish People (Jerusalem), ru. 11; SAR to Gintsburg, 4/13(26)/1912.

12. Sergeeva, "Etnograficheskie ekspeditsii," 101–102.

13. Gurevich to SAR, 8/30/1907, IR IFO NBUV 339:388; on an influential 1897 questionnaire, see *Byt velikorusskikh krest'ian-zemlepashtsev: Opisanie materialov etnograficheskogo biuro kniazia V. N. Tenisheva,* ed. B. M. Firsov, I. G. Kiselev (St. Petersburg, 1993), 7–11; Lukin, "Ot narodnichestva," 133; SAR to Gintsburg, 4/13(26)/1912.

14. Gintsburg to SAR, 5/30(6/12)/1912.

15. S. M. Dubnov, "Iz vospominanii S. M. Dubnova," ed. V. E. Kel'ner, *Arkhiv Evreiskoi Istorii* (2007) 4:22; Maksim M. Vinaver, "Kak my zanimalis' istoriei," *ES* (1909) 42; Simon Rabinovitch, "Positivism, Populism, and Politics: The Intellectual Foundations of Jewish Ethnography in Late Imperial Russia," *Ab Imperio* (3/2005), 250; Benjamin Nathans, "On Russian-Jewish Historiography," in *Historiography of Imperial Russia: The Profession and Writing of History in a Multinational State,* ed. Thomas Sanders (Armonk, New York, 1999), 417–418.

16. Dov Noy, "Mekomo shel Sh. An-ski bafolkloristika hayehudit," *Jerusalem Studies in Jewish Folklore* (1982) 2:106. Cf. Noy, "An-ski hameshulah: beyn hashmiati vehahizoni batarbut haamamit," *Behazarah leaayarah: An-ski vehamishlahat haetnografit hayehudit, 1912–1914,* ed. Rivka Gonen (Jerusalem, 1994).

17. Mark Kiel, "Vox populi, vox dei: The Centrality of Peretz in Jewish Folkloristics," *Polin* (1992), 7; Mark William Kiel, *A Twice Lost Legacy: Ideology, Culture, and the Pursuit of Jewish Folklore in Russia until Stalinization (1930-1931)* (Jewish Theological Seminary, PhD Dissertation, 1991), 400; Pinkhes Graubard, *An ander lebn* (Warsaw, 1928), 5–7, 108–110; Graubard to SAR, IR IFO NBUV 339:353–354.

18. Giuseppe Cocchiara, *The History of Folklore in Europe,* trans. John N. McDaniel (Philadelphia, 1981); Alan Dundes, "The Devolutionary Premise in Folklore Theory," *Analytic Essays in Folklore* (New York, 1975); Dan Ben-Amos, "Jewish Folk Literature," *Oral Tradition* (1999) 14/1:201–207, and "Context in Context," *Western Folklore* (4/1993) 53; Howell, 12; *Study of Russian Folklore.*

19. SAA, "A goyisher kop," GS 14; "Go Talk to a Goy!" trans. Golda Werman, DOW; SAA, "Sredi iudeistvuiushchikh," SS 4:306, 305; Mikhail Krutikov, "The Russian Jew as a Modern Hero: Identity Construction in An-sky's Writings," in *Worlds.*

20. Z 4/11(24)/1911; Roskies, "S. Ansky and the Paradigm of Return," 254N28.

21. Jack Kugelmass, "The Father of Jewish Ethnography?" in *Worlds.*

22. SAR to Gintsburg, 6/30(7/13)/1912.

23. Irina Sergeeva, "O Iulii Dmitrieviche Engele," *Paralleli* (2004), 4–5; on Yudovin, see SAR to Yehuda Pen, Shvadron Collection, JNUL; Iu. Engel, "Evreis-

kaia narodnaia pesnia: Etnograficheskaia poezdka," in *Arkhivna spadshchina Semena An-s'kogo u fondakh natsional'noi biblioteki Ukrainy imeni V. I. Vernads'kogo*, ed. Irina Serheyeva (Kiev, 2006), 467–468.

24. Engel, "Evreiskaia narodnaia pesnia," 464, 467, 469; SAA, "Tsadik Zalman Shneerson: Biograficheskii ocherk," 1–2, IR IFO NBUV 339:10.

25. Engel, "Evreiskaia narodnaia pesnia," 469.

26. SAA, expedition diary fragments, July 9 and 12 (1912? 1913?), YIVO 3:53:3260, 112022, 112022, 112028, 112030; Z, erev Yom Kippur 1912.

27. Expedition diary fragments, 112031, 112022, 112030.

28. Bialik to SAR, 10/17/1912; Engel, "Evreiskaia narodnaia pesnia," 473.

29. Irina Sergeeva, "Etnograficheskie ekspeditsii," 105–108; Zilberman to SAR, 5/7/1914, IR IFO NBUV 339:469.

30. Labunsky to SAR, 6/4/1912, IR IFO NBUV 339:591; will of Samuel Kaufman, the Miropol Rabbi (1935), 2; his family believes Kaufman's modest personality inspired the rebbe character in *The Dybbuk* (interview with Adelaide Goodman Sugarman, 5/20/2003); Engel, "Evreiskaia narodnaia pesnia," 468; Avrom Rekhtman, *Yidishe etnografye un folklor* (Buenos Aires, 1958), 37.

31. Z, erev Yom Kippur 1912; on this material, see *Al'bom evreiskoi khudozhestvennoi stariny*, ed. Sergeeva and Kantsedikas; *Tracing An-sky: Jewish Collections from the State Ethnographic Museum in St. Petersburg*, ed. Mariella Beukers and Renée Waale (Amsterdam, 1992); *Behazarah laayarah; Photographing the Jewish Nation: Pictures from S. An-sky's Ethnographic Expeditions*, ed. Eugene Avrutin, Valerii Dymshits, Alexander Ivanov, Alexander Lvov, Harriet Murav, Alla Sokolova (Brandeis, Mass., 2009).

32. Lukin, "Ot narodnichestva," 137; they went to Nikolaev, Tul'chin, Nemirov, Khmel'nik, Shargorod, Bogopol', Letichev, Medzhibozh, Satanov, Mogilev-Podolskii, and Proskurov in Podolia; Olyka, Kovel', Trisk, Zaslav, Kremenets, Polonnoe, Dubno, Rovno, Korets, Derazhniia, Lutsk, Sudilkov, Muravitsa, Shepetovka, Slavuta, Annopol, and Vladimir-Volynskii in Volynia; see Sergeeva, "Etnograficheskie ekspeditsii," 114–117; SAR, "A idishe etnografishe ekspeditsie," *Haynt* (6/19[7/2]/1913) 140; and *Moment* (7/13/1913) 4:149, 4; Vaynshteyn to SAR, IR IFO NBUV 339:197, 200, 203 (6/20, 7/19, 9/24/1913); Osher and Sosia Manusovich to SAR, IR IFO NBUV 339:678 (7/31/1913).

33. Rekhtman, 37; SAA, "Alte shuln un zeyere legende," GS 15; Shalit, "Sh. Anskis referatn," *Fun noentn over* (1938) 4:312; SAR to Gintsburg, n.d. (Gluboko uvazhaemyi . . . Vse eto vremia my bespreryvno . . .); Programma 2-oi lektsii, "Legendy i verovaniia evreev v iugo-zapadnom krae" [1912–1913, Kiev], IR IFO NBUV 339:91.

34. "Evreiskoe Istoriko-etnograficheskoe Obshchestvo v zale Tenishevskogo uchilishcha: Sostoitsia v pol'zu Obshchestva publichnaia lektsiia Sh. A. Rappoporta (An-skogo) na temu Evreiskoe narodnoe tvorchestvo," 2/25/1913, RNB RO 352:1561; SAA, "Zagovory ot durnogo glaza," 75, 77; Rekhtman, 291–292.

35. Rekhtman, 123–124, 130–131, 136–139, 175–178, 275–277; cf. Graubard, 108–111.

36. Engel, "Evreiskaia narodnaia pesnia," 472; Rekhtman, 243, 249.
37. Rekhtman, 247, 248.
38. Rekhtman, 250–251; the citation, "Dibrei adam gadol selkin leelieh," does not in fact appear in the Zohar.
39. Engel, "Evreiskaia narodnaia pesnia," 471; Yitzkhak Gur Arye, "An-ski, haish umifal hayav," *Yeda-Am* 2:177.
40. Gur Arye, 116; Z 8/26(9/8)/1913; on folklorists as anal personalities driven to collect, see Alan Dundes, "On the Psychology of Collecting Folklore," *Analytic Essays in Folklore* (New York, 1975).
41. M. Lirov [Moyshe Litvakov], "Reaktsionnaia mut'," *Kievskaia Mysl'* (4/6/1913) 2; see *Kievskaia Mysl'* calling card with Litvakov's note, IR IFO NBUV 339:649; SAR to Bialik, n.d. (*Goldene keyt*, 204); Z 5/28(6/10)/1913.
42. Kugelmass, 351–352; Rekhtman, 47N; SAR to Gintsburg, n.d. (Ochen' izviniaius', chto tak dolgo).
43. Sh. Shrira, "Im Anski bemaasotav," *Davar* (11/8/1940) 3; Rekhtman, 120.
44. Z 5/9(22)1914.
45. Alan Dundes, "The Ritual Murder or Blood Libel Legend: A Study of Anti-Semitic Victimization through Projective Inversion," in Dundes, ed., *The Blood Libel Legend: A Casebook in Anti-Semitic Folklore* (Madison, Wisc., 1991), 358.
46. Solomon Gurevich to SAR, 7/23/[1910?], IR IFO NBUV 339:410; "Smolensk," *Elektronnaia evreiskaia entsiklopediia*, www.eleven.co.il/article/13861.
47. O. O. Gruzenberg, *Yesterday: Memoirs of a Russian-Jewish Lawyer*, trans. Don C. Rawson and Tatiana Tipton (Berkeley, Calif., 1981), 105.
48. SAR to Korolenko, 12/8/1911, IRLI 266:3:225; SAA, "Iz narodnykh legend o 'Goileme,'" *Novyi Voskhod* (1/19–26/1912) 3–4; SAA, "Ritual'nye navety v evreiskom narodnom tvorchestve," RB (1912) 1:57–60, 61.
49. Iona Makhover to SAR, 1/4/1912, IR IFO NBUV 339:698; Y. Makhover, "Sh. An-ski: Zikhronot," *Haolam* (11/25/1920); Hans Rogger, "Anti-Semitism and Politics in the Reign of Nicholas II," *Slavic Review* (12/1966) 25:4; G. M. Reznik, "Sud nad M. Beilisom i mif o ritual'nom ubiistve," in *Delo Mendelia Beilisa: Materialy chrezvychainoi sledstvennoi komissii Vremennogo pravitel'stva o sudebnom protsesse 1913 g. po obvineniiu o ritual'nom ubiistve*, ed. R. Sh. Galenin, V. E. Kel'ner, I. V. Lukoianov (St. Petersburg, 1999), 48.
50. Illeg. to SAR, *Rech'* stationery 9/21/1913, YIVO 3:54:3269, 112614.
51. Z 10/9(22)1913; SAA, "Vpechatleniia," *Rech'* (9/26(10/9)/1913) 263:3.
52. An-sky sent his Beilis articles to twenty-eight provincial newspapers, Z 10/9(22)/1913. *Lodzher tageblat* printed fourteen of his articles over the thirty-four-day trial. SAA, "Shtrikhn un ayndrukn," LT (10/7[20]/1913) 230:2, (10/8[21]) 231:3, (10/14[27]) 234:2, (10/16[29]) 236:2; "Dos ende fun der gerikhts-oysforshung," (10/18[31]) 238:2; "Shtrikhn un ayndrukn," (10/20[11/2]) 239:2, (10/22[11/4]) 241:2, (10/23[11/5]) 242:2, (10/25[11/7]) 244:3, (10/27[11/9]) 245:3, (10/29[11/11]) 247:2, (10/31[11/13]) 249:2, (11/1[14]) 250:3, (11/4[17]) 251:3 (all 1913); on LT, see Nathan Cohen, "The Yiddish Press," 155; LT 244.

53. LT 230:1, 234:1, 241, 250, 247, 249.

54. LT 242, 251.

55. See "Trying a Man for 'Ritual Murder,' and in 1913," *New York Times*, 9/7/1913, and "Many Divines Rejoice. Philadelphians of All Faiths Pleased with Kieff Verdict," *New York Times*, 11/11/1913; SAR to Aleksandr Izmailov, 10/20/1913, IRLI 115:3:271.

56. SAR to Dinezon, 11/18/1913; SAR to Bialik, 11/13/1913.

57. David Aberbach, *Bialik* (New York, 1988); unknown to SAR, 1/30/1912, IR IFO NBUV 339:931.

58. LT 239; Nathan Cohen, "The Yiddish Press," 153–155.

59. "Volynskaia guberniia, Naruzhnoe nabliudenie," GARF 102(DP)1914: 9–15-v, 4591; Graubard, 116; SAA, "Fastovskaia tragediia," RGALI 1666:1:2097; Igor' Manevich, "Fastovskoe delo," *Shabat Shalom*, 6/2003, http://jew.dp.ua/ssarch/arch2003/06/sh2.htm.

60. *Pace* Shmuel Werses, in "S. An-ski's 'Tsvishn tsvey veltn (Der Dybbuk)'/'Beyn shney olamot (hadybbuk)'/'Between Two Worlds (The Dybbuk)': A Textual History," *Studies in Yiddish Literature and Folklore* (Jerusalem, 1986), 113–114, who dates the conception of the play to 1912, following Sh. L. Tsitron, "Tsu der geshikhte fun 'dibek,' " *Almanakh tsum 10-yorikn yubileum fun "Moment"* (Warsaw, 1920), 166; cf. Tsitron, *Dray literarishe doyres* (Vilna, 1922), 85; Z 1/11/1914; Gintsburg to SAR 1/13(26)/1914. This play must have been in Russian, since Gintsburg did not read Yiddish.

61. Gintsburg to SAR, 1/24(2/6)1914; Vladislav Ivanov, "An-sky, Vakhtangov, and *The Dybbuk*," trans. Anne Eakin, in *Worlds*, 362–363.

62. Vladislav Ivanov found the Russian text in 2001 in the St. Petersburg Theater Library. SAA, "Mezh dvukh mirov (Dibuk)," ed. Ivanov, in *Polveka evreiskogo teatra, 1876–1926*, ed. Boris Entin (Moscow, 2003); trans., Craig Cravens, in *Worlds*.

63. Yoram Bilu, "Dybbuk and Maggid: Two Cultural Patterns of Altered Consciousness in Judaism," *AJS Review* (1996) 21:2:346–347; J. H. Chajes, "Judgments Sweetened: Possession and Exorcism in Early Modern Jewish Culture," *Journal of Early Modern History* (1997) 1:2.

64. *Mishpat Hadibuk: Din vehcshbon stenografi* (Tel Aviv, 1925), 63, cited in Werses, 105; Tsitron, "Tsu der geshikhte," 168.

65. M 2/18/1916.

66. He dons her body as "a kind of drag." Naomi Seidman, "The Ghost of Queer Loves Past: Ansky's 'Dybbuk' and the Sexual Transformation of Ashkenaz," *Queer Theory and the Jewish Question*, ed. Daniel Boyarin, Dan Itzkovitz, Ann Pellegrini (New York, 2003), 236; Petrovsky-Shtern, " 'We are too late.' "

67. Ben-Tsiyon Klibansky, *The Lithuanian Yeshivot in Eastern Europe between the Two World Wars* (in Hebrew) (Tel-Aviv University, PhD Dissertation, 2009).

68. Frederick Engels, *The Origin of the Family, Private Property, and the State* (New York, 1942), 50; Kan, esp. chap. 2; for more detail, see Safran, "Jews as Siberian Natives," 13:4.

69. Z 3/29/1894, 5/21/1896; question 938 is "Do you know of any cases or stories from the past concerning people who made a match between children who were not yet born?" *Der mentsh: Dos yidishe etnografishe program,* ed. I. L. Shternberg (Petrograd, 1914); the idea of betrothing unborn children reflects the Talmudic saying that forty days before a baby is born, a divine voice announces whom he or she will marry (Sotah 2a; Sanhedrin 22a) (personal communication from Shalom Sabar, Hebrew University of Jerusalem, 10/24/2005).

70. DOW 6.

71. Z 8/30/1920, *Literarishe bleter* (1924) 11; translation adapted from *The Dybbuk and the Yiddish Imagination,* 1.

72. SAA, *Tsvishn tsvey veltn (Der dibek),* GS 2:32–33; DOW 16–17.

73. GS 2:25–26, 36–37; DOW 13–14, 18; SAA, "Mezh dvukh mirov (Dibuk)," 343.

74. SAA, "Ritual'nye navety," 57–60, 61.

75. GS 2:73.

76. Bilu, "Dybbuk and Maggid"; Christine Worobec, *Possessed: Women, Witches, and Demons in Imperial Russia* (DeKalb, Ill., 2001); Tsitron, *Dray literarishe doyres,* 85.

77. Z 8/30/1920, translation adapted from *The Dybbuk and the Yiddish Imagination,* 1.

78. Kittler, *Gramophone, Film, Typewriter.*

79. Gruzenberg, 107; Louis Ginzberg, the author of the 1911 *Legends of the Jews,* presented the blood libel as an unstoppable bit of folklore. Dundes, *The Blood Libel Legend,* 360.

80. Noy, "Anski hameshulah"; Lukin, "'An Academy,'" 297–300; it opened to the general public after WWI began; Sholem Aleichem's speech appears on the compact disc *Treasure of Jewish Culture in Ukraine* (Kiev, 1997).

81. SAR to Gintsburg, n.d. (453); Gintsburg to SAR, 6/21(7/4)1914; Lukin, "Ot narodnichestva," 140; Rekhtman, 15; Moisei Solomonovich Libenson to SAR, 5/3/1914, IR IFO NBUV 339:631.

82. Letter from Kulisher on EIEO stationery, 7/13/1914, in Rekhtman, 24; Sergeeva, "Etnograficheskie ekspeditsii," 119; Rekhtman, 15–16; Y. Y. Trunk, "Homer bilti yaduah shel 'mishlahat an-ski' beshanim 1912–1916," *Gal-Ed: On the History of the Jews in Poland* (1982), 6.

83. *Artige khistorishe program farpast fun Sh. An-ski* (St. Petersburg, 1913), cited in *Photographing the Jewish Nation,* 64, and described in Benjamin Lukin, "'An Academy,'" 288, 294; translation from "From the Ethnographic Expedition," *The Dybbuk and the Yiddish Imagination: A Haunted Reader,* ed. and trans. Joachim Neugroschel (Syracuse, N.Y., 2000), 55–56; Rekhtman, Shrayer, and Fikangur, the students who had worked on the expedition, helped compile the questionnaire; Sh. Vaynshtayn, A. Yuditsky, Sh. Lakshin, Y. Lur'e, Y. Niusikhin, Y. Kimelman, and Y. Ravrebbe are among the editors.

84. Rekhtman, 17; SAA, *Dos yidishe etnografishe program,* pt. 1 (Petersburg, 1914), 10–12; trans. David G. Roskies, "Ansky Lives!" *Jewish Folklore and Ethnology Review* (1992) 14:1–2:67.

9. A Passion for Bloodshed

1. Dubnov, *Kniga zhizni,* 334, 336, 337; M. Altshuler, "Russia and her Jews—the Impact of the 1914 War," *Wiener Library Bulletin* (1973–1974) 27:13.

2. SAA, "Tri nedeli v plenu v Rostoke," IR IFO NBUV 339:76; GS 4:13; N 8; cf. SAA, *Hurban hayehudim bePolin, Galitsie uBukovinah,* trans. S. Tsitron (Berlin, 1929); SAA, "Putevye zametki," *Rech'* (10/16[22?]/1914) 279; Dubnov, *Kniga zhizni,* 342; [SAA], "V evreiskom lazarete," *Den'* (11/28/1914) 324:3.

3. Peter Holquist, "'In the Russo-Turkish War of 1877–78 Russian Forces Conducted Themselves Differently—But That Was a Different Era': Forms of Violence in the First (1914–1915) and Second (1916–1917) Russian Occupations of Galicia and Bukovina" (unpublished paper); E. Iu. Sergeev, *"Inaia zemlia, inoe nebo," Zapad i voennaia elita Rossii (1900–1914)* (Moscow, 2001), cited in Semyon Gol'din, "Russkoe komandovanie i evrei vo vremia pervoi mirovoi voiny: Prichiny formirovaniia negativnogo stereotipa," in *Mirovoi krizis 1914–1920 godov i sud'ba vostochnoevropeiskogo evreistva,* ed. O. V. Budnitsky, O. V. Belova, V. E. Kel'ner, V. V. Mochalova (Moscow, 2005), 36; cf. Holquist, "The Russian Army's Violence Against the Jews in 1915: Causes and Limits," in *Towards Total War: The Turning-Point of 1914–15/Vers la guerre totale: Le tournant de 1914–15,* ed. John Horne (forthcoming), 6; Zosa Szajkowski, "The German Appeal to the Jews of Poland, August 1914," *Jewish Quarterly Review* (4/1969) 59:4; Szajkowski, "The German Ordinance of November 1916 of the Organization of Jewish Communities in Poland," *Proceedings of the American Academy for Jewish Research* (1966) 34.

4. Holquist, "In the Russo-Turkish War," 17, 23; Ianushkevich to Goremykin, 9/19/1914, RGIA 1276:10:895, 29–31ob; reproduced in *Mezhdunarodnye otnosheniia v epokhu imperializma,* III, 6, 1, doc. 349; cited from Holquist, "The Role of Personality in the First (1914–1915) Russian Occupation of Galicia and Bukovina" in "Anti-Jewish Violence: Reconceptualizing 'the Pogrom' in European History, 17th–20th Centuries," ed. Jonathan Dekel-Chen (forthcoming), 12; the Cossacks were in a better position to carry out anti-Jewish policies, per Klier, "Kazaki i pogromy: Chem otlichalis' 'voennye' pogromy?'," in *Mirovoi krizis.*

5. Steven J. Zipperstein, "The Politics of Relief: The Transformation of Russian Jewish Communal Life during the First World War," *Studies in Contemporary Jewry: An Annual, IV: The Jews and the European Crisis, 1914–1921* (New York, 1988), 25; EKOPO to SAR, 11/20/1914, IR IFO NBUV 339:441; M. Gintsburg, "Pervye shagi," *Voskhod* (9/8/1914) 31; Sliozberg, *Dela minuvshikh dnei* 3:331; M. Altshuler, "Russia and Her Jews," 15; Gintsburg to SAR, 10/18(31)1914, 11/22(12/5)/1914.

6. He wrote about these rumors in 9/1914. Shargorodskaia, "O nasledii Anskogo," 309; GS 4:16N9; EKOPO to SAR, 11/20/1914, IR IFO NBUV 339:441; An-sky was still doing aid work in 1918; F. Lander to SAR, 1/2/1918, IR IFO NBUV 339:597; Ettinger, 15–16.

7. Dinezon to SAR, 8/6/1914, cited in Shalit, "Naye Protim vegn I. L. Peretz," 331; William R. Griffiths, *The Great War* (Wayne, N.J., 1986), 44; he kept in touch with the nurse, Regina Markovich; see Markovich to SAR, 5/12/1916, 2/15/1916, 12/3/1915, 10/20/1915, 2/12/1917, IR IFO NBUV 339:680, 687–690.

8. SAA, "Narod i voina," *Vestnik Evropy* (3–4/1910) 45:3–4, 4:142, 150; see M. Korolitsky, "S. A. An-sky, *Narod i kniga,* 1914," *Literatura, isskustvo, nauka: Besplatnoe prilozhenie k N. 341 gazety Den'.*

9. GS 4:29, 38, section 4; N 17, 20–21.

10. I. L. Peretz, Yankev Dinezon, S. An-sky-Rappoport, "Oyfruf," *Haynt* 12/19/1914(1/14/1915) 292:3; translation adapted from "Appeal to Collect Materials about the World War," in *The Literature of Destruction,* 209–210; SAA, "Vozzvanie o pomoshchi bezhentsam," IR IFO NBUV 339:3; Shargorodskaia, 309–311; Lev Aba to SAR (1912–1916), IR IFO NBUV 339:608–617, 619–624; Lev Aba, "Razgrom galitsiiskikh evreev v krovavye gody voiny: otryvok iz dnevnika," *Evreiskaia letopis'* (1924) 3:169–176.

11. Peter Gatrell, *A Whole Empire Walking: Refugees in Russia during World War I* (Bloomington, Ind., 1999), 37, 39; Vladimir Andreevich Obolensky, *Moia zhizn': Moi sovremenniki* (Paris, 1988), 484–494.

12. Diary 1, 1/6/1915.

13. Holquist, "In the Russo-Turkish War," 34ff; John Reed, *The War in Eastern Europe* (New York, 1916), 132–133; Diary 1, 1/16/1915.

14. Diary 1, 1/28/1915; Reed, *The War,* 159, 219.

15. Diary 1, 1/16–20/1915, 1/22/1915, 1/29/1915.

16. Diary 1, 2/9/1915, 2/13/1915.

17. Diary 1, 1/20/1915.

18. Dubnov, *Kniga zhizni,* 341; Alexander Prusin writes that Jews collaborated with the German and Austro-Hungarian armies, in Prusin, *Nationalizing a Borderland: War, Ethnicity, and Anti-Jewish Violence in East Galicia, 1914–1920* (Tuscaloosa, Ala., 2005), ix–x; GS 4:131; N 67.

19. Rozalia Monoszon, a jeweler's daughter, who had a PhD in psychology, did aid work in Gomel and Kiev, 1919–1920. She was unmarried in this period; An-sky calls her Monoszon, not Ettinger (her married name), in his will. GS 4:187, 190, 195–202; M 1/20/1917; SAR to Sologub and Chebotarevskaia, 3/18/1915, IRLI 289:5:225.

20. GS 5:8–9; N 115.

21. GS 4:153, 155–156; N 80–81; Yankev Shatzky wrote that An-sky's description of Galician Jews was "false through and through" in Shatzky, "Sh. An-ski (Shloyme-Zanvl Rapoport), Gezamelte shriftn," *Bikher-velt* (1922) 2:171.

22. "'Skorb' i obida': Pis'mo S. An-skogo—Sologubam," ed. Viktor Kel'ner, *Vestnik Evreiskogo Universiteta v Moskve* (1995) 3:10 (1995):210–211 (incorrectly dated 6/3/1916; it refers to events of 6/1915).

23. *The Jews in the Eastern War Zone* (New York, 1916), 48–49.

24. Holquist, "The Russian Army's Violence," 24–26; Vl. Kosovsky, *Razgrom Evreev v Rossii* (7/1915), 32–33; cf. "Iz 'chernoi knigi' rossiiskogo evreistva," *ES* (1918) (10), 223ff; "From the Debate on the Jewish Question in the

Duma, August 16, 1915," *The Jews and the War: Memorandum of the Jewish Socialist Labor Confederation Poale-Zion* (The Hague, 1916), 53; "Interpellation on the Illegal Measures of the Authorities towards the Jewish Population," *The Jews and the War,* 48.

25. Gatrell, 22; Boris Kolonitsky, "Evrei i antisemitizm v delakh po oskorbleniiu chlenov rossiiskogo imperatorskogo duma (1914–1916gg)," in *Mirovoi krizis;* Leonid Andreev, "Pervaia stupen'," in *Shchit: Literaturnyi sbornik,* ed. L. Andreev, M. Gor'kii, and F. Sologub (Moscow, 1915), 9; cf. Dubnov, *Kniga zhizni,* 342; Diary 1, 3/1/1915.

26. Viktor Kelner, "The Jewish Question and Russian Social Life during World War I," *Russian Studies in History* (Summer 2004) 43:1:2; Dubnov, *Kniga zhizni,* 347; the thirty-six contributors included Symbolist poets Bal'mont, Briusov, Viacheslav Ivanov, Gippius, and Merezhkovsky; neo-realists Gorky, Korolenko, and Ivan Bunin; political figures P. Miliukov and Count Ivan Ivanovich Tolstoy; and scholars D. Ovsianiko-Kulikovsky and I. Badouin de Courteney.

27. Diary 1, 1/16/1915; "Gorod Moskva: Perepiska po raznym predmetam," GARF 102(DP):00(1916):48:46(29193), 72ob. Police noted that the manuscript was distributed by an "Office to gather information on the hostile attitude of the government to the Jews." This may be the Russian summary of the first two sections of *Destruction of Galicia,* published as An-sky, *Razrushenie Galitsii,* ed. I. A. Sergeeva, *Arkhiv Evreiskoi Istorii* (2006) 3.

28. Radivilov is on the map of towns An-sky visited, prepared by Benjamin Lukin, *Worlds,* xiv.

29. Grabar' diary, 10/14/1914, Manuscript Division, Tartu University Library, f. 38 [V. E. Grabar'], s. 50, 44ob (I thank Peter Holquist for showing me this source); Prusin, 28, 30–44; "Letters from Galicia" (anonymous report of a Jewish activist serving as a military doctor in the Russian army, c. mid-1915) PRO FO 371 (1915), vol. 2445, file 155, doc. 124265, 381–382, cited in Holquist, "In the Russo-Turkish War."

30. GS 4:13, 132–136, 6:185; N 8, 68–70, 305.

31. GS 4:38, 170; N 20, 88; this is one of the few direct quotations in *Razrushenie Galitsii,* 19.

32. Sliozberg, *Dela minuvshikh dnei,* 3:333; Diary 1, 1/27/1915, 3/2/1915; GS 4:91, 5:52; N 48, 133; Shatzky, 171. Shatzky was annoyed by the interpolated narratives and complained the memoir was poorly edited, and Ber Karlinski (B. Karlinius) agreed it was full of errors. Karlinius, "Sh. An-ski's shriften (notitsen)," *Moment* (12/11/1912) 280:5 (YIVO 3:53:3274, 112670); Neugroschel's abridged translation responds to some of their concerns.

33. GS 6:133–134; N 280.

34. *The Anchor Bible: Revelation,* intro., trans. J. Massyngberde Ford (New York, 1975), 4; "Sefer Zerubbabel," trans. Martha Himmelfarb, in *Rabbinic Fantasies: Imaginative Narratives from Classical Hebrew Literature,* ed. David Stern and Mark Jay Mirsky (Philadelphia, 1990), 67; SAR, translations of Ezekiel 34 and Isaiah 6, IR IFO NBUV 339:34, 44; SAR, "Kniga znamenii (evreiskii apokalipsis)," 12/20/1914, IRLI 289:1:44; SAA, "Ten Signs of the Messiah"; Lev to SAR, n.d., IR IFO NBUV 339:624.

35. GS 5:43–44, 6:56; N 247; SAR to Monoszon, 11/12/1916.
36. GS 4:165; N 85; Diary 1, 1/30/1915.
37. Diary 1, 2/7/1915; GS 4:167, 172–173; N 86, 88–89. Cf. Randall A. Poole, "Religion, War, and Revolution: E. N. Trubetskoi's Liberal Construction of Russian National Identity, 1912–1920," *Kritika: Explorations in Russian and Eurasian History* (Spring 2006) 7:2.
38. GS 4:175; N 89–90; Diary 1, 2/1/1915. For more detail, see Safran, "Zrelishche krovoprolitia."
39. GS 6:113–114; N 273.
40. GS 6:61–61; N 250.
41. David Roskies points out that An-sky rejects older Jewish destruction tales but recycles elements of them. Roskies, *Against the Apocalypse: Responses to Catastrophe in Modern Jewish Culture* (Syracuse, N.Y., 1999), 54; An-sky uses Russian apocalypticism in the same way; Hamutal Bar-Yosef, *Mistika beshira haivrit bemea haesrim* (Tel Aviv, 2008), 297–298; GS 6:63; N 251.
42. See *An Inventory to the Records of the Central Relief Committee 1914–1918* (Yeshiva University Archives) (New York, 1986); Griffiths, 55.
43. Eric Lohr, *Nationalizing the Russian Empire: The Campaign against Enemy Aliens during World War I* (Cambridge, Mass., 2003), 137–150.
44. GS 5, secs. 7, 8.
45. GS 5:102, 129; N 157, 169, 185.
46. GS 5, pts. 15–17.
47. Gintsburg to SAR, 11/22(12/5)1914.
48. M. Rivesman, "Vospominaniia i vstrechi," *Evreiskaia Letopis'* (1924) 3:84; Ettinger, 15; Trunk, "Homer bilti yaduah," 42; M 12/4/1916; *Al'bom evreiskoi khudozhestvennoi stariny Semena An-skogo;* Yudovin to SAR, 2/25/1917, IR IFO NBUV 339:669; Kiselhof to SAR, 9/23/1916, 1/31/1917, IR IFO NBUV 339:548–549.
49. Gershon Levin, "Zikhroynes vegn An-ski," *Literarishe Bleter* (1929) 6:934–935, cited in Werses, 109, 118–120; Diary 2, 10/5/1915; Ettinger, 14.
50. A. Berkhifand, "Mezh dvukh mirov (Novaia p'esa S. A. An-skogo)," *Evreiskaia Nedelia,* 12/25/1916, 52:49–52; Diary 2, 9/12/1915, 9/20/1915, 10/1/1915; Vladislav Ivanov, "The Dybbuk: Censored Version"; M 11/12/1916; Ettinger, 17.
51. Dubnov, *Kniga zhizni,* 355.
52. Jabotinsky to SAR, 5/12/1914, IR IFO NBUV 339:447; Joseph Schechtman, *The Life and Times of Vladimir Jabotinsky: Rebel and Stateman, The Early Years* (Silver Spring, Md., 1986), 210, 216; Diary 2, 9/2/1915, 9/27/1915; "Doklad o evreiskom legione," *Den'* (5/28/1915) 267:3. For more detail, see Safran, "'The Trace of a Falling Sun;'" GS 8:156; Z 12/4/1905, 5/28(6/10)/1913; Boris Kolonitsky, "Antibourgeois Propaganda and Anti-'Burzhui' Consciousness in 1917," *Russian Review* (April 1994) 53; Katerina Clark, *Petersburg, Crucible of Cultural Revolution* (Cambridge, Mass., 1995).
53. Hillel Zlatopolsky was declared guilty of Zionism in 1916, and An-sky was reminded of the Beilis trial. "Iz zala suda," IR IFO NBUV 339:5; *American Jewish Yearbook* (Philadelphia, 1899-), 1918–1919, 300; Diary 2, 9/13/1915.

54. Michael Stanislawski, *Zionism and the Fin de Siècle: Cosmopolitanism and Nationalism from Nordau to Jabotinsky* (Berkeley, Calif., 2001), 219–221.
55. Kelner, 27, 36; he cites *Evreiskaia Mysl'* (1916) 1:8–10; "Pis'mo V. Zhabotinskogo M. Gor'komu, avg. 1915 g.," *Vestnik Evreiskogo Universiteta v Moskve* (1992) 1; Diary 2, 9/20/1915; Brian Horowitz, "Russian-Zionist Cultural Cooperation, 1916–1918: Leib Jaffe and the Russian Intelligentsia," *Jewish Social Studies: History, Culture, Society* (Fall 2006) 13:1, 101–102.
56. SAA, "Evreiskii narodnyi teatr," *Evreiskaia Nedelia* (1/10/1916) 2:50; "Gorod Moskva, Perepiska po raznym predmetam, 1/9/1916," GARF 102(DP):00(1916):48:46; SAR to Sologub, 12/30/1915, IRLI 289:5:225.
57. A. Ar., "O nastroeniiakh intelligentsii," *Odesskie Novosti* (1/28/1916), 9960:3.
58. Obshchestvo dlia okazaniia pomoshchi evreiskomu naseleniiu to SAR, 6/12/1916, IR IFO NBUV 339:821; Bialik to SAR, summer 1916; Isak Lur'e to SAR, 6/29/1916, 8/9/1916, 9/17/1916, 11/12/1916, IR IFO NBUV 339:662, 663, 666, 668; M 1/16/1916.
59. M 1/8/1916.
60. M 12/4/1916.
61. Lia Melamud to SAR, 9/3/1915, 1/28/1916, n.d., IR IFO NBUV 339:721, 725, 729, 732, 737.
62. Holquist, "In the Russo-Turkish War," 40.
63. GS 6:8; N 225; on Lander, see Elias Heifetz, *The Slaughter of the Jews in the Ukraine in 1919* (New York, 1921), iii.
64. GS 6:63, 6:134–135; N 251, 281.
65. M 1/28/1917; GS 6:38–39, 6:42; N 241, 243.
66. GS 6:83; N 260; cf. M 2/4/1917.
67. GS 6:151; N 290.

10. All Flesh Is Grass

1. GS 6:147; N 288.
2. Orlando Figes, *A People's Tragedy: The Russian Revolution, 1891–1924* (New York, 1996), 307–353; Tsuyoshi Hasegawa, "The February Revolution," Michael Melançon, "The Socialist-Revolutionary Party," and Nikolai N. Smirnov, "The Constituent Assembly," in *Critical Companion to the Russian Revolution, 1914–1921,* ed. Edward Acton, Vladimir Cherniaev, William Rosenberg (Indianapolis, Ind., 1997); Alexander Rabinowitch, *Prelude to Revolution: The Petrograd Bolsheviks and the July 1917 Uprising* (Indianapolis, Ind., 1968), chap. 1.
3. GS 6:147; N 288, 289; D. Sussman to SAR, 3/3/1917, IR IFO NBUV 339:479.
4. GS 6:150, 6:158; N 290, 294.
5. GS 6:166; N 296; Melançon, "The Socialist-Revolutionary Party;" S. A. [SAA], "Iz zhizni partii s-r. Kiev: Pervyi miting sotsialistov-revoliutsionerov v Kieve (ot nashego korrespondenta)," *Delo Naroda* (3/22/1917) 7:3. The memoir gives earlier dates (GS 6:164–166), but the newspaper is probably correct.

6. Richard Stites, "The Role of Ritual and Symbols," *Critical Companion,* 567; Orlando Figes and Boris Kolonitsky, *Interpreting the Russian Revolution: The Language and Symbols of 1917* (New Haven, Conn., 1999), 46–48; Sofiia Dubnova-Erlikh, *Khleb i matsa,* 167–168.

7. Tauride Palace committee identification, 3/29/1917, IR NBUV 190:83; *Zhurnal zasedaniia vremennogo pravitel'stva,* 5/25/1917, and "Rassledovanie zloupotreblenii staroi vlasti v Galitsii," *Armeiskii Vestnik* (5/26/1917) 543:3, cited in Holquist, "In the Russo-Turkish War," 40; Ministerstvo zemledeliia to Romanian authorities (in French), 7/12/1917, IR NBUV 190:97; identification of SAR as a lecturer of the Cultural-Educational Division of the District Headquarters, 7/29/1917, IR NBUV 190:84; Melançon, "The Socialist-Revolutionary Party"; Petrograd City Duma councilor identification, IR NBUV 190:87; letter from the Petrograd city secretary, 8/28/1917, IR NBUV 190:90; S. Gardzonio, "Materialy k biografii Grigoriia Il'icha Shreidera," *From the Other Shore: Russian Writers Abroad Past and Present* (2004) 4:35–48; notice from Duma, 10/3/1917, IR NBUV 190:92; notice from Provisional Government, 10/20/1917, IR NBUV 190:94; the IYP lists fourteen articles by An-sky in *Unzer togblat* (*Togblat*), 5/1917–6/1918.

8. GS 6, chaps. 18, 19; O. V. Budnitsky, *Rossiiskie evrei,* 307, 347.

9. "Nash Sinai," IR NBUV 190:82:1.

10. Figes, *A People's Tragedy,* 407; Rabinowitch, chap. 2.

11. SAA, "Lozungi mira," *Volia Naroda* (6/6/1917) 32:1; Minutes, 5/28/1917, *Politicheskie Partii Rossii,* 3:1:275, 277; "Nash Sinai," 2; SAA, "Nepomniashchie . . . ," *Volia Naroda* (5/25/1917) 22:2; SAA, "Kharakternyi dokument," *Volia Naroda* (5/18/1917) 17:3; M 5/30/1917.

12. M 5/30/1917.

13. SAA, "Kerenskis ofensive," GS 11:73, 74.

14. SAA, "Der ershter nisht-gelungener bolshevistisher oyfshtand," GS 11:64, 65, 67.

15. "Nash Sinai," 2; "Kornilovs fershverung," GS 11; Z 8/6/1919; SAA, "Spasiteli Rossii," *Delo Naroda* (8/13/1917) 126:1; SAA, "Oprichnina, zemshchina i 'bezumnye fanatiki,' " *Delo Naroda* (8/30/1917) 141:1.

16. Z 8/6/1919.

17. SAA, "Bunt buntov," *Delo Naroda* (7/16/1917) 102:1.

18. EE 11:153–160; Melançon, "The Socialist-Revolutionary Party;" M (draft) 10/3/1917, IR NBUV 190:99.

19. Dubnov too opposed Russia leaving the war: Dubnov, *Kniga zhizni,* 414, 487; Sophia Dubnov-Erlich, *The Life and Work of S. M. Dubnov: Diaspora Internationalism and Jewish History* (Bloomington, Ind., 1991), 171; Russian Zionist organization to SAR, 5/20/1917, IR NBUV 190:101; Yitzkhak Maor, *Hatenuah hatsiyonit berusiya,* trans. O. Mintz (Jerusalem, 1977), http://www.il4u.org.il/il4u/history/maor/4/4–2.html; S. L. Mil'ner to SAR, 5/4/1917, IR IFO NBUV 339:739; Ia. Gens to SAR, 10/10/1916, IR IFO NBUV 339:282; untitled drafts, IR NBUV 190:82, 2ob, 190:80; Z 8/6/1919.

20. SAA, "Prizrak koshmarnogo proshlogo," *Delo Naroda* (7/14/1917) 100:1–2; SAA, "Pis'mo v redaktsiiu," *Volia Naroda* (8/23/1917) 99:4.

21. *Politicheskie Partii Rossii* (October 1917–1925) 3:2:181–182, 222, 223; Z 8/6/1919; SAA, *Kak narody Rossii dolzhny ustroit' svoiu sovmestnuiu zhizn' (Avtonomiia i federatsiia)* (Petrograd, 1917).

22. M 5/5/1917; Budnitsky, *Rossiiskie evrei*, 74, citing A. A. Gol'denveizer, "Iz Kievskikh vospominanii," *Arkhiv russkoi revoliutsii* 5–6:184–185.

23. M 12/4/1916; Bialik to SAR, 1917; SAR to Bialik, 4/23/1918 (the haggadah reached RGALI with his 1915 diaries); SAA, *The Jewish Artistic Heritage Album/Al'bom evreiskoi khudozhestvennoi stariny*, ed. Kantsedikas and Serheyeva, 80–85; cf. the earlier edition, SAA, *The Jewish Artistic Heritage: An Album*, ed. Vasily Rakitin, Andrey Sarabianov, trans. Alan Myers (Moscow, 1994).

24. Dubnov, *Kniga zhizni*, 411; Moss, *Jewish Renaissance*, esp. chap. 1; Z 8/6/1919; Werses, 121; Horowitz, "Russian-Zionist Cultural Cooperation"; Avraham-Yusf Stybel, "Zikhroynes vegn An-ski," *Haynt* (7/18/1930) 165:7, (8/15/1930) 189:7.

25. Bialik to SAR, early summer 1916; the notice that Bialik would translate the play was published 2/1917, and An-sky was away from Moscow 12/1916–3/1917; M. Gnesin, *Darkeai im hateatron haivri, 1905–1926* (Tel Aviv, 1946), 119–121.

26. Gnesin, 121; see S. Rubinstein, *Shriftn fun a yidishn folklorist* (Vilna, 1937), 100–101, cited in Werses, 133; Shmuel Chernovits to Bialik, 1/1917 (12/1916 crossed out), Bet Bialik (I thank Shmuel Avineri at Bet Bialik for locating this letter); cf. Moshe Ungerfeld, *Bialik vesofrei doro* (Tel Aviv, 1974), 24; SAR to Bialik, 1917 (Yedidi vehavivi kenefshi).

27. See Steven J. Zipperstein, *Elusive Prophet: Ahad Ha'am and the Origins of Zionism* (Berkeley, Calif., 1993), esp. "The Politics of Culture"; Bialik, "Darkei hateatron haivri," *Dvarim shebealpeh* (Tel Aviv, 1935), 112–113; Adam Rubin, "Hebrew Folklore and the Problem of Exile," *Modern Judaism* (2005) 25:1:62–83; Kiel, "A Twice Lost Legacy," 208N232; David Vardi, "Sh. An-ski vehadibuk shelo," *Heavar* (1964); cf. David Vardi, "Vospominaniia ob S. An-skom," *Rassvet* (12/24/1922) 37; S. T. (Tshernovits), "Hadibuk (kehatsagah be'TA"I')," *Haarets* (2/9/1929) 2; "Gabima," *Evreiskaia Nedelia* (2/26/1917) 9.

28. Gnesin, 121; Bialik to Frishman, 7/1917, *Igrot Bialik* 2:179, cited in Werses, 145; Vardi, "Sh. An-ski vehadibuk shelo," 79–80; Werses, 140–149; on the legend that Bialik changed An-sky's text significantly, then An-sky translated it back into Yiddish, see Tsitron, "Al davar hatargum haivri shel hahezion 'beyn shnei olamot,'" in SAA, *Kol kitve*, ed. Sh. L. Tsitron (Vilna, c. 1921); SAA, *Tsvishn tsvey veltn (Der Dibek)—a dramatishe legende*, ed. Israel Kviat (Vilna, 1919); SAR to Bialik, 4/23/1918.

29. Bialik to Mania Bialik, 3/20/1921, *Igrot Bialik* 2:204, cited in Werses, 137; M 8(21)/3/1918; see Ivanov, "An-sky, Evgeny Vakhtangov, and *The Dybbuk*," 254.

30. He may actually have arrived in Petrograd earlier, since he says that he left Mogilev on the 22nd in SAA, "Pozhaluista, bez chudes!" *Delo Naroda* (12/20/1917) 237:1; John Reed, *Ten Days that Shook the World* (New York,

1934), 58; SAA, "Mayn bagegenish mit Kamenevn," GS 11:93, 94, published in part in Russian as "Posle perevorota 25-go oktiabria 1917g.," *Arkhiv Russkoi Revoliutsii* (1923) 5; V. M. Kruchkovskaia, *Tsentral'naia gorodskaia duma Petrograda v 1917g.* (Leningrad, 1986), relies on An-sky; Figes, *A People's Tragedy,* 487–488.

31. Notice that SAR was selected to attend the Vikzhel conference, 10/29/1917, IR NBUV 190:86; Kruchkovskaia, 104, 106.

32. Stybel, "Zikhroynes."

33. "Mayn bagegenish," 103–112; Figcs, 498.

34. "Mayn bagegenish," 112–115; Abraham Coralnik, "Anski: Russia's negotiator," *Across the Great Divide: The Selected Essays of Abraham Coralnik* (New York, 2005), 1.

35. Figes, 499, 507–513; "Mayn bagegenish," 115–122; Notice from the Constituent Assembly that SAR has the right to enter the Tauride Palace, 11/29/1917, IR NBUV 190:89; Editors of the guide to the Constituent Assembly to SAR, 12/16/1917, IR NBUV 190:96; *Politicheskie Partii Rossii* 3:2 (October 1917–1925): 251, 262; M (draft) 10/3/1917, IR NBUV 190:99.

36. "Pozhaluista, bez chudes!"

37. Figes, 513–517.

38. Shmidt, "Iubilei 'Russkogo Bogatstva,'" 303.

39. M 3/8(21)/1918, 3/23(4/5)/1918.

40. Chernov, *V partii,* 143; Dubnov, *Kniga zhizni,* 437–438; SAR to Bialik, 4/23/1918.

41. Committee of the Jewish Delegations, *The Pogroms in Ukraine under the Ukrainian Governments (1917–1920)* (n.p., 1927), 11–12; SAA, "Tretii navet," *Syn Otechestva* (7/3/1918), reprinted in *Evreiskaia Gazeta* (3/12/1991), 7; cf. SAA, *O evreiakh* (n.p., n.d.).

42. SAA, "Tretii navet."

43. M 3/23(4/5)/1918; SAA, "Der turem in Roym," *Vayter-bukh,* ed. Sh. Niger and Zalmen Reyzen (Vilna, 1920); Russian typescripts exist at RGALI 2583:1:1; as "Velikaia i strashnaia istoriia s tel'tsom (iz evreiskikh narodnykh skazok)," IR IFO NBUV 339:2; and at Shvadron Collection, An-ski II, JNUL.

44. Bialik, *Kol shire,* 362; cf. SAA, "Emigrantn-lid," *Unzer togblat* (6/28[7/11]/1918) 101:3; *Vuhin* (11/1911) 1:5–6; *The Book of Legends: Sefer ha-Aggadah, Legends from the Talmud and Midrash,* ed. Hayim Nahman Bialik and Yehoshua Hana Ravnitzky, trans. William G. Braude (New York, 1992), 390; DOW, p. xxxiv; David Biale, "Counter-History and Jewish Polemics Against Christianity: The *Sefer toldot yeshu* and the *Sefer Zerubavel,*" *Jewish Social Studies: History, Culture, and Society* (Fall 1999) 6:1; Elliott Horowitz, "'The Vengeance of the Jews Was Stronger than Their Avarice': Modern Historians and the Persian Conquest of Jerusalem in 614," *Jewish Social Studies* (Winter 1998) 4:2.

45. Daniel Gerould, "The Apocalyptic Mode and the Terror of History: Turn-of-the-Century Russian and Polish Millenarian Drama," *Theater* 29:3; Hamutal Bar-Yosef, "The Zionist Revolution as an Apocalypse in the Poetry of H. N. Bialik and N. Alterman," *Trumah* (2000) 10:46; David Bethea, *The Shape of*

Apocalypse in Modern Russian Fiction (Princeton, N.J., 1989); for more detail, see Safran, "The Trace of a Falling Sun," 317–337.

46. Dubnov, *Kniga zhizni,* 429.

47. SAR to Bialik, 4/23/1918; he published it serially in *Unzer Togblat* (6–12/1917), per IYP; Stybel, "Zikhroynes"; M 8/15/1918, 6/6/1918; G. Estraykh, "Evreiskaia literaturnaia zhizn' v poslerevoliutsionnoi Moskve," *Arkhiv Evreiskoi Istorii* (2005) 2:191.

48. Figes, 629–632.

49. Werses, 141–142; Ts. Shabad, "Sh. An-ski (shtrikhn un erinerungen)," *Lebn: Heftn fun tsayt tsu tsayt* (12/1920) 7–8:16; Monoszon identifies the estate as Malakhovka, but it may have been Avraham Stybel's dacha at Korzinkino, per Rimgaila Salys, *Leonid Pasternak: The Russian Years, 1875–1921: A Critical Study and Catalogue* (Oxford, 1999), 2:52, cf. 1:46–47; M 8/15(2)/1918, 9/27/1918; SAR to Dinezon, 10/1/1918; L. Jaffe, "Al kivro shel Sh. An-ski," *Hatsefira* (1/7/1921) 6; SAR to L. Y. Libovits, 9/24/1918, Shvadron, JNUL; Shimon Toder, "Sh. An-ski hafolklorist," in *An-sky, Jewish Folklorist: Memorial Exhibition* (Tel Aviv, 1971), 33.

50. Gennady Estraykh, "Yiddish Vilna: A Virtual Capital of a Virtual Land," *Zutot* (2003).

51. Timothy Snyder, *The Reconstruction of Nations: Poland, Ukraine, Lithuania, Belorus, 1569–1999* (New Haven, Conn., 2003), 52; Kh. Lunski, "A halb yor zikhroynes vegn An-ski," *Lebn* 7–8:20; Reyzen, "Sh. An-ski," 48N7; the wartime diaries at RGALI correspond to the first volume of *Destruction of Galicia,* and thus the absence of later diaries suggests they were sent to Vilna; SAR to Dinezon, 10/1/1918, 1/1/1919; Notes, An-sky files, Shvadron, JNUL; SAR to Libovits, 11/24/1918, Shvadron, JNUL.

52. Shraga Antovil, "Sh. An-ski beVilna," *Heavar,* 71; SAR to Shalit, n.d., in Moyshe Shalit, "Tsu der kharakteristik fun Sh. An-ski," *Lebn* 7–8:58; Shalit, "Tsu der kharakteristik," 60; Jacob Wygodzki, "Sh. An-ski: Zikhroynes," *Lebn* (12/1920) 7–8:42; Ts. Shabad, "Sh. An-ski," *Lebn* 7–8:15.

53. Lunski, "A halb yor zikhroynes," 21–22; SAR to Niger, 10/28/1919, 12/28/1919; Cecile E. Kuznitz, "An-sky's Legacy: the Vilna Historic-Ethnographic Society and the Shaping of Modern Jewish Culture," in *Worlds,* 320–321; Shalit, "Sh. An-ski als mitglid fun gegnt-komitet 'Yekopo' in Vilne," in *Af di khurves fun milkhomes un mehumes: Pinkes fun gegnt-komitet "Yekopo" in Vilne,* ed. Shalit (Vilna, 1931).

54. Mikh, "Semyon Akimovitsh An-ski: A kapitel zikhroynes," *Teatr un kino,* 12/1/1922; Lunski, 21, 23; Eleanor Mlotek, ed., *S. Ansky (Shloyme-Zanvl Rappoport), 1863–1920: His Life and Work, Catalog of an Exhibition* (New York, 1980), 18; Shalit, 62–63.

55. Wygodzki, "Sh. An-ski," 41; "Shtadlonus bay di bolshevikes," GS 11:125–127.

56. Shabad, 14; "Shtadlonus," 129–132; Z 8/1/1919.

57. Lunski, 23; see Horowitz, "Russian-Zionist"; SAA, "Baym keyver fun a koydesh," in *Vayter bukh;* Antovil, 73; see Khana Gordon-Mlotek, "Der toyt fun A. Vayter un zeyer nokhfolgn," *YIVO Bleter,* new ser. (1994) 2.

58. SAA, "Der Shtumer Yiush," *Moment* (11/21/1919) 265:5.
59. Wygodzki, 41; SAR to Libovits, 3/1/1919, 6/14/1919, 10/24/1919; M. Shalit, "Sh. An-ski als mitglid"; Z 8/1/1919; Dinezon to SAR, 5/10/1919; "A briv fun I. Dinezon tsu S. An-ski," *Bikher-velt* (9–10/1923), 5:413–416; SAA, "A naye dershaynung in undzer literatur: Alter Kacyzne, 'Der gayst der melekh,' dramatishe poeme, Warshe 1919," *Moment* (10/24/1919) 241:5, (10/31/1919) 247:5; Tsitron, 76–77; "Tsu Dinezons ondenkung: Di rede oyfn fayerlikhn troyer-ovnt tsu shloshim nokh Dinezons toyt," *Moment* (10/7/1919) 230:4.
60. Figes, 773; Peter Kenez, "Pogroms and White Ideology in the Russian Civil War," in *Pogroms;* Budnitsky, *Rossiiskie evrei,* 299.
61. SAA, "A por verter vegn artikl fun H' VV. Bograd," *Moment* (12/23/1919) 292:3; "Petlura un Margolin," *Moment* (9/16/1919) 214:3; "Nikolai Chaikovsky un Boris Savinkov in Varshe."
62. SAR to Niger, 10/9/1920; Lunski, 22; "Zaveshchanie An-skogo," 312–313. This censorship occurred only with the Monoszon correspondence.
63. The IYP lists sixty-two articles by An-sky in *Moment* in 1919 and 1920 and thirty-three articles in other Yiddish newspapers during that period. He told Dinezon in 1919 that he had seven to eight volumes of his collected works ready, in SAR to Dinezon, n.d. (Ikh shrayb behipozen); SAR to Niger, 5/8/1920, 10/9/1920 and later; "Zaveshchanie"; Z 10/11/1920; interview with Luba Kadison Buloff, New York Public Library (NYPL) Theater Division archive; Steinlauf, "'Fardibekt!'"; Tsitron, "Al davar hatargum," and "Di letste fun di dray"; SAR to Bialik, 4/23/1918; Z 2/27/1920, 7/20/1920, 10/11/1920.
64. Z 10/11/1920; "Zaveshchanie."
65. M 1/8/1916; Lunski, 22; Z 8/6/1919.
66. SAR to Niger, 9/5/1920, 10/9/1920; Z 4/24/1920, 5/31/1920, 7/20/1920, 10/11/1920; cable to Charney, 4/13/1920, YIVO 360:57.
67. GS 8:169–171; SAA, "Otets i syn," *Evreiskoe Slovo* (9/8/1920) 6:14–15; SAA, "Der foter mit zayn zun," *Lebn* (6/1920) 3–4; SAA, "Solidarishkayt," *Moment* (7/15/1919) 161:2.
68. Shabad, 16–19.
69. SAA, "Bay undz fargist men nit keyn blut," *Lebn* (1920) 7–8:8; GS 10: 111–122.
70. SAA, "Zeyer 'Hagadah Shel Peysakh,'" *Moment* (4/2/1920) 79:5; GS 8:123– 131; "The Egyptian Passover," trans. Joachim Neugroschel, Tony Kushner, and Neugroschel, *A Dybbuk and Other Tales.*
71. SAR to Lunski, 11/8/1920, *Lebn* 7–8:10; Z. Reyzen, "Sh. An-ski," 56.
72. "Zaveshchanie," 313; Z. Senalovitsh, *Tlomatske 13 (fun farbrentn nekhtn)* (Buenos Aires, 1946), 86–87; Shabad, 19; "Pratim vegn An-skis levaye," *Idishe shtime,* n.d. (clipping at Shvadron, JNUL).

Epilogue

1. See Steinlauf, "Fardibekt!" SAR to Niger, 10/9/1920; Zemtsovsky, "Appendix: Musical Productions of *The Dybbuk,*" *Worlds,* 229–231; "Tog un nakht," GS

2; "The Devil's Sabbath," NYPL Theater Division archive; "Dervishi i dan-singi (po povodu p'esy An-skogo 'Den' i noch')," *Za Svobodu* (10/11/1925) 235:2–3; Alperin, "Der Al-khet," *Teater un kunst* (11/30/1922) 1:4:2; Karlin-ius, "Sh. An-ski's shriften (notitsen)," *Moment* (12/11/1921) 280:5; Z 2/27/1920; SAA, *Der yidisher hurbn*; SAA, *Hurban hayehudim*; Chernov, *V partii*, 151. Tsitron edited one volume of a Hebrew collected works, SAA, *Kol kitve*, ed. S. L. Tsitron (Vilna, 1920).

2. *Behazarah laayarah; Tracing Ansky; The Jewish Artistic Heritage;* L. V. Sholo-khova, *Fonoarkhiv ievreiskoi muzychnoi spadshchyny* (Kiev, 2001); *Dos Oyf-kumen; Treasure of Jewish Culture in Ukraine* (Kiev, 1997); *Materials of J. Engel Ethnographic Expedition 1912,* vol. 1 (Kiev, 2001); *Historical Collec-tion of Jewish Musical Folklore 1912–1947,* vol. 2 (Kiev, 2004); *Photograph-ing the Jewish Nation;* Valery Dymshits is preparing a Russian translation of Rekhtman's memoir of the expedition; *The Dybbuk and Other Writings; The Dybbuk and the Yiddish Imagination; The Enemy at His Pleasure; The Worlds of S. An-sky;* Nathaniel Deutsch, *The People's Torah: Life, Death, and Ethnog-raphy in the Pale of Settlement* (forthcoming; includes a translation of *Man*); Michael Katz is producing an annotated translation of *Pioneers.*

3. Lunski, 21.

4. M. Broderson, "Vegn Sh. An-ski," clipping, YIVO 3:53:3274, 112670; Safran, "Dancing with Death."

5. I thank Valery Dymshits for this metaphor.

6. SS 5.

Acknowledgments

Among the scholars whose work I have used, some require more attention than I could give them in my narrative of An-sky's life. I was inspired by the observation of Seth Wolitz that An-sky, like other prerevolutionary Russian-Jewish writers, calibrated his depictions of Jews for a broad imperial audience. David Roskies, using the published Yiddish sources, beautifully rendered the life in the terms that the writer himself proposed, as a youthful departure from Jewishness followed by repentance and return; although the archival sources and the Russian record belie An-sky's self-construction as a prodigal son, Roskies's contribution as a sympathetic critic remains crucial. Jonathan Frankel's *Prophecy and Politics* helped me find my way in Russian-Jewish revolutionary history; I draw on his depiction of a shared Russian and Jewish atmosphere of messianism and dread at the fin-de-siècle and appreciate his careful illustration of individual lives whose trajectories intersect obliquely with others in their generation. My conversations with Valery Dymshits about An-sky and revolutionary culture have inspired me. Most often I have found myself returning to an essay on "An-sky and the Guises of Modern Jewish Culture" by Steve Zipperstein, my colleague and co-editor, whose themes—An-sky's delight in disguise, and his longing for love—have become those of this book as well.

I owe a huge debt to Zachary Baker, Nathaniel Deutsch, Valery Dymshits, Lazar Fleishman, Joseph Frank, Michael Kahan, Benjamin Nathans, Michelle Oberman, Alex Orbach, David Roskies, Barry Scherr, and Steven Zipperstein, who generously read my entire manuscript and gave me the benefit of their expertise. Lynn Cowley, Amir Eshel, Gregory Freidin, Monika Greenleaf, Heather Hadlock, Peter Holquist, the late John Klier, Andrew Koss, Mikhail Krutikov, Jessie Labov, Lynn Patyk, Sasha Senderovich, Marci Shore, Chris Stroop, Sara Pankenier Weld, Deborah Yalen, Eugene Zelikman, and participants in conferences and colloquia at Stanford, the University of Pennsylvania's Center for Advanced Judaic Studies, and elsewhere, commented on chapters and drafts. Michael Alpert, Israel Bartal,

Caryl Emerson, Edward Frankel, the late Jonathan Frankel, Amelia Glaser, Bruce Grant, Brian Horowitz, Nathan MacBrien, Edward Manouelian, Inessa Medzhibovskaya, Dan Miron, Ken Moss, Norman Naimark, Abraham Nowersztern, Ada Rapoport-Albert, David Shneer, Michael Steinlauf, Nancy Unger, Jeff Veidlinger, Julia Verkholantsev, and Seth Wolitz all answered questions and encouraged me.

Peter Holquist, Brian Horowitz, Mikhail Krutikov, Adelaide Goodman Sugarman, and Irina Sergeeva shared archival materials with me, and Eugene Zelikman, An-sky's distant relative, showed me photographs and told me family stories. The staff at the archives and libraries where I worked were helpful, especially Irina Sergeeva and Anna Rivkina at the Vernadsky Library Judaica section, Carol Leadenham at Hoover, Shmuel Avineri at Bet Bialik, and Zachary Baker and Karen Rondestvedt at Green Library. Roberta Newman found me images at YIVO. Marian Bassett, Irina Denischenko, Amelia Glaser, Ilia Gruen, Martha Kelly, Matthew Klayman, Olga Kochurova, Claire Le Foll, Hanna Meckler, Lauren Nelson, Tom Roberts, Natalie Rouland, and Margo Watson tracked down sources and helped with other tasks. My research was speeded by two bibliographic aids: the Index to Yiddish Periodicals at the Hebrew University and Beth Shalom Aleichem, and the detailed finding guide to the Vernadsky Library An-sky papers; I am grateful to the people who created both of them. I also thank Chaim and Vera Zhitlowsky, Roza Monoszon Ettinger, Shmuel Niger, Moyshe Shalit, Gleb and Alexandra Uspensky, Chaim Nachman Bialik, An-sky's other friends and correspondents, and the Soviet archivists who saved his letters and manuscripts, sometimes at personal risk, because they believed that someday someone would want to write about him.

I am grateful to Joyce Seltzer and her assistant Jeannette Estruth at Harvard University Press for working with me to strengthen my manuscript. I have benefited from the expertise of copyeditor Pat Cattani, master proofreader Rebecca Ritke, and indexer Barbara Roos.

Finally, I want to thank my family – my parents, William and Marian Safran, my husband Michael Kahan, and my daughters Eva and Frieda – for tolerating An-sky for so long. I am grateful for their forbearance, and I hope that he will now leave all of us in peace.

Index